D1522317

Metafísica
para lograr la felicidad

Metafísica
para lograr la felicidad

Editorial Época, S.A. de C.V.
Emperadores No. 185
Col. Portales
C.P. 03300, México, D.F.

Metafísica para lograr la felicidad
© W. Sheldoon
Traducción: Pamela Cortéz A.

© Derechos reservados 2010
© Editorial Época, S.A. de C.V.
Emperadores No. 185, Col. Portales
C.P. 03300-México, D.F.
www.editorialepoca.com
email: edesa2004@prodigy.net.mx
Tels: 56-04-90-46
         56-04-90-72

ISBN: 970-627-844-3
            978-970-627-844-9

Impreso en México — *Printed in Mexico*

INTRODUCCIÓN

Acerca de la felicidad Aristóteles decía: "Puesto que la felicidad (o placer) es *aquello que acompaña a la realización del fin propio de cada ser vivo*, la felicidad que le corresponde al hombre es la que le sobreviene cuando realiza la actividad que le es más propia y cuando la realiza de un modo perfecto; es más propio del hombre el alma que el cuerpo por lo que *la felicidad humana tendrá que ver más con la actividad del alma que con la del cuerpo*; y de las actividades del alma, con aquella que corresponde a la parte más típicamente humana, el alma intelectiva o racional."

Y es que ciertamente la felicidad es el bien más buscado, aunque como lo manifestó el filósofo griego es una actitud que se toma y se siente desde el centro de cada persona. El alma humana tendría que ser su portadora, reguladora y guardiana. No obstante, aunque estamos hablando de un principio universal, comprenderlo no es nada sencillo, de hecho resulta bastante complicado, quizá por ello malgastamos la mitad de nuestra vida buscando algo que realmente no se puede encontrar hasta que no se está dispuesto a sentir.

Éste es un libro que en gran medida le orientará a despertar la felicidad basándose en una de las ciencias más enigmáticas de todos los tiempos, la metafísica. Le ayudará a descifrar una acertada corriente filosófica, alentando a su inconsciente a buscar dentro de sí lo que muchos han estado persiguiendo de forma desorientada en el exterior, en el mundo y en algunas personas. *¡La felicidad está en ti!* Es una frase que tomará forma en usted, querido lector; concepto que no olvidará y amoldará como estilo de vida.

La felicidad se hará aquí y ahora, empleando enseñanzas de maestros como lo han sido Saint Germain, el mismo Jesús, Mahoma, Moisés, Aristóteles, Andrónico de Rodas, entre muchos otros. Lista a la que se sumará alguien tan importante como ellos: usted. Comience hoy a labrar un futuro más feliz, positivo y armónico. *¡Que la verdad os sea revelada!*

METAFÍSICA, ORÍGENES Y VERDAD

El objeto de la metafísica fue escrito en un tratado sistemático (metódico) por el filósofo griego Aristóteles; sin embargo, el término no fue de su autoría, porque los datos pertenecen a Andrónico de Rodas (siglo I a. de C.), quien fuera traductor y recopilador del primero y, al no saber a ciencia cierta de lo que se trataba la obra aristotélica decidió llamarle "ta meta tá physicá", que significa "más allá de la física", que en un modo más sintetizado vendría siendo el término tal cual lo conocemos hoy en día. No es de extrañar, que dicho término connote un tipo de conocimiento transfísico utilizado por numerosas doctrinas ocultistas de toda índole.

Ciertamente, el término fue acogido con excelencia y utilizado para denominar a aquella parte de la física que versa sobre el ser. Pero ¿fueron éstas las intenciones de Aristóteles? El objeto del estudio del filósofo designa no sólo a la ciencia más general que existe (la del ser en cuanto a lo que es y a sus atributos fundamentales) sino que hace alusión a una filosofía primaria (*proton philosophia*) o sabiduría, entendida como teología.

Siendo así, la metafísica al igual que otras ciencias como las matemáticas, son axiomas (principios fundamentales e indemostrables sobre los que se construye una teoría), por ende irrefutables, que sirven de fundamentación a las demás ciencias particulares. Por esta sencilla razón podemos encontrar a la *metaphisica generalis*, o ciencia del ser y la *metaphisica speciallis*, la del ser supremo, una de cuyas ramas es la teología. Claro que para llegar a este punto tuvieron que pasar muchos cientos de años.

Hoy en día se intenta hacer creer que la metafísica no es una ciencia, por no aceptar que esta totalidad le da cabida al "ente". Esta multiplicidad de sentidos es la que probablemente hace confusa a esta ciencia que, por sus modos definitorios, resulta completa. En cuanto a su método de conocimiento éste no es experimental (*a posteriori*) o empírico, sino que se basa en deducciones *a priori*; es decir, independientes de la experiencia. Todos estos conocimientos son malinterpretados, siendo la razón principal por la que han cambiado drásticamente, y es un privilegio de algunos conocerla en su totalidad.

Muchos de los principios de la metafísica ahora son mitos; uno de ellos es el pilar fundamental que explica la creación del mundo *ex nihilo*. Otro muy importante es la facultad de devolverle la vida a un cuerpo inanimado, crear vida por medio de una masa parecida a la arcilla, entre muchos que son difíciles de citar en su totalidad. Ciertamente la obra desarrollada por Aristóteles ha sido ampliamente tratada por autores que le han dado un giro inesperado y hoy en día esos principios no son más que una leyenda consumada.

La metafísica actual deja atrás el problema del ser para centrarse en la sustancia. El esquema categorial aristotélico quedó reducido a tres: sustancia (lo que no necesita de otra cosa más que de sí misma para existir), atributos (características esenciales y definitorias) y modos (modificaciones y cualificaciones) de la sustancia.

Según Aristóteles, la felicidad más humana es la que corresponde a la vida teorética o de conocimiento, de ahí que se considere al filósofo el hombre más feliz en cuanto que su razón se dirige al conocimiento de la realidad más perfecta; Dios. Pero el filósofo griego también acepta que para ser feliz es necesaria una cantidad moderada de bienes exteriores y afectos humanos.

¿Qué significa eso? Basándonos en el hecho de que la metafísica es una ciencia capaz de describir el principio de la vida, buscaremos la fórmula de la felicidad completa, total, para hacerla un hábito de bienestar constante. Nos apoyaremos de autores que le han dado a esta ciencia su interpretación.

LA FELICIDAD: SAINT GERMAIN

Todo el mundo anda buscando la felicidad, a veces llamada dicha, y, sin embargo, muchos de los que la buscan con tanto ahínco continúan pasando de largo ante la llave de esa felicidad. La llave simple de la dicha perfecta y el poder inherente que la mantiene constante es el autocontrol y la autocorrección. Pero esto es facilísimo de lograr una vez que se aprende la verdad de que uno mismo es la presencia "Yo soy", y la inteligencia que controla y ordena todas las cosas.

Alrededor de cada individuo hay todo un mundo de pensamientos creados por él mismo. Dentro de este mundo mental está la semilla, la Presencia Divina, el «YO SOY», que es la única Presencia que actúa en el Universo y la cual dirige toda energía. Esta energía puede ser intensificada más allá de todos los límites por medio de la actividad consciente del individuo.

La Presencia Divina Interior puede ser comparada con la semilla de un durazno. El mundo de pensamientos que la envuelve semeja la pulpa. La pulpa representa no sólo el mundo mental creado por el individuo, sino la sustancia electrónica universal, siempre en espera de ser activada por la determinación consciente del individuo, para ser precipitada a su uso visible en la forma que a él le convenga o desee.

El camino seguro hacia la comprensión y uso de este poder consciente nos viene por medio del autocontrol. ¿Qué quiero decir con esa palabra «autocontrol»?: el reconocimiento de la inteligencia «YO SOY» como única presencia activa; que sabiendo esto, sabemos también que no existen límites o limitaciones para el poder de su uso, y que los humanos, habiendo recibido libre albedrío, libre selección y libre actuación, aquello que crean en su mundo circundante *es todo aquello en que fijan su atención.*

Ha llegado el momento por fin cuando todos deben comprender que el pensamiento y el sentimiento forman el poder creador más grande en la vida y en el universo. La única forma de usar ese pleno poder de pensamiento-sentimiento, que llamamos «DIOS EN ACCIÓN», es empleando el autocontrol y la autocorrección, con los cuales se puede rápidamente alcanzar la comprensión, y con la cual se puede usar y dirigir este poder del pensamiento, sin limitación alguna. Cuando se ha logrado el suficiente autocontrol, el individuo puede mantener su pensamiento fijo en cualquier deseo, al igual que una llama de acetileno que se mantiene inmóvil sobre una soldadura. Así, cuando se mantiene inamovible la conciencia en cualquier deseo, sabiendo que la presencia «YO SOY» es la que está pensando, o sea, que es Dios en acción, entonces se comprenderá que se puede traer a la visibilidad, o precipitar, lo que quiera que se desee o se necesite. No es que no se pueda pensar en otra cosa; si así fuera, ¿cómo podría uno realizar los mil y un deberes que colman nuestros días? Es que cada vez que se tenga que recordar el punto en cuestión, se recuerda invariablemente que es DIOS, o la presencia «YO SOY» con todo su poder, la que está actuando para precipitarnos el deseo.

Oye bien; ha sido comprobado en miles de formas que el efecto de una cosa no puede traer felicidad. Sólo por la comprensión de la causa que opera es que el individuo se hace maestro o dueño de su mundo.

El autocontrol se ejerce pensando y diciendo inmediatamente frente a todo lo inarmonioso que se presente: "No señor. Esto no puede ser verdad porque mi «YO SOY» es perfecto. Borro, pues, todo lo que esté hecho por mi conciencia exterior y no acepto sino la perfección manifestada". ¿Qué pasa entonces? Que le has abierto la entrada a Dios «YO SOY», y Él endereza todo lo exterior.

Dice Saint Germain: "Amado estudiante, si pudieras comprender el esplendor magnificente que se manifiesta en ti, cuando afirmas así tu autocontrol ante la actividad exterior, duplicarías todos tus esfuerzos para lograr ese autocontrol y maestría sobre toda expresión exterior. Así es que se le permite a la Magna Presencia «YO SOY» liberar su gran Poder en nuestra conciencia y uso exterior".

Ahora vamos a quitar de la mente de los amados estudiantes el sentido de tiempo, espacio y distancia.

La llave que abre la entrada a todas las esferas superiores, los planos superiores, está en la sencillez y firmeza del autocontrol. Todo estudiante debe recordar esa gran verdad de que «DONDE ESTÁ TU CONCIENCIA ESTÁS TÚ», y que el «YO SOY» está en todas partes.

La conciencia de que hay espacio, distancia y tiempo es sólo una creación del hombre. Pasar a través del velo finísimo que separa la conciencia de su pleno poder y actividad interior es sólo un asunto de estado de conciencia, o sea, de pensamiento y sentimiento. Aquellos que están esforzándose por alcanzar la Luz, están viviendo constantemente en esas altas esferas. La belleza de estas esferas sobrepasa toda imaginación. Cuando entres en ellas consciente y voluntariamente, encontrarás que todas las creaciones que existen allí son tangibles como cualquiera de nuestros edificios de aquí.

Con la afirmación «YO SOY EL PODER DE MI AUTO-CONTROL COMPLETO PARA SIEMPRE SOSTENIDO» será más fácil lograr esta maestría. Los estudiantes deben hacerse conscientes de que cuando ellos reconozcan la actuación de la Presencia «YO SOY», es imposible que ella sea interrumpida o que se le interfiera en forma alguna. Al saber que no hay ni tiempo ni espacio, se tiene al alcance el conocimiento de la eternidad.

Para entrar en una esfera más alta que el mundo físico, plenamente consciente, sólo hay que ajustar o cambiar la conciencia. ¿Cómo hacerlo? Sabiendo que ya estás ahí, conscientemente.

Afirma a menudo: *Por el poder del círculo electrónico que yo he creado en contorno mío, no puedo ser afectado ya por dudas y temores. Yo tomo gozoso el cetro de mi "yo soy" y piso resueltamente cualquiera de las altas esferas en que yo quisiera entrar, y conservo la clara y perfecta memoria de mis actividades allí.*

Con esta práctica te encontrarás rápidamente gozando de la libertad ilimitada y la felicidad perfecta de actuar en cualquier plano que tú escojas.

El estar consciente de las cosas que están mil años adelante es tan fácil y tan accesible como ir a tus repisas a tomar un libro que necesites. El gran obstáculo para la libertad humana ha sido la gran ilusión del tiempo y el espacio en la creencia general.

Aquellos que han llegado a la gran desilusión de ver que la riqueza y los efectos exteriores de las cosas no pueden traer la dicha, comprenden la gran bendición que dentro de su propio pensamiento creativo, su propio poder y su propio pensamiento, tienen toda la dicha, la libertad perfecta y el dominio.

Cuando el estudiante comprenda que aquello en que él conecta su atención se le adhiere, se convierte en él, o él se convierte en aquello con toda la intensidad que él emplee, verá la importancia de mantener su atención lejos de todo lo destructivo en la experiencia humana. Aprende a invocar en estos momentos a la Amada Presencia «YO SOY», antes de fijar la atención en las cosas destructivas.

El discutir y comentar los defectos de nuestros amigos, familiares y asociados, comunica esos defectos a nuestras propias conciencias y parece que aumenta el defecto que vemos en el otro. Esto es fijar la atención en lo destructivo y nos convierte en ello.

El hecho de que existen magos negros en el mundo (brujos), o sea, ciertos hijos de Dios que dirigen mal y contaminan la energía electrónica que les viene de su Presencia YO SOY, no es razón para que permitamos que nuestra atención se fije en ese hecho, simplemente porque conocemos los hechos. Lo que nos incumbe es que mantengamos nuestra atención libre para que se fije en nuestro propio autocontrol impulsándolo a que se pose en lo que nos conviene.

Pocos se dan cuenta de que cuando vuelven a pensar o a estudiar un caso negativo y destructivo, o que cuando alguien les ha desagradado en alguna forma y ellos se permiten volver a repasar el incidente, se están grabando y fabricando ese caso en sus conciencias puras, ensuciándolas y atrayendo el resultado para que vuelva una y otra vez a ocurrir.

Pero yo quiero imprimir en las mentes de los estudiantes que es tonto dejarse afectar y perturbar por actividades, reales o imaginarias, de la conciencia exterior, ya que una vez que sepan «YO SOY LA ÚNICA PRESENCIA TODOPODEROSA ACTUANDO EN MI MENTE, MI CUERPO Y MI MUNDO», ya no podrán ser afectados ni perturbados por ninguna asociación del mundo exterior. Deben saber que están enteramente inmunes de las molestias y perturbaciones de la mente de otros, no importa lo que traten de hacernos.

Cuando el individuo se da cuenta de que su propio pensamiento y sentimiento le puede producir todo lo que él necesite, se sentirá libre del deseo de las riquezas y todo lo que el mundo exterior pueda ofrecerle.

Les aseguro que no existe un mundo «sobrenatural». En cuanto pisamos una esfera superior a ésta, aquella se hace tan real y verdadera como ésta. Es simplemente otro estado de conciencia. Para alegría de tus familiares te diré que de aquí a cien años habrá centenares de personas que podrán usar los rayos cósmicos para limpiar y conservar sus casas, y cuando ya no sientan la necesidad de seguir las modas creadas por las ideas comercializadas, tejerán sus mantos «de un solo hilo y sin costuras» hechos con los rayos cósmicos.

Muchos estudiantes me preguntan cómo es que los maestros, con todos sus poderes creadores, prefieren vivir en habitaciones humildes. La explicación es sencilla. La mayor parte de sus actividades son en altas esferas, dirigiendo magnos rayos de Luz para la bendición de la humanidad desde sus hogares de Luz y Sabiduría tan bellos y trascendentes, como para hacerse invisibles a aquellos que aún ocupan cuerpos físicos. Si los estudiantes lograran comprender esto les evitaría mucha confusión y les quedaría más tiempo para usar en la actividad de la Gran Presencia «YO SOY».

Esto los llevará al estado trascendente que consume la ansiedad por las riquezas del mundo exterior, todas las cuales no son sino basura en comparación al poder creador inherente en todo individuo. Éste puede traer a la manifestación el poder trascendente a través del autocontrol y maestría. Yo te digo, amado estudiante, hijo del Dios Único: ¿No vale la pena usar tu más sincero esfuerzo cuando sabes que no puedes fallar? Empuña el cetro de tu Magno Poder Creador y libérate para siempre de todas esas ataduras y limitaciones que han torturado a la humanidad a través de las edades. Yo te aseguro que todo el que se empeña en adquirir el cetro y esta maestría recibirá toda la ayuda necesaria.

Aquel que tenga la comprensión de su habilidad creadora debe saber que él puede crear todo lo que se le antoje, no importa cuál sea el rango vibratorio, en la Luz, o en cualquier otra condensación que él desee mantener.

Tú sabes que tienes la habilidad de transferir tu pensamiento de Caracas a New York en el mismo instante, lo mismo que cambiar tu pensamiento desde una condición de Luz a una condensación muy espesa, tal como el hierro. Esto te hará ver que lo que tú haces en cada momento consciente y voluntariamente, puedes hacerlo con mucho más poder si fijas tu atención conscientemente manteniéndola en aquello que deseas manifestar.

El hecho de que tú no hayas precipitado aún de lo invisible a lo visible es lo que produce esa duda que te molesta. Hasta el día en que manifiestes una sencilla precipitación, tu valor y confianza surgirán, y en el futuro no tendrás inconveniente en precipitar lo que quieras. *LA ATENCIÓN* ES EL CANAL POR MEDIO DEL CUAL LA MAGNA ENERGÍA ATRAÍDA FLUYE A SU REALIZACIÓN.

La humanidad, a través de las centurias, se ha formado estos muros de limitación. Ahora hay que derrumbarlos y consumirlos de cualquier manera que podamos. Al comienzo se necesita determinación para lograrlo, pero cuando uno sabe que el Poder de «YO SOY» es el que está actuando, también sabe que no es posible fallar. En exterior sólo tienes que mantener la atención fija sobre el objeto que quieres hacer visible, te concentras, y de pronto lo encuentras plasmado y te asombras al constatar que has vivido tanto tiempo sin hacer uso de este poder.

La longitud del rayo que se desprende de la sustancia precipitada o condensación de Luz, es controlada por la conciencia del que lo usa. Si esa conciencia se eleva muy alto el fulgor es muy grande.

La «JOYA DE LUZ» está aún en su trascendente estado de perfección. La Joya es una sustancia condensada, tal como el diamante, esmeralda o rubí, pero, naturalmente, tomará la condición del que la lleva. Si el rango vibratorio de éste es bajo, la joya o piedra perderá su brillo, mientras que si el pensamiento es trascendente, esta piedra se pondrá muy luminosa.

Si el temor te hace creer en una presencia perturbadora, tú eres el responsable, ya que si hubiese una presencia perturbadora y tú la calificas con la presencia "Yo soy", verás cuán imposible sería que ella te pudiera perturbar. No hay sino una sola energía actuando, y en el propio momento en que tú reconoces en ella la presencia "Yo soy", has recalificado aquella actividad con perfección.

La expectativa es una poderosa conciencia calificadora. La expectativa intensa es una cosa estupenda; siempre manifiesta. El hombre, a través de las centurias, ha creado un velo que le oculta estas esferas trascendentes. Ahora, si él lo ha creado, entonces el sentido común y la razón le dicen que él puede disolver esa creación.

Una radiación poderosa ha salido hacia los estudiantes, radiación que será sostenida hasta que ellos reciban este trabajo que se ha dictado hoy. Pero transmitirles la sencillez, la facilidad y la seguridad con que puede ser materializada la idea, por medio del pensamiento y sentimiento creativos, es cosa que se debe meditar. Esto disolverá la acción de: «¿podré yo?», y en su lugar dirá «YO PUEDO» y «YO SOY». A toda afirmación y decreto agreguen que desean conservar la memoria de cada experiencia y resultados.

Si los estudiantes se mantienen, de tiempo en tiempo recibirán la iluminación que les dará toda la confianza necesaria. Manténganse asidos a una idea y sepan que cualquier conocimiento que necesiten les vendrá instantáneamente.

Cuando permites que tu atención se fije en algo, en ese momento le estás dando el poder de actuar en tu mundo, es decir, que no puede existir una cualidad o una apariencia en tu mundo sino aquella que tú mismo le des.

INTERPRETACIÓN

La metafísica está llena de leyes que están en constante acción. Debemos estar conscientes que estas leyes han guiado a la civilización desde el principio de los tiempos. No hay nada en el universo que éstas no puedan explicar. El maestro Saint Germain, hombre místico a quien la historia nos lo revela en fecha y tiempo no precisos, cita para ser felices la *Ley de Correspondencia:* "El secreto para ser feliz se encuentra en el interior de cada ser humano." Esta ley se basa en el hecho de que lo afín atrae a lo afín.

En tiempos de Abraham, el maestro Hermes Trismegisto aseguraba que toda la información sobre un hombre se podía encontrar en solo una gota de su sangre y que dentro de cada hombre se hallaba representada la totalidad del universo. Formuló entonces un principio al que llamó la *Ley de la Correspondencia* que decía: "Como es arriba es abajo, y como es abajo es arriba". Con estas palabras creó Hermes un método deductivo que permitió vislumbrar la grandeza del universo creado, donde lo más grande de lo más grande es igual a lo más pequeño de lo más pequeño. Donde todos los niveles de existencia comparten la misma esencia, organizados en un sistema de hologramas dentro de hologramas, dentro de hologramas, hasta el infinito.

La *Ley de la Correspondencia* tiene aplicaciones sin fin. Por ejemplo: considerando en un hombre el cuerpo físico como el "abajo" y su mente como el "arriba" decimos: "como es el pensamiento de un hombre así es su cuerpo". Puede ser: "mente sana en cuerpo sano", o cuerpo enfermo como manifestación de pensamientos distorsionados. Afortunadamente en las enseñanzas de Hermes, "el tres veces sabio", la enfermedad viene de la mano con el remedio: "Cambia el pensamiento y sanarás tu cuerpo."

Esta ley también es conocida como de Afinidad, por el hecho de que lo afín atrae lo afín, por lo que nos debe quedar claro que está íntimamente ligada con el proceso del mentalismo. "Somos lo que pensamos" dice un dicho popular, y en este caso es una realidad

señalada por una ciencia que al parecer posee el secreto de la vida.

¿Por qué buscar la felicidad afuera? Todos los seres
humanos aspiran llegar a la felicidad, pero siempre
sitúan ésta más allá de lo que tienen en ese momento,
la ven como si fuera algo que tuviera que alcanzarse,
como si fuera algo por lo que tuvieran que luchar, como
si fuera algo que llegara justo en el momento en que
ellos consiguen hacer determinadas cosas, pero esta
forma de ver a la felicidad, en realidad los aleja de ella.
Pensar que se encuentra en algún futuro indetermi-
nado, implica que ese futuro nunca se va a hacer presente, pues siempre estará más allá de lo que el propio
individuo ha conseguido; sin embargo, la felicidad se
encuentra presente en todo momento alrededor de
las personas y, más aún, dentro de ellas.

¿QUÉ ES LA FELICIDAD?

El ser humano ha tendido siempre a perseguir la
felicidad como una meta o un fin, como un estado de
bienestar ideal y permanente al que llegar; sin embargo, parece ser que la felicidad se compone de pe-
queños momentos, de detalles vividos en el día a día,
y quizá su principal característica sea la futilidad, su

capacidad de aparecer y desaparecer de forma constante a lo largo de nuestras vidas.

La felicidad, concepto con profundos significados, incluye alegría, pero también otras muchas emociones, algunas de las cuales no son necesariamente positivas (compromiso, lucha, reto, incluso dolor). Es la motivación, la actividad dirigida a algo, el deseo de ello, su búsqueda, y no el logro o la satisfacción de los deseos, lo que produce en las personas sentimientos positivos más profundos.

El término felicidad, cabe mencionar, proviene del griego "ευδαιμονια", que de forma generalizada podría interpretarse como un estado de satisfacción, debido a la propia situación en el mundo. El concepto de felicidad es humano y mundano. Nació en la antigua Grecia, cuando Tales de Mileto afirmó que es sabio *"quien tiene un cuerpo sano, fortuna y un alma bien educada"* (Diógenes Laercio, I, 1, 37). La buena salud, el buen éxito en la vida y en la propia formación, que constituyen los elementos de la felicidad, son inherentes a la situación del hombre en el mundo y entre los otros hombres. Demócrito, de modo más o menos análogo, definió la felicidad como *"la medida del placer y la proporción de la vida"*, o sea como el mantenerse alejado de todo defecto y de todo exceso

(*Fragmentos,* 191, Diels). De cualquier modo, felicidad e infelicidad pertenecen al alma (*Fragmentos,* 170, Diels), ya que sólo el alma *"es la morada de nuestro destino"* (*Fragmentos,* 171, Diels). Por otro lado, Platón negó que la felicidad consistiera en el placer y, en cambio, la consideró relacionada con la virtud. *"Los felices son felices por la posesión de la justicia y de la temperancia, y los infelices, infelices por la posesión de la maldad"* (508 b).

¿Dónde está la felicidad entonces? La felicidad no es un estado futuro, es una posibilidad en el presente, es algo que se tiene, que simplemente no se ha observado no se ha sabido experimentar, no se ha aprendido a verla. Es una palabra que las personas no han aprendido todavía en su correcto significado; generalmente se piensa que la felicidad va asociada a una casa, a un automóvil, a la salud, al cariño, al estado del tiempo, al bienestar económico, a muchas cosas, y por sí sola no se le comprende, ésta es otra de las grandes mentiras, la felicidad es independiente de cualquier objeto, de cualquier cosa, incluso espiritual; es un estado de conciencia, es un momento en la vida del individuo, es una forma distinta de sentirse, de verse a sí mismo, y de ver a todo lo que le rodea.

Contrario a lo que podría pensarse, la felicidad no llega necesariamente con las cosas materiales, ni siquiera con las espirituales, se es feliz por medio de un estado de conciencia. Así pues, no esperemos encontrar la felicidad en un momento futuro de nuestras vidas, ni tampoco esperemos hallarla en el momento en que logremos conseguir tal o cual cosa; la felicidad está en este momento, ha estado siempre presente y estará siempre dentro de nuestras posibilidades.

Estas son las enseñanzas que Saint Germain ha querido legarnos por medio del capítulo ocho de su *Libro de Oro*.

BIENAVENTURADOS...
DIJO JESÚS, EL CRISTO METAFÍSICO

A nadie le resulta extraño el hecho de que se considere a Jesús un metafísico consumado, un maestro ascendido. Si es así, y así es como se acepta, en el mundo occidental Jesucristo es uno de los nombres más conocidos, sin importar la religión a la que se pertenezca. Desde el momento en que tenemos edad suficiente para comprender sobre el mundo y la vida se nos habla de Jesús, el hijo de María, a quien cuidó con gran esmero José, pero que realmente era hijo del Espíritu Santo. Para recordar su nacimiento, año con año nos vemos reunidos en la noche del 24 de diciembre con los familiares. Eso hace del cumpleaños de Jesús el acontecimiento más especial y difundido del año.

No obstante, de su vida poco se conoce y la poca información que se tiene nos ha sido brindada por medio de las Sagradas Escrituras, las cuales han sido calificadas de malinterpretadas y hasta mutiladas. Y es que ciertamente a lo largo de dos mil años se han desarrollado cientos de sectas cristianas, todas ellas con sus propias ideas acerca de lo que dijo y quiso decir Jesús, y acerca de cómo un ser humano debería llevar la vida de un verdadero creyente.

¿Qué realmente quiso decir el Mesías con sus parábolas, y por qué utilizarlas en vez de hablar con claridad? Este problema de variación es posible que se haya suscitado en la traducción, aunque también es muy probable que Jesús no haya querido legar sus enseñanzas de una forma más sencilla. Como quiera que sea, en Jesucristo se encierra el misterio del que habla Saint Germain; es decir, vuelve a aparecer la tríada en el "yo".

Desde este punto de vista, Jesús es la representación de la esencia del amor de Dios. Fue amor en sí mismo y tuvo que venir a la Tierra de una forma especial, como un individuo sobrenatural para enseñar. Pero, ¿fueron sus enseñanzas algo novedoso para la humanidad? Es muy probable que para la época en que vivió sí, aunque por otro lado cuatro siglos antes de su nacimiento, Aristóteles dijo: *"Al juzgar de las vidas que viven, la mayoría de hombres identifica el bien, o la felicidad, con placer"*, y él, habiendo sido iniciado en la metafísica, no compartió aquel punto de vista. Al contrario, él consideraba que para que el hombre fuera feliz debía dedicarse a la acción virtuosa y a la contemplación, aguantando los cambios de la vida en una forma noble y completamente decorosa (Ética A Nicomaco, Libro 1, capítulo 10). Todo lo anterior, si podemos compararlo con la vida de Jesús, es exactamente lo que llevó a cabo el Mesías.

La búsqueda de una vida virtuosa era realmente la base de estas enseñanzas; representaban la oportunidad para reconectarse con la energía suprema; ese es el fin único de la metafísica, mostrarnos un modo de trascender. En ese tiempo —hablo de cuatrocientos años antes del nacimiento de Cristo— los autores que más admiraron la vida virtuosa fueron Aristóteles y Séneca. Ellos analizaron con profundidad las virtudes como valentía, justicia, prudencia y templanza. Séneca dijo: *"Si la virtud nos precede, cada paso de la vida estará segura."*

Jesús, por su parte, nos dice porqué es posible ser dichosos en medio de las aflicciones. Antes de todo, hay que notar que él asume la búsqueda de la virtud. Por ejemplo, que la persecución viene "a causa de la justicia" y que las cosas malas que hablan de nosotros son "falsas." Pero para Jesús, la base de la felicidad es más profunda que la conciencia tranquila que resulta de una vida de virtud. Jesús añade una frase pequeña: "por causa mía". Es decir, lograremos la felicidad si abrazamos la desgracia por Jesús.

Esto cobra sentido cuando lo comparamos con lo dicho por Séneca; si la virtud nos precede, cada paso de la vida estará segura. Jesús, por su parte, añade la frase "por causa mía". De esto resulta que sin importar los cambios que traiga el destino por causa nuestra somos y debemos ser felices. Veamos las palabras de Cristo:

- Bienaventurados los pobres de espíritu porque de ellos es el Reino de los cielos.

- Bienaventurados los mansos porque ellos heredarán la Tierra.

- Bienaventurados los que lloran, porque ellos serán consolados.

- Bienaventurados los que tienen hambre y sed de justicia porque ellos serán hartos.

- Bienaventurados los misericordiosos, porque ellos alcanzarán misericordia.

- Bienaventurados los limpios de corazón, porque ellos verán a Dios.

- Bienaventurados los que buscan la paz, porque ellos serán llamados hijos de Dios.

- Bienaventurados los perseguidos por causa de la justicia, porque de ellos es el Reino de los cielos.

- Bienaventurados serán ustedes cuando los injurien y persigan y digan —mintiendo— todo mal contra ustedes, por causa mía. Alégrense y regocíjense, porque es grande la recompensa que ustedes tendrán en los cielos. Pues así persiguieron a los profetas anteriores a ustedes.

En este sentido, Jesús nos vino a mostrar una corriente filosófica en la que se basaron distintas religiones para fundarse. De esto es creencia metafísica que Jesucristo fue uno de los maestros de más alta ascendencia que visitaron jamás la Tierra. Vino para darnos la verdad, amor y ejemplo. Mientras estuvo aquí fueron muchos los que escribieron acerca de lo que hizo, dejándonos un magnífico registro de su estancia aquí. Después de que se marchara, también fueron muchos los que «canalizaron» sus enseñanzas del «espíritu» (que llamaron Espíritu Santo), e impartieron instrucción en la verdad y en el amor. Algunas de esas canalizaciones son los libros del Nuevo Testamento, traducido y vuelto a traducir numerosas veces y transmitido entre los hombres desde hace dos mil años.

LA FELICIDAD SEGÚN EL EVANGELIO

Una pregunta que surge es: ¿fue Jesús feliz?, y si analizamos con detenimiento su vida nos daremos cuenta de que tuvo una senda llena de dificultades, y por último, una muerte injusta y criminal. Sin embargo, Jesucristo no era una persona triste, sino serena, bondadosa y llena de gozo. A pesar de sus carencias, podría ser considerado el hombre más rico del mundo, porque si bien no poseía bienes materiales, era capaz de hacerse de todo lo que necesitaba. Recordemos esos pasajes en los que multiplica los panes, convierte el agua en vino, resucita a su amigo; en fin, ¿qué más podía pedir si lo poseía todo?

Las enseñanzas de la montaña son quizá el mayor legado del Mesías. Decíamos líneas atrás "bienaventurado"; pero, ¿qué significa esta palabra? Según la Real Academia de la Lengua Española, se dice de la persona que goza de Dios en el cielo, así como de la persona afortunada, sencilla y cándida, y ¿acaso esto no es lo que dice Séneca sobre la felicidad? Recordemos que el filósofo griego dice que la felicidad puede ser alcanzada por medio de la virtud.

Así pues, ahora conocemos que para ser felices hace falta comenzar a sentirlo, despertando la conexión con nuestro interior sin importar las dificultades del mundo exterior.

PRINCIPIOS METAFÍSICOS
DE LA FELICIDAD

Si está en nosotros el secreto para ser felices, ¿por qué simplemente no serlo? Se dice que el cambio fundamental ocurrirá cuando el Pensador cambie de mentalidad. Y ¿quién es el pensador? La respuesta es: cada uno de nosotros en su individualidad. Para que esto ocurra hace falta despertar siete principios en nosotros.

1. Del mentalismo.
2. De correspondencia.
3. De vibración.
4. De polaridad.
5. Del ritmo.
6. De causa y efecto.
7. De generación.

Los siete principios fueron escritos por Hermes en el antiguo Egipto. Hermes es considerado el Padre de la Sabiduría y descubridor de la Alquimia. Toda su enseñanza se mantuvo guardada en forma secreta para la gente y sólo fue revelada a unos pocos escogidos en aquel entonces. De allí viene el concepto de "herméticamente" guardado.

Originalmente, toda la información se transmitió de boca en boca, sin material escrito. Luego se inició la recopilación de estas enseñanzas en un conjunto de axiomas y máximas, en el libro llamado *El Kybalión*, escrito por tres iniciados. Muchas de las enseñanzas metafísicas también se han difundido bajo la autoría del Conde de Saint Germain, quien según aseguran los estudiosos del tema, fue una de las reencarnaciones del maestro Hermes. Los estudiantes y maestros herméticos modernos consideran a la Alquimia como un "arte de transmutación mental", por el cual se reemplazan pensamientos de baja naturaleza por otros más elevados. Ellos sostienen que la llamada "piedra filosofal", capaz de transmutar metales en oro, era sólo un símbolo que los antiguos tomaban para representar la transformación del hombre de "plomo" en hombre de "oro".

El conocimiento de las leyes del Universo nos da la oportunidad de transformarnos a nosotros mismos y a la materia que nos rodea. Cabe mencionar que estos siete principios son la base de todo, no solamente de la felicidad, pero ésta, queda claro, es un bien buscado que se encuentra dentro de cada ser humano. Dichas enseñanzas fueron conocidas por Aristóteles, Platón, Mahoma, Jesús, Moisés, Andrónico de Rodas, Saint Germain, entre otros, y gracias a la predicación de los mismos es que podemos conocerlas sin ningún tipo de censura.

PRINCIPIO DEL MENTALISMO

El Principio del Mentalismo dice textualmente: **"EL TODO es Mente; el Universo es mental."**
Para analizar este principio tenemos que partir de la base de que en el Universo donde vivimos existe un solo Dios. A pesar de las grandes diferencias culturales y religiosas que existen en el mundo, Dios es Uno solo y es el mismo para todos. *El Kybalión* utiliza la palabra "Todo", y de esta manera se sintetiza la idea de una Única Presencia.

De acuerdo con esto, en el Universo hay una sola Mente y absolutamente todo lo que existe está comprendido dentro de esa Mente. Cada uno de nosotros es una partícula o pensamiento inmerso en este gran cuerpo mental y de esta manera se explica cómo se dan los fenómenos parapsicológicos, tales como la transmisión de pensamientos o las premoniciones acerca del futuro.

En síntesis: "Todos estamos conectados por una sola Mente"; al existir una sola Mente, como consecuencia, existe una sola Ley, y ésta se manifiesta a través de los siete principios. Si aceptamos la idea de que Dios es Infinito, Omnipresente y Eterno, algunas de las preguntas que surgen son: ¿Cómo creó Dios al Universo? ¿De dónde extrajo el material necesario para hacer todo lo que hizo? Si Dios extrajo material de algún lugar, entonces no sería ni Infinito ni Omnipresente. La respuesta correcta a esos interrogantes es una sola: Todo lo que Él creó, lo creó en Su propia Mente. Es decir que todo lo que existió, existe y existirá está incluido en esa gran Mente Universal.

El hombre fue hecho "a imagen y semejanza" de su Creador. El hombre puede crear utilizando materiales del mundo concreto pero, cualquiera que sea su creación, siempre comenzará en su propia Mente. El Universo es mental y esto significa que "cada una de las cosas que vivimos depende de nuestro pensamiento". Para algunos, la vida es una gran oportunidad para crecer y disfrutar; para otros, la vida sólo es un gran sacrificio y una continua lucha. La gran diferencia entre ellos está en su propia mente, en su manera de percibir el mundo. Nuestro "Universo Personal" depende de nuestro Pensamiento.

Todo lo que uno llegue a creer de sí mismo es lo que va a ver reflejado en los demás. Si una persona se siente exitosa, merecedora y poseedora de buena suerte, entonces atraerá hacia sí misma situaciones y personas que reflejarán su creencia. Lo mismo ocurre con las personas negativas que creen todo lo contrario. El Universo en que vivimos es mental y responde a lo que elegimos pensar en cada momento. No existe nada aleatorio en la vida: "Todo lo que ocurre siempre está reflejando alguna pauta de pensamiento que llevamos dentro."

Si el Universo es mental y todo depende de nuestro pensamiento, entonces la primera tarea será aprender a "Controlar el Pensamiento".

Ahora bien, todo lo que nosotros llamamos Universo o Dios, se manifiesta a través del "Espíritu". El espíritu tiene una parte obediente que es el "Alma", ella se encarga de manifestar lo que llamamos "Cuerpo" u "Objeto". Cuando llevamos esta estructura a nuestra vida humana, dicha estructura se identifica de la siguiente manera: lo que llamamos "Espíritu" es nuestra Mente Consciente; el "Alma" es la Mente

Inconsciente y, finalmente, el "Cuerpo" se corresponde con nuestro cuerpo físico. Por lo tanto, lo que nos conecta con nuestro Creador es nuestro Espíritu, que tiene su asiento en la Mente Consciente. Allí es donde radica nuestra Voluntad y nuestro Poder de Decisión. Se llama "Libre Albedrío" a la capacidad que tenemos de elegir nuestros propios pensamientos.

De acuerdo con nuestro libre albedrío, nosotros podemos elegir el "cielo" o el "infierno" según lo que aceptemos como verdadero en nuestra conciencia. Muchas personas creen que el libre albedrío significa escaparle al Karma o hacer lo que se les da la gana, pero esto no es así. Es solamente nuestra libertad de elegir lo que queremos pensar.

Nuestro Poder de Acción radica siempre en la Mente Consciente. De acuerdo con esto, a partir de ahora debemos abandonar la idea de que somos víctimas de nuestro destino y tenemos que empezar a aceptar que "Todo lo que nos ocurre lo estamos eligiendo, de alguna manera".

Muchas de estas elecciones se dan en tan sólo fracciones de segundos y se depositan en nuestra Mente Inconsciente, donde germinan y luego se manifiestan en nuestras vidas.

Así es como funciona todo el Universo. Vivimos en un Universo que siempre dice "Sí" a todo lo que elegimos creer. La mayoría de nuestras creencias se ha ido formando a través del tiempo, de acuerdo con la familia, cultura, sociedad, religión y las instituciones de educación a las que asistimos. Muchas de nuestras ideas ni siquiera son nuestras, sino que han sido impuestas por nuestros mayores a lo largo de nuestra crianza. Es importante saber que todo aquello que ya está depositado en nuestra Mente Inconsciente se puede remover. Podemos crear nuevos pensamientos, aceptar nuevas ideas y diseñar un porvenir mucho más conveniente y favorable.

PRINCIPIO DE CORRESPONDENCIA

El estudio del Principio del Mentalismo nos enseñó que "Con nuestro Pensamiento creamos una realidad...". El segundo Principio, denominado "de Correspondencia", nos permitirá entender cómo y por qué a veces creamos situaciones negativas o desfavorables; por qué atraemos a personas que nos mienten, nos engañan, nos roban dinero, y demás. La comprensión de este principio es la clave para encontrar soluciones a esos problemas.

De acuerdo con el libro *El Kybalión*, el Principio de Correspondencia dice textualmente: "Como arriba es abajo; como abajo es arriba." En el Universo todo se corresponde entre sí: tal como es aquí abajo, va a ser allá arriba; cuando uno logra entender todo lo que ocurre en el mundo material, entonces podrá entender todo lo que sucede en el mundo espiritual. Este principio es un auxiliar de la mente que nos permite entender lo que ocurre en el resto del Universo conociendo solamente una de sus partes. Si se estudia el funcionamiento de una estrella, como consecuencia se entenderá el funcionamiento de las galaxias. Si se estudia el comportamiento de un habitante de una sociedad, se podrá llegar a entender cómo funciona dicha sociedad.

Estudiar una parte del todo nos permite comprender el resto. Éste es el principio de la analogía que nos da la posibilidad de entender la relación presente entre los distintos planos de existencia. Cuando llevamos este principio al nivel humano, podemos modificar las palabras y decir: "Como adentro es afuera; como afuera es adentro." Todo lo que sucede alrededor de una persona refleja lo que le está ocurriendo por dentro. Esto significa que cuando una persona es desordenada con sus cosas, está demostrando su desorden interno. Por el contrario, quienes están en el otro extremo y son muy rígidos con el orden están reflejando una rigidez mental en sus ideas. Lo de adentro es como lo de afuera y viceversa.

PRINCIPIO DE VIBRACIÓN

Hemos aprendido anteriormente que "Dios crea todo a partir de su Mente". Nosotros, creados a Su Imagen y Semejanza, hacemos lo mismo. Por lo tanto, llegamos a la conclusión de que vivimos en un Universo Mental: "Aquello que llegamos a Creer es lo que se manifiesta en nuestra vida."

La mente humana está dividida básicamente en dos partes: la Consciente y la Inconsciente. La última es la depositaria de todas nuestras programaciones y recuerdos; mientras que en la primera radica todo nuestro Poder de Decisión. La Mente Consciente es la que se encuentra conectada con el Espíritu. Solamente al ser consciente de lo que se vive se puede cambiar. La Mente Subconsciente es la equivalente al Alma; es el gran archivo de las experiencias de esta vida y de las anteriores. Finalmente, tenemos nuestro Cuerpo Físico, que es el vehículo principal para vivir las experiencias en este plano.

Aprendimos que existe una correspondencia entre lo que vivimos por fuera y lo que llevamos adentro;

que la realidad no es más que un espejo de nuestro interior. Esto significa que si vivimos un caos, sin amor, con problemas económicos, o enfermos, es porque existe una idea o programación que nos lleva a elegir eso. A partir de esta unidad, vamos a dar un paso adelante y estudiaremos una de las maneras de producir cambios profundos en nuestra realidad. Textualmente, el Principio de Vibración dice lo siguiente: **"Nada está inmóvil, todo se mueve, todo vibra."**

Esto significa que en el Universo donde vivimos no existe nada que sea totalmente firme o estable. Todo se encuentra en un continuo movimiento, una continua vibración y transformación. Cada parte del Universo tiende a transformarse en algo mejor, evoluciona hacia un nuevo nivel de existencia. En nuestro orden personal, la vida nos empuja siempre a vivir de una manera mejor. Las crisis aparecen cuando permanecemos rígidos o inflexibles en una posición. Cuanto más cerrados estemos en una posición o idea, más fuerte será el esfuerzo que hará el Universo para movernos de allí. Por eso es que la gente sufre fuertes crisis y luego cambia. Algunas personas necesitan pasar por enfermedades, accidentes o pérdidas para darse cuenta del valor que tienen ciertas personas o su propia vida. Hay otras personas que caen en la inercia y no toman decisiones; cuando eso ocurre. el Universo mismo toma las decisiones por ellos. De acuerdo con el Principio de Vibración "debemos aprender a prepararnos para los cambios en la vida". Según este principio, tendemos a aferrarnos a una vivienda, una pareja, un trabajo, una amistad, o a cualquier objeto que da seguridad, lo más probable es que tarde o temprano sufriremos. ¿Por qué? Porque en el Universo no existe nada que se encuentre inmóvil. El creer que todo será eterno es una vía segura de frustrarse.

Este principio hermético nos enseña que cada objeto que vemos está compuesto de millones de átomos. Estos átomos se encuentran formados por partículas que giran a grandes velocidades alrededor de un núcleo. Podemos decir que existen dos formas extremas de vibración: una baja, que corresponde a la materia y otra alta, que pertenece al terreno del Espíritu. Cuando la vibración es muy baja, decimos que la materia está en reposo, permanece inerte para nuestros sentidos y parece sólida. Sin embargo, la materia está compuesta de millones de átomos que se encuentran en pleno movimiento y transformación. Por otra parte, cuando la vibración es muy alta, llegamos al extremo del Espíritu y decimos también que la materia está en reposo. Aquí la materia vibra en una frecuencia tan alta que nos da la sensación de que tampoco tiene movimiento. El eslabón entre la materia y el Espíritu es el éter.

Los órganos de nuestro cuerpo físico están formados por células, que, en última instancia, están compuestas de átomos. Por lo tanto, aquello que percibimos como un cuerpo sólido no es tan sólido. Nuestro cuerpo físico está formado por un 99,999% de espacio vacío, y solamente 0,001% de materia; este último porcentaje, según la Física Cuántica, es también espacio vacío. La Física Cuántica es la que estudia el comportamiento del átomo. Ella nos enseña que nuestro cuerpo físico se encuentra continuamente intercambiando átomos con el medio. Al inhalar aire tomamos los átomos con el medio y los átomos del entorno; al exhalar devolvemos átomos de nuestro propio cuerpo físico.

La pregunta inevitable es: ¿qué hace que el cuerpo cambie o se deteriore? Hay una sola respuesta... la mente. Lo que lleva a los átomos a agruparse y a producir cambios en el cuerpo es la idea que gobierna la propia mente, que está compuesta por un cerebro.

El cerebro humano está compuesto por millones de células llamadas "neuronas". Cuando una persona toma una decisión, las neuronas llevan el mensaje o la orden al resto del cuerpo físico para producir la acción. A través de muchos experimentos, se ha descubierto el "mapa del cerebro", según el cual se conocen las actividades que desarrollan las distintas partes del cerebro y su relación con el cuerpo físico. Sin embargo, los investigadores no han encontrado jamás dónde está la parte que elige realizar un determinado movimiento. La conclusión a la que se ha llegado es asombrosa. La mente no está en el cuerpo. La mente ocupa el cerebro físico pero no está en él. La mente es más grande que todo el cuerpo físico y se encuentra en cada parte del mismo, no solamente en el cerebro.

Todo el Universo está compuesto básicamente de la misma sustancia y nosotros, a través de nuestra intención, podemos manejarla para manifestar la realidad que deseamos. De acuerdo con el Principio de Vibración, debemos ir creando la vibración necesaria para atraer la sustancia necesaria.

El Principio de Vibración nos enseña que "las energías iguales se atraen". Por eso vemos que los deportistas van a entrenar a un mismo lugar, al igual que los religiosos se reúnen en una iglesia, los intelectuales en una biblioteca, o los metafísicos en algún lugar de estudio. De esta manera, cada uno se rodea de gente y lugares que están vibrando en la misma frecuencia.

En el Universo existen tres niveles elementales de vibración: baja, media y alta. Son tres escalones con características propias. De acuerdo con nuestro nivel vibratorio personal, estamos ubicados en algunos de estos tres escalones y, como consecuencia, atraemos las cosas de dicho nivel. Es imposible atraer situaciones u objetos que tienen una vibración alta si uno se encuentra en el escalón más bajo.

La depresión, la angustia, el miedo, las enfermedades y todas las emociones más negativas nos llevan a vibrar en el nivel más bajo de esta escala. Mientras una persona se mantenga "vibrando bajo", sólo atraerá a su vida a personas o situaciones que aumentarán su malestar. Éste es el nivel de la "mala suerte". Mucha gente dice: "No termino de salir de un problema que ya tengo otro." La respuesta a esto es muy simple: mientras la persona se mantenga vibrando en ese nivel, continuará atrayendo las cosas de dicho nivel. Hasta que esa persona no cambie su vibración personal, no se manifestarán ni la salud, ni la alegría, ni el amor, ni la felicidad en general.

En el nivel vibración media aparecen las soluciones y la vida fluye. Los obstáculos y problemas de este nivel son más fáciles de resolver y la persona que se encuentra en esa vibración siempre muestra una actitud optimista hacia la vida.

Finalmente, el nivel de vibración más alta corresponde al de la iluminación, la paz y el amor perfecto. Aquí no existen problemas, miedos o enfermedades. Cuando uno vibra en este nivel, lo que uno piensa se manifiesta inmediatamente. El reconocimiento del poder personal es total y absoluto y, por lo general, se lo utiliza para servir a la humanidad.

La vibración más baja corresponde al terreno de nuestro ego, es el nivel del miedo y por eso se generan toda clase de problemas. La vibración media es el terreno de la esperanza, de esta manera, comienza a producirse la "suerte". Finalmente, la vibración más alta corresponde al terreno del Espíritu, es el nivel de la Fe Absoluta, en el cual se producen los milagros. Esta vibración está libre de miedos.

PRINCIPIO DE POLARIDAD

El Principio de Polaridad se encuentra justo en el medio. La comprensión cabal del mismo permite producir grandes cambios en la vida. El Principio de Polaridad dice textualmente: **"Todo es doble; todo tiene dos polos; todo, su par de opuestos; los semejantes y los antagónicos son lo mismo; los opuestos son idénticos en naturaleza, pero diferentes en grado; los extremos se tocan; todas las**

verdades son semiverdades; todas las paradojas pueden reconciliarse."

Para comprender mejor el Principio de Polaridad, lo vamos a estudiar por partes. Está claramente explicado que en el Universo donde vivimos todo es doble, todo tiene su par de opuestos. Algunos son: blanco/ negro, hombre/mujer, calor/frío, arriba/abajo, este/ oeste, bueno/malo, rico/pobre, amor/odio, sucio/ limpio, culpable/inocente. Nuestra función al querer ser felices debería ser armonizar los opuestos.

Venimos al planeta Tierra a desarrollar la habilidad de encontrar el justo equilibrio entre los distintos polos. Tenemos que aprender a pararnos justo en la parte de enmedio. *El Kybalión* dice que "los opuestos son iguales en naturaleza, pero que difieren en grados". Para entender mejor esto debemos imaginarnos un termómetro. En él vemos cómo el mercurio sube o baja la escala de grados indicando la temperatura del ambiente. Pero aquí surge una pregunta clave, ¿dónde empieza el frío y dónde empieza el calor? El límite no está en el grado cero. Cuando hace cero grados se siente mucho frío en cualquiera de las dos escalas conocidas (Centígrados o Farenheit). De acuerdo con los grados centígrados, para algunos el frío comienza a sentirse a los 15 grados, para otros, a los 10. La interpretación es completamente subjetiva.

La conclusión final es que no existe diferencia entre el frío y el calor. Los dos son extremos de una misma cosa, son polos opuestos, la única diferencia entre ellos es el grado en el que se están manifestando. Cuando el termómetro marca los grados menores, tenemos la sensación del frío. Por el contrario, cuando la marca llega a grados mayores decimos que hace calor. Pero en esencia, estamos hablando siempre de la misma cosa: la temperatura.

Tal como lo afirma *El Kybalión*, los opuestos son lo mismo. Cuando vemos a una persona demasiado buena y luego la comparamos con otra que es muy mala, en esencia sabremos que estamos hablando de la misma cosa pero en diferentes grados de manifestación; cada una de ellas está ubicada en un extremo. Todos tenemos distintos grados de bondad y también de maldad. Las personas extremistas, para las cuales todo es blanco o negro, tienen más trabajo por hacer, porque a ellas les resulta más difícil ser parciales o encontrar el punto medio. ¿Cuál es la razón por la cuál debemos aprender a armonizar los opuestos? La respuesta es sencilla: encontrar la unidad en todo.

Recordemos lo estudiado anteriormente: en el Universo existe un solo Dios, una sola Fuente, una sola Energía, un solo Amor; por lo tanto, la diferencia que percibimos entre polos opuestos no es real. Lo que existe en esencia es la Unidad. Si queremos acceder al estado de paz y armonía en la cual habita Dios, debemos aprender a encontrar la unidad en todo lo que nos rodea. Mientras más separación percibimos, más lejos estaremos de encontrar el amor y la paz de Dios. Cuanto más separación percibimos más se manifiestan los conflictos. Debemos aprender a reconocer que el "culpable" también es inocente; que nadie es tan bueno ni tan malo como parece; que nada es tan lindo o tan feo como lo catalogamos; que nada es tan caro o tan barato. Cuando empezamos a ejercitarnos para encontrar la unidad en todo, el resultado que se obtiene es la paz.

Cuando estudiamos el Principio de Vibración, vimos que vibración más alta corresponde al Espíritu; por otra parte, la vibración más baja le corresponde a la materia. Ahora sabemos que, en esencia, los dos extremos son la misma cosa. Sólo cuando aprendamos a pararnos en el punto medio encontraremos la paz. Dicho de otra forma: no se puede vivir feliz en el mundo material sin tener espiritualidad y no se puede ser espiritual si no se tiene orden en el mundo material.

Los dos extremos necesitan ser conciliados para lograr una vida armoniosa y feliz.

Otra parte de este mismo principio sostiene que "los extremos se tocan". Para entender esto, veámoslo en otro ejemplo práctico: si yo decido viajar siempre en dirección este y pudiera dar toda la vuelta al mundo, entonces terminaría en el mismo punto de partida. La pregunta que surge entonces es: ¿Dónde está el oeste? La respuesta más acertada de acuerdo con este principio, sería que el este y el oeste son lo mismo. Debemos recordar que "como arriba es abajo, como abajo es arriba", lo más probable es que si yo viajara a través del Universo siempre en la misma dirección, finalmente terminaría en mi punto de partida. En el Universo todo tiene un movimiento circular cíclico.

¿Pero cómo se aplica esta parte a la vida diaria? La respuesta es muy sencilla: cada vez que te encuentres viviendo una situación extrema, es decir, que estés ubicado en uno de los polos y desees revertir o neutralizar la situación, deberás comenzar a crear la energía de la polaridad opuesta. De esta manera, llevarás el "termómetro" a su punto medio.

Esto es muy importante porque no se puede cruzar de un par de opuestos a otro y esperar un resultado en el primero. Si deseas transmutar una situación, tendrás que utilizar la energía envuelta en ese par, no en otro. Las personas que tienen problemas de dinero o están en la pobreza deben empezar a dar algo de lo poco que tienen; es decir, deben fingir que están en el otro polo y comenzar a actuar como "ricos" o, al menos, como alguien que tiene algún dinero.

Por otra parte, el Principio de Polaridad sostiene que "todas las verdades son semiverdades". En pocas palabras, esto significa que nadie en el planeta Tierra es poseedor de la verdad completa, sino que todos tenemos nuestra cuota de verdad. Es decir que al igual que con las piezas de un rompecabezas, uniendo nuestra semiverdad con la de los demás, encontraremos la verdad completa. Por eso es importante escuchar a otros. Siempre se aprende algo nuevo de los demás.

Cuando nos encontramos defendiendo ciegamente nuestro punto de vista, en realidad, estamos errando porque "ninguno de nosotros es portador de la verdad completa". Cuando criticamos a alguien que piensa o actúa de una manera diferente de la nuestra, en realidad nos estamos cerrando a la posibilidad de aprender otra parte de la verdad. Cada persona, aunque nos parezca errada, tiene su porción de conocimiento. El mantener nuestra mente abierta nos ayudará a escuchar y aprender otra forma de lógica que, finalmente, nos llevará a encontrar el punto medio, o sea, aquello que definimos técnicamente como la armonización de los opuestos.

PRINCIPIO DEL RITMO

El Principio del Ritmo dice textualmente: **"Todo fluye y refluye; todo tiene sus períodos de avance y retroceso; todo asciende y desciende; todo se mueve como un péndulo; la medida de su movimiento hacia la derecha es la misma que la de su movimiento hacia la izquierda; el ritmo es la compensación."**

En el Universo todo tiene un movimiento similar al de las olas, de avance y retroceso. Los científicos ya han comprobado este movimiento a través de la evolución de los planetas, las estrellas, los soles y demás. La vida tiene movimiento pendular y el proceso de nacimiento, crecimiento, desarrollo y muerte se repite incesantemente en todo. El mismo movimiento que se da en el plano físico, también se da en los planos emocional y mental. Esto quiere decir que tanto nuestro humor como nuestros pensamientos también responden a ese ritmo. Como ejemplo, podemos decir que después de un período de gran tristeza, pesadumbre o dolor, se sucede otro lleno de gran alegría, felicidad y satisfacción. A veces, los cambios de humor se dan en el mismo día; uno se siente optimista y alegre, y al rato, triste y preocupado.

El principio está muy relacionado con el anterior: el Principio de Polaridad. En cada punta del péndulo podemos ubicar uno de los polos opuestos y así vemos claramente cómo oscilamos de un extremo al otro. Raramente llegamos a los extremos totales. Nuestro péndulo oscila en diversos grados y, así, alcanzamos ciertos grados de felicidad o de tristeza. *El Kybalión* define a este ritmo como compensación. Aunque el movimiento es difícil de medir en números y no sabemos en qué grado se da, podemos determinar en qué fase del movimiento nos encontramos.

Cuando una persona se encuentra en el polo de la tristeza, debe saber que en algún momento la vida lo llevará hacia el polo de la alegría, lo desee o no. Cuanto más profunda sea la primera, mayor será la segunda. El ritmo siempre comienza por el polo negativo. De esto se deduce que la medida del movimiento negativo será igual a la del movimiento positivo. El Principio del Ritmo nos advierte también que los momentos de felicidad o éxito no son permanentes, tarde o temprano, el péndulo nos llevará a retroceder para luego volver a avanzar. Esto no significa que uno tenga que perder lo que ha logrado, pero es necesario saber que el período de crecimiento o de dicha no es constante. Entonces, debemos prepararnos tomando la mayor ventaja posible de los buenos momentos, hasta que aprendamos a manejar el Principio del Ritmo a voluntad. Por ejemplo, si estoy viviendo un momento de crecimiento económico, tendré que aprovechar para ahorrar parte de ese dinero.

Existen casos en que las personas parecen haberse quedado estancadas en uno de los extremos del péndulo; se dice que esas personas se han "polarizado". La mayoría tiende a estancarse en los polos negativos: pobreza, soledad, enfermedad, y demás. Utilizando ciertas técnicas metafísicas, la persona puede llegar a despolarizarse y mejorar su vida. El estudio del Principio del Ritmo nos permite sintonizarnos con nuestro propio movimiento pendular para aprovechar los momentos de avance.

¿Cómo? El Espíritu se corresponde con la Mente Consciente. Gracias a la acción de nuestro Espíritu tomamos decisiones y nos movemos en cierta dirección; aquí se localiza nuestra "voluntad". El Alma se corresponde con la Mente Inconsciente, es el gran archivo donde almacenamos todas las experiencias vividas. El Alma es la fiel servidora del Espíritu y ejecutará aquello que elija. Finalmente, el cuerpo se corresponde con nuestro cuerpo físico, vehículo necesario para vivir las experiencias en este plano. Si ordenamos estos niveles de existencia de arriba abajo (Espíritu, Alma y Cuerpo) y ubicamos el eje del péndulo en la parte superior, podemos deducir que lo que más sufre el embate de su movimiento es el cuerpo físico, ya que le toca el recorrido más amplio del péndulo. Le sigue el mundo emocional o el terreno del Alma y, finalmente, el plano del Espíritu, donde las situaciones no cambian, aquí el movimiento pendular es muy leve o inexistente. Por lo tanto, en la medida en que ascendemos a planos superiores, el embate del péndulo se reduce hasta que desaparece. Esto se logra cuando ingresamos plenamente en el plano del Espíritu, el plano del eterno presente y la dicha constante.

Uno de los instrumentos más eficaces para acceder al plano del Espíritu es la práctica de la "Meditación". Cuando se entra en meditación, se permanece en un estado sin tiempo, donde las presiones de la vida cotidiana y las de nuestro propio ego desaparecen. Hay muchas maneras de meditar. Básicamente, significa concentrar la mente en un solo pensamiento, que puede ser una palabra determinada (amor, justicia, paz), algún sonido de la naturaleza (el canto de los pájaros, la lluvia, el viento), alguna música o la repetición de un mantra ("Ohm"). Cuando uno realiza una actividad concentrándose totalmente en la misma, se encuentra meditando. Esta actividad puede ser tanto pasiva (por ejemplo: leer un libro o contemplar la naturaleza) como activa (por ejemplo: la práctica de un deporte o el trabajo de jardinería).

En el Universo, todo tiene su propio ritmo: las actividades, los trabajos, las relaciones y demás. Cuando uno aprende a fluir con ese ritmo no sufre. Por ejemplo, hay negocios que funcionan más en verano que en invierno; hay mercaderías que son más requeridas en ciertas épocas del año que en otras; hay actividades que se incrementan hacia fin de año, como las ventas de Navidad. Las relaciones humanas también tienen su ritmo y cumplen ciclos. Si una persona cree que ya ha encontrado el ritmo de su vida y que todo estará bien, tarde o temprano se decepcionará porque se encontrará sumida en alguna crisis o problema. Esto no es un mal augurio sino que, por el contrario, implica reconocer que la vida tiene este movimiento pendular.

Según el Principio del Ritmo, todo en la vida tiene un pendular. Cuanto más lejos ha llegado el péndulo en el polo negativo (tristeza, dolor, sufrimiento etc.), más se inclinará luego hacia el otro extremo (alegría, éxito, felicidad, etc.). De acuerdo con *El Kybalión*, el movimiento siempre comienza en el extremo negativo y nunca al revés. Es decir que si se está viviendo un momento feliz, no significa que luego se va a sufrir. En realidad, el proceso es al revés: si se ha sufrido un gran dolor, la vida luego nos compensa con una gran alegría. El movimiento pendular se reduce en la medida en que nos elevamos espiritualmente y se termina cuando nos hallamos en el terreno del Espíritu. Es entonces cuando se alcanza el estado de dicha constante y paz. Cuando uno logra llegar a ese punto, en el cual se puede sentir bien con pareja o sin ella, dinero, familia, y demás, es cuando uno se ha situado sobre el péndulo. Mientras uno oscila emocional o mentalmente es porque todavía está siendo arrastrado por aquél.

El balance puede lograrse en ciertas áreas primero y luego en las demás. Por ejemplo, una persona puede tener solucionada su vida económica pero no su vida afectiva, o viceversa.

El planeta Tierra también tiene su ritmo. No solamente gira en su órbita alrededor del Sol sino que también gira sobre su propio eje. Además el planeta tiene su ritmo interno, gobernado en gran medida por la influencia de la Luna. De la misma manera en que la Luna produce el aumento o la disminución de las mareas, también produce cambios en el humor de las personas. Básicamente, el movimiento de la Luna muestra dos fases: Creciente y Decreciente; cada una de ellas dura aproximadamente 14 días. A su vez, estas fases se dividen en cuartos que duran alrededor de siete días. Lo que todos debemos saber es que a partir del día en que hay "Luna Nueva" comienza su fase creciente. Mientras la Luna se encuentra en esta fase, el planeta está recibiendo una energía de crecimiento ideal para iniciar cualquier tipo de actividad. Todo lo que se inicia durante este tiempo crecerá con facilidad, especialmente en los siete primeros días. Las personas que quieran que su cabello crezca más rápido y fuerte deben cortárselo en ese momento. En general, esta fase es buena para iniciar negocios, contraer matrimonio, viajar, firmar contratos, cambiar de trabajo, comenzar estudios, mudarse, hacer dieta, empezar a escribir un libro o comenzar cualquier tipo de proyecto o diseño.

Por otra parte, a partir de la "Luna Llena" comienza su fase decreciente. Esta fase es ideal para finalizar todo lo iniciado con anterioridad, especialmente en los siete primeros días Es el momento de terminar un trabajo incompleto, finalizar algún trámite legal, divorciarse o separarse (de esta manera no se vuelve a la misma persona), regresar de viaje, cerrar una compañía, finalizar un libro o proyecto, renunciar a un puesto, cortarse el cabello para que crezca lentamente y demás.

De acuerdo con las fases de la Luna podemos iden-
tificar el ritmo del planeta y elegir el momento más
apropiado para nuestras actividades personales. Técnicamente, los horarios que hay que evitar son aquellos en que la Luna está "fuera de curso". Esto ocurre
cada dos días y medio y su duración es variable. En
los calendarios se muestran estos horarios con la si-
gla: "vc" (en inglés: "*void of course*", o fuera de curso)
y, además, se indica la hora y los minutos en que comienza y termina dicho período.

Es entonces cuando aumenta la "marea emocional"
de la gente y todas las decisiones que se toman en ese
momento son erróneas. Si uno conoce a una persona bajo el influjo de la Luna fuera de curso, es muy
probable que nunca llegue a nada con ella porque la
relación estará basada en puras fantasías. También
ocurre que si la persona se ha peleado con su pareja
durante esas horas, la separación será sólo momen-
tánea. Si una persona viaja con este influjo, terminará
en un destino que no era el programado o se le ex-
traviará su equipaje. En esencia, nunca ocurre lo que
uno cree, ya sea que se tenga un pensamiento positivo o negativo. Cuando la Luna está fuera de curso,
se planean viajes, reuniones, matrimonios o negocios
que nunca llegan a concretarse.

Otra de las manifestaciones del Principio del Ritmo que encontramos a diario es la "música". En esencia, la música es ritmo y tiene su propio movimiento pendular. El tipo de música que uno prefiere denota en gran medida la velocidad del péndulo en el cual uno está oscilando. Si a uno le gusta la música romántica, el péndulo oscilará más lentamente; si uno prefiere la salsa o el rock, estará moviéndose a mucha mayor velocidad. Hemos aprendido que para programar nuestra mente debemos tener presente lo que hablamos, lo que visualizamos y aquello que sentimos. La música, por lo general, reúne a estos tres elementos y, en muchos casos, lo hace para expresar dramas o dolor.

Algunos ejemplos de letras dramáticas son: No podré vivir sin tu cariño; no podré resistir sin tu amor... Vuélveme a querer, no me lastimes... Por lo general, cuando uno canta estas canciones repite las palabras con entusiasmo; se visualiza con claridad lo que se está cantando y, finalmente, se pone el condimento más importante: la "emoción o sentimiento". En pocas palabras, se están usando todos los ingredientes metafísicos necesarios para manifestar algo. Por lo tanto, si una persona canta "No soy nada sin ti", la mente tomará esa frase como una "orden" y hará todo lo posible para ejecutarla, haciendo que la persona se sienta en la miseria al estar separada de su pareja.

La "música" reúne todo lo necesario para producir la manifestación. El peligro real existe cuando la persona se identifica con el drama. Al cantarlo, lo afirma con las palabras, lo visualiza claramente y lo siente en lo más profundo de su corazón. La "música instrumental" también "habla" y cuenta historias. Hay ciertas músicas instrumentales que levantan el ánimo y otras que, por el contrario, deprimen. Cada tema musical tiene su vibración propia. Debemos ser muy cuidadosos y elegir todo lo que nos lleve a elevarnos y a sentir dicha.

PRINCIPIO DE CAUSA Y EFECTO

El sexto principio metafísico es uno de los más difundidos y dice textualmente: **"Toda causa tiene su efecto, todo efecto tiene su causa; todo sucede de acuerdo con la Ley; la suerte no es más que el nombre que se le da a una Ley no conocida; hay muchos planos de causalidad pero nada escapa a la Ley."**

Absolutamente todo lo que estamos viviendo en el presente ha sido generado en algún momento, lo hemos creado ya sea consciente o inconscientemente en ésta o en otra vida. Cuando decimos que algo nos sucede "por casualidad", sólo estamos refiriéndonos a una ley que desconocemos, pero en realidad era un evento que nos tocaba vivir porque lo habíamos generado de alguna manera.

Es agradable pensar que todo lo bueno que nos ocurre es el producto de nuestras buenas acciones; pero por el contrario, nos cuesta aceptar que las situaciones negativas que se nos presentan también las hemos creado. Se nos hace difícil llegar a entender por qué y cuándo generamos lo negativo. Este principio nos da la respuesta al explicarnos que son muchos los planos de causación; algunos de ellos provienen desde muy atrás en el tiempo y están dormidos en la memoria, son eventos que pudieron darse tanto en la infancia como en vidas anteriores.

Además, genéticamente recibimos la "influencia" de nuestros padres, a eso le agregamos la de los cuatro abuelos y, si seguimos, vemos que también recibimos la influencia de ocho bisabuelos. Así, esta cadena continúa infinitamente. También recibimos las influencias de la sociedad en la que crecemos, la religión que practicamos, las instituciones de enseñanza a las que asistimos, los lugares de trabajo, los clubes, los amigos que nos rodean, y demás. Éstos son sólo algunos ejemplos para indicar que existen muchos planos de causación y nosotros somos el resultado de la suma de dichos planos. Llamamos "planos de causación" a los lugares, personas y eventos que nos han enseñado un "patrón mental o creencia" que tomamos como verdaderos.

Cada persona debe analizar el conjunto de información que ha recibido a lo largo de su vida; conscientemente debe seleccionar aquello que desea mantener en su mente y lo que debe desechar. En este proceso se debe reconocer lo que pensaba nuestro padre, nuestra madre, nuestros abuelos, y qué es lo que elegimos pensar nosotros. También es conveniente recordar lo que uno acostumbraba pensar tiempo atrás y lo que elige pensar ahora. Siempre tenemos la libertad de poder elegir en el presente, que es el único momento que existe. Recuerda que lo que llamamos "libre albedrío" no es más que la oportunidad que se nos da de elegir nuestros pensamientos. En esto radica nuestro verdadero poder y es así como tomamos las riendas de nuestra vida.

En este proceso de selección de pensamientos debemos ser responsables y evitar en todo momento caer en el papel de víctima. Para la mayoría, es más fácil culpar a alguien o a algo por la infelicidad y, por lo tanto, se deja de lado la posibilidad de "cambiar y crecer". Hay personas que culpan al gobierno, la situación económica, su pareja, su familia, sus hijos, jefes, y además, algunos llegan a culpar al clima (humedad, calor, frío) por su insatisfacción.

Tal como aprendimos al estudiar el Principio de Correspondencia, debemos recordar que "todo lo que ocurre por fuera está reflejando nuestro estado interno". Cuando algo externo nos produce insatisfacción o dolor, eso sólo nos está recordando que tenemos una herida que sanar; de otra manera, no nos alteraríamos.

Es muy recomendable investigar el origen de las situaciones presentes. Si estás viviendo un momento de soledad, no se debe a que tienes "mala suerte" y no encuentras a nadie adecuado para ti. Esa soledad tiene un significado en tu vida; es una lección que debes aprender. La manera más rápida de encontrar respuestas a los conflictos que vivimos es formulando la pregunta a nuestro Yo Superior o Dios Interno. Esto se debe hacer preferiblemente en estado de meditación. Las respuestas que uno recibe siempre son claras y concretas; por lo general, se resumen en pocas palabras o en una sensación.

Las aparentes injusticias que vemos en la vida diaria encuentran su fundamento en este principio. A lo largo de numerosas vidas anteriores hemos ido generando causas, que determinan nuestra situación presente. Hay personas que han hecho mucho bien en el pasado y ahora les toca vivir su recompensa. A estas personas las percibimos como "afortunadas". Por otra parte, hay otros que han cometido muchos errores, han quebrado ciertas leyes universales y ahora se encuentran atrapados en problemas y dificultades. Por eso es que nace gente pobre, enferma o con "mala suerte", mientras que otros nacen saludables, en un hogar confortable y con buenas oportunidades. Sin embargo, sin importar cuál es la apariencia o situación que nos toca vivir, todos venimos al planeta con la única función de sanarnos a nosotros mismos. Por tal motivo, los problemas desaparecen cuando terminamos de aprender nuestra lección. Así vemos que todo lo malo que vivimos no es más que la oportunidad de abrir nuestra conciencia a un conocimiento nuevo.

Se llama "karma" a la deuda que tenemos con nuestro destino y "dharma" a la recompensa que recibimos por nuestras buenas obras del pasado. Por ejemplo, una persona puede estar atravesando una crisis y, en el momento menos esperado, aparece alguien que la ayuda desinteresadamente. Ese "alguien" quizá sea una persona a la cual ha beneficiado antes. Todo el bien que hacemos a los demás vuelve en algún momento a nosotros multiplicado. Ocurre lo mismo con todo lo malo.

Si alguna vez hemos perjudicado a alguien, tarde o temprano alguien nos va a perjudicar. Esto es lo que la Biblia explica como la "Ley del Talión", que dice textualmente: "Ojo por ojo, diente por diente." Esta ley ha sido mal interpretada y muchos la entienden como la ley de la venganza; sin embargo, lo que afirma no es más que la ley de causa y efecto. El karma y el dharma pueden entenderse como actividades en dos bancos diferentes. Al primero le debemos dinero y nos perseguirá hasta que le paguemos. Por el contrario, el segundo nos paga intereses por lo que hemos depositado. Estos bancos no tienen conexión entre sí; es decir que por más buenas obras que hagamos en el presente, igual tendremos que saldar nuestras deudas con el destino.

La cadena del karma puede llegar a ser eterna: una persona quizá sea víctima de alguien en una vida y luego se vuelva vengadora en la siguiente, para luego volver a ser la víctima y así sucesivamente. La cadena se corta cuando una de las partes involucradas decide perdonar. El karma se disuelve por completo gracias a la práctica del perdón.

Perdonar no es tan fácil como uno cree. Muchas personas que dicen haber perdonado sólo hacen un juego intelectual; cuando vuelven a tener otro problema con la persona "perdonada", el resentimiento y los reproches aparecen instantáneamente. Esto es lo que conocemos como "perdono pero no olvido", lo que sólo nos indica que el perdón no ha tenido lugar aún. El verdadero perdón otorga paz.

Básicamente, hay dos maneras de cortar el karma. Para entender cómo funcionan estas dos maneras, vamos a imaginarnos una relación entre un hombre y una mujer en la cual el primero ha perjudicado a la segunda. En esta vida, ella sentirá un gran deseo de vengarse y perjudicarlo, pero como se ha elevado espiritualmente y conoce la Ley de Causa y Efecto elige perdonarlo y NO responde al impulso negativo. El karma ha sido interrumpido gracias a su decisión de perdonar.

Imaginemos ahora el mismo caso pero, en esa oportunidad, con la diferencia que la mujer no está tan iluminada y elige perjudicar al hombre. Es ahora él quien acepta la responsabilidad de lo que le ocurre porque conoce la Ley de Causa y Efecto, y entonces elige perdonarla. El karma ha sido interrumpido nuevamente.

En pocas palabras, sólo hace falta que una de las partes involucradas tenga la buena voluntad de elegir el perdón como solución al conflicto. La mayoría de las personas que no perdonan actúan así porque sienten que alguien tiene que pagar por lo que les ha sucedido; existe en ellas una sed de justicia que, en apariencia, no se da en este plano. En consecuencia, debemos aprender a ser conscientes de nuestros actos. Cada pensamiento o acción que iniciamos es una causa que, indefectiblemente, tendrá su efecto. Si peleamos y discutimos con la gente a nuestro alrededor (causa), el resultado será un gran conflicto (efecto). Sin embargo, si hacemos favores y ayudamos a otros (causa), también recibiremos lo mismo en algún momento (efecto), aunque quizá los favores nunca provengan de las personas a quienes hemos ayudado. Por eso es que todas las religiones del mundo enseñan a hacer el bien. La única manera de vivir bien es generando buenas acciones.

PRINCIPIO DE GENERACIÓN

El Principio de Generación dice textualmente: **"La generación existe por doquier. Todo tiene sus principios masculino y femenino. La generación se mantiene en todos los planos."**

El Principio de Generación se refiere a la Creatividad. Lo que nos dice *El Kybalión* es que para crear algo nuevo, es necesaria la conjugación de dos energías: la masculina y la femenina; si esta conjugación no se da, entonces no se da la manifestación. Este principio está muy relacionado con el de polaridad porque habla de dos energías opuestas, pero se diferencia de aquél porque se refiere exclusivamente al proceso de creación.

Este principio no tiene que ver con el sexo; el sexo es una de sus manifestaciones. Más allá de nuestro sexo, todos somos portadores de energías masculinas y femeninas y tenemos que lograr la perfecta conjugación de éstas para obtener éxito en la vida. El hombre que es muy machista, es decir, que se ha polarizado en el extremo de la energía masculina, tarde o temprano sufrirá por la falta de su lado receptivo, intuitivo o imaginativo. Por otra parte, la mujer muy dependiente o sumisa, polarizada en la energía femenina, también sufrirá por la falta de iniciativa y confianza en sí misma. Sin importar nuestro sexo, cada uno tiene que desarrollar tanto su parte masculina como femenina para sentirse equilibrado.

Debemos recordar que para que exista la electricidad tiene que haber dos polos: el positivo y el negativo. Solamente la combinación de ambos produce la electricidad. El símbolo del Yin-Yang representa la perfecta armonía entre las energías masculina y femenina. La parte negra simboliza la energía "Yin" o femenina; la parte blanca es la energía "Yang" o masculina. De acuerdo con este símbolo, exactamente donde termina la energía femenina comienza la masculina y viceversa. Además, observamos que dentro de la parte negra existe un círculo blanco; esto significa que en el corazón de la energía femenina existe la energía masculina y también ocurre lo mismo con la parte blanca. Cada una de ellas necesita de la otra para complementarse y lograr el equilibrio perfecto.

La energía Yin o femenina es la receptiva, creativa, imaginativa y pasiva. La energía Yang o masculina es la dinámica, activa, agresiva y es la que regula la capacidad de dar.

Es conveniente tener el símbolo Yin-Yang a la vista, en una medalla o cuadro para que nos recuerde en forma permanente el equilibrio que debemos encontrar. La energía tiende a complementarse y por eso, atraemos a nuestras vidas a las personas con la polaridad que nos falta. Cuando una persona es muy tranquila, pasiva o tímida, es muy probable que atraiga a su vida a amigos más agresivos, dinámicos y extrovertidos. Por el contrario, la persona más peleadora siempre busca rodearse de gente más pacífica o sumisa. Cada uno de nosotros atrae la energía que le está faltando.

Pero sabemos que los polos opuestos son iguales en naturaleza; solamente difieren en su grado de manifestación. También hemos estudiado que uno de los objetivos de nuestra vida aquí en el planeta es aprender a armonizar los opuestos. El sentido de atraer a personas o situaciones con la polaridad que nos falta es el de ayudarnos a encontrar la armonización o punto de equilibrio. Cuanto más tímida sea una persona, más extrovertido será quien le atraiga. Aunque al principio esta atracción de los opuestos puede generar cierta dependencia entre ambos, con el tiempo cada uno brindará su energía al otro para ayudarlo a encontrar su punto medio. Quien era más tímido dejará de serlo y quien era más extrovertido aprenderá a mediar más sus actos. La idea no es que cada uno se convierta en el bastón de apoyo para el otro, sino todo lo contrario. Cuando finalmente una persona encuentra su punto de equilibrio, a la vez comienza a sentir la unidad con el Universo y verdadera paz interior.

En el proceso de la creación, debemos aprender a conjugar estas energías para obtener el resultado que buscamos. No hay creación si no conjugamos correctamente nuestras energías masculinas y femeninas.

En nuestra sociedad está muy valorizada la energía Yang o masculina, la que nos inclina a asumir responsabilidades y funcionar dentro de una estructura organizada. Pero cuanto más nos introducimos en esa estructura, más limitamos nuestra capacidad creativa.

El estudio del Principio de Generación nos recuerda nuestra naturaleza creadora y la importancia de desarrollarla para la expresión del Espíritu. Fuimos creados a "imagen y semejanza" de nuestro Padre. Dios creó el Universo; por tanto, nosotros tenemos la habilidad para crear nuestro propio Universo también.

Para desarrollar la energía Yin, es necesario aprender a jugar con la vida. La creatividad aumenta notablemente cuando nos dedicamos a algún pasatiempo, si nos relajamos y disfrutamos del presente, o cuando estamos concentrados en el estudio de algo que nos interesa.

La energía Yin es la energía femenina y gobierna la parte izquierda del cuerpo. Si se es diestro, entonces es aconsejable que se comience a usar más la mano izquierda.

Aquí es importante reconocer que el Universo está en continua expansión y crecimiento. Dios nos creó como una extensión de Sí Mismo, con la finalidad de que, a la vez, nosotros continuáramos creando. Tal como lo hemos estudiado, para poder crear debemos equilibrar nuestras energías masculinas y femeninas adecuadamente. La vida organizada nos lleva a pensar que nuestro talento nos tiene que dar dinero, fama o cierto mérito social. Sin embargo, en el mundo espiritual no es así. A veces, la misión de algunos es servir a otros para que alcancen fama y reconocimiento. En otros casos, la misión es cuidar, alimentar o educar a los demás. Cualquiera que sea la forma que tome la misión, siempre será nuestra felicidad, nos dé o no dinero. Cuando cumplimos con nuestra misión, toda la vida se nos facilita; llegan a nosotros los medios para sustentarnos económica y emocionalmente, y es así como llega la felicidad.

ANEXO 1

Cuando comenzamos a transitar el camino espiritual, buscamos la perfección en nuestras vidas. Tratamos de mejorar nuestro carácter, costumbres, ideas, alimentación, y hasta la vida social. A veces, hacemos sacrificios con el fin de alcanzar una vida más plena y feliz; sin embargo, muchas veces no llegamos al estado de éxtasis o plenitud que anhelamos. La decepción puede llevarnos a rechazar la disciplina que habíamos emprendido, o en el peor de los casos, puede desmoralizarnos a tal punto de pensar que "Dios se ha olvidado de nosotros". Cualquiera que sea la reacción, ésta sólo nos está señalando que hemos cometido un error, y un error puede ser corregido.

El Universo funciona como una gran computadora: hay que saber presionar las teclas adecuadas para obtener lo que se desea. Cuando no lo estamos haciendo, la computadora se detiene, espera fría y silenciosamente la señal eléctrica correcta.

ANEXO 2

Una de las ideas más generalizadas en nuestra cultura es que estamos aquí para cumplir un "karma". Esto significa que tenemos, por ejemplo, que pasar por ciertas pruebas, sufrir dolencias físicas, enfrentar crisis y problemas cotidianos. Los más avanzados encuentran las razones al analizar sus vidas pasadas, recordando hechos y situaciones que se repiten una y otra vez con el fin de ser sanadas. Otros se inclinan por convencerse de que son las influencias astrológicas las generadoras de los malos y buenos momentos. Los menos esotéricos encuentran que la razón de nuestros sufrimientos se debe a desequilibrios psicológicos, a los hábitos adquiridos durante la infancia, a la herencia genética, y demás. Y aquellos que no tienen ni una pizca de esotéricos culpan al gobierno y a la economía por su insatisfacción. Tanto aquellos de pensamiento más elevado como los más primitivos están convencidos de que hay un motivo real para sufrir.

Vivimos en el planeta Tierra, que, dentro de la organización de este Universo, es el planeta del Chakra Corazón. En pocas palabras, esto significa que venimos aquí para aprender a amar. A través de las distintas religiones nos llega el mensaje de que Dios es Amor, y que debemos aprender a amarnos los unos a los otros; sin embargo, todo parece quedar en las palabras porque nuestro ego se niega a aceptar que dentro de la persona que nos trae problemas también está Dios. Estamos convencidos de que Dios sólo habita dentro de la "gente buena" y de que los demás están "descarriados" o lejos del sendero espiritual. Dios es Todo y está en Todos, y aunque cueste creerlo, nos ama a todos por igual.

La función selectiva y discriminatoria de nuestro ego terrenal nos llena de justificaciones y razones lógicas que apoyan la teoría personal del amor. El ego nos dice: "Esta persona merece mi amor, esta otra no". Generalmente, confundimos "amar" con "ser amados". Si no tenemos respuesta de la otra parte, nos cerramos, guardamos los sentimientos y nos frustramos. El ego dice: "No vale la pena que ponga mi energía en esta relación", o en el peor de los casos, después de haber hecho mucho por alguien, el ego dice: "Todo fue una pérdida de tiempo."

Ya estamos viviendo la Era de Acuario, regida por Urano. Este símbolo significa, en primer lugar, que hay que entender el amor romántico de otra manera para luego dirigirlo hacia un solo lugar: su fuente original, Dios. Muchas veces, lo que entendemos por amor romántico no es más que una demostración de un alto grado de neurosis. El amor es aceptación, colaboración, impulso, humildad; jamás exige nada a cambio. También decimos que hay muchas clases de amores y que el amor se manifiesta en distintos grados. Lo cual sólo se vuelve una justificación a nuestros miedos interiores. Sólo existe una clase de amor: el amor de Dios, el amor incondicional.

Hemos aprendido durante años que debemos evolucionar, elevarnos, dirigirnos hacia Dios, y sin embargo, siempre estamos en Dios. No existe un lugar en el Universo que esté fuera de Él. La Era de Acuario nos trae una luz diferente y nos dice simplemente que los problemas que enfrentamos no son sino oportunidades para brindar amor. Aquellas personas que nos complican la vida, que pelean y discuten, que están nerviosas están pidiendo amor con desesperación, internamente y en secreto. Muchos adultos actúan como niños y no saben pedir con claridad lo que quieren.

Más importantes aún son aquellos errores que cometemos nosotros mismos, a causa de los cuales nos sentimos culpables, y creemos que merecemos un castigo (o karma). Tenemos muy arraigada la idea de que debemos pagar por nuestros errores. Esos momentos no son sino una "gran oportunidad" para aprender a perdonarnos a nosotros mismos, a aceptarnos y a amarnos incondicionalmente.

Nos preocupamos demasiado por curar las heridas del pasado, o por desarrollar estrategias para prevenir situaciones futuras, y en esta carrera nos olvidamos de que "curando el presente lo demás se cura automáticamente". Por eso, no debemos preocuparnos tanto de si fuimos piratas, ladrones o asesinos en otra vida; o si en este momento Saturno hace una cuadratura a mi Sol natal; o si el gobierno no está tomando las medidas que yo considero adecuadas. Cada momento de mi vida es una valiosa oportunidad para extender amor. No debemos dejar que nuestro pensamiento se distraiga y se pierda.

Nosotros tenemos poder creativo que nos fue otorgado por el Creador y podemos utilizarlo erróneamente. El ego es una creación de nuestra mente, es la idea que tenemos de nosotros mismos y a veces, en esa idea general hay pensamientos muy poco positivos o hay miedos muy perturbadores que inhiben nuestra capacidad de amar. El ego genera la culpa y el castigo, y nos hace ver algunas situaciones como terribles o catastróficas.

Para remediar esto, nuestro Creador nos ha dado una guía muy eficaz: la Conciencia Superior, que nos vuelve a conectar con nuestra fuente y nos recuerda nuestra única misión: amar. Podemos recurrir a esta luz todas las veces que queramos y, en especial, en aquellos momentos en que nos encontramos atrapados por la realidad. La manera más eficaz y directa de encontrar una respuesta es renunciando primero a lo que nos indica la lógica; así dejamos a un lado a nuestro ego y damos paso al Espíritu.

La Conciencia Superior nunca habla con muchas palabras. Su mensaje es breve y generalmente se dirige a nuestra mente inconsciente a través de un símbolo. Lo más importante de este paso es renunciar a aceptar la situación como dolorosa o irreparable, "cancelando" básicamente la idea que estamos percibiendo. El segundo paso consiste en confiar y entregarse a nuestra Guía Interna. Las crisis son necesarias porque abren canales a Dios. Cuanto más cerrada está la persona, probablemente más fuertes sean sus crisis.

Finalmente, la idea que debemos afirmar dentro de nosotros es que en este Universo TODOS SOMOS UNO, no estamos separados. Cuando muestro amor, recibo amor (aunque mi ego a veces afirme lo contrario). Ya entramos en la Era de Acuario, la de la Amistad Universal, donde aprenderemos a aceptar a los demás tal como son, encontraremos en cada uno el Ser Perfecto que habita en nuestro interior, y dejaremos de lado los mensajes erróneos de nuestro ego. En esta Era se termina para siempre el karma porque comienza la Era del Amor.

DECRETO DE LA FELICIDAD

Parecería que estos principios son difíciles de llevar a cabo pero no es cierto. Basta con habituarnos a ellos para que podamos ser plenamente felices. Ahora que conoces el principio de la felicidad, hace falta que aprendas el siguiente Decreto metafísico:

1. YO no hablo, ni permito que se me hable nada contrario a la perfecta salud, la felicidad y la prosperidad.

2. YO le hago sentir a todo ser viviente que lo considero valioso.

3. YO le busco el lado bueno a todo lo que me ocurre, y a todo lo que veo ocurrir a otros.

4. YO pienso en todo lo mejor. Espero todo lo mejor. Trabajo únicamente por lo mejor.

5. YO siento igual entusiasmo por lo bueno que le ocurre a otro, que por lo que me ocurre a mí.

6. YO olvido mis errores del pasado y sigo adelante a mayores triunfos.

7. YO llevo una expresión agradable en todo momento, y sonrío a todo ser que contacto.

8. YO no tengo tiempo para criticar a los demás, ya que paso tanto tiempo mejorándome.

9. YO me hago tan fuerte que nada puede perturbar la paz de mi mente.

10. YO SOY demasiado grande para preocuparme. Demasiado noble para enfurecerme. Demasiado fuerte para temer. Demasiado feliz para permitir la presencia de algo negativo.

Índice

Esta obra se terminó de imprimir en los talleres de

LITOGRÁFICA TAURO S.A. Andrés Molina Enríquez no.4428

Col. Viaducto Piedad. C.P. 08200 México, D.F.   Marzo de 2012

Tel.5519-3669 y 5519-7744. Se tiraron 1,000 ejemplares más sobrantes.

CONTENTS

ACKNOWLEDGEMENTS

The editors gratefully acknowledge the following reviewers who played a pivotal role in ensuring quality contributions to this volume.

2013 Editorial Review Board
for *Advances in Service-Learning* Series

Jeffrey Anderson
Jessie Guidry Baginski
Kathy Bussert-Webb
Anthony Collatos
Margaret M. Ferrara
Marjori Krebs
Antonina Lukenchuk
Carol A. Marchel
Paul H. Matthews
Todd A. Price
Carol Revelle
Nancy Ruppert
Robert Shumer
Michelle I. Spain
Kathleen C. Tice
Barri Tinkler

FOREWORD

Across the globe, service-learning in primary and secondary schools continues to grow. Argentina, Australia, Canada, Chile, England, Germany, Ireland, Singapore, Venezuela, and the United States are just a few of the countries that have adopted initiatives to advance the practice of service-learning in primary and secondary education. In the United States, service-learning remains a pedagogy that receives steady, modest support from advocates who champion the engagement of K–12 students in authentic, community-based learning experiences that simultaneously address community needs while enhancing students' academic learning.

The advancement and institutionalization of service-learning in K–12 education is predicated on having teachers and instructional leaders who understand the pedagogy and its value and potential for student academic success and achievement. Consequently, programs that educate and prepare prospective teachers play a critical role in the future of service-learning, as they are responsible for ensuring that teachers who enter the classroom are qualified and prepared to use the pedagogy.

Research studies have explored the status of service-learning in U.S. teacher education programs and the various ways in which service-learning is taught and practiced in preservice teacher preparation programs. Other studies have assessed the impacts of service-learning on preservice teacher education students. Overall, to date, more than one hundred studies have been published on the impacts, implementation, and institutionalization of service-learning in teacher education programs.

However, many questions remain unanswered, and more research is this area of study is needed. The Research Special Interest Group of the

Transforming Teacher Education Through Service-Learning, pages ix–xii
Copyright © 2013 by Information Age Publishing
All rights of reproduction in any form reserved.

International Center for Service-Learning in Teacher Education has identified many of these questions in a research agenda (available at www.educationprogram.duke.edu/icslte/research-agenda), which was produced to encourage researchers to conduct investigations on these important questions. To advance the field, it is critical for researchers to familiarize themselves with this knowledge base, reference it in their studies, and design and conduct studies that explicitly add to this knowledge base. To build a more robust body of knowledge on service-learning in teacher education, researchers should identify gaps in the knowledge that they are addressing or clarify how their study will expand previous findings. We also encourage researchers to conduct studies that examine service-learning outcomes across multiple courses and from different programs and institutions; many of the existing studies are based on single course or program experiences. Larger, more comprehensive studies are beneficial because they often include a greater depth and breath of data as they expand the investigation beyond the convenience samples that are all too common in teacher education research.

This volume sheds much needed light on how the depth and breath of research on service-learning in teacher education is expanding, and how the rigor of the research continues to improve. The authors tackle a broad range of issues regarding the quality, focus, emphasis, and methods of service-learning in teacher education research. They offer both a critical analysis of the current state of research on service-learning in teacher education and strategies for producing better research that can strengthen the case for advancing service-learning in teacher education.

One of the key drivers of service-learning expansion both in teacher preparation and throughout higher education has been the work of faculty service-learning "champions". Individuals performing this role have been found in virtually all programs and institutions that have experienced success with service-learning. They go above and beyond their job description to do whatever is necessary to integrate service-learning with the academic curriculum, especially in the early stages of service-learning inclusion in a teacher education program. To achieve continued growth of service-learning in preservice teacher education it will be essential for these champions to continue their work, but also for everyone knowledgeable about the power of service-learning to transform lives and educate students to take an advocacy role in support of service-learning integration.

Many employ service-learning to heighten students' and preservice teachers' commitment to being life-long active democratic citizens. Teachers educators committed to service-learning must take on this type of advocacy role as a part of their professional service. For too long teacher educators have labored in the trenches, working hard with teacher candidates on campus and in K-12 schools to prepare them for the challenges of teaching while wondering why school and teacher preparation reform seem to be headed in directions not aligned with what they see as the optimal road to improvement. These teacher educators now need to become active, kind-hearted, assertive advocates for what they know to be the most effective approaches to educate our new teachers, including service-learning. They can advocate at levels within the university for increased inclusion and support for service-learning. Advocacy is also necessary with state and national professional organizations such as AACTE (American Association of Colleges for Teacher Education), ATE (Association of Teacher Educators), and CAEP (Council for the Accreditation of Educator Preparation). A significant portion of advocacy is education. Teacher educators can speak with their legislators, and testify before government committees at the local, state, and national levels to help these decision-makers understand how service-learning can support achievement of many key school reform objectives. If we want a better future for our children and our country we must move beyond frustration and fear and resolve to share our vision by providing decision-makers with solid rationales for why this vision makes sense and specific actions to take in order to optimize the benefits of service-learning. Sharing research results will be an essential component of this process. We must model the thinking and actions we expect our teacher candidates to engage in. It is time to find our courage, connect it to our intellect and heart; and take action. This volume sets the stage for advocates of service-learning in teacher education to take the next step in advancing and improving current practice and research.

This type of advocacy is challenging given teacher educators' already heavy work loads and history of being seen as a low status department of the university. Yet teacher educators have a great deal of wisdom to offer, and when we share our most deeply held beliefs and knowledge in a kind and compassionate manner we are helping to shape the future of education, strengthening our democracy, and modeling for our students what we desire for them to become. Parker Palmer describes this as exercising the "habits of the heart" we need to revitalize our politics. He writes:

For those of us who want to see democracy survive and thrive—and we are legion—the heart is where everything begins; that grounded place in each of us where we can overcome fear, rediscover that we are members of one another, and embrace the conflicts that threaten democracy as openings to new life for us and our nation.

Transforming teacher education through service-learning is a noble goal and a monumental challenge. Yet if those of us committed to service-learning take it on we will be living fuller lives by aligning our words and actions with our core beliefs. To do any less diminishes us and raises questions regarding the authenticity of those beliefs. This volume offers many valuable findings, new insights, diverse perspectives and expanded theories that support and enhance the use of service-learning in teacher education. Given the great influence teacher candidates and newly minted teachers have on literally millions of children every year we owe it to them and to ourselves to read the chapters in this book closely, examine our own practices, and take heartfelt actions to transform teacher education. Michael Fullan's comment from 1993 still rings true: "Teacher education has the honor of being simultaneously the worst problem and the best solution in education."

—**Jeffrey Anderson**
Andy Furco

PREFACE

Why Service-Learning Now?[1]

During the past several years, we have heard several long-time advocates of service-learning integration into teacher education complain that teacher education has descended into a quagmire of micro-management and unnecessary burdensome regulation in the name of "accountability." These advocates point to high-stakes testing approaches such as the Teacher Performance Assessment (TPA) and a proposed nationally standardized test of teacher knowledge such as the one advanced by American Federation of Teachers President Randi Weingarten in a recent *Wall Street Journal* Op-Ed: a national bar exam for teachers. Does service-learning fit into this picture? Why service-learning now?

The push to reform P–12 teacher preparation in the United States is a front-burner issue for many policymakers. In our push to remake and improve teacher preparation, we must not lose sight of the core mission of American education: to prepare our children and our nation to live and prosper. While no one strategy of preparing teachers captures all facets of this goal, community service-learning is one method that holds tremendous promise. Service-learning (the learning method that combines rigorous academic learning with authentic community service) has been demonstrated to deliver measurable improvement for both students' thinking and behaving. When reforming teacher preparation, don't forget service-learning.

For many years, critics have described deficiencies and dysfunction in the ways we prepare our P–12 teachers. Critiques such as *Cracks in the Ivory*

Transforming Teacher Education Through Service-Learning, pages xiii–xviii
Copyright © 2013 by Information Age Publishing

Tower[2] cite anachronistic techniques and attitudes among teacher educators as an ongoing impediment to improving our nation's P–12 schools. There's hardly a teacher educator who hasn't heard the criticisms of teacher preparation. At best, teacher educators are characterized as "reluctant reformers," or at worst, "obstructionist pawns of teachers' unions." Others cite frustratingly long, complicated, and unnecessary state licensure rules.

In response to these criticisms, new initiatives such as the Boston Teacher Residency, Tennessee's Teaching Quality Initiative, Chicago's Academy for Urban School Leadership, and others have attempted to remake and improve the performance of teacher candidates through innovative immersive residency programs. These programs emphasize on-the-job training mixed with nontraditional academics.

Private foundations seeking revolutionary and fast-paced change in the way we prepare teachers often fund these initiatives. Very often these programs bring together school districts, higher education institutions and teachers' unions. They recruit nontraditional candidates from the corporate sector as well as traditional-age college students. They focus on research-based strategies of teaching and learning that have been demonstrated to quickly and efficiently improve student performance.

While we support earnest efforts to improve teacher preparation, we want to make sure that in our rush to remake teacher preparation, we remember that efficiency and effectiveness are not the same thing. We want to ensure that as we reform teacher preparation we don't lose sight of the core duties of America's schools. That means that students not only need to read and compute, but also must relate, conflict, reconcile, judge, decide, and reflect. Teaching methods that only emphasize the cognitive outcomes of learning miss the broader mission of schools. Education enables our children to do more than make a living; it enables them to make a life.

Over 20 years of research on service-learning has demonstrated impact for both the teacher candidates and our children in how they think and relate to one another. Service-learning helps students and teachers improve their test scores, deepen their community engagement, and develop skills and attitudes necessary for a well-rounded life. It also shows promise as a means to assist learners in meeting national and state standards. Service-learning is one of only a few teaching strategies to have evidence of impact across the whole spectrum of school outcomes.

So why isn't service-learning the centerpiece of all teacher preparation in the United States? The answer lies in our tendency to seek and recognize only solutions that conform to our expectations of how teacher preparation should look. Some reformers seek solutions that are relatively inexpensive, quick, and easy to measure. But we mustn't let the tail wag the dog. Standardization and efficiency are useful only if they assist us in reaching more children and helping them to achieve their goals. Whether standardization helps us accomplish these goals is an empirical question to which more careful study should be brought, but just because something is easy to count, doesn't mean it counts. The policy decision shouldn't only be made on the pragmatic grounds of what we can monitor and summarize; it should also emphasize what it is we really want to accomplish. Service-learning helps students achieve both the academic and civic goals of education. It does what we want education in America to do. Service-learning takes students out of the four walls of the classroom and into the community seeking to understand the world as it is—messy, complicated, and real!

Since at least the early 1990s, teacher preparation programs have attempted to integrate service-learning into teacher education. The penetration of service-learning practice into teacher preparation is by most estimates broad but thin. A majority of teacher education programs talk about it with their students, but few carry this practice to the level necessary to ensure candidates for licensure are fully prepared to use service-learning in their classrooms. In order to achieve the benefits that research suggests are available to service-learning practitioners, our teacher preparation reform efforts must push our candidates past mere familiarity with the method.

As we continue our work to reform and strengthen teacher preparation, there is a risk that policymakers will confuse pragmatic efficiency with authentic effectiveness—an oversimplification that may be seductive in our fiscally tight times. As Neil Postman observed, "What does it matter if we can get the trains to run on time if they don't go where we want them to go?" We must remember that the most effective teachers are frequently not narrowly focused in any one specialty or technique, but instead employ different strategies for different learning situations and therefore possess the power to reach more students. If we really want to impact the entire spectrum of cognitive and behavioral skills that students need to be fully participating citizens, then service-learning is a teaching strategy we must feature in our reform efforts. Service-learning truly is, as Meta Mendel-Reyes puts it, "a pedagogy for citizenship." So when reforming teacher preparation, let's not forget to include service-learning in the process.

This volume seeks not only to reform but to transform teacher education through promoting service-learning pedagogy. Within this book we adhere to the National Service-Learning Clearinghouse definition:

> Service-learning is a teaching and learning strategy that integrates meaningful community service with instruction and reflection to enrich the learning experience, teach civic responsibility, and strengthen communities.

The pedagogy of service-learning has significant implications for teacher education. Its transformative aspects have far-reaching potential to address teacher candidate dispositions and provide deeper understanding of diversity. Knowledge of the pedagogy and how to implement it in candidates' future classrooms could alter education to a more powerful experience of democracy in action and enhance the civic mission of schools. The current and ongoing research found within this volume is meant to continue support of the notion of educational reform.

We appreciate the seminal work of Erickson and Anderson (1997), *Learning with the Community: Concepts and Models for Service-Learning in Teacher Education,* which initially explained and defined service-learning pedagogy within the field of teacher education. This book broke new ground on which we currently tread. They addressed head-on the issues educators gave as reasons not to embed service-learning pedagogy in their preservice coursework. They gave us answers, "... service-learning has been successfully used to enhance student understanding of motivational theory, authentic assessment, the meaning of active citizenship, interdisciplinary units, and cooperative learning. It can also be effective in influencing preservice teachers' awareness of multicultural issues, individual differences, and the realities of issues of educational reform and collaboration" (p. 6). While we have made some inroads with advancement of service-learning inclusion in teacher education since the late 1990s, we still have a long way to go.

We acknowledge the work of Anderson, Swich, and Yff (2001) as they continued defining the pedagogy and what service-learning means within the field of teacher education. Their influential book, *Service-Learning in Teacher Education: Enhancing the Growth of New Teachers, Their Students, and Communities,* set the stage for national and international discussion on the topic. We adhere to the ideas they put forth at the beginning of the century. Throughout our current volume we assume the 10 principles/ideals they suggested for successful service-learning inclusion in teacher education programs:

1. Preservice teachers should prepare to use service-learning as a pedagogy by participating in service-learning experiences as well as in-class study of principles of good service-learning practice.
2. Teacher education faculty involved with service-learning should have a clear understanding of service-learning theory and principles of good practice and model these principles in their use of service-learning as a teaching method.
3. Teacher education courses that include service-learning should be grounded in theories and practices of teaching and learning that are congruent with service-learning.
4. The design, implementation, and evaluation of service-learning projects should reflect all stakeholders' needs and interests, including

those of preservice teachers, P–12 students, and other community members.

5. Reciprocity and mutual respect should characterize the collaboration among teacher education programs, P–12 schools, and the community.
6. Preservice teachers should participate in multiple and varied service-learning experiences that involve working with diverse community members.
7. Preservice teachers should participate in a variety of frequent and structured activities and prepare to facilitate reflection with their future students.
8. Preservice teachers should learn how to use formative and summative assessment to enhance student learning and measure service-learning outcomes.
9. Teacher educators should align service-learning outcomes with program goals and state and national standards for teacher certification and accreditation.
10. The teacher education program, institution, and the community should support service-learning by providing the resources and structural elements necessary for continued success.

Service-learning has the power to transform teacher education. Under the current conditions of competing educational best practices and reforms, service-learning often remains peripheral to the realm of possibilities with regard to innovative initiatives. Research and scholarship regarding service-learning in the field of teacher education are particularly sparse. Projects such as this book can contribute, in important ways, to developing teacher candidate and faculty identities committed to civic engagement—one of the most enduring purposes of American education.

While there are a number of publications that also suggest "transforming teacher education" (Carroll, Featherstone, Feiman-Nemser, & Roosevelt, 2007; Hill-Jackson & Lewis, 2010; NCATE, 2010; Sockett, DeMulder, LePage, & Wood, 2001), none propose the transformation through service-learning. Within the four parts of this book we highlight service-learning pedagogy best practice for teacher education. The authors in the first part offer conceptual frameworks to provide philosophical, theoretical, and visionary context. We look at the spaces service-learning can make available for teacher candidates in the second and third parts of the book. And finally, we discuss the pedagogy of service-learning for implementation in P–12 classrooms in the last section. We hope the ideas gleaned from reading the chapters spark excitement, curiosity, and understanding as you relate them to your own teaching and learning experiences and ponder the question, Why service-learning now?

NOTES

1. The Education Commission of the States in their newsletter *Citizenship Matters* originally published portions of this introduction in January 2011.
2. *Cracks in the Ivory Tower? The Views of Education Professors Circa 2010* was written by Steve Farkas and Ann Duffett and published by FDR Group, Thomas B. Fordham Institute in September 2010.

REFERENCES

Anderson, J. B., Swich, K. J., & Yff, K. (Eds.). (2001). *Service-learning in teacher education: Enhancing the growth of new teachers, their students, and communities.* Washington, DC: AACTE.

Carroll, D., Featherstone, H., Feiman-Nemser, S., & Roosevelt, D. (2007). *Transforming teacher education: Reflections from the field.* Cambridge, MA: Harvard Education Press

Erickson, J. A., & Anderson, J. B. (Eds.). (1997). *Learning with the community: Concepts and models for service-learning in teacher education.* Washington, DC: American Association for Higher Education.

Hill-Jackson, V., & Lewis, C. W. (Eds.). (2010). *Transforming teacher education: What went wrong with teacher training, and how we can fix it.* Sterling, VA: Stylus Publishing.

NCATE (2010). *Transforming teacher education through clinical practice: A national strategy to prepare effective teachers.* Washington, DC: Author.

Sockett, H. T., DeMulder, E. K., LePage, P. C., & Wood, D. R. (Eds.). (2001). *Transforming teacher education: Lessons in professional development.* Westport, CT: Bergin & Garvey.

PART I

CONCEPTUAL FRAMEWORKS

Virginia M. Jagla

INTRODUCTION

Framing the concept of transformation in teacher education through service-learning is a formidable task. Yet to many who have utilized this powerful pedagogy, this notion is clearly felt. Many teacher candidates have disclosed their sense of transformation during service-learning through reflection on the experience.

Theoretical or conceptual frameworks are often used to lend clarity and vision to the idea being discussed. Such a framework can provide a rationale or focus. This first part of the book sets the stage with interesting perspectives regarding the ways service-learning can transform teacher education. The ideas are complex and many are abstract, yet all share the vision that the experientially based powerful pedagogy of service-learning has the capacity to reform the way we prepare educators. While the field of teacher education has historically relied on forms of experiential learning such as practica and student teaching to help prepare future educators, the particular form of experiential education known as service-learning has not been widely embraced in the field.

As you read through the three chapters that comprise this first section of the book you will notice that the frameworks discussed in each have unique

Transforming Teacher Education Through Service-Learning, pages 1–3
Copyright © 2013 by Information Age Publishing
All rights of reproduction in any form reserved.

elements, yet they are all relatable as we concern ourselves with effective ways to educate teachers. Each chapter provides a set of coherent viewpoints the authors wish to communicate to stimulate conceptual understanding of this distinctive and intricate idea. Each chapter attempts to group concepts that are broadly defined and systematically organized to provide a focus, a rationale, and a tool for the integration and interpretation of information. As you read through this section, you will encounter word models, metaphors, and other abstract concepts to frame the work we do with novice and continuing educators in order that they may gain deeper understanding of the immense undertaking of teaching with the heart and mind at the same time. They provide us with an organized way of thinking about how and why we use service-learning pedagogy as a part of our teacher education programs. They offer a basis for thinking about what we do when utilizing service-learning pedagogy and about what it means for us, for our teacher candidates, and for the field of teacher education in general. Each of the conceptual frameworks propounded here is greatly influenced by the ideas and research of others, yet each one presents a distinct perspective.

In the first chapter, "Tensions as Catalysts for Transformation: Multidisciplinary Education Faculty Perceptions While Implementing Service-Learning," Stenhouse, Dooley, and Feinburg focus on teacher education faculty and the experiences they faced while implementing service-learning endeavors with teacher candidates in various disciplines. As you read about the experiences of the group of faculty who embed service-learning pedagogy into their diffuse teacher education courses, you will surely find yourself relating to some of the tensions uncovered by them. The authors' particular framework looks at these tensions as catalysts for deeper understanding, which uncovers some essential beliefs held by faculty and how they use these insights to inform important decisions. The concept of perceiving tensions in this more productive manner has implications well beyond the scope of this study (Alexander, 1998; Freedman & Ball, 2004). The faculty members in this study worked together in a professional learning community, which met regularly to consider their experiences as they implemented service-learning. You will read about identified philosophical, pedagogical, and logistical tensions that afford enhanced understandings of the role faculty plays in effective service-learning.

Boggs presents an interesting image of "running against the wind" in Chapter 2, "Teacher Education as Partnership: Service-Learning and the Audacity of Listening." This concept may remind some readers of the 1980 Bob Seger song, but the author brings up a sailing reference. While runners tend to move slower and exert more energy when going against the wind, sailors know how to harness the wind to allow them to sail more quickly. This metaphor provides a thought-provoking conceptual framework for faculty perusing service-learning pedagogy. The chapter frames relational epistemologies through the understandings of Dylan, an instructor of a service-learning course. Read how Dylan tacks back and forth as he sails with the wind and often against the wind.

In the final chapter of this section, "Critical Discourse Analysis of Service-Learning Perspectives and Models: Transforming Teacher Education," Lukenchuk, Jagla, and Price bring together images from philosophy, social theory, and relational ethics with the metaphor of heterotopia. Written in the form of critical discourse analysis (Fairclough, 2003; Gee, 2005), it leads us through discussion of power, transformation, ethics and caring, and education reform. As we seek to transform teacher education through service-learning pedagogy, to be more progressive, imaginative, and caring, we hope to promote the teaching profession as genuinely honorable as it becomes known for its public service.

REFERENCES

Alexander, P. A. (1998). Positioning conceptual change within a model of domain literacy. In B. Guzzetti & C. Hynd (Eds.), *Theoretical perspectives on conceptual change: Multiple ways to understand knowing and learning in a complex world* (pp. 55–76). Mahwah, NJ: Erlbaum.

Fairclough, N. (2003). *Analyzing discourse: Textual analysis for social research.* New York: Routledge.

Freedman, S. W., & Ball, A. F. (2004). Ideological becoming: Bakhtinian concepts to guide the study of language, literacy, and learning. In A. F. Ball & S. W. Freedman (Eds.), *Bakhtinian perspectives on language, literacy, and learning* (pp. 6–74). Cambridge, UK: Cambridge University Press.

Gee, J. P. (2005). *An introduction to discourse analysis. Theory and method* (2nd ed.). New York: Routledge.

CHAPTER 1

TENSIONS AS CATALYSTS FOR TRANSFORMATION

Multidisciplinary Education Faculty Perceptions While Implementing Service-Learning

Vera Stenhouse
Caitlin McMunn Dooley
Joseph Feinburg

ABSTRACT

The findings from this study demonstrate how tensions shaped 16 faculty members' implementation of service-learning in their courses at Georgia State University's College of Education. We frame tensions not as problems to be solved but as experiences that ground ones' understanding, reveal underlying values, expose contradictions, and inform decisions. The participating faculty members integrated service-learning in a variety of educator preparation courses, from PK–12 kinesiology to elementary language arts to secondary social studies. They worked together in a professional learning community to discuss their experiences and perceptions throughout an academic year. The faculty members described three types of tensions: philo-

Transforming Teacher Education Through Service-Learning, pages 5–30
Copyright © 2013 by Information Age Publishing

sophical, pedagogical, and logistical. These tensions yielded deepened concepts about service-learning pedagogy, its ideological underpinnings, and the role of faculty in both areas. Such tensions are ongoing considerations that should be shared and discussed among faculty and teacher preparation students to further advance the transformation of teacher education through service-learning.

We describe tensions experienced by a group of 16 university faculty members as they participated in professional development to improve service-learning integration in their teacher education courses. The Community Opportunities that Motivate People and Enhance Learning and Service (COMPELS), a grant-funded project, brought together this group of faculty members who had diverse disciplinary expertise, but who all shared an interest in service-learning. A primary goal of COMPELS was to enhance and expand service-learning initiatives as part of teacher education. Warner and Esposito (2009) assert that "little attention has been given to the experience of faculty teaching service-learning courses.... Yet, the impact of service-learning on faculty and their teaching is an integral factor in the outcome of student engaged learning" (p. 510). This chapter describes how faculty participation in a professional learning community (hereafter called COMPELS) revealed tensions that catalyzed their implementation of service-learning in their undergraduate and graduate courses. Discussing these tensions provided faculty opportunities to examine how their teaching aligned with or contradicted the tenets of service-learning they sought to impart to their students.

This inquiry arose through COMPELS in Georgia State University's College of Education and brought together education faculty from six departments. Each faculty member came with unique prior experiences with service-learning and community service. During an academic year, faculty engaged in professional development activities designed to support the implementation of service-learning in their courses. In this chapter, we first offer a review of COMPELS activities and then share the tensions that faculty members expressed along the way. Examining tensions is important because they were catalysts for faculty members' decision making about how to implement service-learning. Tensions are significant because they are a factor that shapes our thinking, choices, and actions (Alexander, 1998; Assaf & Dooley, 2006; Freedman & Ball, 2004). In short, tensions transformed faculty perceptions about their role in advancing service-learning integration in teacher education coursework. Harking back to Anderson, Swick, and Yff's (2001) principles and ideals for successful service-learning discussed in the introduction of this volume, we emphasize how teacher educators influence whether and how service-learning can be successfully implemented.

FACULTY INVOLVEMENT WITH SERVICE-LEARNING

With so many potential benefits at stake for students, faculty members are germane in establishing and shaping service-learning integration in coursework with pre- and in-service teachers. Faculty members are essential to the success (and limitations) of service-learning initiatives in higher education (Warner & Esposito, 2009). Evidence confirms the myriad benefits of student engagement through service-learning (Furco & Root, 2010; Gross, 2010; Porfilio & Hickman, 2011). Research on faculty is growing and includes needed information about the personal, institutional, and professional dimensions that influence faculty engagement in service-learning (Wade & Demb, 2009). Service-learning literature provides detailed information on faculty pedagogical beliefs and motivators that can lead higher education faculty to engage service-learning (Banerjee & Hausafus, 2007; Bowen & Kiser, 2009; Bringle & Hatcher, 2009; Garcia & Robinson, 2005; Mundy, 2004, Wade & Demb, 2009). Obviously faculty beliefs inform service-learning pedagogy, and we discuss what is understood about those beliefs.

Faculty members' own investment in service-learning, sense of social or civic duty, and student, community, and institutional contexts have all been shown to influence how service-learning is implemented (O'Meara & Niehaus, 2009; Pribbenow, 2005; Stenhouse & Jarrett, 2012). For example, Pribbenow (2005) described the nature of how service-learning affected teaching and learning within 35 faculty members' courses at one university. Pribbenow detailed six themes indicating how service-learning increased faculty understanding of student learning processes and deepened their relationships with students. Among the six themes, the type of the course and whether faculty required or offered optional service-learning projects influenced students' overall service-learning experiences. In addition, Pribbenow noted shifts in practice related to increased student authority in the classroom and enhanced collegial relationships. In another study, O'Meara and Niehaus (2009) reviewed the personal narrative essays of 109 Thomas Ehrlich Civically Engaged Faculty Award nominees. The Thomas Ehrlich Civically Engaged Faculty Award,[1] offered by the Campus Compact, is comprised of a national coalition of almost 1,200 institutions of higher education. This annual award recognizes tenured faculty for their leadership in advancing students' opportunities for civic and community engagement. O'Meara and Niehaus were interested in faculty members' explanations of service-learning and how they perceived themselves, their students, and communities. Four themes emerged, one of which focused on teaching and learning. Faculty viewed service-learning as (1) a strategy for learning disciplinary knowledge and skills (89%); (2) a form of experiential learning (90%); (3) a way to shape civic and moral dispositions (53%); and (4) a means of exposing students to diversity (32%). Another example of how pedagogical views influence service-learning implementation was shared by Stenhouse and Jarrett (2012). They detail the experiences of one faculty member who implemented a type of critical service-learning approach with five cohorts of pre-service teachers over a 5-year period. The instructor approached service-learning from a critical perspective to support the pre-service teachers' development of skills in exercising autonomy and agency in learning—skills intended to support their P–5 students' learning opportunities. A critical pedagogy approach to service-learning led the researchers to conclude that power dynamics affected the instructor's and students' project management, leadership roles, and decision making. The preceding studies show how faculty members shape service-learning pedagogy, while the subsequent discussion highlights the influential role of communal professional learning about service-learning.

Service-learning research suggests that participation in professional learning groups/communities has a positive differential effect on service-learning implementation. Such communities of practice provide a space for faculty to discuss, share, and reflect on their own service-learning teaching. Banerjee and Hausafus (2007) reported that integrating service-learning in coursework was enhanced when faculty shared advice with each other and were engaged in faculty development. Bowen and Kiser (2009) found that faculty believed that participating in a fellows program improved their service-learning teaching.

COMPELS served as a professional learning community for our multidisciplinary group of teacher education faculty as they engaged with service-learning. As a result of participating in professional development opportunities, they learned from and informed their colleagues about their pedagogical successes, challenges, and dilemmas. This study offers insights from their experiences implementing service-learning. Thus far, service-learning researchers continue to explore what motivates and deters faculty service-learning involvement (Banerjee & Hausafus, 2007; Bowen & Kiser, 2009; McKay & Rozee, 2004). Researchers are also developing an understanding of faculty beliefs and attitudes regarding service and service-learning (Banerjee & Hausafus, 2007; Carracelas-Juncal, Bossalier, & Yaoyuneyong, 2009; Hou, 2010; Mundy, 2004). In light of what is known about faculty and service-learning, we specifically focus on the tensions faculty experienced in the planning, implementing, and assessing of coursework that involves service-learning and how these tensions shaped their decisions as course instructors.

EXAMINING TENSIONS AS TRANSFORMATIVE

Service-learning scholars (Banerjee & Hausafus, 2007; Bowen & Kiser, 2009; Hou, 2010) have focused on challenges or inhibitors for faculty involvement in service-learning; however, we discuss tensions as catalysts that demonstrate a deepened involvement by faculty in service-learning. We use the term *catalyst* as a metaphor to show how tensions can serve a function similar to a chemical catalyst. In chemistry, a catalyst is a substance that changes or accelerates a reaction, yet is not expended in the process. In this instance, tensions can catalyze reflective practice. Tensions are not resolved (or expended) but function as continuous opportunities to learn and enhance understanding. Therefore, we do not view tensions as inherently negative. Instead, tensions can ground understanding, reveal underlying values, expose contradictions, and inform decisions. Experiencing and identifying tensions are integral to human development because they teach us how we cope with the realities of doing what we do on a daily basis.

Engaging tensions can lead to transformative learning (Dooley, 2008). In this case study, we guided teacher educators to learn about service-learning. Our data suggest that as these educators experienced tensions, they were also transforming into *service-learning educators*. The idea that tensions can lead to transformative learning is not new. Indeed, in literature on multicultural teacher education, tensions are viewed as common to transformative experience (Dooley, 2008; Freedman & Ball, 2004; O'Grady, 2000). Freedman and Ball (2004) advise that teachers must guide learning by "find[ing] ways to create and manage tensions and conflicts that are critical to learning" (p. 14). As learners grapple with new concepts and new worldviews, they often experience tensions. In order to engender transformative (adult) learning experiences, Mezirow (1997) states "the process [of transformative learning] involves transforming frames of reference through critical reflection of assumptions, validating contested beliefs through discourse, taking action on one's reflective insight, and critically assessing it" (p. 11). These elements of transformative learning mirror desired components of service-learning as well. In particular, a key piece of service-learning is reflection that yields introspection and praxis. In order to cultivate transformative experiences, tensions serve as catalysts.

Alexander (1998) posits notions of micro-transformations that more specifically apply to this research context (Dooley, 2008). "Micro-transformations are smaller, less widespread changes in conceptions (as opposed to large-scale changes in frames of reference or perceptual changes indicated by the word 'transformative'), yet they posit the possibility that these smaller changes can be essential elements of a larger shift in thinking, or transformation (Alexander, 1998)" (Dooley, 2008, p. 65). Micro-transformations "are slight starts toward new, broadened conceptions" (Dooley,

10 ■ V. STENHOUSE, C. M. DOOLEY, and J. FEINBURG

2008, p. 65). We wondered whether and how the faculty members' tensions evidenced their deepening commitment to service-learning.

CONTEXT

Participants

Sixteen faculty members participated, at least one from each of the six departments in the College of Education: Seven were in Early Childhood Education; four in Middle Secondary and Instructional Technology (MSIT); two in Kinesiology and Health (KH); and one each in Counseling and School Psychology (CSP), Education and Policy Studies (EPS), and Educational Psychology and Special Education (EPSE). They all integrated service-learning into their teacher education courses. Of the 16, five became core researchers involved in the study presented here (two from MSIT, two from ECE, and one from KH). As teacher educators, the faculty members prepared teachers for a variety of grade-level and demographic settings within their respective disciplines. These faculty members were part of a professional learning community that was made possible through a grant from the U.S. Corporation for National and Community Service. As previously noted, we called this project and the professional learning community COMPELS.

Also involved in the COMPELS project (but not as research participants) were the Director of the University Center for Teaching and Learning (CTL) and two grant administrators. All but the CTL Director were housed in the College of Education. The CTL Director worked with the first author to facilitate sessions addressing faculty experiences as they engaged service-learning in their work.

The COMPELS project required several responsibilities of faculty members. They had to (1) attend at least five of nine faculty development workshops over the course of an academic year; (2) contribute written reflections at the end of each workshop; (3) collect student work samples; (4) provide an end-of-semester written synthesis of implemented projects; and (5) attend a one-day summer gathering institute for celebration and dissemination featuring guest speakers and community partners. Additional support activities included one-on-one collaborative mentoring; classroom observations; attendance at local and national conferences; and research projects.

Faculty members' experience with service-learning fell along a continuum, from no prior experience and minimal knowledge of service-learning to years of experience and significant knowledge regarding service-learning. Some members of the group have written publications about the topic; others had never read a publication about the topic. Those in the middle of the continuum had some understanding of service-learning, may have implemented service-learning in their courses prior to participating in the project, or were planning to implement it in courses. All participants came to the project with shared goals to enhance their knowledge, gain insight, and advance their practices with service-learning regardless of where they fell on the continuum.

We, the authors, were closely involved with the COMPELS project. Stenhouse, the first author, was the COMPELS Project Director. Dooley, the second author, was the Principal Investigator. Feinberg, the third author, was a faculty participant. We each have experience with implementing, researching, and writing about service-learning.

Service-Learning Courses

The faculty participants implemented service-learning in 22 courses collectively teaching 336 pre- and in-service educators (i.e., teacher education students, hereafter referred to as candidates, except within quotations). All participants followed a generic model similar to the IPARDC Model,[2] which includes investigation, planning and preparation, action, reflection, and demonstration/celebration. The participants' service-learning courses varied in structure and format. With slight variations, faculty implemented three models of service-learning: (1) full class immersion; (2) individual teacher projects; and (3) action research service projects. In *full class immersion*, all members of the teacher education course worked collaboratively to identify the needs of a community (e.g., a homeless shelter for children, an elementary school, a high school math department, etc.). Full class immersions were conducive for field-based courses or courses that required candidates to participate in teaching experiences "outside" of the higher education classroom. *Individual teacher projects* meant that candidates conducted a service-learning project in their individual P–12 classrooms. They worked with their students to identify an issue, design a solution (tied to curricular standards), carry out the solution, and assess the solution as well as the curricular standards. This model was more conducive for candidates who were graduate students and who had their own classrooms. Lastly, *action research service projects* meant the candidates carried out the assigned service-learning project in small groups. Each group selected a school community within which to focus its project. Similar to Japanese Lesson Study (Lewis, Perry, & Murata, 2006), the group worked together to design the project and link to curricula, at least one group member carried out the project, and the whole group collaboratively reflected on the efficacy of the project. At least one classroom (in which the service project is carried out) acted as the intervention site.

In addition, faculty courses were bound by time and class session frequency in different ways. Some courses met during 3-week mini-semesters, other courses met over 15-week semesters, and a few were two parts of a two-semester (30-week) sequence. Data for this research comes from one academic year.

DATA SOURCES AND COLLECTION

This research was conducted within the first and only year of the COMPELS project (funding was cut due to federal budget cuts to the Learn and Serve Higher Education grant program). Data sources (see Table 1.1) included (1) end-of-semester synthesis reports about courses ($n = 14$); (2) faculty development workshop reflections ($n = 60$); and (3) questionnaires ($n = 6$).

End-of-semester synthesis reports from each faculty member detailed the nature of the course, an overview of the course-related service-learning assignment(s), and a brief reflection on the experience. These reports provided information required by the funding agency and extended feedback for the project director (see Appendix A).

Workshop reflections elicited participants' beliefs about their pedagogy, practice, understanding, and experiences with service-learning. Reflections were collected monthly after every faculty development workshop. Participants' responses also guided the workshop content; in other words, the project leadership team used the responses iteratively to determine the content of subsequent workshops. Reflection prompts specifically focused on whether and how each workshop was useful and what additional workshop topics would be helpful for future sessions (see Appendix B).

After initial analyses of the above-mentioned data, the research team created and administered a questionnaire that was sent to all COMPELS

TABLE 1.1   Data Type, Description, and Time of Collection

Data Type	Description	Time of Collection
End-of-semester synthesis reports	Faculty written reflections about successes, changes, challenges, and future modifications to their course.	Dec. 2010, May 2011
Workshop reflections	Faculty written reflections about what they learned and what they want to learn more about after each workshop.	Oct. 2010–April 2011
Questionnaire	Ten questions about faculty engagement. Prompts were created after initial analyses by the group-identified emergent themes from above data sources.	May–June 2011

faculty members to further investigate emerging themes. The additional prompts were meant to garner more detailed, deeper qualitative information regarding faculty members' personal histories; perspectives and tensions pertaining to implementing service-learning; and the influence of the COMPELS grant activities. The questionnaire (see Appendix C) was developed after initial coding of the other two data sources to further investigate emerging themes. Table 1.1 shows the data type, description, and data collection time line.

DATA ANALYSIS

This chapter represents a small piece of a larger study. We describe the broader analysis and then the more finite analysis of tensions as a prominent theme. Our analysis followed a grounded theory protocol (Bogdan & Bilken, 2007; Charmaz, 2006) in that we engaged in inductive and deductive coding throughout the process of analysis. Five members of the faculty analyzed the end-of-semester synthesis reports as well as the workshop reflections (submitted by all 16 faculty participants). Each individual separately open-coded the synthesis reports and reflections. Then, we came together to discuss our codes. From this discussion, we came to a shared list of themes to describe *faculty engagement* with service-learning: identifying tensions, changes in faculty practice, and community influences that shape service-learning experiences. From those themes, the group decided to further investigate by developing a questionnaire.

The group developed a questionnaire to elicit more information about faculty engagement. The questionnaire asked about faculty members' inclination toward, engagements with, and perspectives/reflections on service-learning. The same five faculty members read the questionnaire answers, inductively coded the answers, then deductively looked for the three themes across all answers (tensions, changes in practice, and community influences). After reading the questionnaire responses in pairs and identifying initial categories, two additional researchers read through all questionnaires to confirm (or disconfirm) the group's categories. The group came together twice during this process to summarize their categories to ensure trustworthiness (Charmaz, 2006).

As a final phase of analysis, the first two authors (who were not participants in the study) returned to the larger data set to ensure credibility of the findings. We targeted "tensions" as an area ripe for theoretical grounding because tensions seemed to be important for faculty members as they learned about and engaged in service-learning pedagogy. The varied data types, data collection mechanisms, and iterative analyses among and across data sets served to augment the trustworthiness and credibility of our efforts. Below is a reflection of the collective work and discussion regarding faculty participants' expressed tensions.

FINDINGS

The faculty experienced three types of tensions: philosophical, pedagogical, and logistical. Although the tensions are presented as discrete categories, they were, in fact, interconnected. Furthermore, each category yielded a series of subheadings that detail the nature of the tensions and in doing so, we use the term "or" to distinguish the types of tensions experienced. Using "or" is not meant to position tensions as dichotomous but merely reflects the ideas that faculty members considered. Tensions led to faculty growth in thinking about the pedagogy of service-learning, its ideological underpinnings, and the role of faculty in both areas.

Philosophical Tensions

Philosophical tensions included contradictions, concerns, and questions that challenged faculty perceptions of genuine motivations for engaging students in service-learning. Four interrelated topics prompted considerable discussion and reflection by faculty. They wondered: How can a candidate feel empowered by mandates? In what ways is the candidate's voice made a tangible facet of the service-learning experience when elements of the experience are prescribed (and what elements need to be prescribed by the faculty member)? Would candidates still engage without a grade or assignment to validate their participation? Should assessments of service-learning measure process (as demonstrated via candidates' dispositions, initiative, and/or reflective stance) or product (such as quality ratings for knowledge about service-learning, the successful implementation of service-learning projects, and/or demonstrations of project effectiveness)? What candidate outcomes really count? COMPELS faculty members raised these questions, but did not come to shared conclusions. Instead, these questions demonstrated the enduring tensions they felt as they became more deeply involved integrating service-learning in their courses.

Faculty contemplated how to reconcile mandating service-learning with notions of service as voluntary. In other words, could they still call it *service-learning* if they mandated that students take part in service activities? Specifically, some faculty members believed that requiring service-learning is "oppositional to democratic citizenship ideals" espoused by service-learning pedagogues. One stated:

Requiring students to serve is oppositional to democratic citizenship ideals and potentially hinders the possible development of intrinsic motivation or a personal desire to serve or embrace social justice. Mandating service-learning may cause resistance and fail to gain the support of our students.

Several faculty members echoed similar concerns regarding the intrinsic motivation of candidates and expressed reservations about mandating service-learning. Although all of the faculty participants agreed that this was a tension, each negotiated it differently. One faculty member noted:

In a way, requiring service seems like a contradiction. However, I think requiring it was probably necessary. Given all their other requirements, I doubt whether they would have done it if it had not been required. . . . If their experience is good, I hope that they will continue with service-learning when it is not required.

Other faculty members reasoned that although they prefer to offer optional service-learning opportunities, requiring service-learning through course assignments was necessary for preparing teachers to conduct service-learning projects with their P–12 students. Faculty believed that not all candidates would participate in service-learning unless it was required. Despite this rationale, the majority of the faculty tended to agree with one faculty member who said, "I struggle with the concept of mandatory service and wonder if it is possible to require it for a course without mandating it."

As faculty expressed discomfort with requiring service-learning, they also struggled with their obligations to grade candidates' work and participation. Some faculty felt that accountability would negatively affect candidates' intrinsic motivation. However, other faculty members thought that candidates would be motivated to learn more simply by experiencing service-learning. Several faculty members were also convinced that if they did not hold candidates accountable, typically in the form of points for completion of a service-learning assignment, the candidates might not follow through on service-learning. One faculty member told about this tension:

"No accountability, no task" reflects my thoughts regarding the requirements on service-learning projects. . . . Students are trained to operate based on assignments they get credit for. If we just expect students to do something *for the soul,* it may or may not happen.

Nonetheless, all faculty members held candidates accountable and assigned a portion of the final grade to service-learning projects.

Moreover, all but two (14 of 16; 88%) associated grades with the *process* of implementing service-learning rather than grading the quality of the *product.* This tension between assessing process or product is reflected in the following comments: "I was interested in the process more than how well they implemented it. So, my accountability was tied to the process . . . if they went through it and completed the process, they received full credit on that assignment" and "They were held accountable for the completion of the project, as it was part of their grade." Although faculty became more aware of the distinction between process/product assessments, they overwhelmingly required process assessments ("Did you do a service-learning project? How did you feel about it?"), rather than product assessments ("Was the service-learning project of high quality?").

Another recurring philosophical tension involved candidate voice and faculty dictation of service-learning experiences. Faculty expressed concern about whether the faculty or candidates should choose community partners. A few faculty members wanted more candidate involvement in determining the partners and project focus. A few others struggled to involve candidates in these decisions because candidates were not asking to be involved—in fact, many candidates were asking *not* to be involved in planning the service-learning projects. As stated by one faculty member, "In the future, I will encourage my students to choose their own community organization or project to complete. This will hopefully allow students to seek out projects that they are passionate about and experience great professional development." Yet, several faculty members emphasized that candidates preferred more direction with choosing projects—candidates wanted more input from faculty about what communities to partner with and establishing a project goal. One stated, "In the end, asking students to find their own service project appeared to add stress to the assignment."

Most faculty members undertook considerable preparation and relationship building with community partners to shape candidates' service opportunities and connect course content. Unfortunately, this sometimes limited candidates' ability to directly select the focus of the service-learning. In these cases, faculty spent time trying to secure candidates' buy-in about the value and intent of the project as indicative of the following faculty testimonial: "I shared my personal and current service experience with my students to improve the validity of the requirement. I believe the majority realized that the course requirement was relevant and would help with their future teaching skills."

Pedagogical Tensions

Faculty named two experiences prompting pedagogical tensions: one related to curricular content, the other to candidate expectations. Both were related to time. One faculty member put it this way:

My most persistent challenge is not having enough time to fully implement service-learning projects in an already packed curriculum. I also experienced resistance from several students/preservice teachers, who felt the service requirement was a burden and made it difficult for them to balance family and other school obligations.

Faculty members consistently mentioned tension between implementing service-learning and addressing subject-specific curricular content for the course. In other words, faculty constantly negotiated course content and service-learning activities. Interestingly, faculty fully expected the service-learning activities to align and deepen candidates' knowledge of course content; however, they also felt obliged to use direct instruction to address a broader curriculum. When asked what candidates learned from service-learning, faculty identified mostly nonacademic (e.g., dispositional, social aspects of teaching and learning) and far fewer specific academic outcomes (e.g., knowledge about math instruction or literacy instruction).

Faculty members also conveyed their tensions related to the time it took to integrate service-learning and candidates' expectations of their course. Faculty reported candidates' feedback regarding service-learning experiences/expectations, as follows:

Initially, I gave students the option to choose a service-learning project, ranging from volunteering at a local community organization to implementing a service-learning project within their respective classrooms. I also provided information on various community organizations. . . . Many students were unsuccessful in their attempts to find a community organization that fit their schedules, so I made an executive decision and decided that all students would tutor on Mondays before the course at [a local] Boys and Girls Club.

This tension identified by the COMPELS faculty echoed Bowen and Kiser's (2009) finding that the issue of time caused faculty a great deal of consternation in their implementation of service-learning. We believe that this issue will never dissipate entirely—faculty will likely continue to grapple with how to pace and organize their time as they integrate service-learning.

Logistical Tensions

In addition to philosophical and pedagogical tensions, faculty experienced logistical tensions. Three tensions informed logistical aspects of implementing service-learning for faculty: (1) access to community, (2) locale/space, and (3) course structure. With respect to community access, faculty members struggled with whether the community should be familiar or unfamiliar. Select faculty members explicitly required candidates to seek out communities that they were *unfamiliar* with to prepare them for teaching unfamiliar P–12 student populations (and to begin familiarizing them with those populations). When they led the service-learning, all faculty members reached out to familiar communities. Faculty who asked candidates to seek out their own communities reported that candidates most often selected familiar communities as well. Sometimes the familiar community partner lacked relevance or was not the best fit for the academic course content. For instance, a course preparing middle-secondary teachers included a service-learning activity at an elementary school. Although the experience proved useful as a service activity, it was not a useful way to provide experiences for teachers to interact with the kinds of candidates whom they would eventually teach.

Lastly, course structure influenced decisions faculty members made about whether candidates would autonomously select projects. Most often when courses were in mini-semesters, faculty orchestrated service-learning opportunities. But in the instances when courses stretched across multiple semesters, faculty members were more likely to allow candidates to gradually design and undertake their own service-learning projects. Such findings, in part, suggest that course structure may influence tensions regarding candidate autonomy in decision-making and more prescriptive approaches. Overall, faculty recognized differences in candidates who independently engaged in the process from the very beginning (finding a community on their own) and candidates who were led through the process by faculty who had already engaged the foundational stages of service-learning (locating community, establishing rapport, determining community needs, orchestrating options/opportunities for candidates). Upon reflecting on these differences in candidate engagement, three faculty members shared that:

> I still grapple with initially assigning the [community partner] as a . . . partner from the beginning [versus] allowing them [candidates] to find an organization they would like to support. . . . Do I take away the [community partner name] completely? Do I open the doors for them searching for . . . nonprofits in the community? Where's that line? I'm not sure. More freedom this semester felt better.

> I am planning to engage my preservice teachers . . . where they brainstorm service they will do *together*. . . . I am hoping a collaborative project might generate more creativity, excitement, and engagement. . . . My hope is that I can model with preservice [teachers] what it looks like for students to create their projects, instead of instructors and teachers dictating what will happen and how it will happen.

> In the future, I will encourage my students to choose their own community organizations or project to complete. This will hopefully allow students to seek out projects that they are passionate about and experience personal development.

As represented in the quotations above, faculty explored tensions as part of their process in making decisions about their service-learning implementation. Phrases such as "I still grapple . . . ," "I am planning . . . ," and "In the future . . ." were sentiments expressed as they discussed logistical tensions but were indicative of how they also processed philosophical and pedagogical tensions. In other words, the three identified tensions—philosophical, pedagogical, and logistical—all served to shape faculty members' current and anticipated implementation of service-learning.

DISCUSSION

Tensions as Deepened Understanding

The faculty experienced philosophical, pedagogical, and logistical tensions that other scholars deemed as inhibitors to implementing service-learning (e.g., Banerjee & Hausafus, 2007; Hou, 2010; Mckay & Rozee, 2004), yet we suggest that these tensions were conducive to (and evidence of) faculty members' deepening commitment to implementing service-learning. We invite service-learning researchers and teachers to build on the categorical tensions presented here as a means of extending the literature on faculty service-learning efforts.

Several of the philosophical tensions are likely rooted within service-learning pedagogy itself. For instance, the faculty members wrestled with how to forge agentive, autonomous, and intrinsically motivated dispositions among the candidates while requiring service-learning; they wrestled with the irony of requiring agency and autonomy. These philosophical issues were further exacerbated by the grading process. Faculty members grappled with whether and how to assign value to the process and/or product outcomes of service-learning. Given the reality of institutions of higher education, we do not believe that these tensions will dissipate; rather, we contend that faculty members can critically analyze the structures that define not only their course design, but also candidates' expectations.

Another philosophical tension related to whether and how faculty directed service-learning experiences. They repeatedly discussed the pros and cons of mandating service-learning participation and who should dictate the nature of the project. The faculty members agreed that candidate voice is important to service-learning, but the boundaries of what that meant were undefined. For instance, some candidates did not want to do service-learning activities at all—is resistance to service-learning legitimate voice? These faculty members felt that *not* requiring service-learning could cause candidates to miss out on the opportunity to engage *and subsequently benefit* from such experiences. Furthermore, when given opportunities for choice and voice in their service-learning experience, many candidates expressed stress and a desire for more faculty direction. Faculty members struggled to define how much (and how little) to intervene as they negotiated each service-learning experience with their candidates. Service-learning is commonly positioned as an approach different from "traditional" schooling (Clayton & Ash, 2004; Hurd, 2006); consequently, faculty members are often working against candidates' expectations for required faculty-driven, faculty-centered, faculty-graded assignments (Shor, 1996; Stenhouse & Jarrett, 2012). This issue of candidates' expectations was underscored by faculty members' concerns in this study. Faculty should directly engage such tensions by inviting candidates to critically reflect on how they have been socialized in education in ways that counter a service-learning philosophy (Cipolle, 2004; Clayton & Ash, 2004; Stenhouse & Jarrett, 2012).

From a pedagogical perspective, faculty participants wanted candidates to implement service-learning to deepen content knowledge, yet faculty struggled to connect a broad array of curricular content objectives to service-learning. Faculty members expressed tensions related to time for addressing academic content and time for providing service-learning experiences. Consequently, faculty identified fewer academic outcomes for service-learning activities and more nonacademic outcomes (such as affective, democratic/civic, and social objectives). Advancing content knowledge and academic learning is a significant service-learning expectation; however, they are not the sole outcomes (Clayton & Ash, 2004; Stenhouse & Jarrett, 2012; Warner & Esposito, 2009). What kinds of outcomes are worthy: civic, social, emotional, perceptual, academic, or all of the above? The problem with *all of the above* is that faculty members seem to expect service-learning to provide more affective and civic outcomes than academic outcomes. Based on their experiences with students in an immersion service-learning course, Warner and Esposito (2009) offered that student learning is not just about academic course content "but also influenced by the experiential and relational aspects of immersion. This may not be a surprise to those who use service-learning in their courses, but it may point to the inadequacies of our assessment of student learning" (p. 515).

Service-learning itself clouds distinctions among pedagogical outcomes. Pribbenow (2005) suggests that faculty should be supported in maximizing candidate outcomes and being more explicit about the desired learning. Yet even when faculty members are explicit about their instructional objectives, the distinction between academic content and affective content is blurry. This was especially true for faculty members who believe that their goal is civic education and/or who are oriented toward a sociocultural perspective. For example, one faculty member, who focuses on social studies and civics education, mentioned that learning about service-learning is *itself* a content-area academic outcome. Another faculty member used service-learning as a conduit for talking about teacher and student empowerment.

Within service-learning research, faculty identified logistical aspects of service-learning as deterrents to service-learning (Banerjee & Hausafus, 2007; Hou, 2010; McKay & Rozee, 2004). Such logistics might include service-learning site support or university support in carrying out service-learning projects. Faculty, in this case, expressed logistical tensions, such as issues of access, locale/space, and course structure that should also be considered within the context of service-learning. Logistics were an area that often directly affected how faculty members introduced and carried out service-learning assignments. For instance, candidates' inability to secure their own service-learning communities led one professor to intervene and select a common site for everyone. Courses with limited class sessions prompted faculty to accelerate the process by engaging in the preparation and planning themselves on behalf of their candidates or providing a limited selection of specific choices.

Intersecting Tensions

As we gain further insights into the tensions experienced by faculty, the overlap with candidates' service-learning engagement might prove useful to how service-learning educators position and perceive their efforts. We highlight how these intersecting tensions—faculty tensions and candidates' tensions—might inform the design, description, and implementation of service-learning in courses.

Extrinsic motivation merits consideration in light of the role it plays in prompting faculty and candidate participation in service-learning. For example, as faculty members negotiated their tensions with candidates' accountability and grading, they are also subjected to institutional accountability structures (such as course evaluations, promotion and tenure guidelines, etc.). Faculty tensions with desired rewards might echo candidate tensions with grading and accountability. Banerjee and Hausafus (2007) and others (Hou, 2010; McKay & Rozee, 2004) have consistently found that faculty desire validation of service-learning efforts through promotion, tenure, or other reward systems. However, the research trends further indicate that faculty members are more likely to persist in pursuing service-learning despite not receiving external institutional rewards (Wade & Demb, 2009). In courses that include service-learning, faculty and candidates can negotiate what extrinsic motivations can and/or should apply.

Faculty further suggested that candidates perceived service-learning as an "add on" rather than a conduit for learning academic content. Other service-learning proponents have noted that service-learning should not be perceived as isolated acts or tangential to real learning (e.g., Clayton & Ash, 2004; Eyler & Giles, 1999); yet, faculty expressed their own tensions with balancing service-learning experiences and other course content. Having to decide between content and service-learning is antithetical to the underlying academic focus of service-learning. If this perception is not explicitly addressed, candidates' perception of service-learning as add-on, extra, or isolated from content can undermine the academic goals of service-learning. Lilly (2001) cautions that "for the most part, new teachers practice what they have seen—which is precisely why it is so important for teacher educators to practice what we preach" (p. 215). Given that service-learning distinguishes itself from other forms of service because of an explicit focus on academic learning, faculty should consider how they negotiate that expectation with their candidates. Therefore, we recommend that faculty and candidates explicitly (and honestly) address whether and how service-learning maps on to academic course content.

Tensions, Microtransformations, and Learning Communities

Recognizing the similarities and differences among faculty and candidates' experiences presents an opportunity for faculty to continue to closely examine how their philosophical, pedagogical, and logistical tensions shape their implementation of service-learning in their teacher preparation courses. Extending beyond notions of challenges as necessarily resolvable, faculty tensions catalyzed discussion and reflection that led to shifts in practice, perception, and reorchestration of service-learning assignments. We view these shifts as microtransformations.

Clayton and Ash (2004) discuss "shifts in perspective" to explain the conceptual and pedagogical changes in the understanding and doing of service-learning. Microtransformations, as we posit, also occur conceptually and pedagogically. We further assert that tensions describe the catalytic process that faculty experience as they toggle between choices that influence their service-learning courses toward transforming them into service-learning educators.

Illuminating tensions and microtransformations were a result of faculty participation in COMPELS. COMPELS provided faculty with opportunities for critical reflection and dialog as a means of critiquing, assessing, and taking action (Mezirow, 1997). As is underscored throughout what we know about enhancing faculty service-learning practices, participating in learning communities like COMPELS is a relevant factor in affecting service-learning pedagogy for the better (Jones, 2001; McKay & Rozee, 2004; Wade & Demb, 2009).

IMPLICATIONS

The tensions we report here suggest that in order to transform teacher education through service-learning, faculty should explicitly address the tensions they experience—and recognize the connections to the tensions candidates might be experiencing as well. As previously argued, we contend that these tensions may not have definitive solutions; instead, they provide ongoing considerations that should be discussed among colleagues and, in some instances, with candidates. Much of what is shared about service-learning is positive, whether it is its influence on candidates' academic learning, community engagement, or civic responsibility (Furco & Root, 2010). At the same time, semester after semester, faculty are in a position to maximize learning outcomes for candidates who participate in service-learning or candidates learning how to implement service-learning themselves. Discussion of the following questions may reveal important tensions and inform effective service-learning practices:

- How do faculty members model, in their own service-learning teaching, their desired pedagogical practices?
- To what degree are limitations faculty members perceive in implementation and outcomes related to philosophical, pedagogical, or logistical tensions?
- What affordances are faculty members given to engage in dialogue and to consider the tensions in their teaching that could yield transformative outcomes in their service-learning practices?

Articulating tensions serves to make explicit what faculty should consider as they implement service-learning. Doing so may provide faculty with language that enables more refined understandings of their intentions, practices, and outcomes. As faculty enhance their understanding of service-learning and examine their own classroom practices, they should consider how they explicitly model their decision-making process (Loughran & Berry, 2005).

The COMPELS grant initiative supported faculty through embedded faculty development and provided a space to systematically reflect and inform/transform their practice. Faculty members praised the routine meetings as opportunities for professional learning. Institutions that support service-learning initiatives should embed consistent opportunities for faculty to discuss these tensions just as faculty may provide candidates with such opportunities in their courses. As a result, faculty can continue to improve their efforts to provide effective service-learning in teacher education.

ACKNOWLEDGMENTS

We are grateful for the contributions of our colleagues who assisted with the research presented here: Rachel Gurvitch, Lydia C. Mays, Janet Z. Burns, and Olga S. Jarrett.

NOTES

1. For additional details on the Thomas Ehrlich Civically Engaged Faculty Award, go to http://www.compact.org/initiatives/campus-compact-awards-programs/the-thomas-ehrlich-civically-engaged-faculty-award/
2. To further review the IPARDC Model for service-learning, go to http://www.servicelearning.org/topic/quality-components-standards/k-12-cbo-service-learning-core-components.

APPENDIX A
End-of-Semester Synthesis Reports

Please share the following information in your synthesis report:

- Name, Course title/number, identify undergraduate or graduate course
- Number of GSU students/teachers (Please indicate number of pre-service and/or inservice teachers)
- Total number of service activities/projects in which GSU students/teachers engaged
- Briefly describe how community needs were determined (e.g., professor, students/teachers, pupils, etc.)
- Describe the types of service activities/projects (what did people do, with whom were they doing service, location, and approximately how long) (e.g., tutoring 10 first-grade (~7 years old) refugee students at the privately run Schley County Refugee Community Center, 3 hours a week for 5 weeks).
- Describe the population(s) they worked with demographically (i.e., socioeconomic status, ability, race, gender, language(s), and any other characteristics helpful to know about the population).
- Note if and how you utilized any community partners.
- Feel free to offer any overall comments/reflections on the experience of engaging service-learning in your coursework this semester.

APPENDIX B
COMPELS Faculty Development Workshop
Reflection Prompts

10/5/10 (10)

  I. Was this session useful to you or not? Why or why not? (all sessions)
  II. Considering you own teaching,
  – If you have engaged service-learning before in your coursework, how has doing so affected your instruction?
  III. – If you have not engaged in service-learning in your coursework before, how do you envision your participation affecting your instruction?

11/3/10 (9)

  IV. Considering you own teaching,

  Describe any challenges you are experiencing or have experienced in one or more of the following aspects regarding implementing service-learning:
  (a) managing the logistics of the project;
  (b) eliciting meaningful reflections from students;
  (c) supporting democratic decision making;
  (d) addressing deficit views of the community being served;
  (e) integrating projects into academic coursework;
  (f) other:

11/30/10 (8)

  V. If you have been integrating service-learning in your course(s) this semester, describe your overall impression and up to three key things you have learned regarding conducting service-learning in your coursework.
  VI. If you have not been integrating service-learning in your course(s) this semester, ask up to three key questions that remain for you as you anticipate integrating service-learning in your upcoming course(s).
  VII. As we plan our spring dates, we need to know your schedule. What days/times would work best for you next semester to participate in additional workshops?

2/2/11 (6)

VIII. What do you think about Learn and Serve's definition of service-learning? How does it converge or diverge from your understanding of service-learning?

IX. Based on the discussion today, how could the next session best serve your current goals regarding implementing and understanding service-learning?

2/15/11 (6)

X. What, if any, "quality indicators" or "standards" do you use in assessing your students' service-learning projects?

XI. Based on the discussion today, how could the next session best serve your current goals regarding implementing and understanding service-learning?

3/8/11 (7)

XII. If you had to describe "service-learning" as a metaphor, simile, or a symbol, what would it be and why?

XIII. Based on the discussion today, how could the next session best serve your current goals regarding implementing and understanding service-learning?

XIV. If you have not been integrating service-learning in your course(s) this semester, ask up to three key questions that remain for you as you anticipate integrating service-learning in your upcoming course(s).

3/23/11 (9)

XV. Do you engage in community service, charity, or service-learning? If so, briefly share what you do. If not, and it is something you wish to do, what inhibits your engaging in such endeavors?

XVI. Based on the discussion today, how could the next session best serve your current goals regarding implementing and understanding service-learning?

4/19/11 (5)

XVII. What surprised and/or interested you regarding service-learning research and why?

XVIII. Based on the discussion today, how could the next session best serve your current goals regarding implementing and understanding service-learning?

APPENDIX C:
Questionnaire Prompts

1. Describe your *personal* history associated with service-learning and community service (growing up, school, K–12, undergraduate, graduate) and how it has impacted your life.
2. If and how did your engagement with COMPELS affect (a) your practice of teaching and learning? (b) your relationship with your students? (c) your relationship with other faculty (in or outside this grant activity)? and (d) your service engagement in the community?
3. If you had any challenges in implementing service-learning projects this academic year, how did you overcome them?
4. What went well for you this academic year in implementing service-learning projects?
5. What factors assisted you as you implemented the service-learning project(s) in your classes (e.g., readings, websites, workshops, presentations, conferences, faculty colleagues, staff, students, community partners, etc.)? Please describe how.
6. Do you plan to implement service-learning project(s) in your future academic courses? Why or why not?
7. Did you require your students to participate in a service-learning project this past academic year? Was it a group- or individual-based project? Did you hold them accountable for completion of this project? If yes, describe how.
8. What are your thoughts about requiring service-learning projects?
9. What did you expect your students to learn from participating in service-learning this academic year?
10. How do you think your students benefited from their service-learning engagement in your course? Please describe.

REFERENCES

Alexander, P. A. (1998). Positioning conceptual change within a model of domain literacy. In B. Guzzetti & C. Hynd (Eds.), *Theoretical perspectives on conceptual change: Multiple ways to understand knowing and learning in a complex world* (pp. 55–76). Mahwah, NJ: Erlbaum.

Anderson, J., Swick, K. J., & Yff, J. (Eds.). (2001). *Service-learning in teacher education: Enhancing the growth of new teachers, their students, and communities.* Washington, DC: American Association of Colleges for Teacher Education.

Assaf, L. C., & Dooley, C. M. (2006). "Everything they were giving us created tension": Creating and managing tension in a graduate-level multicultural education course. *Multicultural Education, 14*(2), 42–49.

Banerjee, M., & Hausafus, C. O. (2007, Fall). Faculty use of service-learning: Perceptions, motivations, and impediments for the human sciences. *Michigan Journal
of Community Service*, pp. 32–45.
Bogdan, R., & Biklen, S. (2007). *Qualitative research for education: an introduction to
theories and methods*. Boston: Pearson.
Bowen, G. A., & Kiser, P. M. (2009). Promoting innovative pedagogy and engagement through service-learning faculty fellows program. *Journal of Higher Education Outreach and Engagement, 13*(1), 27–43.
Bringle, R. G. & Hatcher, J. A. (2009). Innovative practices in service-learning and
curricular engagement. *New Directions for Higher Education, 147*, 37–45.
Carracelas-Juncal, C., Bossalier, J., & Yaoyuneyong, G. (2009). Integrating service-
learning pedagogy: A faculty reflective process. *InSight: A Journal of Scholarly
Teaching, 4*, 28–44.
Charmaz, K. (2006). *Constructing grounded theory: A practical guide through qualitative
analysis*. Thousand Oaks, CA: Sage.
Cipolle, S. (2004). Service-learning as a counter-hegemonic practice: Evidence pro
and con. *Multicultural Education, 12*(4), 12–23.
Clayton, P. H., & Ash, S. L. (2004, Fall). Shifts in perspective: Capitalizing on the
counter-normative nature of service-learning. *Michigan Journal of Community
Service*, pp. 59–70.
Dooley, C. M. (2008). Multicultural literacy teacher education: Seeking micro-trans-
formations. *Literacy Research and Instruction, 47*(2), 55–75.
Eyler, J., & Giles, D. E. (1999). *Where's the learning in service-learning?* San Francisco:
Jossey-Bass.
Freedman, S. W., & Ball, A. F. (2004). Ideological becoming: Bakhtinian concepts
to guide the study of language, literacy, and learning. In A. F. Ball & S. W.
Freedman (Eds.), *Bakhtinian perspectives on language, literacy, and learning*
(pp. 6–74). Cambridge, UK: Cambridge University Press.
Furco, A., & Root, S. (2010, February). Research demonstrates the value of Service
Learning. *Kappan*, pp. 16–23.
Garcia, R. M., & Robinson, G. (2005). *Transcending disciplines, reinforcing curricula:
Why faculty teach with service learning*. Washington, DC: American Association
of Community Colleges.
Gross, T. (2010, February). Service learning builds bonds to school for young learn-
ers. *Kappan*, pp. 24–26.
Hou, S. (2010, Spring). Developing a faculty inventory measuring perceived service-
learning benefits and barriers. *Michigan Journal of Community Service Learning*,
pp. 78–89.
Hurd, C. A. (2006). Is service-learning effective?: A look at current research. Re-
trieved from *http://tilt.colostate.edu/sl/faculty/Is_Service-Learning_Effective.pdf*.
Jones, S. R. (2001). The service-learning scholar's roundtable: A model for engaging faculty in service-learning theory and practice. In J. B. Anderson, K. J.
Swick, & J. Yff (Eds.), *Service-learning in teacher education: Enhancing the growth
of new teachers, their students, and communities* (pp. 220–233). Washington, DC:
American Association of Colleges for Teacher Education.
Lewis, C., Perry, R., & Murata, A. (2006). How should research contribute to in-
structional improvement: The case of Japanese Lesson Study. *Educational*

Researcher, 35(3), 3–14. Lilly, S. (2001). A dean's perspective on service-learning in teacher education. In J. B. Anderson, K. J. Swick, & J. Yff (Eds.), *Service-learning in teacher education: Enhancing the growth of new teachers, their students, and communities* (pp. 212–219). Washington, DC: American Association of Colleges for Teacher Education.

Loughran, J., & Berry, A. (2005). Modeling by teacher educators. *Teaching and Teacher Education, 21*, 193–203.

McKay, V. C., & Rozee, P. D. (2004, Spring). Characteristics of faculty who adopt community service learning pedagogy. *Michigan Journal of Community Service,* pp. 21–33.

Mezirow, J. (1997). Transformative learning: Theory to practice. *New Directions for Adult and Continuing Education, 74*, 5–12.

Mundy, M. E. (2004). Faculty engagement in service-learning: Individual and organizational factors at distinct institutional types. In M. Welch and S. H. Billig (Eds), *New Perspectives in Service Learning: Research to Advance the Field* (pp. 169–193). Greenwich, CT: Information Age Publishing.

O'Grady, C. R. (Ed.) (2000). *Integrating service learning and multicultural education in colleges and universities.* Mahwah, NJ: Erlbaum.

O'Meara, K. A., & Niehaus, E. (2009, Fall). Service-learning is...: How faculty explain their practice. *Michigan Journal of Community Service Learning,* pp. 17–32.

Porfilio, B. J., & Hickman, H. (Eds.). (2011). *Critical-service learning as a revolutionary pedagogy: an international project of student agency in action.* Charlotte, NC: Information Age Publishing.

Pribbenow, D. A. (2005, Spring). The impact of service-learning pedagogy on faculty teaching and learning. *Michigan Journal of Community Service Learning,* pp. 25–38.

Shor, I. (1992). *Empowering education: Critical teaching for social change.* Chicago: University of Chicago Press.

Stenhouse, V L., & Jarrett, O. S. (2012). In the service of learning and activism: Service learning, critical pedagogy, and the problem solution project. *Teacher Education Quarterly, 39*(1), 51–76.

Wade, A., & Demb, A. (2009, Spring). A conceptual model to explore faculty community engagement. *Michigan Journal of Community Service Learning,* pp. 5–16.

Warner, B., & Esposito, J. (2009). What's not in the syllabus: Faculty transformation, role modeling and role conflict in immersion service-learning courses. *International Journal of Teaching and Learning in Higher Education, 20*(3), 510–517.

Vera L Stenhouse is an internal evaluator and research coordinator for three federally funded grants that support urban teacher preparation in Georgia State University's Department of Early Childhood Education. Prior to this position, Stenhouse served as the project director for the federally funded Community Opportunities that Motivate People and Enhance Learning and Service (COMPELS) grant that supported service-learning professional development for Georgia State University College of Education teacher preparation faculty. Stenhouse has coauthored two publications focused on service-learning and critical pedagogy that appear in *Teacher Education Quarterly* and *Urban Education*, respectively: "In the Service of Learning and Activism in Teacher Education: Service Learning, Critical Pedagogy and the Problem Solution Project" (2012) and "Transforming Curriculum and Empowering Urban Students and Teachers" (2011). Current research centers on teacher education, teacher educators, and matters related to diversity and multicultural education. Stenhouse's doctorate is from the Division of Educational Studies at Emory University.

Caitlin McMunn Dooley is an Associate Professor in the Early Childhood Education Department at Georgia State University. Her research investigates early emergent comprehension, literacy instruction and testing in elementary grades, and teacher development. She serves as Co-Editor for the National Council of Teachers of English premier journal *Language Arts* (2011–2016). Dooley has led and participated in funded research totaling more than $16.2 million. She is currently a co-PI for a $13.5 million Teacher Quality Partnership grant from the U.S. Department of Education. Dooley's research has been published in national and international refereed journals and chapters published by the Literacy Research Association, the International Reading Association, and the National Council of Teachers of English, among others. She is the lead author of "Literary Meaning Making," a chapter in the *Literacy Research Handbook* (Sage). Dooley is also the Director for the PhD program in Early Childhood and Elementary Education at Georgia State University. In addition to having taught elementary grades, Dooley has served as a consultant to education nonprofits as well as several urban schools and districts across the United States.

Joseph R. Feinberg is an Associate Professor of Social Studies Education at Georgia State University. He taught social studies at Campbell High School in Smyrna, Georgia, where he received a Martin Luther King Humanitarian Award, which recognizes excellence in humanitarian service to the school and community. One of Joseph's first publications was the product of a Kezai Koho Fellowship to Japan. He wrote "Service Learning in Contemporary Japan and America" (2002) for *The Social Studies*, which helped him develop a greater passion and understanding of domestic and international service-learning. He also published a service-learning chapter in *Real World Investigations for Middle and High School Social Studies* (2004). His current research interests include simulation games, teacher education, and service-learning.

CHAPTER 2

TEACHER EDUCATION AS PARTNERSHIP

Service-Learning and the Audacity of Listening

George L. Boggs

ABSTRACT

Service-learning pedagogy invites teacher education programs to weigh the consequences of *local* versus *mass teacher education* and to consider the value of listening and community partnership as vital features of teacher preparation. Concepts of language-mediated becoming and prefigurative politics reveal a revolutionary aspect of service-learning pedagogy and unique challenges for utilizing it in teacher education. Reflecting on multiple research programs in service-learning, both within and outside teacher education programs, the educators' role in developing relational epistemologies that produce knowledge embedded in and for the benefit of local communities is considered. Such an understanding of service-learning can enable sophisticated adaptation and redeployment of traditional academic activities as part of a powerful and transformative listening project.

Transforming Teacher Education Through Service-Learning, pages 31–50
Copyright © 2013 by Information Age Publishing
31

Teachers teach students and serve their families and communities, but their training and employment make them accountable elsewhere. Colleges of education across the United States are publishing mission statements that express a desire to improve the communities in which they are located (e.g., Mission Statement, 2012), which raises the question whether teachers trained in such programs will have experience attending to the motivations and interests of communities in which they practiced their craft. Listening is messy; it necessitates "continuously adaptive action, not seeking definitive solutions" (Nicolaides & Yorks, 2008, p. 56). It therefore frustrates noble efforts to improve x unilaterally, opening instead the possibility of mutual aid, on which some conceptual forerunners of service-learning have been based (Bunge, 2011). Schools and teacher preparation programs function smoothly when *they* get to articulate the needs of their constituents, when they dictate treatments, and when they select tools for measuring their success. However, as any parent knows, the efficiencies generated by subordination do not always deliver the goods. Attending to stakeholders' goals represents an "opening" in effective teacher education (Fleener, Jewett, Smolen, & Carson, 2011, p. 14).

Psychologist and teacher Lev Vygotsky (1978) had brilliantly subtle advice for literacy teachers that expresses the necessity of systematic listening: "[It] should be organized in such a way that reading and writing are necessary for something.... [W]riting must be 'relevant to life'" (p. 24). Without listening to students and their communities, it is impossible to accomplish this organizational task (Parker, 2010). Impositional curricular elements unravel under Vygotsky's optimal conditions, yet structural obstacles to listening to students are added yearly, with the Common Core, value-added programs and nationally standardized tests among the highest-profile examples. Voices like these demanding teachers' attention have become part of the structure of schooling. Along with long established features of schooling—performances of competence, competition, and individual achievement—they act as a kind of headwind resisting organizing teaching by listening to students' motivations or goals present in their families and communities.

Service-learning can transform teacher education by making teacher education necessary for something. To do so, it must justify its place in higher education (Butin, 2006), despite widespread agreement that educational institutions are in need of restructuring. Two processes in particular provide especially rich opportunities for growth in teacher education. First, teacher educators, preservice teachers, and teachers can use service-learning pedagogies to *listen* to the interests of students and their communities as prerequisites to or, in Vygotskian terms, histories of instruction, planning, and assessment. Second, all stakeholders, including students, families, and school administrators, can use service-learning practices to repurpose or resituate (Lather, 2007) academic tools to *work against the wind* of structural marginalization of community goals. Powerful conceptual tools are available and practical examples abound that position locally relevant teacher education as a form of authentic, attentive civic engagement. This article suggests no turnkey model for transforming teacher-education but attempts to coordinate optimal conditions for development described by Vygotsky (1978), Bakhtin (1981), and others with the prefigurative ethical possibilities (Franks, 2003) of service-learning.

CONCEPTUAL FRAMEWORK FOR SERVICE-LEARNING IN TEACHER EDUCATION

The preparation of teachers should attend to the intersection of their languages, of the school worlds in which they work, and of the communities in which they seek legitimacy. Among the meanings of attend and attention, the notion of focused listening is perhaps the most appropriate. Colleges of education have a reputation for being ideologically at odds with schools—speaking a different language—and structurally immune to community concerns. To the extent this reputation is based in the training teachers receive, it hampers the development of robust concepts of teaching. The training offered by service-learning experiences, by contrast, can strengthen humane impulses to listen before speaking, to wait one's turn, and to show respect.

Part of the problem is that teacher education typically occurs prior to a teaching career, another feature of the structured way in which teacher education impedes listening, but the ingredients of teacher education are subject to change. Alternative teacher education pathways have been around for a long time, but Teach for America and similar programs have raised the profile of alternative teacher preparation together with a critique of traditional methods. Interestingly, although Teach for America and traditional teacher education approaches organize their clients differently, they are scarcely distinguishable in terms of their orientation toward the development of just, sustainable communities: They assume that success in school, as measured by test performance, is the be-all and end-all of a teacher's contribution to a child's life.

Conceptual grasp of teaching (Grossman, Smagorinsky, & Valencia, 1999; Grossman, Hammerness, & McDonald, 2009) can be elusive because of contradictory goals in teaching settings for what education should accomplish. Confusing control and teaching (Packard, 1988; Smagorinsky, Boggs, Jakubiak, & Wilson, 2010; Willower, Eidell, & Hoy, 1967), a significant concern in the development of teachers' conceptual understanding, may be an error counted against a novice teacher, but this obstacle to teaching expresses a problematic political arrangement exemplified institutionally by conventions favoring teacher authority, fixed curricula, district demands, or credentialing requirements. From a Vygotskian (1987) perspective, the whole lot, along with writing, grades, and reading, are tools in teachers' and students' hands whose role in learning depends on the context of their use, just as, for example, using grades to control behavior shapes teachers' and students' perception of school achievement. Developing service-learning culture therefore involves much more than deemphasizing performance-based grading or eliminating formal writing: It involves the nurturance of relational epistemologies, which will in time suggest new uses for old physical, verbal, and conceptual tools.

Changing a Community of Practice

Communities of practice (Lave, 1988) are saturated with their own concerns. This condition of social life calls for theories of teaching based on listening, problem-posing, and respect. In teacher education, "apprenticeship of observation," the ingrained, atheoretical notions people have about teaching based on their experience as students (Lortie, 1975), has justified insidious forms of deficit-based education, despite our calling critical and emancipatory (Ellsworth, 1989). With preconceived notions of the needs of others in the forefront, deficit approaches in education schools reveal to preservice teachers that the world is not white, middle class, English speaking, and so on. The captive audience of preservice teachers may make disrupting hegemonic perspectives appear too easy (Mewborn & Tyminski, 2006), and teachers are left to work out in their placement schools the moral consequences and effectiveness of deficit-based instruction.

Political and epistemological affordances of service-learning are not absolute or autonomous, but situated and context-dependent. In other words, distinctive modes of learning do not happen because descriptions are entered into a university bulletin or uttered by an instructor; they are embodied, practiced, and enculturated each semester and moment by moment, by participants as well as teachers, hence the notion of a community of practice (Lave, 1988). The radical localness of service-learning shows up first in this need to awaken and share epistemologies, politics, and language of experiential education. Then as service-learning is enacted (Grossman et al., 2009)—participants embrace their immediate context and each other as the curriculum—the primary, prefigurative space enables service-learners to extend the space to include communities in which they may participate. Service-learning, as a basis for teacher education, acknowledges the goals of target communities where student teaching alone does not. In other words, student teaching as a means of learning to teach is silent with regard to the relationship among student teachers and between teachers and the communities they serve, while service-learning places that relationship at the prefigurative center. Reminiscent of Martin Buber's (1923/2004) *I–thou* relationship, Dewey's (1902) conception of life as curriculum, and Bakhtin's (1981) notion of the self in dialogue, there is transformative potential for listening in basic human interactions.

The second part is incorporating I–thou, life-as-curriculum, or listening culture in contexts saturated with established meanings for what school is and how it's done. When the instructor of a human geography service-learning course, whom I call Dylan, said, "You will not be turning in formal essays or any of that crap for this class," he was working the sails of service-learning, suggesting meanings for practices privileged in school (i.e., academic writing) in order to open the prefigurative spaces in which participants recognize themselves and others around them as the curriculum. Dylan admitted it was "political theater" with real consequences: He surrendered a means of assessing development of critical perspectives in order to convince his audience of the egalitarian organization of his course.

Dylan justified the risks in terms of his unwillingness to sit in judgment over the quality of their contributions, and he was convinced of the autonomous significance of not judging his students as a crucial first step toward expanding prefigurations of just, local, transformative action. Dylan's plan was to awaken ownership of community partnership by managing the symbols of schooling: "That crap" was a scapegoat meant to drive out what participants, in interviews, called "school as usual." These efforts to inscribe a service-learning subsetting within the university and even his own teaching were "experimental" and "trial and error." He imagined himself and the course "tacking back and forth," alternatively including and excluding writing assignments semester-by-semester, trying to work out the orientation toward typical academic activities that nurtured the development of a culture of listening. He wanted to run against the wind of school as usual, which involved *learning* to run against the wind. A shift in orientation from external manipulation of schooled practices (i.e., writing) as symbols with fixed meaning to optimizing advantages of academic tools through a dynamic listening and learning process marks a conceptual development for Dylan as a teacher. Recognizing the rich overlap between typical academic activities and the broader practices of community activism in which he had participated, he nurtured collaborative production of a newspaper article as a way of building momentum for community projects.

Prefiguration and Prefigurative Ethics

I conducted case studies of participants in Dylan's courses to determine their development of concepts related to the course and to community engagement. Concepts pertaining to participants' ability to contribute meaningfully to their communities ran the gamut but correlated fairly neatly with conceptions of the service-learning course itself. One participant, Elspeth, saw the service-learning experience as a dry-swim for future community action. Correspondingly, she saw Dylan as the most important player in a "very theoretical" class (Boggs, 2011), and she suggested a "second class that was about growing food" to complement the academic, intellectual work she felt she had done *under* Dylan. Sara played out her "good student" identity in the opposite fashion. She accepted the radical curriculum Dylan acted out and used the theoretical tools privileged by the new model (e.g., mutual aid, agency, and food system) to revalue agricultural practices among extended family members and new acquaintances in the community. She projected a vision of community sovereignty as a guiding feature of her career plans, and she narrated past experiences as examples of informal, mutually beneficial learning. Leda, one of the nonmajors, didn't use the course to find ways to engage locally. She saw the course as a fixed social entity with hidden rules and a full agenda. She didn't feel the need to "break in," even though ongoing personal and family experiences closely paralleled and might have greatly enriched the course. In interviews she explained the intergenerational, international cookbook she was creating with family members seeking to protect and extend a rich food heritage for the benefit of children growing up in a cheap food generation. Chandra resented those who sat on the periphery because they detracted from the collective power the group had to bring about change. The course was a moment for action.

Hidden curricula in the course made it resemble a "choose your own adventure" novel, as discussions, decisions, and activities occurred in the context of the concepts they developed about the course. Prefiguration in the sense of hidden curricula is inevitable. Means are always present in ends. The three participants above differently identified salient ways of doing service-learning, which not surprisingly shaped how and what they learned. Sara's teacher-centered course offered a lot of great ideas; Leda's intact-social-group course was treated as a person might treat an irritating but important clique. Chandra's collective action course was an opportunity to maximize community, personal, and educational impact. These cases point to the prefigurative relation between means of conducting service-learning and its ends, namely concepts and benefit to the community.

Prefiguration connects endpoints to the means of reaching them. Aristotle theorized education in prefigurative, pragmatic terms: Efforts to impose a form of government, whether monarchy or democracy, will fail "unless the citizens have been trained by force of habit and teaching in the spirit of the constitution" (V, 9, 1310, a 17). Prefiguration is not an ethical orientation but a concept of politics, socialization, and social construction of reality. Aristotle's ethical imperative is simply that educational practices should align with outcomes. Prefigurative ethics, by contrast, is rare, specific, and powerful.

Prefigurative ethics is laden with value judgments. Its ends are justice, equity, and mutual aid, and it rejects means of reaching these goals that depend on violence and hierarchy. Prefigurative ethics collapses the distinction, so often problematic, between means and ends, attacking the uneven power relations on which many expedient forms of action, from violence to deception, depend. Nonviolent resistance is the most famous and recognizable example of prefigurative ethics, in which eschewing violent resistance to violent oppression steps toward a more just society by breaking with a tradition of oppression and violent means of social change, robbing opposition of public support and justifications for violent retaliation. Despite the appearance of significant leader-power in the Civil Rights and Indian Nationalism movements, their organizational models were local, nonhierarchical, and participatory.

Prefigurative Ethics and the Importance of the Local

While teacher education and service-learning researchers have engaged aspects of political and social hierarchies having to do with teacher performance, teacher education largely depends on structural efficiencies that limit exchange between those learning to teach and the communities those teachers will ultimately serve. In other words, every course in a college of education could critique teacher-centered notions of the "sage on the stage," but the credentialing and placement process by which teachers enter the workplace are no less likely to subordinate the interests of the families and communities to the interests of the school, the college, the state, and the nation. This subordination is a structural feature of the preparation of teachers that service-learning is theoretically positioned to disrupt due to its concern for just prefiguration.

The revolutionary potential of service-learning in teacher education rests in the status afforded to local contexts and their stakeholders. Job training is not an obstacle; epistemological and institutional hierarchies are. Prefigurative ethics thus draws attention to immediate contexts of engagement, not as a way to ignore or distract ourselves from global problems, but as a just starting point for action.

Focusing on the local context as an ethical matter restates and refocuses the well-known paradox of the school—the learning advantages and consequences of the artificial school setting. Focusing on the local necessitates managing the relationship between school and nonschool worlds, a process Dylan described as "tacking back and forth." Working with the wind is a metaphorical theme threaded throughout this chapter. The lateen sail, which enabled people to sail almost directly into the wind, is a perfect example of the way cultural and psychological tools can transform the impossible into the routine. The impossible that can become routine in teacher education involves superseding ingrained understandings of performing teacherness (Mewborn, 2006) and contradictory motives of institutional settings (Wertsch, 1991), which often conspire to restrict access to transformative education and trap teachers in roles they find uninspiring and unsustainable. Framing the wind and the sail as a conceptual problem, I ask how cultural and psychological tools available in service-learning pedagogy afford reflective supersession of unconscious, ingrained concepts of teaching and authorial agency to use institutional educational contexts to foster peer-assisted learning, inspire civic engagement, and strengthen communities.

As I enter my eighth semester of formal observation of courses designed to run *against the wind* of school as usual, the teachers I work with appear to be acquiring the ability to *use the wind* more productively as a nonviolent, productive force. They are even going on the offensive, in a way. One drafted a successful grant proposal marrying the human geography course to a program co-administered by the college of agriculture. Another doubled down on her administrator's need to promote human geography within and beyond the university by offering to take over the maintenance of the building's green roof. A third is taking service-learning into the highly contested domain of online instruction. Over the past 4 years of teaching and studying service-learning and teacher education together, I have been researching (1) local, consensus-based models of teacher education away from the factory floor and (2) synergies between literacy and other forms of concept development and out-of-school learning.

Service-Learning Pedagogy and Epistemology

Teacher education has been categorized as a form of service-learning pedagogy because of the belief that reflection upon authentic experiences with students outside the walls of the university facilitates deep learning within and across disciplines (Gordon & Debus, 2002). But it is next to impossible to define teacher education without reducing the extreme range of purposes of schooling (Smagorinsky & O'Donnell-Allen, 2000). The idea that structured exposure or action coupled with systematic reflection benefits those learning to teach is thus quite complicated if we take seriously the philosophical, political, and epistemological diversity of pedagogies and the unique sociocultural situation of the contexts in which one or more pedagogical approaches are simultaneously realized.

Preservice teachers are invited, if the thousands of PowerPoints comparing Vygotsky, Piaget, and Montessori are any indication, to pick and choose from a salad bar of epistemologically inflected approaches to instruction (Richman, 1996), their choices to be refined in the fires of the classroom and critical reflection—a kind of experiential education distinguished from in a number of ways, but in particular by the possibility of listening to constituents. A service-learning approach to teacher education that audaciously listens to people with whom service-learners work can have revolutionary consequences in a national schooling context by test-oriented instruction engineered with little regard for student and community concerns (Miller, 2012).

Elements of service-learning epistemology. Two epistemological orientations that capture the spirit of service-learning offer means of escaping the trap of unwanted and often spurious liberation: heterogeneous ways of knowing and relational epistemology. First, acknowledging multiple ways of knowing, without collapsing the everyday into the scientific or the tacit into explicit knowledge, can resolve ethical vulnerabilities of teacher education processes in which researchers, theorists, and research provide hegemonic languages into which teaching knowledge must be translated. Service-learning pedagogy strategically combines tacit, hands-on epistemologies with scientific, school-based epistemologies to producing more robust and flexible knowledge that is culturally aware, morally sophisticated, and politically conscious. This first epistemological distinction goes hand in hand with a second. Epistemic heterogeneity results from listening to the voices that swirl around us, that compose us (Bakhtin, 1981).

Listening to ideological diversity present in classrooms, schools, students, families, and communities should be part of teacher education, yet is often missing. The notion of funds of knowledge popularized in the work of Luis Moll and his colleagues (Gonzalez, Moll, & Amanti, 2005) is a perfect example of the importance of listening in the community, even as the schools involved worked against the listening project. The burden fell upon the teachers and researchers to make the lives of children intelligible in the school context. Service-learning in teacher education has the theoretical resources to turn the funds of knowledge problem on its head by coordinating the language and practices of school with the funds of knowledge of students, rather than the other way around. The question that their research raises to this present inquiry is whether listening is more an anthropological tool or act of human decency, the *sine qua non* of knowing something about another person.

Mastery-oriented and relational epistemologies. In conceptualizing the kinds of learning needed for the preparation of teachers, discourses of mastery remain dominant. The notion of mastery inscribes male-dominated epistemologies, imagining learning as conquest, private property, independence, and competition. In this framework, knowledge is static, passive, and ontologically separate from knowers. Framing teacher knowledge in terms of mastery, as a thing to be gained or owned, lowers the bar for teacher knowledge. Contrary readings of knowledge and development can provide teachers with better tools for interpreting the challenges they face and the sort of knowledge they can develop.

In contrast to fictions of independent epistemic agency belonging to mastery, relational epistemologies described by poststructural feminists (e.g., Code, 2006) acknowledge social networks as epistemic agents who share ways of seeing and saying the world. Their knowing together is the root phenomenon of human knowing. This approach resonates with the Vygotskian notion of goal-directed, tool-mediated action, framing knowledge as a tool in the hands of people who negotiate its value and use together. The legend of Archimedes shouting "Eureka" while bathing and running naked through the streets of Syracuse illustrates how mastery narratives (eureka=I found it!) may obscure the prerequisite social context for knowledge, which his roaming the streets signifies.

Social imaginary. Eureka expresses the joy of the lone (male) miner, scientist, or mathematician through a "social imaginary," which, in many European American knowledge domains, suggests that individuals are responsible for the work that matters. From the work of a noted teacher educator comes an important account of the effects of the social imaginary on thinking about teacher education epistemologies; the author explains his anti-collectivist theoretical orientation in terms of a supposedly universal cultural absolute, that "Those of us in the U.S. are raised from birth to think in terms of individuals and independence rather than collectives and group action..." (Smagorinsky, 2011, p. xxxviii). Credit goes to feminist philosophers in particular for articulating and exploring the disproportionate benefit of such powerful social imaginaries to white, Judeo-Christian, middle-class, heterosexual males. Nonetheless, social imaginaries are vital mediators of processes of sharing among epistemic agents. Because my research has focused primarily on the role of language in producing knowledge, I am especially interested in the way communication between preservice teacher and teacher educators shapes epistemic agency.

Representing teacher knowledge as if it were a thing to be mastered by individuals rather than negotiated among members of groups has many more problematic consequences beyond the disproportionate benefit to members of the dominant subculture. Mastery narratives in teacher education, and individualistic approaches, more broadly, mask the importance of knowledge networks that uphold conventional knowledge. In fact those networks typically exclude or marginalize important stakeholders such as parents, students, and other members of a community directly affected by schooling practices.

Other stakeholders have disproportionate sway: textbook companies, testing services, credentialing institutions, and employers.

Repurposing school tools. Relational epistemologies suggest new uses for familiar school tools. Service-learning instructors often attempt to develop an idioculture (Fine, 1987) within the wider institutional context of schooling, as I suggested Dylan did with the banishment of writing. Over time, however, participants negotiated new meanings for focused in-school writing, deadlines, assignments, and criticism that corresponded with their collaborative approach. This transition from preconceptual to conceptual arrangements of service-learning environments that I observed in Dylan's teaching over several years raises questions about the potential for typical features of teacher preparation to be transformed through the application of service-learning pedagogy.

Running against the wind points to the history of sailing and sailing technology: New vision and new tools enabled the transformation of a large portion of impossible sailing situations into routine circumstances, severely limiting the power of oppositional forces to determine where and how (and how efficiently) progress is made. Any effective teaching requires resolving some contradictions—some work with contrary wind—but the challenges to authentic teaching are considerable. Sometimes efforts to work strategically against the wind are left to wither through lack of school support (Smagorinsky, Boggs, Jakubiak, & Wilson, 2010); the notion of a "hidden curriculum" can refer to the ways in which the wind carries us in spite of the direction we've pointed the boat. In teacher education courses, preservice teachers are right to question high-minded pedagogies of teacher educators who appear to have little at stake, their extensive classroom experience and knowledge notwithstanding. Dylan, as many others before him, tried to resolve the contradictions between service-learning and "school as usual" by symbolically excluding the latter, only to find that participants still conceptualized elements of the course, such as an optional reflective journal, as a graded assignment.

SERVICE-LEARNING AND THE AUDACITY OF LISTENING

Service-learning affords the development of epistemological pathways that can position teachers as vital stakeholders in communities and indispensable assets to administrators. What about their subject areas? Doesn't it matter that these people are trained and employed to teach something, not just *experience* the community?

Teacher education and federal teaching policies have long assumed that the production and maintenance of excellent teachers was the responsibility of schools of teacher education and school districts, but new centers of gravity have emerged that intensify the problem of training teachers to listen to students, families, and communities. Entrepreneurs have identified and exploited educational markets for generations, but corporate control of the tools for measuring achievement, in addition to resources that help kids pass the tests, is unparalleled. Similarly, philanthropic interest in education is not new, but contemporary private foundations exert nationwide influence on educational policy, technology, and funding. Again, alternative routes to the classroom have always been around, but newer programs such as Teach for America are raising questions about the role of formal teacher preparation, if not mandate itself. The tragedy of the changing landscape of education in the United States is that corporate control, philanthropic influence, and alternative teacher preparation programs compound fundamental obstacles to effective teaching. Conventional teacher education already suffers from its structural inability to attend and adapt to local concerns. Standardized testing, nationwide philanthropic initiatives, and Teach for America solve imaginary problems and confound the difficult work of reinterpreting schools as mutually beneficial to students and communities.

At least they're doing something though, right? Service-learning straightforwardly recommends listening within a community as a means of learning. The idea is revolutionary in an era in which benevolent despots seem to multiply. I remember asking my father, a farmer and a teacher, what an extension agent was. He said they were people paid by the state and trained in state universities to offer agricultural support to anyone who asked. Evidently, there were good extension agents and bad ones: Some listened carefully to find out what sort of extension services could be of use, others waited for their phone to ring and kept the pamphlets stacked neatly in their displays, their doors open during regular business hours. Daddy gave me no indication of the pressures an extension agent might face, the ways job performance might be measured, whether any peers were adapting instruction to the goals of their communities, but I now see the question of good and bad agricultural support tied up in the priority systems of the wider institutional system. In 2008 news broke of a court case in which a class action suit brought by African American farmers won a huge judgment against the United States Department of Agriculture (USDA) for systematic racism in the provision of agricultural support through local extension offices—belated resolution to years of running against the wind.

The statistic that stood out most to me in the reports of the case was that in the 1910 census there were almost a million black people registered but only around 18,000 90 years later, a drop of more than 98%. The court ruled that the agriculture boards charged with listening to the needs of farmers ignored local concerns intentionally, systematically, and prejudicially by race. The court found that the regional and local agricultural services had organized themselves out of the business of attending to a (consequently) rapidly dwindling population. By analogy, the trial reinvigorates what the student understood of school's relevance: Institutions far larger in terms of budget have been found *legally* liable for not listening to those who they were commissioned to serve. Proliferation of charter schools sends a similar message as the lawsuit against the USDA, yet charter schools are a mixed bag in terms of the organizational affordances and constrains on listening in the communities in which they are located, partly because (for the time being) many of their teachers will be trained in schools of education.

READING THE WIND

Considering the obstacles to learning to teach in the first place—the multiple visions for education, apprenticeships of observation, the mixing of teaching approaches, and the complicated contexts in which people teach—how can someone learn to enact teaching that is epistemologically heterogeneous and effective at sailing against the wind of school as usual? Finding answers will inevitably require critical exploration of the objections to service-learning in general and listening as its distinctive foundation.

TEACHERS AND SCHOOLS AS COMMUNITIES OF PRACTICE

In many teacher education programs, master's comps questions, our standards alignment documents, our teaching evaluations, and our syllabi point ambiguously toward core knowledge and goal-oriented knowledge construction of our student teachers. When I use any of the above tools, I find myself hoping for authenticity above all. At times I am disappointed at the superficial way in which Rosenblatt or Dewey seem "tacked on," but often I am impressed by preservice teachers' ability to tell me what I want to hear in a way that makes them sound like a teacher. One important objection to service-learning and listening is that "fake it till you make it" approach, through which people are socialized as teachers, learn to recognize themselves as teachers, and elicit similar recognition in others. The school and teaching are communities of practice, in other words; teachers should enter communities in the role they will ultimately assume, in order to make best use of limited practice.

Core pedagogical knowledge poses a similar problem to teacher socialization. Teacher knowledge and dispositions have been standardized and codified because of the belief that measuring mastery of teaching knowledge or mastery of performances of teaching are indispensable indexes of future teacher success and the development of respective preparatory programs.

It is beyond the scope of this chapter to challenge all aspects of teacher core knowledge or socialization. The goal here is to recognize structural opposition to the service-learning approach in conventional understandings of teacher preparation. Performance and core knowledge concerns remind me of my mother's main advice for me the summer before my first year teaching seventh-grade language arts: "You gotta start where they are, but really even lower than that!" The potential for service-learning rests in scaffolding preservice teachers' experiences with students "where they are"; it differs from scripted approaches in the way participants are invited to make decisions about students' best interests. Preservice teachers need opportunities to listen carefully to the goals and motivations interwoven in student and community discourse. Otherwise, "where they are" invokes the relationship of the scientist to her data and the doctor to her patient. Likewise, if communities of practice and core knowledge approaches to teacher education do not theoretically and practically integrate attention to students' meaning making, decision making, and relationship making, then "community" and "knowledge" become ethically vulnerable justifications of something other than teaching.

Globalization

The notion of community is not without problems. Because it can suggest homogeneity at the expense of difference, use of the term *community* can be violent. I have argued that the preparation of teachers should include opportunities to listen and learn about the lives, families, and communities in which students live, which must include school, Internet social networks, television, and so on. In arguing for the value of local engagement in service-learning, I invite the criticism that the world is changing too fast to train teachers only to examine, as anthropologists, "what is." Globalization demands global citizens; read the crisis narratives (e.g., Framework for 21st Century Learning, 2011). Teachers should play a role in inviting students into this new world and "play by a set of global rules not of [their] own making" (Burbules & Torres, 2000). Such a view of globalization is problematic because it conceives of globalization as a place rather than a contested set of contemporary economic and cultural processes. Globalization matters because it may be transforming local settings, involving students, teachers, and families. Globalization is not a world "out there" for which students (and their teachers) must be prepared. It is moving factories, changing the environment, and putting global megaphones into the hands of teenagers.

How can we support teachers as they learn how digital, demographic, and economic changes influence the day-to-day lives of their students?

Literacy Education

Closely related to the issue of globalization, the acquisition of primary and secondary literacies is another area of potential conflict in reconsidering the role of experiential education in teacher preparation. Every knowledge domain is becoming simultaneously more multimodal and more print-driven. Perhaps reading is more important today than ever before, but new literacies are now required. If teachers needed training in providing literacy education, the argument goes, they certainly need practice teaching additional literacies. The panic approach to 21st-century literacy instruction is a formidable obstacle to service-learning, yet it can be very difficult for student-teachers, especially, to conceptualize the literacy practices of young people if they view them exclusively from behind a teacher's desk. Paradoxically, the most fertile contexts for learning about 21st-century literacy depend on peer support rather than direct instruction. Considerable philosophical and organizational overlap between service-learning pedagogies and 21st-century literacies has not been explored in the literature, but two gaps in particular appear to limit the responsibility service-learning is permitted to shoulder. First, there is a generational gap in perspectives on literacy that is poorly understood, and they are compounded by teachers' inexperience listening to younger and older members of the communities in which they work. Second, there is an organizational gap in the way technologies are positioned in relation to learning.

Generational gap. In the blog post below, a graphic designer-turned-computer programmer discusses the role of Internet communicative tools.

What's Twitter good for anyway?

Submitted by Hal Misseri on Thu, 02/16/2012–18:16

The other day my mom asked me, "What is Twitter good for? How much can you say in 140 characters?" [I responded,] Sure, you can use Twitter to see what Ashton Kutcher and Kim Kardashian had for lunch. You can also use it to organize an uprising as we saw last summer in the Middle East. I (and I'm not alone in this) use Twitter to learn new things. Like any tool its what you use it for that makes it worthwhile.

When I lost my job a couple of years ago I faced a situation where I was burned out on the sign industry. I wanted to move back into Web development and design but realized quickly that in the past 10 years the world of the Web had moved on and I was in the weeds. With my lack of funds and excess of time I turned to the Internet for help. I quickly realized that every good tutorial I found had that little bird icon at the top. A quick Google search of "top css tweets" led me to a list of industry leaders willing to give away all the knowledge they had on the subject. Ditto for Photoshop, Illustrator, HTML 5, and so on.

Each morning I would make a pot of coffee and start my day by looking through my Twitter feed for links to articles, blogs, and tutorials. Not everything I found was great, but not every teacher I had in school was great either.

Over a couple of months I had weeded out the not so great and was left with a core listing of fantastic resources that posted articles three or four times a week. Within 5 months I was back up to speed on what the latest Web technologies had to offer and was well on my way to mastering the ones that were important to me. I even learned how to rebuild my car's engine but that's another story.

We all know the Internet has more information than you can possibly keep up with. Twitter makes it easy to find and follow the best and brightest of their respective fields.

...I now have a full-time job as a front-end developer with carters.com and make thrice as much as I did in the sign industry. I still don't follow Ashton Kutcher.

Hal's comments on the value of Twitter exemplify the gap in perspectives of literacy instruction between him and his mother and more generally across generations. Literacy instruction has traditionally had the goal of producing analytical thinkers, critical readers, and competent writers. The explosion of available information interweaves literacy with practices far removed from academic learning. The results, as Hal's story suggests, are transforming workforce development by democratizing it. Literacy no longer represents a marker of education or privilege, as it may have in ancient Rome or medieval Britain; now literacy is integral to all kinds of adaptation, from the workplace to the political sphere. Community elders, the group to which teachers and administrators have at times belonged, are likely to conceptualize literate practices in terms of status they may have afforded a generation ago or more.

Service-learning can be a way of preparing teachers to negotiate among these generational literacy goals. Instead of crisis narratives about failure to compete in a global economy, teachers may be trained to broker mutually beneficial agreements about literacy education, help raise awareness about risks associated with globalization, and bridge gaps in what it means to write well.

Technological context gap. Hal's comments draw attention to an organizational gap affecting the way technologies are incorporated. Vygotsky (1978) said teaching should be organized to make necessary the acquisition of desired literacies, and Hal forcefully expresses the importance of systematic, evolving inquiry that makes a technology tool valuable or necessary. He quickly learned to whom to listen as he shifted from one teacher to another while his skills developed. Technology education in schools faces organizational obstacles tied to the assumption that teachers design curricula. Hal's and Vygotsky's positions undermine the notion that teachers can unilaterally make acquisition of a technological literacy necessary.

Service-learning can structure opportunities to attend to and challenge candidates' technology-mediated learning. Experiences with informal education (teachers' and students') can support new paradigms for the integration of technology into the classroom. In comparison to crisis narratives about global competition, listening, careful observation, and problem-posing have much more to recommend them as approaches to creative adaptation of technology in and beyond the classroom.

FURTHER QUESTIONS

Poet Khalil Gibran's (1970) sentiments on teaching echo Hal's and Vygotsky's belief that conceptual understanding proceeds by indirection: "If he [sic] is indeed wise he does not bid you enter the house of his wisdom, but rather leads you to the threshold of your own mind" (p. 56). Dylan offered a related observation about service-learning, and points to ways of moving beyond the threshold through audacious listening:

> I think we can sum up much of this discussion in three words. *With*, not *for*. If we just think about *with, not for*. It gets at the solidarity issues, the dialogic issues that Terri [a course participant] is talking about. It gets at the hierarchies that are problematic. Is [Freire] talking in too binary a language? *With, not for* helps us think about the leveling of that. It reduces the binary in important ways. Any of the bad words he uses, if you use *with, not for*—paternalism, oppression, false charity—*with, not for* takes care of it, and the only way to do *with, not for* is through deep listening, which means asking questions, feeling vulnerable to each other and to groups that we're less comfortable with. It might feel foolish to engage an elderly African American women community. I couldn't be more different and couldn't be more clueless. But after three years, I'm starting to glean community solidarity and interaction. Now it doesn't feel weird, it feels down home.

Vygotsky (1987) used a spiral to show how people can pass the same place at radically different stages of development. The statement could have happened at any point over the years in the study: At the beginning, *with, not for* could have been Dylan's soapbox. In the end it gave words to an ethic that had developed in an emerging community practice. What matters is that his grasp of fundamental service-learning and community engagement concepts spiraled through qualitatively more advanced understandings of schooled literacies, helping him not only run against the wind, but learn to do so.

REFERENCES

Bakhtin, M. M. (1981) *The dialogical imagination: Four essays* (M. Holquist, Ed.; C. Emerson & M. Holquist, Trans.). Austin: University of Texas Press.

Boggs, G. L. (2011). Products and processes of agri-scientific service-learning: Adding harmony to Dopico and Garcia-Vázquez [with Spanish executive summary]. *Cultural Studies in Science Education, 6*(2), 337–346.

Buber, M. (2004). *I and thou.* New York, NY: Continuum. (Original work published 1923)

Bunge, W, (2011). *Fitzgerald: Geography of a revolution.* Cambridge, MA: Schenkman. (Original work published 1973)

Burbules, N. C., & Torres, C. A. (Eds.). (2000). *Globalization and education: Critical perspectives.* New York, NY: Routledge.

Butin, D. W. (2006). Special issue introduction: Future directions for service-learning in higher education. *International Journal of Teaching and Learning in Higher Education, 18*(1). 1–4. Retrieved December 12, 2012, from http://www.isetl .org/ijtlhe/past2.cfm?v=18&i=1

Code, L. (2006). *Ecological thinking: The politics of epistemic location.* Oxford, UK: Oxford University Press.

Dewey, J. (1902). *The child and the curriculum.* Chicago: University of Chicago Press.

Ellsworth, E. (1989). Why doesn't this feel empowering? Working through repressive myths of critical pedagogy. *Harvard Education Review, 59,* 297–324.

Fine, G. A. (1987). *With the boys.* Chicago, IL: University of Chicago Press.

Fleener, M. J., Jewett, L., Smolen, J., & Carson, R. (2011). Creating spaces for service learning research: Implications for emergent action and civic ingenuity. In T. Stewart (Ed.), *Problematizing service-learning: Critical reflections for development and action* (pp. 3–18). Charlotte, NC: Information Age Publishing.

Framework for 21st Century Learning. (2011). Retrieved December 12, 2012, from http://www.p21.org/overview

Franks, B. (2003). Direct action ethic. *Anarchist Studies, 11*(1), 13–41.

Gibran, K. (1970). *The prophet.* New York, NY: Knopf (Original work published 1929

González, N., Moll, L. & Amanti, C. (2005). *Funds of knowledge: Theorizing practices in households, communities, and classrooms.* London: Psychology Press.

Gordon, C., & Debus, R. (2002). Developing deep learning approaches and personal teaching efficacy within a preservice teacher education context. *British Journal of Educational Psychology, 72*(4), 483–511.

Grossman, P., Hammerness, K., & McDonald, M. (2009). Redefining teacher: Reimagining teacher education. *Teachers and Teaching: Theory and Practice, 15*(2), 273–290.

Grossman, P. L., Smagorinsky, P., & Valencia, S. (1999). *Conceptual and pedagogical tools for teaching English: A conceptual framework for studying professional development* (Technical Report No. 12011). Albany: State University of New York, University of Albany, National Research Center on English Learning and Achievement.

Lather, P. A. (2007). *Getting lost.* Albany: State University of New York Press.

Lave, J. (1988). *Cognition in practice.* New York, NY: Cambridge University Press.

Lortie, D. (1975). *Schoolteacher: A sociological study.* Chicago: University of Chicago Press.

Mewborn, D. S., & Tyminski, A. M. (2006). Lortie's apprenticeship of observation revisited. *For the Learning of Mathematics, 26*(3), 39–42.

Miller, V. (2012). The broad challenge to democratic leadership: The other crisis in education. *Democracy and Education, 20*(2), 1–11.

Mission Statement, Mary Lou Fulton College of Education, Arizona State University. Retrieved December 9, 2012, from http://education.asu.edu/about/mary-lou-fulton-teachers-college-mission

Nicolaides, A. & Yorks, L. (2008). An epistemology of learning through. *Emergence: Complexity and Organization 10*(1), 50–61.

Packard, J. S. (1988). The pupil control studies. In N. J. Boyan (Ed.), *Handbook of research on educational administration* (pp. 185–207). New York, NY: Longman.

Parker, W. (2010). Listening to strangers: Classroom discussion in democratic education. *Teachers College Record, 112*(11), 2815–2832.

Richman, K. A. (1996). Epistemology, communities and experts: A response to Goodwin Liu. *Michigan Journal of Community Service Learning, 3*(1), 5–12.

Smagorinsky, P. (2011). *Vygotsky and literacy research: A methodological framework.* Boston, MA: Sense.

Smagorinsky, P., Boggs, G. L., Jakubiak, C., & Wilson, A. A. (2010). The implied character curriculum in vocational and nonvocational English classes: Designing social futures for working class students and their teachers. *Journal of Research in Character Education, 8*(2), 1–24.

Smagorinsky, P., & O'Donnell-Allen, C. (2000). Idiocultural diversity in small groups: The role of the relational framework in collaborative learning. In C. D. Lee & P. Smagorinsky (Eds.), *Vygotskian perspectives on literacy research: Constructing meaning through collaborative inquiry* (pp. 165–190). New York, NY: Cambridge University Press.

Vygotsky, L. S. (1978). *Mind in society: The development of higher psychological processes* (M. Cole, Ed.). Cambridge, MA: Harvard University Press.

Vygotsky, L. S. (1987). *Thinking and speech.* In R.W. Rieber & A.S. Carton (Eds.); N. Minick (Trans.), *The collected works of L.S. Vygotsky, Volume 1: Problems of general psychology.* New York, NY: Plenum Press.

Wertsch, J. V. (1991). *Voices of the mind: A sociocultural approach to mediated action.* Cambridge, MA: Harvard University Press.

Willower, D. J., Eidell, T. L., & Hoy, W. K. (1967). *The school and pupil control ideology* (Penn State Studies Monograph No. 24). University Park: Pennsylvania State University.

George L. Boggs is an Assistant Professor in the School of Teacher Education at Florida State University. He conducts research on disciplinary literacies and how they shape education within and beyond the school. Changing ways of sharing ideas within and beyond academic disciplines are of particular interest, as are efforts to serve the common good through discipline-specific, interdisciplinary, and other ways of knowing involving hybridization of disciplinary and nondisciplinary knowledge. Recent research projects have focused on how disciplinary language, knowledge, and identity shape university students' community engagement.

Epistemological diversity emphasized traditionally by service-learning and popular education open pathways for nurturing teacher development and community sovereignty. As a current teacher educator in northwest Florida, he is eager to work with teachers and community partners to balance the national, state, and university-level demands that have long shaped formal teacher education.

CHAPTER 3

CRITICAL DISCOURSE ANALYSIS OF SERVICE-LEARNING PERSPECTIVES AND MODELS

Transforming Teacher Education

Antonia Lukenchuk
Virginia M. Jagla
Todd A. Price

ABSTRACT

This chapter presents critical discourse analysis (CDA) of service-learning perspectives and models building on the theoretical dispositions and practices of teacher education faculty at National Louis University. Grounded in Bourdieu's social theory, the *Service-Learning Habitus* (*SLH*) model previously considered for conceptualizing our teacher education practice finds its new expression in *SLH²* in which Foucault's discourse of *heterotopia* becomes instrumental in positioning service-learning as a *real* transformative pedagogy. Selected testimonials of our teacher candidates illuminate the generative potential of *SLH²*.

Transforming Teacher Education Through Service-Learning, pages 51–69
Copyright © 2013 by Information Age Publishing
51

As we ponder the remarkable history of service-learning in the United States, we realize how strong the linkages between our university's traditions are with this powerful pedagogy and its origins. The National College of Education of National Louis University was founded on progressive pedagogical traditions. We embrace and continue the work of our predecessors. We advocate for service-learning pedagogy, which appears to be a natural outgrowth of our historical roots. Over the past several years, we have been integrating service-learning in coursework. Our recurring engagement in service-learning endeavors with students and colleagues led us to broaden paradigmatic horizons regarding this pedagogy. This chapter is a result of our sustained effort to conceptualize service-learning in ways that benefit our teacher education programs the most. We find it especially advantageous to advance scholarly discussions on service-learning to the level that illuminates the paradigmatic complexity and diversity of this pedagogy.

The model that we propose in this chapter (SLH^2) is an extension of our previously developed SLH model, which signifies *Service-Learning Habitus* grounded in social theory (Bourdieu, 1990, 1999) and relational ethics (Levinas, 1998, 2006; Noddings, 2003, 2005a, 2005b). SLH^2 underscores the language of postmodern critique of social practices in teacher education and reflects an evolving nature of service-learning and our own conception of this pedagogy. We rely primarily on the methodology of critical discourse analysis (CDA) to unfold the discussion of service-learning with regard to the language of critique of its main dispositions and practices and their relevance to the field of teacher education.

We conceive of service-learning as essentially human practice inseparable from its deliberative, or "theoretical" aspect, for practices are "grounded in understandings that people have about the world, and these understandings are, in turn, influenced by the effect of their practices in the world" (Polkinghorne, 2004, p. 5). Service-learning thus represents a synergy of *praxis* ("action") and *phronesis* (practical reasoning required for *praxis*) (Arendt, 1998, 2005). Such understanding of service-learning challenges the false dichotomy of theory and practice, the dichotomy that still prevails in teacher education, much to the detriment of a greater understanding, generated from diverse contexts regarding the complexity of the knowledge of practice (Cochran-Smith & Lytle, 1999).

We are guided by the assumption that critical analysis of service-learning should include "deeper understanding of the historical, sociological, cultural, economic, and political contexts of the needs or issues being addressed" (Jacoby et al, 1996, p. 7). Finally, we have come to believe that Foucault's metaphor of *heterotopia* captures our social imagination of service-learning as a space of *otherness*, in which empowerment and transformation are *really* possible. In what follows, we consider the discourses of the theory-and-practice of service-learning and its relevance to teacher education drawing from selected academic sources and lived experiences of faculty and students at our university.

FRAMING METHODOLOGICAL DISCOURSE

Methodologically, this study is conceived as critical discourse analysis (CDA), a research paradigm that can be regarded as both the theory and method—or rather, a "theoretical perspective on language and more generally semiosis as one element or 'moment' of the material social process" (Fairclough, 2003, p. 121). Semiosis includes "all forms of meaning making—visual images, body language, as well as language" (p. 122), and these elements are dialectically related. Our focus in this chapter is on the analysis of language/text pertaining to service-learning as social practice in the multiplicity of its meanings.

CDA is derived from discourse analysis that is commonly understood as "language-in-use" (Gee, 2005, p. 1), "language as social practice" (Wodak & Meyer, 2002, p. 4), "situated speech," or the use of "models developed in the analysis of clauses and sentences, in the analysis of connected speech or writing, and in the analysis of units larger than the sentence" (Johnstone, 1996, p. 22). Discourse analysis uses "human language as its data base" (Merriam & Simpson, 1995, p. 88).

Historical and ideological roots of CDA can be found in the critical theory tradition (Frankfurt School) and the works of Jürgen Habermas (b. 1929). CDA is a "network of scholars emerged in the early 1990s, following a small symposium in Amsterdam, in January 1991. Teun vad Dijk, Norman Fairclough, Gunther Kress, Theo van Leeuwen and Ruth Wodak spent two days discussing theories and methods of discourse analysis and specifically CDA" (Wodak & Meyer, 2002, p. 4).

Basic assumptions of CDA include the notion of language as a social phenomenon, the idea that not only individuals, but also institutions and social groupings have specific meanings and values that are expressed in language in systematic ways (Fairclough, 2003). CDA explores the relation between language and power. CDA is "everywhere and always 'political' " (Gee, 2005, p. 1), since we take a particular perspective on the world when we speak or write. The analysis of particular perspectives on service-learning expressed through the texts of selected academic sources and the language of individuals engaged in service-learning are central to this inquiry.

Most contemporary approaches of discourse analysis assume a "*reflexive*" view of the relationship between language and context. 'Reflexive' here means that, at one and the same time, an utterance influences what we take the context to be and context influences what we take the utterance to mean" (Gee, 2005, p. 57). Accordingly, we approach the analysis of service-learning as social practice embedded in different ideological and sociocultural contexts while reflecting on the influences of the contexts in which our own assumptions of this pedagogy have been rooted.

It is significant for the purposes of this study to distinguish between what Gee (2005) calls Discourse (big *D*) and discourse (little *d*). A lowercase *d* designates discourse as language-in-use. Hence, discourse is a preoccupation of linguists who are interested in how language is used "on site" to enact activities and identities. When a lowercase *d* is "melded with non-language 'stuff' to enact specific identities and activities..., Discourse comes into play when [we] "produce, reproduce, sustain, and transform a given form of life or Discourse" (Gee, 2005, p. 7). We are interested in uncovering the meanings of service-learning as a form of life capable of generating transformative experiences, and we seek to contribute to important issues and problems in "applied area[s] that interest and motivate [us]" (Gee, 2005, p. 8).

Building on Wittgenstein (1998–1951) and Habermas, Foucualt (1926–1984) conceives of discourse as a way of representing social practice as a form of knowledge and as the things people say about social practice (cited in Wodak & Meyer, 2002). Wodak and Meyer (2002) emphasize that:

> A defining feature of CDA is its concern with power as a central condition in social life, and its efforts to develop a theory of language which incorporates this as a major premise.... Power is signaled not only by grammatical forms within a text, but also by a person's control of a social occasion by means of the genre of a text. It is often exactly within the genres associated with given social occasions that power is exercised or challenged. (p. 11)

Our intention in this chapter is to analyze the existing paradigmatic conceptions of service-learning pedagogy in teacher education as the discourses of meaning and power, to examine local meanings of service-learning models created within our institution, and to reflect on subtle structures of power that underpin service-learning within teacher education. By critically analyzing our own experiences with service-learning pedagogy, we expect to deepen understanding of the transformational aspects of service-learning in teacher education.

Our turn to the critique of language of the dominant discourse of teacher education (and service-learning within it) signals the form of resistance to "the politics of the new global order" (Fairclough, 2001). By "dominant discourse," we assume "North Atlantic" political discourse of globalization (Fairclough, 2001). The discourse of globalization is a "discourse of power—a discourse which is used in conjunction with other potent resources by those in power to enhance their power" (Fairclough, 2001, p. 207). This study largely represents critical social research, which is "oriented to human emancipation" (Fairclough, 2001, p. 215).

SERVICE-LEARNING: LOCAL DISCOURSES AND MEANINGS

The roots of our university are embedded in service. Elizabeth Harrison, who, in 1886, founded the college that later became National Louis University, dedicated her life to service and encouraged her students to do the same. She founded the National College of Education as a progressive institution, and we are certain she would be proud of our efforts to promote service-learning throughout the university. We embrace and promote service-learning as an activist, progressive pedagogy and philosophy (Jagla & Lukenchuk, 2009; Lukenchuk, 2009).

Service-learning began at National Louis as a single-faculty initiative that has inspired and led many others into a memorable and empowering journey. Comprised of about a dozen faculty members, our Civic Engagement Team has had a number of significant accomplishments since its inception in 2004. We implement annual university-wide service-learning symposia and model service-learning to our faculty and students through conference participation at local, national, and international levels, as well as through our own social activism. Our service-learning activities and events are documented on our Civic Engagement Center (CEC) website. The website reflects the CEC's lively and empowering undertakings such as collaborative-action research projects, links among the university and local partners, professional-development sessions with pre- and inservice teachers, and urban school initiatives. Uniquely to the context of our institutional practices, service-learning has received its widest implementation in the National College of Education.

Over the years of our personal engagement in service-learning, we have internalized many of its existing definitions and extended their boundaries. Service-learning resembles what Arendt (1998, 2005) calls *praxis*—the highest form of human activity; an expression of the condition of plurality, our collective social and political engagement; and an embodiment of critical democratic practices. Stemming from our ethical beliefs is an understanding of service-learning as an infinite responsibility to others, before us (Levinas, 1998, 2006), expressed through the ethics of care in education (Noddings, 2003, 2005a, 2005b, 2007). We think of service-learning as "living pedagogy" (Whitehead & McNiff, 2006) and as a philosophy of "human growth and purpose, a social vision, an approach to community, and a way of knowing" (Anderson, Swick, & Yff, 2001, p. 23). The above conceptions correspond to Billig and Furco's (2002) notion of service-learning as grounded in interdisciplinary constructs and theories and as a "boundary-spanning activity" having multidimensional capabilities.

Service-learning has been inspirational within the stepping-stones of our careers as we teach, research, and perform university service. We strongly believe that for our service-learning initiatives to be successful, there "must be a shared understanding of what service-learning is and a commitment by at least some faculty to use it as a teaching methodology" (Stacey & Foreman, 2006, p. 47). As faculty we are "ultimately responsible for providing service-learning experiences for students" (Stacey & Foreman, 2006, p. 47). The pedagogy of service-learning empowers those who participate. In a college of education, we are responsible for demonstrating this pedagogy to our teacher candidates for use in the P–12 schools in which they will teach.

Our ongoing engagement in service-learning has been informed by multiple and often contending theoretical perspectives on this pedagogy, which, in turn, prompted us to consider the language of critique, within the critical discourse analysis, of the theory and practice of service-learning.

SERVICE-LEARNING: THE DISCOURSE OF POWER, EMPOWERMENT, AND TRANSFORMATION

Debates on Service-Learning in Higher Education

The debates on service-learning in higher-education have been revolving around justification claims as to what constitutes proper practice of this pedagogy. For some, the focus of service-learning is external and interpersonal; it "enhances a student's educational experience, sustains democratic culture, strengthens democratic institutions, and advances social justice" (Abel, 2004, p. 46). Yet for others, service-learning is limited to internal, philanthropic justifications that do not seek to transform societal or educational institutions.

The civil rights movement of the 1960s challenged the institutions of higher education and students to participate in the demands for social justice. As various other forms of experiential education, service-learning established itself on many college campuses in the late 1960s. The movement continued with different levels of success through the 1970s and 1980s. The federal government's interest and support of service-learning increased in the 1990s with the passage of the *National and Community Service Trust Act of 1990*. The expansion of service-learning programs in higher education has led to the development of multiple models of service-learning pedagogy.

The emergence of the civic engagement model broadly addresses the paradoxical role of higher education in the larger society—higher education is influenced by the larger society, but it is also a part of the dominant culture. The civic engagement model is based on the premise that "democracy demands equal participation and voice by all citizens" (Watson, 2004, p. 75). The strength of this model is in its "utility in leveraging the resources of higher educational institutions to address pressing social problems" (Watson, 2004, p. 77). Civic engagement encourages a truly collaborative relationship among community and university partners. Civic engagement "renews and alters the focus of higher education institutions on service as the focal point of their mission of teaching, research, and professional service" and represents a "new voice at the table in discussions of reform within higher education" (Watson, 2004, p. 77).

Jacoby et al. (1996, 2003, 2009) echo the above assumptions and claim that colleges and universities can reinforce their public service mission through service-learning and that university faculty ought to invite communities into the academy, build successful partnership relationships, and develop high-quality civic engagement experiences for students.

More importantly, service-learning in higher education can be a "potentially transformative pedagogical practice and theoretical orientation" (Butin, 2005, p. vii). Accordingly, Zlotkowski (1998) asserts that service-learning "transforms and renews the educational enterprise as a whole" (p. 3). Service-learning activities thus "foster a sense of community not just with off-campus groups but also among on-campus units—faculty and student affairs staff, faculty and students, and faculty across department lines" (Zlotkowski, 1998, p. 6).

Central to the language of critique of the higher education discourse is its static notions of teaching and learning, which can be challenged by service-learning that exposes links between power, knowledge, and identity. As such, service-learning carries the promise for higher education programs geared toward teaching for social justice (Butin, 2005).

The idealism of our aspirations to enact service-learning as transformative praxis is tempered by the realities in which higher education often finds itself concerning changing historical and socioeconomic conditions. In this regard, we share Butin's (2005) concerns:

> Tight budgets, federal mandates, limited free time, and the incessant drive to quantify impacts of service-learning...challenge the ideal of providing the length of time, space, and dialogue that compels a free-flowing exchange of ideas and thoughts on our self-understanding and identity with professional practice. (p. 201)

Those of us who advocate for service-learning and promote this pedagogy among both students and faculty are acutely aware of the trappings of formal institutional structures that can hinder such efforts and prevent us from integrating progressive practices such as service-learning into larger units of curricula than particular courses. Clearly, "without [the] deeply seated concept of why it is that we integrate academic and experiential learning, we risk making experience tangential to the academic objectives of the course and, therefore, disconnecting knowledge and experience" (Butin, 2005, p. 202).

Service-Learning as Discourse of Power

Service-learning is certainly a "complex concept: social capital, citizenship, democratic participation/practice, public work, [and] political engagement" (Jacoby et al., 2009, p. 6). The complexity and paradigmatic diversity of service-learning become evident as we consider an expanded *SLH*² model that integrates the elements of technical-rational, sociocultural, political, ethical, and postmodern dimensions.

Contemporary practice theorists regard cultures not as unified or universal constructs but rather as composites of various groups with conflicting interests (Polkinghorne, 2004). They focus on the study of individuals who engage in a variety of everyday activities (or practices) and they seek best ways for individuals to express their subjectivities and freedom within the constraints of given societies or cultures (Polkinghorne, 2004). French sociologist Pierre Bourdieu (1930–2002) is one of the foremost investigators of the social theory of practice.

Bourdieu conceives of practice as an everyday activity of people and institutions, and the approach to practice as a mode of relational thinking. Relational thinking "focuses on networks or bundles of relationships, such as a field or *habitus*" (Polkinghorne, 2004, p. 58). Practices therefore are consequences of interactions between an individual's historically developed dispositions (*habitus*) and a specific field of contention (institutional dispositions, or external structures). *Habitus* is a "product of history" and a "system of durable, transposable dispositions, structured structures predisposed to function as principles which generate and organize practices" (Bourdieu, 1999, p. 442).

Bourdieu (1999) underscores the importance of moving beyond the habitual antinomies in order to properly understand *habitus* as "infinite yet strictly limited generative capacity" (p. 444), that is, transcending the dichotomies of determinism and freedom, conditioning and creativity, or the individual and society. This point is especially commendable for a consideration of service-learning habitus as generative practice that "makes possible the free production of thoughts, perceptions and actions inherent in the particular condition" (p. 444).

Much like Bourdieu's habitus, service-learning appears to be an "embodied history" and an "active presence of the whole past of which it is the product" (Bourdieu, 1999, p. 444). Bourdieu's (1999) anti-dualistic social conception of habitus enables individuals to exercise their freedom of thought production, but also institutions to attain their realization: an institution "is complete and fully viable only if it is durably objectified not only in things . . . , but also in bodies, in durable dispositions to recognize and comply with the demands immanent in the field" (p. 446). Accordingly, educational institutions can be viewed as such viable places ("fields") within which service-learning habitus works as a micro-level generative structure thereby connecting individuals and the institution (macro structure) through the bundles of relationships engaged in practice.

Bourdieu's social theory inspired our conception of service-learning as *Service-Learning Habitus* (*SLH*). The generative capacity of relational thinking as espoused in Bourdieu's philosophy seems to have a special merit for the practice of service-learning geared toward progressive education. This generative capacity, in our view, finds even stronger expression in Foucault's (1967) discourse of *heterotopia.*

Heterotopia (*heterotopion* in singular) is a medical term signifying a neurological disorder caused by clumps of gray matter supposedly located in the wrong part of the brain. Foucault appropriates the term to provide a sharp criticism of advanced modern societies with rigid and punitive regimes of power. Unlike utopias, *heterotopia* are real places, human geographies, spaces of potential nonhegemonic conditions. Foucault reminds us that we do not live in a void. We occupy spaces that reflect our cultural, social, and political realities. We live in the "epoch of juxtaposition," the epoch of "near and far," sameness and otherness (Foucault, 1967, p. 1). Not only are *heterotopia* the spaces of affirmation of difference, but they are also a means of escape from oppression.

Heterotopia evoke institutional exclusionary and oppressive politics presented in Foucault's earlier works (e.g., *Madness and Civilization,* 1961; *Birth of the Clinic,* 1963). In the West, as Foucault claims, leprosy and madness have been treated as *dis-eases* and the people who had them needed to be isolated completely from the rest of the so-called "civilized" society. *Heterotopia* are the haven-bearing spaces for all *others* "shipped" away; they are the places of inclusion and acceptance.

Translated into the language of progressive education, service-learning can be thought of as the discourse of *heterotopia,* namely, the conditions that create, sustain, and/or disrupt the boundaries and norms by which we make sense of ourselves and the world, to reiterate Butin's (2005) previous arguments. It appears that *heterotopia* provide individuals with much more powerful generative discourses than habitus in terms of their capacity to disrupt the limited and potentially oppressive institutional dispositions and practices ("the field") and therefore not simply to freely produce thoughts, but more importantly, to transform the very practice of education in general and teacher education specifically.

Service-Learning as Discourse of Ethics and Caring

Transformative and generative practices of service-learning in teacher education entail a serious consideration of the ethics as the "first philosophy" (Levinas, 1998, 2006). Ethical questioning is about what ought to be (and not what is—ontological question). To Levinas, ethics occurs prior to essence of being in that we do not exist as absolutely autonomous beings. We are inevitably involved with one another and therefore should feel responsible for each other. Each of us ought to feel moral responsibility to and for the other person, which, as Levinas argues, should lead to the demand for justice for all others and for all humanity. The ethical question posits our infinite responsibility for other human beings: "I speak of responsibility as the essential, primary and fundamental structure of subjectivity. I understand responsibility as responsibility for the Other" (Levinas, 2006, p. 95).

Pertinent to Levinas's "first philosophy" is our more than a decade-long practice of engagement in service-learning pedagogy that brings forth the argument of unconditional service enacted and embodied within the teacher education curriculum (see examples in the following sections). Levinas (1998) describes the evolving sense of our true humanity as the process of "awakening of our moral obligation" (p. 114). True selfhood therefore occurs precisely *in and as service*. Stemming from Levinas's ethics are the very precepts of service-learning as we conceptualize and internalize this pedagogy in our scholarship and teaching.

Nel Noddings (2003, 2005a, 2005b) advocates the ethics of care, which, to an extent, echoes Levinas's philosophy. Noddings's (2003) philosophy of care is rooted in caring relations and happiness: "People want to be happy, and since this desire is well-nigh universal, we would expect to find happiness as an aim of education" (p. 74). Noddings (2003) links happiness to the life of community, democracy, and service: "Community life and a democratic mode of living provide a foundation upon which [the] primary goods are built and thus make a substantial, if indirect, contribution to happiness" (p. 236). Accordingly and as our preservice teacher candidates testify (see further sections), service-learning is precisely such a mode of living that fulfills us as moral and social human beings, as well as professionals.

Noddings alerts us of the responsibility and a "demand of *caring for*" (2005a, p. 7); and caring is a "way of being in relation" (2005b, p. 17). She further deliberates extensively on the conception of caring relations that extend from people to animals, plants, and the earth by presenting an argument that "our lives are interdependent with those of nonhuman animals and plants" (2005b, p. 126). Caring relationship thus, in its most basic form, constitutes a "connection or encounter between two human beings—a carer and a recipient of care, of cared-for" (Noddings, 2005b,

p. 15). These relationships infiltrate all of our service-learning endeavors as teachers and students care for the elderly and the young, work with community members to better neighborhoods, address issues such as the environment, animals in danger, hunger and homelessness, immigrants, literacy, social change, and special needs and disabilities. After all, the essence of teaching is relationships. Teachers and students relate to each other, the curriculum, the environment, the community, and so on. Service-learning pedagogy amplifies and elucidates these relationships in worthwhile and meaningful ways.

Teacher Education Habitus: The Discourse of Education Reform

Teacher education does not exist in a vacuum. From *No Child Left Behind* to *Race to the Top*, teacher education is increasingly subject to political forces that in turn seem to call for an increased monitoring and accountability surveillance. These measures, in our view, reflect a "new" sociopolitical framework, the neoliberal condition, wherein decentralization of centralized bureaucratic administration forms corresponds with the development *in their place* of semi-autonomous privatized bodies that exercise regulatory control. In essence we as teacher educators are witness to a paradigm shift where the aims and means of the public good as producing highly qualified and effective teachers is increasingly aligned with the ends of "the market." Bourdieu's theory of practice can be helpful for understanding the field of teacher education in this new period, this radical shift, in several ways. For instance, his notion of habitus can be looked at as a "third way" to teacher candidate development. We have seen and continue to believe that teaching and learning in the field of the "community" give our teacher candidates the opportunity to encounter, experience, and overcome challenges that are posed, becoming authentic, reflective practitioners in the process. It is, in fact, our sense that done well, service-learning is a habitus unto itself, creating the means by which aims and ends of progressive education are enabled, beyond that which could take place in the classroom, during clinical hours, or even through traditional student teaching periods.

While, as we mentioned previously, we are continually guided by the assumption that service-learning should include a "deeper understanding" of the issues that teacher candidates and faculty face, we are aware of the challenges to implementing service-learning itself, given that the field of teacher education is increasingly buffeted by forces outside of the profession. In other words, we are concerned with these outside forces and strive to develop SLH^2 that moves the field of teacher education forward, beyond a fairly narrow framing.

Teacher education has become victim to a narrowly defined and large-ly ideological struggle that has little to do with improving the lives of stu-dents (Cochran-Smith & Fries, 2001). To be specific, contestation over who manages and controls the teacher education field has fallen down on two lines: one line being those who would advocate significant *deregulation,* so that other alternative certification entities may compete in "teacher train-ing," and the second line being those who would sustain the traditional teacher education institutions while augmenting the *professionalization* as-pects (Cochran-Smith & Fries, 2001) such as intensifying the standards for teacher candidate admission and increasing the number of clinical hours spent by those teacher candidates admitted to the teacher education pro-grams. That demarcation of broad lines of contestation, deregulation, and further professionalization are lines that nonetheless share the implicit and explicit aim of wresting control of teacher education from educators. This neoliberal *teacher education habitus* has only grown in the post–No Child Left Behind era, where the current federal administration seems intent to draw even further on the criticism of teacher education institutions while at the same time calling for increasingly more "rigorous" standards and data systems for measuring progress, not only of the teachers in the field but of the teacher education institutions who credential them.

At the heart of our argument is the idea that while there are insights to be gained by the ideologies of deregulation and professionalization, both ideologies fall short. The process of preparing a teacher who is fully quali-fied and effective is not sufficient; service-learning suggests that empathy and reflection are developed through carefully directed service-learning experiences, and these qualities only enhance the qualified and effective attributes given such close attention by the federal government and teacher education institutions.

Service-learning is a means of developing the teacher candidate who is empathic and engaged in the ethics of learning. The model of SLH^2 that we propose can foster relationships that sustain learning not only for increas-ing student achievement, but also to augment love of knowledge and an appreciation of social justice means, aims, and ends.

The challenge, however, for service-learning is to live up to this promise, to develop the mindful, empathic, and engaged teacher candidate in spite of what many are claiming to be an attack on institutions of the public good and higher learning (Ravitch, 2010; Lipman, 2011; Watkins, 2012). Teacher education seems to be at a crossroads. During the turn of the 21st century, teacher education institutions came under increased scrutiny. In effect, as teacher researcher Peter Taubman (2009) was apt to put, teach-ing and learning in the nation's public schools was placed under an "audit culture." Without much let-up under the current Obama administration, a "Race to the Top" was launched where states and their school districts were placed in competition for coveted federal dollars. Many teachers are now as a result evaluated using pay-for-performance measures, which effectively ties their compensation to merit pay schemes and other performance assessment systems. They pit teachers against each other, rather than encourage cooperation, which our SLH^2 model fosters.

Yet it is the complexity of the idea of "service" and service-learning, in particular, which captures our attention and may refocus teacher education on a more collaborative and less competitive approach. Indeed, service-learning has grown in interest on the national front, once again under *Race to the Top*. To the point, the *Edward M. Kennedy Serve America Act*, signed by President Barack Obama in 2009, is really just a revision of the *National Service Act*, signed in 1990 by then President William Clinton. At the heart of this "new" revised call for national service is the idea of increasing the number of paid volunteers from 75,000 to 250,000 by 2017. The mission is to provide volunteers in order to help with mentoring students, provide relief from natural disasters, sustain service learning projects deemed to be in the community/public interest, and research, review, and recommend service projects for general dissemination. With respect to teacher education institutions, the revised *Serve America Act* aims at improving the "curricula" of the institution to strengthen the instructional capacity of teachers to provide service-learning at the elementary and secondary levels.

What is of note to the changing nature of the *habitus* of teacher education is that in the revised act, the practice of teacher education is expanded, and the curricula of service-learning are understood to be developed in realms outside of the traditional teacher education institution. The education of the teacher, in other words, is lifted outside of the boundaries of the university itself, located within a government or private agency that may or may not partner with the college of education. This is a critical point, an interesting departure from the manner in which teacher education has emerged in the past. Service-learning may play a part in effectively shifting the teacher education *habitus* to a level in which the federal government is increasingly using alternative organizations to produce "curricula."

Teacher Candidate Discourse for Transformation

We are continually guided by the assumption that service-learning should include a deeper understanding of the issues teacher candidates and faculty face. Service-learning is an excellent means of developing teacher candidates who are empathetic and engaged in the ethics of learning. SLH^2 fosters relationships that sustain learning not only for increasing candidates' future P–12 students' academic achievement, but to augment those students' love of knowledge and commitment to social justice means and aims. As our teacher candidates find themselves in alternate spaces, *heterotopia* of place, and circumstances, we witness transformation as they reflect on the *habitus* of self and others.

We have been embedding service-learning in foundational and research courses for our teacher candidates for years in our many teacher education programs. Our students perform direct service within schools and other community agencies. Our assumptions about service-learning as relational and transformative practice prove themselves true as we read through the pages of our candidates' reflections. Their stories reveal important and precious moments of "truth"—our conviction that the rational is intertwined with the emotional as we build our relationships with others through engaging in dialogue and reciprocal service *and* learning. When working with children as their mentors and tutors, our candidates experience firsthand the hidden treasures of the teaching profession—the value of building relations beyond the mastery of subjects. Within a reflection of a service-learning project in a school, a candidate tells us, "I think the most important thing that I have learned from my service learning project is that I still really want to be a teacher.... I feel that I can truly make a difference in someone's life."

Through engagement in service-learning, our teacher candidates' selves become naturally connected to their students and thus the relation of care is being formed. Simultaneously, as our candidates testify, their sense of self is being transformed and elevated to a higher ethical plane: "Service-learning provides the reward of teaching you more about yourself while you are helping others. It may change some of your perceptions and beliefs, and confirm others in the process. In any case, a true service-learning experience will make you a better person."

The critical lessons in professionalism and citizenship that we teach our candidates become their living and lived reality once they experience the plurality of the world through engagement in service-learning. One of our teacher candidates reflects on learning in an alternate space. "My primary realization as I have volunteered with refugees is that I have so much to learn from them. Their life experiences are full of much trauma and pain, yet they have weathered and survived these things. As a result, they have life stories that have the power to affect others. I hope that I can continue to volunteer for World Relief and continue to deepen my friendships with the refugees I know. I hope that I can encourage others to welcome refugees into their lives."

By actively involving candidates in the process of constructing their own knowledge, they more readily see how it relates to the real world as opposed to just learning the theoretical concepts in isolation. These natural connections enhance understanding and retention. Many are transformed through the heterotopian view of alternate spaces. As one of our undergraduate students put it: "This service learning project has really impacted me in a positive way. Being able to work with students one-on-one in a classroom setting really opened my eyes to how differently every student learns. During my schooling I have learned that every student learns differently, but seeing this information firsthand really showed me how in depth you must go when teaching a lesson." Allowing her time in this alternate space provided the needed insight to what a teacher must understand to be effective.

Besides experiencing service-learning as direct service endeavors, our teacher candidates are taught to use the pedagogy with their P–12 students. We feel this is a major aspect of transforming the *habitus* of teacher education. Service-learning offers a unique opportunity for students to get involved with their communities in a tangible way by integrating service projects with classroom learning. Service-learning engages students in the educational process, using what they learn in the classroom to solve real-life problems. Students not only learn about democracy and citizenship, they become actively contributing citizens and community members through the service they perform.

TRANSFORMING TEACHER EDUCATION THROUGH SERVICE-LEARNING: FINAL REFLECTIONS

Through service-learning pedagogy we believe teacher education becomes more dynamic. Service-learning, once integrated in the programs that prepare teachers for their service in increasingly diverse classrooms, is an effective pedagogical strategy. Our teacher candidates testify that service-learning experiences "take social justice out of the realm of academic, theoretical discussions and into the realities of the lives of people" (Lucas, 2005, p. 172). Service-learning supports the acquisition of effective multicultural education by "allowing preservice teachers to become familiarized with diverse communities, families and children in contexts outside of school and thereby providing them with the skills needed for effective community collaboration" (Anderson et al., 2001, p. 93).

Service-learning in teacher education represents a *semiosis* of social practices carried out within specific and multiple institutional and historical discourses and thereby acquiring multiple meanings for all those engaged in this pedagogy. The discourses and meanings of service-learning establish, in turn, the context of shaping our professional expectations and purposes. To paraphrase Gee (2005), service-learning discourse is always political in that it signifies our capacity to produce, reproduce, sustain, or transform existing power structures. It is political because within itself it carries generative forces to transform the very practice and experience of teacher education.

Service-learning conceived as an alternative pedagogy based on caring relations and an acute sense of ethical responsibility has the potential to transform teacher education curricula and pedagogical practices from the traditional to more progressive, collaborative, and creative, as well as to elevate the status of the teaching profession to a more authentic and honorable public service. Service-learning is the scholarship of engagement. Once embedded in the core of the mission of higher educational institutions, it has "potential for addressing a crisis of community, the crisis that signifies social, political, intellectual, and moral fragmentation" (Hoppe, 2004, p. 147).

Proposed in this chapter, SLH^2 demonstrates the dynamics and complexity of service-learning discourses as social practices—deliberative, relational, reflexive, activist, and ethical. With a critical eye on each of the elements that constitute SLH^2, we acknowledge the necessity to draw from educational scholars, philosophers, and social theorists what we deem as most valuable for service-learning pedagogy as a vehicle for preparing effective and empathic teacher candidates. The service-learning discourse of *habitus* represents a model of shared dispositions than enable teacher educators to practice their art as a free-thinking and generative activity within the institutional boundaries. The service-learning discourses of *heterotopia* generate the power that can break the boundaries of potentially oppressive external structures and to transform the practice of education.

The power to produce, to sustain, and to transform arises from our innermost ethical core. Serving others brings forth our humanity, which is defined by our responsibility to and care for other human beings. Those who choose service-learning over other socially engaged activities share the understanding of service as a moral obligation that supersedes prescribed professional duties and expectations. As a counterpoint of social escapism and nihilism, service-learning pedagogy has the potential to transform the *habitus* of teacher education.

REFERENCES

Abel, C. F. (2004). A justification of the philanthropic model. In B. W. Speck & S. L. Hoppe (Eds.), *Service-learning: History, theory, and issues* (pp. 45–57). Westport, CT: Praeger.

Anderson, J. B., Swick, K. J., & Yff, J. (Eds.). (2001). *Service-learning in teacher education: Enhancing the growth of new teachers, their students, and communities.* Washington, DC: AACTE.

Arendt, H. (1998). *The human condition.* Chicago: University of Chicago Press.

Arendt, H. (2005). *The promise of politics.* New York, NY: Schoken Books.

Billig, S. H., & Furco, A. (Eds.). (2002). *Service-learning through a multidisciplinary lens.* Greenwich, CT: Information Age Publishing.

Bourdieu, P. (1990). *The logic of practice* (R. Nice, Trans.). Palo Alto, CA: Stanford University Press.

Bourdieu, P. (1999). *Structures, habitus, practices.* In C. Lemert (Ed.), *Social theory: The multicultural and classical readings* (pp. 441–447). Boulder, CO: Westview Press.

Butin, D. W. (Ed.). (2005). *Service-learning in higher education: Critical issues and directions.* New York, NY: Palgrave Macmillan.

Cochran-Smith, M., & Fries, M. K. (2001). Sticks, stones, and ideology: The discourse of reform in teacher education. *Educational Researcher, 30*(8), 3–15.

Cochran-Smith, M., & Lytle, S. L. (1999). Relationships of knowledge and practice: Teacher learning in communities. *Review of Research in Education, 24,* 249–305.

Fairclough, N. (2001*). Language and power* (2nd ed.). Upper Saddle River, NJ: Pearson.

Fairclough, N. (2003). *Analyzing discourse: Textual analysis for social research.* New York, NY: Routledge.

Foucault, M. (1967). *Of other spaces.* Available at http://foucault.info/documents/heteroTopia/foucault.heteroTopia.en.html.

Gee, J. P. (2005). *An introduction to discourse analysis. Theory and method* (2nd ed.). New York, NY: Routledge.

Hoppe, S. L. (2004). A synthesis of the theoretical stances. In B. W. Speck & S. L. Hoppe (Eds.), *Service-learning: History, theory, and issues* (pp. 137–149). Westport, CT: Praeger.

Jacoby, B. et al. (Eds.). (1996). *Service-learning in higher education: Concepts and practices.* San Francisco, CA: Jossey-Bass.

Jacoby, B. et al. (Eds.). (2003). *Building partnerships for service-learning.* San Francisco: Jossey-Bass.

Jacoby, B. et al. (Eds.). (2009). *Civic engagement in higher education: Concepts and practices.* San Francisco: Jossey-Bass.

Jagla, V., & Lukenchuk, A. (2009). Our journey toward institutionalizing service learning: Emergent paradigms and integrative practices. In M. Moore and P. L. Lin (Eds.), *Service-learning in higher education: Paradigms and challenges.* Indianapolis, IN: University of Indianapolis Press.

Johnstone, B. (1996). *The linguistic individual: Self-expression in language and linguistics.* New York, NY: Oxford University Press.

Levinas, E. (1998). *On thinking-of-the-Other: Entre nous* (M. B. Smith & B. Harshav, Trans.). New York, NY: Columbia University Press.

Levinas, E. (2006). *Ethics and infinity: Conversations with Philippe Nemo* (R. A. Cohen, Trans.). Pittsburg, PA: Duquesne University Press.

Lipman, P. (2011). *The new political economy of urban education: Neoliberalism, race, and the right to the city.* New York, NY: Routledge.

Lucas, T. (2005). Fostering a commitment to social justice through service-learning in a teacher education course. In N. M. Michelli, & D. L. Keiser (Eds.), *Teacher education for democracy and social justice* (pp. 167–187). New York, NY: Routledge.

Lukenchuk, A. (2009). Living the ethics of responsibility through university service and service-learning: *Phronesis* and *praxis* reconsidered. *Philosophical Studies in Education, 40,* 246–257.

Merriam, S. B., & Simpson, E. L. (1995). A guide to research for educators and trainers of adults (2nd ed.). Malabar, FL: Krieger.

Noddings, N. (2003). *Happiness and education.* New York, NY: Cambridge University Press.

Noddings, N. (2005a). *The challenge to care in schools: An alternative approach to education* (2nd ed.). New York, NY: Teachers College Press.

Noddings, N. (2005b). *Educating citizens for global awareness.* New York, NY: Teachers College Press.

Noddings, N. (2007). *When school reform goes wrong.* New York, NY: Teachers College Press.

Polkinghorne, D. E. (2004). *Practice and the human sciences: The case for a judgment-based practice of care.* New York, NY: State University of New York Press.

Ravitch, D. (2010). *The death and life of the great American school system: How testing and choice are undermining education.* New York, NY: Basic Books.

Stacey, K. H., & Foreman, C. W. (2006). Faculty incentives: A necessity for integrating service-learning. In D. Dodge & B O. Murphy (Eds.), *Voices of strong democracy: Concepts and models for service-learning in communication studies* (pp. 47–60). Sterling, VA: Stylus Publishing.

Taubman, P. M. (2009). *Teaching by numbers: Deconstructing the discourse of standards and accountability in education.* New York, NY: Routledge.

Watkins, W. H. (2012). *The assault on public education: Confronting the politics of corporate school reform.* New York, NY: Teachers College Press.

Watson, Jr., J. B. (2004). A justification of the civic engagement model. In B. W. Speck & S. L. Hoppe (Eds.), *Service-learning: History, theory, and issues* (pp. 73–83). Westport, CT: Praeger.

Whitehead, J., & McNiff, J. (2006). *Action research: Living theory.* Thousand Oaks, CA: Sage.

Wodak, R., & Meyer, M. (Eds.). (2002). *Methods of critical discourse analysis.* Thousand Oaks, CA: Sage.

Zlotkowski, E. (Ed.). (1998). *Successful service-learning programs: New models of excellence in higher education.* Bolton, MA: Anker Publishing.

Antonina Lukenchuk is an Associate Professor at National Louis University in Chicago, where she teaches graduate courses in educational foundations and research. Her research and scholarly interests are in philosophy of education, epistemology, critical discourse analysis, semiotics, cross-cultural studies, service-learning, and imaginative education. Some of Antonina's recent publications include *Paradigms of Research for the 21st Century: Perspectives and Examples from Practice* (Peter Lang, 2013), "Itinerary of the Knower: Mapping the Ways of Gnosis, Sophia, and Imaginative Education" (in I. Semetsky, *Jung and Educational Theory*, 2012), and "Exploring Cultural Dynamics of Self–Other Relations: University Faculty and Students Engage in Service-Learning with Refugees" (with E. Barber, in T. Stewart and N. Webster, *Exploring Cultural Dynamics and Tensions within Service-Learning*, 2011).

Virginia M. Jagla is an Associate Professor of Education at National Louis University. She has been a teacher and administrator in urban schools, museums, and arts organizations. She has taught for various colleges and universities.

Currently Dr. Jagla leads the NLU Civic Engagement Team. She is an editor of the online journal *i.e.: inquiry in education,* She is the chair of the Middle Level Educators SIG of the Association of Teacher Educators and the chair of the Service-Learning and Experiential Education SIG of the American Educational Research Association. Dr. Jagla is the series editor for *Advances in Service-Learning Research* (Information Age Publishing). She also wrote a book, *Teachers' Everyday Use of Imagination and Intuition: In Pursuit of the Elusive Image* (SUNY Press). Dr. Jagla has numerous published chapters and articles in various juried journals. She is a frequent presenter at local, national, and international conferences and symposia. Her research interests include imagination and intuition in education; the use of the visual and creative arts in education, with particular emphasis on creative drama; urban education; and service-learning, particularly as it applies to middle-level education.

Todd Alan Price is an Associate Professor at National Louis University. His work includes the study of educational policy and the implications of corporate-sponsored education reform on curriculum and instruction at all levels. His previous books include *Defending Public Education from Corporate Reform* (2013); *Classrooms without Walls: An Exploration in the Management of Video Distance Learning (VDL)* (2010); *The Myth and Reality of No Child Left Behind: Public Education and High Stakes Testing* (2009); as well as several chapters and articles. He has lectured in China, Great Britain, and Germany and has received a diploma from Cuba for his study Las Estapas de Educacion y Revolucion in 1994. Dr. Price teaches educational foundations and qualitative research courses. He frequently applies video documentation of policymaker interviews and K–12 classroom observations in his research. He has also presented at conferences in Vietnam and has traveled to Nicaragua, Mexico, and El Salvador.

PART II

FIELD EXPERIENCES: PROVIDING THE SPACE FOR DEEPER UNDERSTANDING

Alan S.Tinkler

INTRODUCTION

When Shulman discusses the importance of advancing teaching practice in *The Wisdom of Practice: Essays on Teaching, Learning, and Learning to Teach*, he argues that teaching, as a profession, is "inherently public and communal" (2004, p. 536). To this end, Shulman argues for teaching that fosters a dynamic and synergetic relationship between theory and learning from experience. In other words, teacher preparation programs, as professional programs, should value and affirm certain attributes, including: "the exercise of *judgment* under conditions of unavoidable uncertainty" (p. 530). The two chapters in this section offer ways to think about how service-learning in teacher preparation offers opportunities for deeper understanding. To put it another way, the two chapters in this section allow readers a space to reflect on the complexity of practice and the need to offer space (and time) for preservice teachers to develop understanding and self-efficacy across the community.

In the first chapter of this section, Tice and Nelson offer a model that includes four interdependent factors of service-learning experiences that influence gains in efficacy. This model recognizes the complexity of teacher

Transforming Teacher Education Through Service-Learning, pages 71–72
Copyright © 2013 by Information Age Publishing
71

preparation as an ecological system that includes many interconnected parts. In fact, the service-learning experiences examined in the chapter represent a range of complex experiences for preservice teachers that are analogous to those the preservice teachers would experience as they enter the practice of the profession. For Tice and Nelson, service-learning offers a chance to enhance efficacy through the practice of service-learning.

In Chapter 5 of this section, Tinkler and Tinkler also identify the opportunities associated with service-learning, specifically how work with English language learners affects the growth of teacher candidates and develops culturally responsive practice. By expanding the conceptual framework for field experiences, Tinkler and Tinkler examine the practice of teaching and learning across the community. Not only does this expanded model allow for preservice teachers to practice across the community, this attention to community-based service-learning also identifies the importance of developing social capital. This is particularly important because 21st-century learning is not limited to the traditional content-area classroom.

Taken together, the two chapters offer interesting insights into teacher preparation and how teacher preparation programs continue to be remodeled to effectively meet the demands and the complexities of the 21st century. Given modern society's complex ecology, it is all the more important to align learning outcomes with service since it matters how we practice our teaching and learning. After all, "What people are able to do in the course of their lives, in large measure, is a function of the opportunities they have to learn. The school curriculum is the major vehicle through which we define those opportunities" (Eisner, 1998, p. 16). The two chapters in this section make a compelling argument to incorporate service-learning as part of the teacher preparation curriculum, for, as noted by Tice and Nelson in their chapter: "The service-learning experience yielded multiple concrete and complex experiences, akin to what preservice teachers would be expected to experience as teachers." In other words, advancing their understanding through the authentic practice of service-learning provided preservice teachers an opportunity for deeper learning.

REFERENCES

Eisner, E. (1998). *The kind of schools we need: Personal essays.* Portsmouth, NH: Heinemann.

Shulman, L. (2004). *The wisdom of practice: Essays on teaching, learning, and learning to teach.* San Francisco: Jossey-Bass.

CHAPTER 4

TOWARD UNDERSTANDING EFFECTIVE COMMUNITY FIELD EXPERIENCES

Kathleen Tice
Larry Nelson

ABSTRACT

This chapter features a series of studies and a model that has emerged, thereby yielding guidance in planning community field experiences in teacher preparation. The research has studied a service-learning project of a physical education course, spanning a period of eight semesters, or 4 years. Through service-learning, preservice teachers have worked with youth from lower socioeconomic, minority backgrounds in communities characterized by gang recruitment. Using mixed methods, the studies examined whether preservice teachers experienced gains in efficacy beliefs and factors that play a role. The results of the quantitative analyses have shown that the preservice teachers mostly experienced substantial gains in efficacy. Findings of the qualitative analyses have complemented the quantitative analyses in understanding the gains in efficacy. The model that has emerged shows an array of interdependent factors that seem to play a role in beneficial service-learning experiences. The model also has been substantiated and extended through theoretical underpinnings and related empirical findings.

Transforming Teacher Education Through Service-Learning, pages 73–98
Copyright © 2013 by Information Age Publishing
All rights of reproduction in any form reserved.

73

Research has shown us that teacher education should gauge not only what teachers can do, but also what teachers believe they can do. A teacher's confidence about being able to influence students' learning, or sense of efficacy, is one of the most well-documented aspects of effective teaching (Henson, Kogan, & Vacha-Haase, 2001). Teachers who believe they can be successful actually are more apt to be successful in making a positive impact. Although the notion of efficacy beliefs is not new, the importance of knowing how to foster efficacy is increasingly important in view of increases in poverty and a population of students who have traditionally been marginalized in our schooling. All children deserve and count upon effective teachers, and children from lower socioeconomic, nonmainstream populations especially rely upon excellent teachers to succeed. Research has revealed particular learning experiences that help preservice teachers develop efficacy beliefs: successfully implementing strategies presented in coursework (Scott, 2003); engaging in collaborative problem solving and reflection (Rushton, 2000); and offering recommendations to each other when collaborating (Henson, 2001). Service-learning is promising in offering these types of experiences that research has found enhance efficacy. Furco (2001) notes that "... service-learning is a teaching strategy that enhances students' learning of academic content by engaging them in authentic activities in which they apply the content of the course to address identified needs in the local and broader community" (p. 67). Along with reflection, service-learning can offer opportunities for collaboration that supports personal, social, and academic growth (Baldwin, Buchanan, & Rudisill, 2007; Hale, 2008; Wade, 2000).

This chapter features findings from a series of studies we have conducted over a period of eight semesters, or 4 years, where we have examined gains in efficacy of preservice teachers who engaged in service-learning as part of their preparation to become physical education teachers. The series of studies we have conducted have not been designed to serve as replications because actual projects have been designed with community partners whose needs have differed. However, the series of studies has made it possible to document whether preservice teachers experienced gains in efficacy during a semester where they engaged in service-learning, with gains in efficacy being measured in the same way. Additionally, the inherent similarities and differences of projects provide understanding of underlying features of the service-learning experiences that are sources of efficacy beliefs according to theory. These underlying features of the service-learning experiences also seem to be associated with the levels of gains in efficacy of the preservice teachers who engaged in a given service-learning experience.

The service-learning projects of each semester have not been exactly alike, but they have been alike in major ways. Through engaging in service-learning, preservice teachers of these studies have worked with youth from lower socioeconomic, minority backgrounds in communities character-ized by gang recruitment. The second author of this chapter has been the instructor of the course in the program of study where service-learning is incorporated. The instructor worked closely with community partners from the outset in discussing types of service-learning projects that would meet the needs of the community partner while also being projects that would make it possible for the preservice teachers to engage in the plan-ning and implementation of a major project where they applied knowl-edge of curriculum models in physical education. The preservice teachers worked in small groups, where the size of the groups varied, depending on the number of youth at a certain site in the community and the needed child-to-adult ratio.

The other learning experiences of the service-learning course studied also have been alike in major ways. The instructor provided information about curriculum models and other information in physical education to help the preservice teachers be prepared as physical education teachers and to plan the project successfully. The instructor also helped the pre-service teachers know how to respect the interests and needs of the com-munity partners. As the small groups of students planned, they received feedback and support from the instructor and other class members. Simi-larly, groups of preservice teachers received support and feedback once a project was underway, through class discussion and email correspondence with the instructor. Along with oral reflection during class meetings once a project was underway, all preservice teachers engaged in written reflection at the end of the project.

The longitudinal aspect of this research has made it possible for us to substantiate findings that show that the service-learning projects of this re-search have generally fostered gains in efficacy beliefs of preservice teach-ers. At the same time, however, our research has uncovered differences in findings across semesters, which has refined understanding of when ser-vice-learning did and when service-learning did not foster efficacy beliefs of preservice teachers. As suggested above, the series of studies has made it possible to uncover underlying features of projects that align with theo-retical notions of how to foster efficacy and that also are associated with service-learning experiences where preservice teachers experience gains in efficacy.

We have used mixed methods, where the quantitative approach revealed whether preservice teachers who engaged in service-learning experienced substantial gains in efficacy beliefs during a semester. A qualitative approach has complemented the quantitative approach and has included analyzing written reflections. A tentative model has emerged from this research that has uncovered interdependent factors that seem to play a role in service-learning fostering efficacy beliefs.

CONCEPTUAL FRAMEWORK

Efficacy Beliefs and Service-Learning

Teacher efficacy is based on work of Bandura (1977, 1986), who purports that efficacy beliefs affect human agency in various ways, including people avoiding tasks and not putting forth effort where they do not feel confident. Efficacy also affects emotional reactions and choices, such that people with low efficacy attribute difficulty to lack of ability rather than viewing effort as a way to overcome difficulty. Additionally, people tend to avoid situations where they feel they cannot succeed. Thus, as suggested previously, levels of efficacy affect how teachers interact with students and the amount of effort teachers are willing to put forth in meeting educational outcomes. Bandura (1986) also sets forth four sources of efficacy that can be applied to teacher education: mastery experiences, vicarious experiences, social persuasion, and affective states. Mastery experiences serve as the most influential source, whereby teachers experience success and predict they will be successful in future situations. Through vicarious experiences, teachers see others like themselves being successful and perceive that they also can be successful. Another source of efficacy relates to social persuasion, such as people cultivating teachers' beliefs that they can succeed while also ensuring success is attainable. A fourth source relates to physiological/affective states, or emotions that affect teachers' sense of being able to succeed.

Research has included studies that show that highly efficacious teachers are more effective in motivating students (Tschannen-Moran, Woolfolk-Hoy, & Hoy, 1998), and these teachers foster higher student achievement (Woolfolk-Hoy & Davis, 2006; Anderson, Greene, & Loewen, 1998; Shahid & Thompson, 2001). Highly efficacious teachers are also more persistent in striving to help students (Ashton, 1984), and they are more likely to embrace instructional innovation (Ghaith & Yaghi, 1997). Conversely, teachers who are not confident are pessimistic about students' success and undermine students' self-assessments (Pajares, 2000). Given what is at stake, teacher education should strive to foster a sense of efficacy in deliberate ways. However, the literature on teacher preparation programs shows that different programs vary in learning experiences offered and in how well-prepared graduates feel (Darling-Hammond, Chung, & Frelow, 2002).

Hybrid Spaces and Service-Learning

Zeichner (2010) points out that a major problem in teacher preparation has been the lack of congruence and collaboration between prospective teachers' coursework and their field experiences, thwarting opportunities for prospective teachers to learn from practice even though field experiences have expanded in programs. Zeichner adds that a growing consensus underscores the need for prospective teachers to learn from practice in the field while challenging the traditional approach of preparing for practice. Ball and Forzani (2009) call for teacher preparation to shift its emphasis from providing knowledge to providing repeated opportunities for prospective teachers to engage in the interactive experiences of teaching, learning what they need to know to be effective. Gallego (2001) points out that prospective teachers need more than knowledge of culturally relevant curriculum and culturally responsive instruction. Teacher preparation needs to make it possible for prospective teachers to interact with the children and communities representative of those with which they will interact as classroom teachers. Zeichner (2010) also discusses benefits of a third space, in particular, hybrid spaces in teacher preparation, where academic expertise is not relegated to a superior role and where schools and communities are seen as sources of knowledge, with community-based service-learning being a promising hybrid space for fostering effective teaching.

According to hybridity theory (Bhabha, 1994), people make sense of the world by drawing upon multiple discourses, or funds of knowledge. In a third space, separate or competing discourses actually can work together to create new knowledge. Applied to field experiences in teacher preparation, third spaces provide opportunities for learning, where academic and practice knowledge are brought together in ways that are less hierarchical (Zeichner, 2010). Theoretical underpinnings of service-learning recognize knowledge offered by students and other members of communities (Baldwin et al., 2007; Wade, 2000). Reciprocal relationships foster prospective teachers' learning to teach, including the development of cultural competency and commitment to working with historically underserved students (e.g., Wade, 2000).

Although various factors play a role in fostering teacher quality, teacher preparation programs have a responsibility and opportunity to make a difference. As suggested previously, levels of efficacy affect how teachers interact with students and the amount of effort teachers are willing to put forth in meeting educational outcomes. Service-learning has the potential to foster efficacy beliefs, given sources of efficacy. Similarly, research has documented the potential of service-learning to foster cultural competence and responsiveness of prospective teachers to teach marginalized students, including reducing negative conceptions (e.g., Flannery & Ward, 1999). At the same time, not all field or service-learning experiences are necessarily beneficial, and could actually reinforce preconceived ideas about marginalized students and increase a sense of hopelessness in working with these students (Gallego, 2001; Zeichner, 1996).

SERIES OF STUDIES

Given the importance of efficacy beliefs, teacher educators need to know how to enhance efficacy. A series of studies we have conducted, Study 1 (Tice & Nelson, in press) and Study 2, focused on how service-learning can foster preservice teachers' sense of efficacy. These studies extended our previous research that examined gains in efficacy over four semesters, where findings showed that when preservice teachers engaged in service-learning, they experienced statistically significant gains in efficacy (Nelson, Tice, & Theriot, 2008). In addition to building upon that research by examining additional data obtained over subsequent semesters, we extended the previous study through the qualitative component of the studies we feature here, study 1 and study 2. The quantitative and qualitative components of these studies have complemented one another in yielding understanding of how service-learning could foster a sense of efficacy. From the findings, a model has emerged of interdependent factors that seem to play a role when service-learning fosters efficacy beliefs, findings that could guide planning and implementation of service-learning.

As suggested, each study uses a mixed-methods design, and we examined gains in efficacy of preservice teachers who engaged in a service-learning project. First, we present the methods of each study and the quantitative analyses in showing differences that we found, which were subsequently understood in view of the qualitative analyses. Next we present the qualitative findings for study 1 and study 2, which complemented the quantitative findings. Finally, we present a tentative model that has emerged from these studies and that has been refined in view of the findings over time. As suggested above, this model yields understanding of interdependent factors that play a role in effective community field experiences.

Study 1: Purposes

One purpose of study 1 was to compare efficacy gains of preservice teachers when they did and did not engage in service-learning during a semester of their teacher preparation, with data gathered over a period of six semesters and analyzed through a quantitative approach. For this study, we measured gains in efficacy of each preservice teacher when he or she enrolled in a course that was part of the teacher preparation program but did not include service-learning. We also measured gains in efficacy of each preservice teacher when he or she was enrolled in a course that was part of the teacher preparation program and did include service-learning. A qualitative analysis of the preservice teachers' perceptions about their participation yielded understanding of how service-learning can foster confidence of prospective teachers working with diverse students from low-income backgrounds and factors that seem to play a role.

The research questions of our inquiry that we addressed through quantitative analysis are as follows: (1) Are there significant differences in the gains in efficacy scores of preservice teachers when they engaged in a service-learning experience in a teacher preparation course as compared to when they did not? (2) Are there significant differences in reported gains of efficacy when comparing gains associated with courses across the six semesters? The first question pertained to whether students would show gains in efficacy when they engaged in service-learning based on measures of efficacy administered at the beginning of a course and at the end of a course. The second research question pertained to consistency, or whether comparative gains in efficacy differ, depending on the semester/course/time under consideration.

Study 1: Participants

The 76 participants in this study were teacher candidates who were enrolled in a physical education program of study at a large urban university. As part of their first year of teacher preparation, or as juniors, all of the participants enrolled in non-service-learning courses, including one that is part of this study that was subsequent to their initial courses. During their senior year, the candidates, or preservice teachers, enrolled in a course that included a service-learning component, and they enrolled in the course during the semester before the semester for student teaching. The courses of this study were comparable in that the students had the same instructor, were part of the same cohort, and they all focused on pedagogy. The major difference of the courses was whether the course did or did not include a community-based service-learning component. The course of this study that did not include a service-learning component did not entail working directly with students. Instead, the preservice teachers applied information of the course through providing learning experiences for class members that could be eventually used when teaching youth.

Study 1: Service-Learning Component

The service-learning projects of the service-learning course each semester required preservice teachers to collaborate with others in the course to plan and implement a curriculum-based project that entailed working with approximately 30–160 students from public schools serving mostly low-income, minority families. The preservice teachers provided the students adventure and outdoor activities through a field trip experience. The pre-service teachers worked in a group of 7–14 members, depending on the size of the course and areas of the curriculum that candidates preferred to focus on for the project. Each group designed the service-learning project, so each project was different, and each group worked with a different school. Nevertheless, the types of experiences they provided the students were similar in that they all followed the same criteria in planning and implementing the project. All of the projects had the same basic features in being based on a curriculum model, Project Adventure's methods of adventure education or Outward Bound's expeditionary learning programs. For example, one service-learning project was a team-based scavenger hunt at a state park that featured fitness concepts and science education. Another project at the state park was a camping trip that focused on plant and wildlife ecology, fitness, nature conservation, orienteering, outdoor living, teamwork, problem solving, and first aid. A project at a city park provided an array of outdoor education activities, such as adventure problem solving, archery, orienteering, and disc golf.

Prior to each semester, the instructor for the course met with the community partners to determine whether these types of projects would be viewed as beneficial for their students and to help ensure the success of the projects. The instructor discussed with school administrators and teachers ways they hoped the projects would serve their students. The discussions also focused on guidelines and procedures for preservice teachers to use in planning and implementing their project.

Group planning took place during approximately 8 weeks of the semester, and at two points in the semester, each group presented their planning during a class meeting to receive feedback. Group planning also included conferences with the instructor and communicating with the public school officials/faculty. At the end of the service-learning project, the instructor asked preservice teachers to engage in written reflection, providing a candid, careful reflection about their service-learning experiences, including how these experiences related to their development as teachers.

Study 1: Quantitative Data Sources and Analysis

This study measured pre- and post-efficacy beliefs of preservice teachers when they took the non-service-learning and service-learning methods courses. We collected data to measure the gains of each participant twice during their program of study in teacher preparation, once when a participant enrolled in a non-service-learning course, and once when they took a service-learning course. Although random assignment to courses was not feasible, the same participants enrolled in each type of course under consideration. We collected data for six semesters for each type of course, yielding data for six semesters of the service-learning course and six corresponding sets of data for the non-service-learning course. At the beginning and end of each of the six semesters, preservice teachers responded to an efficacy measure that has been used widely in efficacy research (Woolfolk & Hoy, 1990). The preservice teachers' responses to the efficacy measure made it possible to determine their general sense of teacher efficacy and personal sense of efficacy. Teacher efficacy is the belief that teachers in general/teaching can be effective in reaching teaching goals regardless of educational obstacles. Personal efficacy is defined as the teacher's belief that he or she can be effective in reaching teaching goals (Woolfolk & Hoy, 1990).

In order to account for some of the initial variance between the two types of courses, a two-factor ANCOVA (course type × time) was applied to the model. Covariates included pre-test scores for both the service-learning and non-service-learning courses. This approach made it possible to examine whether student levels of personal efficacy and teacher efficacy changed as a result of experiencing a service-learning project. A significance level of $p < .05$ was used to verify all differences in variability.

Using a mixed-model repeated measures design for data analysis made it possible to consider whether student levels of personal efficacy and/ or teacher efficacy changed as a result of experiencing a service-learning course. This analysis also made it possible to uncover any differences that existed over the six-semester time span of data collection.

Results: Study 1, Quantitative Analysis

The quantitative data analysis addressed the following research questions: (1) Are there significant differences in the gains in efficacy scores of preservice teachers when they engaged in a service-learning experience in a teacher preparation course as compared to when they did not? (2) Are there significant differences in reported gains of efficacy when comparing gains associated with courses across the six semesters? Results indicate that there were significant gains in personal efficacy $(F(1) = 7.53, p = .013)$ and teacher efficacy $(F(1) = 4.61, p = .046)$ for the service-learning course when compared to the non-service-learning course (Table 4.2). Results also indicate that that there were not significant differences in gains in efficacy when comparing courses across time, or semesters. Regardless of which semester courses took place, gains in efficacy were consistent in the way preservice teachers reported personal efficacy $(F(5) = 1.92, p = .172)$ and teacher efficacy $(F(5) = 1.60, p = .242)$ scores. This suggests that each of the six semesters of service-learning projects were similar in regard to preservice teachers' reported gains in efficacy. In other words, teacher candidates in the service-learning course

TABLE 4.1 Personal Efficacy and Teacher Efficacy Scores of Service-Learning and Non-Service-Learning Courses

	N	Pre-Test Mean (SD)	Post-Test Mean (SD)	Mean Difference
PE Service-Learning	76	44.72 (6.50)	46.41 (5.24)	1.69*
PE Non-Service-Learning	76	45.28 (7.37)	45.41 (6.89)	0.13
TE Service-Learning	76	39.43 (6.11)	40.86 (6.15)	1.43*
TE Non-Service-Learning	76	38.34 (5.96)	38.56 (6.67)	0.22

Note: PE, personal efficacy scale; TE, teacher efficacy scale.
*$p < .05$

TABLE 4.2 Efficacy Effects of Course Type and Time Factors

	df	F	p	Observed Power
Personal Efficacy				
Course Type (SL to NSL)	1	7.53	.013*	.957
Time (Semesters)	5	1.92	.172	.565
Teacher Efficacy				
Course Type (SL to NSL)	1	4.61	.046*	.820
Time (Semesters)	5	1.60	.242	.309

*$p < .05$

showed similar gains regardless of when the service-learning project took place or any differences among projects (although the projects were alike in major ways, as discussed previously). These findings also make it possible to know that the gains reported were not due solely to preservice teachers taking the service-learning course after the course that did not include a service-learning component because the analyses considered gains in efficacy, taking into account initial levels of efficacy. As Table 4.1 shows, the participants actually had higher levels of personal efficacy at the outset of the non-service-learning course as compared to their levels of personal efficacy at the outset of the service-learning course, yet they did not make substantial gains in personal efficacy in the non-service-learning course. However, the participants did make substantial gains in personal efficacy during the semester when they took a service-learning course.

These findings substantiated the findings from an initial study (Nelson et al., 2008) that also showed that preservice teachers in this program experienced substantial gains in efficacy when taking a course that included the service-learning component. That being said, the service-learning experience may not be accounting for all of the variance in gains in efficacy because it is possible that the participants' development as teachers contributed in ways not accounted for by the measures of the study. In other words, it is possible that in some ways the participants were more ready to make gains in efficacy as a result of learning more about teaching in previous courses. As Table 4.1 also shows, the participants did have higher levels of teacher efficacy when entering the service-learning course. What the findings do show, however, is that participants of six semesters studied made substantial gains when they engaged in service-learning.

Study 2: Purposes

This study focuses on the effectiveness of community service-learning experiences, where preservice teachers in a physical education program worked as coaches in an after-school soccer program for students at eight middle schools located in communities where the students are from mostly low socioeconomic and minority backgrounds. The change in the type of service-learning project took place in response to a need of the community partners. The school district and a community agency asked for assistance as they initiated an after-school soccer program for youth. A quantitative approach was used to examine effectiveness through assessing gains in efficacy of preservice teachers, comparing pre- and post-scores on two measures of efficacy. The qualitative component complemented the quantitative findings, refining understanding of how service-learning can foster confidence of prospective teachers working with diverse students from low-income backgrounds and specific factors that seem to play a role.

Study 2: Participants

The participants were 72 preservice teachers enrolled in a physical education teacher education program of study and enrolled in a course with a service-learning component. The preservice teachers worked with students and site supervisors at eight middle schools. These middle schools are located in communities characterized by low-performing schools and gang recruitment, with approximately 66% of the parents being immigrants from Mexico. The student population is 90–94% minority from low socio-economic backgrounds.

Study 2: Service-Learning Component

Through the service-learning project of this study, the preservice teachers were coaches for an after-school soccer program throughout a semester.

In planning the service-learning project of the course, the instructor discussed possible projects with potential community partners. The service-learning project of this study was one deemed beneficial for the community because of the need to provide a soccer program for youth. The local school district did not provide a soccer program through the regular curriculum. Therefore, most of the students did not have access to soccer because their parents could not afford to enroll the youth in a soccer program. Through grant funding, the school district and a community program initiated an after-school soccer program, and the university students served by being coaches that were needed for the program to be implemented.

As indicated previously, through previous research we examined gains in preservice teachers' gains in efficacy associated with their participation in service-learning projects of the course. In previous semesters, preservice teachers participated in service-learning projects that were like the current project in that they were based on a curriculum model, although the projects were different. In all projects, the course instructor collaborated with community partners. All preservice teachers followed the same criteria in planning and implementing a project, and the instructor provided guidance throughout. At the beginning of a semester, the instructor presented guidelines of the project and information needed for helping youth succeed. Additionally, the preservice teachers worked together to plan within a group, with group membership depending on the size of the class and needs of the project. Once a project was started, class meetings provided a forum for preservice teachers to share and reflect upon the service-learning experience along with receiving guidance from the instructor. Regardless of the scope and focus, the project of the current study and previous semesters (1) required preservice teachers to synthesize and apply content from the course regarding teaching, (2) were valued by community partners, and (3) included preservice teachers' oral and written reflections upon the experiences.

Study 2: Quantitative Data Sources and Analysis

At the beginning and end of two semesters, preservice teachers responded to the same efficacy measure used in our previous studies and that has been used widely in efficacy research (Woolfolk & Hoy, 1990). The responses to the efficacy measure made it possible to consider teachers' personal sense of efficacy and general sense of teacher efficacy. Again, personal efficacy is defined as the teacher's belief that he or she can be effective in reaching teaching goals. Teacher efficacy is the teacher's belief that teachers in general can be effective in reaching teaching goals regardless of educational obstacles (Woolfolk & Hoy, 1990). A quasi-experimental design using a mixed model repeated measures (pre–post) analysis was used to account for variance among pre-test scores. A two-factor ANCOVA (course × time) was applied in order to increase the ratio of variance explained by efficacy scores. This made it possible to consider efficacy gains within a course, regardless of differing levels of efficacy each student had upon entering either course.

Results: Study 2, Quantitative Analysis

As stated above, we administered efficacy measures to gain understanding of the preservice teachers' levels of personal and teaching efficacy before engaging in the service-learning project and after to determine whether gains in efficacy existed. The first research question focuses on gains when personal and teacher efficacy scores of all preservice teachers are analyzed, and this data analysis was the same as used in previous studies, thereby providing a basis of comparison with the previous semesters and similar service-learning projects. The second research question focuses on gains when a community partner was deemed supportive by preservice teachers and when the community partner was not deemed supportive. More specifically, the quantitative data analysis addressed the following research questions: (1) Are there significant gains in personal efficacy and teacher efficacy scores of preservice teachers when they engage in a service-learning experience in a teacher preparation course? (2) Are there significant gains in personal efficacy and teacher efficacy scores of preservice teachers when they engage in a service-learning experience in a teacher preparation course and work with community partners considered supportive, and are there significant gains in these efficacy scores of preservice teachers who worked with community partners considered not supportive?

The second research question that focuses on supportive and nonsupportive sites originated with this study after an initial analysis of the findings. The initial results of the quantitative analysis showed that there were not substantial gains in personal efficacy and teacher efficacy when all prospective teachers' gains were examined. These findings were not consistent with findings of previous semesters where preservice teachers in a course did experience substantial gains in personal efficacy and teacher efficacy, or gains that were statistically significant. The qualitative data analysis uncovered possible reasons for this discrepancy in findings. Unlike previous semesters, the preservice teachers in the current study wrote about problems that existed in working with the community partner at some sites of the soccer program. The preservice teachers voiced frustration regarding obstacles created by the supervisors at some of the sites. In view of this finding, we analyzed the personal and teacher efficacy data again, according to whether a preservice teacher worked at a site deemed supportive or nonsupportive by preservice

TABLE 4.3 Personal Efficacy and Teacher Efficacy Scores between Supportive and Nonsupportive Service-Learning Environments

	N	Pre-Test Mean (SD)		Post-Test Mean (SD)		Mean Difference
PE Supportive	42	45.52	(6.01)	46.73	(6.29)	1.21*
PE Nonsupportive	34	45.49	(6.17)	45.41	(6.59)	−0.20
TE Supportive	42	40.11	(5.91)	41.60	(6.28)	1.49*
TE Nonsupportive	34	39.04	(5.75)	37.39	(6.03)	−1.65*

Note: PE, personal efficacy scale; TE, teacher efficacy scale; Supportive, supportive service-learning conditions; Nonsupportive, nonsupportive service-learning conditions.
* $p < .05$

teachers assigned to the site. As shown in Table 4.3, further analysis revealed that there were statistically significant gains in personal and teacher efficacy when the community partnership/site supervisor was supportive, but not when the partnership was nonsupportive. Moreover, preservice teachers at nonsupportive sites collectively reported reductions in levels of personal efficacy and teacher efficacy. At the same time, variation existed among the reported gains or reductions in levels of efficacy of those at non-supportive sites. The variance in the reported levels of efficacy can be understood in view of the qualitative analysis, which is discussed next.

Study 1 and Study 2: Qualitative Data and Analysis

The major sources of data were the individual reflections each preservice teacher had written upon completing the service-learning project. Through written reflections, prospective teachers shared their perceptions of their participation in a service-learning project. The course content/class meetings devoted to preparing for the service-learning project also provided data for understanding characteristics of the service-learning experiences. Using a qualitative approach (Lincoln & Guba, 1985), we analyzed the written reflections. In analyzing the data, we individually and then together noted salient, repeated units of meaning to code. This analysis entailed a recursive process of reading, interpreting, and rereading toward recognizing theme and categories that emerged from the data and relationships among categories. Further analysis entailed also examining characteristics of the service-learning experience to uncover an array of factors that seemed to play a role in service-learning fostering a sense of efficacy.

The research questions of our inquiry that we addressed through qualitative analysis are as follows: (1) How do service-learning experiences seem to foster preservice teachers' sense of efficacy? (2) What factors seem to play a role in regard to service-learning experiences fostering a sense of efficacy? We addressed these questions through analyzing reflections of preservice teachers who engaged in service learning and the data describing how service learning was incorporated in the courses.

Findings: Study 1 and Study 2

The qualitative component of this study helped reveal understanding of the gains in efficacy that preservice teachers reported in Study 1 and Study 2. Equally important, the findings of the qualitative analyses uncovered understanding of the variation in reported gains in efficacy of Study 2. The themes that emerged were consistent across studies, yet together, the studies have delineated more clearly factors that play a role when service-learning fosters efficacy beliefs of preservice teachers.

TENTATIVE MODEL FOR UNDERSTANDING EFFECTIVE COMMUNITY FIELD EXPERIENCES

As shown in Figure 4.1, the themes of the qualitative analyses have provided the basis of a tentative framework of interdependent factors of service-learning experiences that influence gains in efficacy: (1) the nature of the

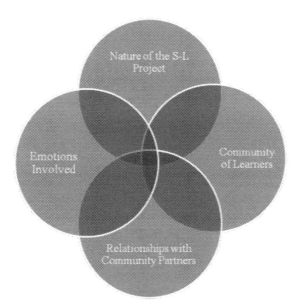

Figure 4.1 Interdependent factors of the service-learning experience that influence gains in efficacy.

service-learning experience, (2) the community of learners, (3) relationships with community partners, and (4) emotions involved for each factor. As indicated previously, preservice teachers of Study 1 indicated that the community partner relationships were supportive, but in Study 2, a lack of support from the community partner was a prominent feature of some written reflections. Further analysis showed that the adults at some school sites, particularly the site supervisors, were deemed consistently supportive and some were not. The lack of support discussed by preservice teachers helps understand why preservice teachers at nonsupportive sites did not as a group experience substantial gains in efficacy. Yet as stated previously, variance existed among preservice teachers when gains in efficacy are observed, and the qualitative findings also lend understanding to why variance in efficacy gains existed among preservice teachers at nonsupportive sites. As is discussed subsequently, some preservice teachers at nonsupportive sites seemed able to capitalize upon what the service-learning experience offered in spite of any obstacles provided by community partners. In the following sections, we discuss findings related to the tentative framework of interdependent factors, with the emotions involved being an integral part of the discussion of each of the three factors and therefore not discussed separately. Although factors are discussed individually, all of the factors are interdependent.

Nature of the Service-Learning Experience

For both studies, the service-learning project yielded multiple concrete and complex experiences, akin to what preservice teachers would be expected to accomplish as teachers. This type of authentic learning was new to the preservice teachers, and initially, many felt reluctant and/or apprehensive. However, the nature of the participation in the service-learning experiences that provided a community of learners could lead to engagement and confidence. As reported for Study 1 (Tice & Nelson, in press), one preservice teacher, Janna, put it this way:

> At first we all had resistance to the project. We wanted a traditional college setting with a syllabus that said we are taking a test on this date and this is what we have to do to pass the class. But soon after the project planning started, I realized that in a year I'm not going to have a syllabus to follow. . . . I think we are better prepared to go into the real world as a result of the authentic experience we got teaching kids.

One preservice teacher, Sam, who was at a supportive site for Study 2, wrote the following, which is akin to comments of other preservice teachers at supportive sites of this and previous research:

This has been an absolute blessing. Every single week, I look forward to coaching on Tuesday and Thursday more than anything I have ever done. I just love what I do, seeing results, and being 100% accountable for a "teaching/coaching" atmosphere. This experience has shown me that my choice through UT Arlington was a great one. The most important part of this program, for me, is the structure. It is like getting your feet wet before being hurled into the massive ocean that is teaching. It gives you a chance to see if what you are getting into as a teacher is really what you want. I wouldn't have known so quickly if I did not take this chance.

This preservice teacher also wrote about specific gains he had made through knowledge he had created as a result of the authentic learning experiences afforded by the service-learning project:

You really have to set up an environment that is conducive to the specific age group, as well as talent level. For example, if it is too easy, the kids get bored; if it is too hard, the kids don't understand or have the specified skill level to achieve success. I find the most important structure for my practices involves a small skill that is built upon throughout the practice session, ending in the skill being applied in a game-like setting. This aids in the game time situation. They have seen it and are prepared for it.

Community of Learners

Through the "scaffolding" they received from class meetings and collaboration, preservice teachers were able to overcome challenges. Laura, who was a participant in Study 1 (Tice & Nelson, in press), wrote the following:

To me, this class was a lot like climbing Mount Everest. The mountain is big and risky...Busywork, excuses, and tests will not get you to the top of that mountain, but a real-life project working with kids forces you to find a way to make it work. We all had to rely on each other, take a leap of faith, and allow those people around us to help push us to the top.

Laura's comment also indicates the interdependence of factors because the authentic nature of the service-learning experience provided for real, complex teaching situations and the nature of the service-learning experience made it possible for preservice teachers to work together, relying upon and learning from others. Sam from Study 2 also wrote the following, which again is akin to what others wrote about being a part of a community of learners:

I enjoyed discussing with the other coaches my plans and hearing their plans for practice that particular day. You most definitely learn from them and sometimes borrow ideas from them. That is how we learn (as coaches) to become better at our job, learning from what works and what doesn't work in practice. If I heard that another coach had a very influential/fun/effective practice, I would want to learn what was done, so maybe I could pull things from it, but still (hopefully) make it my own. The most important thing is to find those practice games that create the atmosphere that draws the kids to keep coming back for more. If it is skill and drill all the time, the kids lose interest. So many coaches, so many ideas: let's put it to use.

Sam also wrote the following, recognizing the reality of working with others while also seeing the benefits:

It was a tedious task to coordinate meetings between the numbers of people involved, at times. In the long run, it has not been a big issue because when it comes down to it, you have your kids and your coworkers alongside you at every single practice.

Relationship with Community Partner

The significance of being a teacher reached new heights as preservice teachers worked closely with the students (who were part of community partner relationship), making it possible to know students as individuals and care about them. Because the preservice teachers felt that much was at stake in working with the students, their success was meaningful for the preservice teachers in Study 1 and Study 2. The preservice teachers witnessed the types of benefits for the students. For example, in Study 2, the after-school soccer club facilitated student interest at the school and improved the attendance of students who previously had not attended school regularly. The school's security officer had this to say about the program:

Soccer mostly changed the mentality of those particular students who were most resistant to come to school in the first place. Many of us saw a real transformation with the soccer kids, as they were definitely more motivated to come to school and at least try a little more than they ever did before.

One student commented, "If we get into trouble or miss class, the consequence would be we wouldn't be able to play on the soccer team . . . so it's motivation for us to go to class and get good grades." Another student said, "It's a good thing coach comes out and supports us. Coach is a good role model and keeps us away from drugs and all the bad stuff." A school official noted that "these students have been waiting for school soccer to become a reality for some time. This is their game and they can easily relate and transfer what they are learning in the soccer program to their home life and the world around them." Sam, a preservice teacher, saw how his work made an impact on students, which shows learning from the students and relates to support from the students as community partners:

> I feel this program has been absolutely terrific for the children. It provides a chance for them to play a sport that may not be accessible by all. I am proud to say that, after this season is over my team has gotten together and decided that they want to form a summer league team. One of the leaders of this is named Eric, who had never played soccer on a team before. He likes it so much; he wants to work out over the summer so that he can play at the high school level! That is great!

Some preservice teachers also commented about how their growth as teachers related to site supervisors as community partners:

> The site supervisor gave me insight into what really goes on in the inner-city school. She was supportive and gave us the freedom to run our side of the program the way we felt best.

Another preservice teacher put it this way: *I was fortunate to have a great community partner who really showed a genuine interest in the kids and was always there even after it was over and the students left.*

Understanding how the experience contributed to gains in efficacy is illustrated in these following final comments by Sam. Especially noteworthy is how the hybrid nature of the service-learning project differs from other traditional, field experiences:

> I have learned numerous things about my ability as a coach throughout this process. I am much more confident when I step on the field each day. I know that practice runs smoothly if I prepare thoroughly. I know that my attitude can alter practice settings for the kids, bring them down or get their spirits up. Most importantly, though, I know I can do these things on my own. I don't need someone standing over my shoulder, helping me. This is a great feeling because when you are in class and have those classroom settings it becomes easy to rely on others to help you out of any situation. This gave me a chance to learn what I have to offer and what I can do on my own.

However, unlike previous semesters, the prospective teachers of this study did not all experience statistically significant gains, and considerable variation in efficacy gains existed. The qualitative analysis yielded understanding of the quantitative findings, indicating that lack of support and organization on part of some community partners was not conducive to successful work with the students. Relationships with the students did not falter totally, and prospective teachers' comments were akin to those of previous semesters in indicating how the authentic nature of the experience was beneficial. These preservice teachers also were able to collaborate with other coaches/class members at a site and during class. Additionally, all indicated they could rely upon support from the instructor. Yet some preservice teachers voiced frustration and disappointment in regard to how site supervisors did not put students first in making decisions. Site supervisors' lack of organization and planning created roadblocks, such as not having equipment. Frank shares it this way:

> I feel that Larry [the instructor] has been more than helpful with the program. I feel that he has gone above and beyond to help us solve problems. I haven't really enjoyed working [community partner]. At the beginning, they were there and wanted to be involved, but as time has progressed, the referees have been rude, and it seems like they are there more for the paycheck than for the kids. Also, at the beginning of the season we had nets at every game, and now the kids show up and wonder why they don't have nets. I don't have an answer for them. Larry has done a great job of being responsive to emails and helping out in whatever way he can. However, I feel that the [community partner] could do a better job of making sure the referees are prepared to referee a soccer game and that they want to be there.

Frank indicated that he felt the project was beneficial, but his remarks also indicate that he did not gain confidence as he worked for the first time with marginalized students:

> I think it is important to get real-world experience with the children, so you can practice what works and doesn't work. . . . I feel that this program has helped and hindered my confidence to teach. Having taught at a private school, where the kids are fairly well mannered and obviously come from a different background, I was coming in feeling great about teaching, and I was ready to go. I have learned, though, that I didn't quite have the skills needed for discipline. I have learned that some kids have to be taught differently, and coming with the strict attitude that I had, wasn't really conducive to their learning style. I feel that I had to lighten up my attitude and emotion, in order to get a better response out of the children.

Frank acknowledges the importance of changing his stance in developing a rapport that would motivate students, but he does not seem to have left the experience feeling completely successful in working with marginalized students even though he did make changes that he saw that made a difference in the response of students.

Yet some preservice teachers did experience gains in efficacy even when at a nonsupportive site. Some prospective teachers recognized the lack of support from site supervisors, but they were not hindered in doing what they needed to do to help the students, and they perceived associated gains. The following series of comments of one preservice teacher illustrates how some students did consider the community partner nonsupportive, but were able to capitalize upon the authentic nature of the opportunity, learn from being part of a community of learners, and feel successful in spite of lack of support from the adults in the community partner relationship. In regard to the community partner, this preservice teacher, Sean, wrote the following, which are characteristic of other comments in its evaluation of site supervisors at nonsupportive sites, yet shows how the preservice teacher used this situation to his advantage in his growth as a teacher:

> Working with the adults at the sites was the only downside to this program. It's a great program and has the potential to do terrific things. However, the staff (mainly the site supervisors) has caused more damage than good for these kids. I will say that seeing the lack of concern by people in charge helped give me reassurance that I really am doing something that I love and am perfect for.

Sean also expressed feeling that he gained from the authentic nature of the service-learning experience rather than being deterred by the "lack of concern" of the community partner. Again, this preservice teacher was able to capitalize upon the recognized hindrances to progress by adults of the community partner relationships.

> Being in the school district gave me a great idea of how things actually work. Granted, this semester seemed to be extremely disorganized because of the site supervisors, but I'm glad that we as students got exposure to this early. It's better to face it in disarray rather than expecting everything to run smoothly because then when it doesn't, you are completely lost.

> After this semester, it has become obvious that planning for the unexpected/worst is far more beneficial than planning as if everything is going to run smoothly. Nothing ever goes as planned and if does, it's easy to manage.

> It's amazing how much confidence this program has given me about coaching. I came into this program completely clueless about soccer, and now I leave with confidence to coach a soccer team on my own.

As in previous semesters, this preservice teacher found value in a community of learners, working with the team: *Collaborating with other coaches introduced me to other management techniques. I started this program with zero knowledge about soccer. I now leave with the knowledge and confidence to coach another soccer team in the future.*

Sean also alluded to learning from the students as community partners, such as here where he sees that the program and his involvement was offering much to students:

> The impact that this program has on the kids is unbelievable. A student on my team told their parents that it was mandatory for them (the student) to be in the program. I spoke with the parent and it turns out the student was saying

it was mandatory because that was the only way the parents would allow them to play in the games. The student showed a ton of emotion and passion for the program when I had a sit-down conversation with the parent and student.

DISCUSSION

Some prospective teachers of Study 2 did experience gains in efficacy, which was consistent with findings of previous semesters of Study 1 in this course where preservice teachers engaged in service-learning. Other preservice teachers did not experience gains in efficacy, and this lack of consistency in gains in efficacy was associated with working with a nonsupportive community partner. As we have discussed previously, the findings indicate that certain factors play a role when service-learning experiences foster a sense of efficacy, and these factors can be understood in view of Bandura's sources of efficacy. The service-learning experience yielded multiple concrete and complex experiences, akin to what preservice teachers would be expected to accomplish as teachers. This type of learning was new to the preservice teachers, and initially, many felt reluctant and/or apprehensive. However, the nature of the participation in the service-learning experiences could lead to engagement and confidence. Preservice teachers knew that team members and students were counting on them. Through the "scaffolding" they received from class meetings and collaboration, preservice teachers were able to overcome obstacles. The significance of being a teacher reached new heights as preservice teachers worked closely with students, making it possible to know students as individuals and care about them. Responses of students validated the importance of the preservice teachers' hard work. The service-learning experiences that preservice teachers had conceptualized, planned, and implemented for students were successful. In other words, the preservice teachers had "ownership" of real teaching, and their efforts were supported, making it possible for them to succeed. Because the preservice teachers felt that much was at stake in working with the students, their success was meaningful.

Bandura stresses the importance of mastery experiences such as these. These service-learning projects also could be sources of efficacy beliefs because collaboration provided vicarious experiences, where preservice teachers saw their peers engage and succeed at various points. Social persuasion is another source of efficacy beliefs according to Bandura, and this could take place implicitly, if not explicitly, as peers/team members assigned responsibilities or asked for assistance, "telling"/telling team members they could succeed while ensuring they could. As suggested above, emotional dimensions played an integral role in fostering a sense of efficacy.

However, not all preservice teachers experienced mastery experiences that lead to confidence and engagement. Rather, some preservice teachers' learning and engagement was thwarted by their work with adults as community partners who not only did not support the preservice teachers but also created obstacles to successful work with the youth by not being organized and dedicated. Although some preservice teachers succeeded in spite of the situation, not all preservice teachers could overcome the obstacles as they worked in a novel, complex teaching situation.

The instructor for the course entered into the collaboration through meetings and discussions characteristic of past collaborations with community partners that were supportive. Yet how the school district and community agency managed the after-school program was not an issue he could control. What can be learned here is that not all service-learning experiences will yield a high, consistent level of beneficial outcomes. Much depends on support from the community partner. All preservice teachers considered the service-leaning experience beneficial for the youth and for themselves to some extent. However, not all made gains in confidence to teach, which is too important to be dismissed, especially as this relates to working with marginalized students. Although it is beyond the scope of this report of our research, more recent analyses has indicated a positive outcome of these findings in that the concerns related to nonsupportive site managers was addressed by managers of the after-school soccer program, and the positive changes have made a difference in reported gains in efficacy of the preservice teachers who now work as coaches for their service-learning component of the course.

LIMITATIONS AND CONCLUSIONS

Although the notion of fostering efficacy beliefs is not new, much remains to be done, and efforts to enhance efficacy can be elusive through relying upon traditional coursework. As discussed previously, a limitation of Study 1 is that a service-learning course and one that was not a service-learning course that were compared were not comparable in regard to the development of each preservice teacher. Although all of the participants had enrolled in teacher preparation courses prior to the course of the study that did not include service-learning, the service-learning course is the last course before student teaching. As stated, the levels of personal efficacy were higher when preservice teachers enrolled in the non-service-learning course, but it could be that learning more about teaching also helps in making gains in efficacy. Other sources of variance also can exist, and future research could uncover other sources of variance that are not accounted for in this research. Nevertheless, the data across six semesters of Study 1 corroborate findings of our initial research that showed that the service-learning projects of this research consistently foster both personal and teaching efficacy beliefs. The data from study 2 corroborate findings from all of the previous studies in showing that the service-learning projects of this research foster both personal and teaching efficacy beliefs and do so consistently when a community partner is supportive.

Given these findings that furnish evidence for incorporating service-learning in teacher preparation, the findings also call for understanding of what is taking place in the type of community-based field experience of this research, which is provided to an extent by the qualitative data. The authentic nature of the service-learning experience where the preservice teachers assumed responsibility akin to what they would assume as teachers through a major project provided opportunities for the preservice teachers to recognize for themselves that what they did mattered. They knew students they worked with were counting on them, and preservice teachers' confidence was bolstered when they saw the students develop through their work with them. The nature of the service-learning experience also included collaboration with the community partner from the outset, and this helped most when the community partners continued to be supportive. The preparation and feedback from the instructor and others that was integral throughout additionally helped preservice teachers be successful.

This research similarly illustrates the importance of considering an array of factors in providing hybrid spaces, particularly in indicating that attributes of prospective teachers and community partners are interdependent and can play a role. One factor that seems to be emerging relates to the ability of preservice teachers to deal with obstacles. Here, we can see how the obstacles created by the site supervisors seemed to hamper some preservice teachers' confidence in being able to work with youth from a background different from their own because they could not experience success, even though the preservice teachers tried and wanted to succeed. Future research is needed to document ways to help preservice teachers overcome obstacles. The obstacles presented by adults as community partners are not unlike those presented by adults in teaching situations. The hybrid nature of service-learning provides opportunities for a learning community where support can be provided by others and knowledge created, including how to overcome obstacles to be able to be effective teachers. As we have indicated, our current research has shown that changes in the actions of the community site supervisors has been associated with consistent gains in efficacy of the preservice teachers serving as coaches in the soccer program.

Future research can delineate more clearly the interdependence of factors and may uncover other factors. Although this research provides support for incorporating service-learning, this research concurrently indicates that we should acknowledge the complexity of teacher preparation and factors that can play a role as we implement service-learning in teacher preparation. Although service-learning experiences across settings never will be exactly the same, we can address the types of factors associated with successful service-learning experiences, making it more likely for preservice teachers to be prepared and feel prepared to work with all students.

REFERENCES

Anderson, R., Greene, M., & Loewen, P. (1998). Relationships among teachers' and students' thinking skills, sense of efficacy, and student achievement. Alberta Journal of Educational Research, 34(2), 148–165.

Ashton, P. (1984). Teacher efficacy: A motivational paradigm for effective teacher education. *Journal of Teacher Education, 35*(5), 28–32.

Baldwin, S., Buchanan, A., & Rudisill, M. (2007). What teacher candidates learned about diversity, social justice, and themselves from service-learning experiences. *Journal of Teacher Education, 58*(4), 315–327.

Ball, D., & Forzani, F. (2009). The work of teaching and the challenge for teacher education. *Journal of Teacher Education, 60*(5), 497–511.

Bandura, A. (1977). Self-efficacy: Toward a unifying theory of behavioral change. *Psychological Review, 84*, 191–215.

Bandura, A. (1986). *Social foundations of thought and action: A social cognitive theory.* Englewood Cliffs, NJ: Prentice-Hall.

Bhabha, H. K. (1994). The location of culture. London, United Kingdom: Routledge.

Darling-Hammond, L., Chung, R., & Frelow, F. (2002). Variation in teacher preparation: How well do different pathways prepare teachers to teach? *Journal of Teacher Education, 53*(4), 286–302.

Flannery, D., & Ward, K. (1999). Service learning: A vehicle for developing cultural competence in health education. *American Journal of Health Behavior, 23,* 323–331.

Furco, A. (2001). Advancing service-learning at research universities. In M. Canada & B.W. Speck (Eds.), *Developing and implementing service learning programs.* San Francisco, CA: Jossey-Bass.

Gallego, M. (2001). Is experience the best teacher? The potential of coupling classroom and community-based field experiences. *Journal of Teacher Education, 52*(4), 312–325.

Ghaith, G., & Yaghi, H. (1997). Relationships among experience, teacher efficacy, and attitudes toward the implication of instructional innovation. *Teaching and Teacher Education, 13*(4), 451–458.

Hale, A. (2008). Service learning with Latino communities: Effects on preservice teachers. *Journal of Hispanic Higher Education, 7*, 819–836.

Henson, R. (2001). The effects of participation in teacher research on teacher efficacy. *Teaching and Teacher Education, 17*(7), 819–836.

Henson, R., Kogan, L., & Vacha-Haase, T. (2001). A reliability generalization study of the teacher efficacy scale and related instruments. *Educational and Psychological Measurement, 61*(3), 404–420.

Lincoln, M., & Guba, A. (1985). *Naturalistic inquiry.* Newbury Park, CA: Sage.

Nelson, L. P., Tice, K., & Theriot, S. (2008). Impact of service-learning on teachers' efficacy. *Academic Exchange Quarterly, 12*(3), 102–107.

Pajares, F. (2000, January). *Schooling in America: Myths, mixed messages and good intentions.* Lecture delivered at the Great Teachers Lecture Series, Emory University, Atlanta, GA.

Rushton, S.P. (2000). Student teacher efficacy in inner-city schools. *Urban Review, 32*(4), 365–383.

Scott, S. (2003). Innovative use of teaching repertoire: A study in transfer of complex strategies into classroom practice by novice teachers. *European Journal of Teacher Education, 26*(3), 365–377.

Shahid, J., & Thompson, D. (2001, April). *Teacher efficacy: A research synthesis.* Paper presented at the annual meeting of the American Educational Research Association. Seattle, WA.

Tschannen-Moran, M., Woolfolk-Hoy, A., & Hoy, W. (1998). Teacher efficacy: Its meaning and measure. *Review of Educational Research, 68* (2), 202–248.

Tice, K., & Nelson, L. (in press). When service-learning fosters efficacy beliefs of preservice teachers. *International Journal of Research on Service Learning in Teacher Education.*

Wade, R. C. (2000). Service-learning for multicultural teaching competency: Insights from the literature for teacher educators. *Equity and Excellence in Education, 33*(3), 21–30.

Woolfolk-Hoy, A., & Davis, H. (2006). Teacher self-efficacy and its influence on the achievement of adolescents. In F. Pajares & T. Urdan (Eds.), *Self-efficacy beliefs of adolescents.* Greenwich, CT: Information Age Publishing.

Woolfolk, A., & Hoy, W. (1990). Prospective teachers' sense of efficacy and beliefs about control. *Journal of Educational Psychology, 82*(1), 81–91.

Zeichner, K. (1996). Designing educative practicum experiences for prospective teachers. In K. Zeichner, S. Melnick, & M. L. Gomez (Eds.), *Currents of reform in preservice teacher education* (pp. 215–234). New York, NY: Teachers College Press.

Zeichner, K. (2010). Rethinking the connections between campus courses and field experiences in college- and university-based teacher education. *Journal of Teacher Education, 61*(1–2), 89–99.

Kathleen C. Tice is Clinical Faculty and Program Coordinator for Literacy Studies in the Department of Curriculum and Instruction at the University of Texas at Arlington. Her research has focused on teacher knowledge development and service-learning in teacher preparation.

Larry P. Nelson is an Associate Professor in the Department of Kinesiology at the University of Texas at Arlington. His research interests include physical education program development, measurement and evaluation, and active-learning strategies in physical education teacher education coursework.

CHAPTER 5

TEACHING ACROSS THE COMMUNITY

Using Service-Learning Field Experiences to Develop Culturally and Linguistically Responsive Teachers

Alan Tinkler
Barri Tinkler

ABSTRACT

A June 2012 presentation from the external evaluator of Project BRITE (Brown's Response to Improving Teacher Education) reported a statistically significant finding that states: "Direct interaction with an ELL student affects the growth of the teacher candidate." Given the increase in the numbers of ELLs in the United States, it is crucial that preservice teachers are prepared to be culturally and linguistically responsive. The challenge is to find field experiences that provide meaningful experiences with ELLs. At our university, one BRITE-related initiative was to collaborate with school and community partners to advance opportunities for teacher candidates to work with ELLs through service-learning field experiences. By embracing service-learning, the teacher education program offers meaningful opportunities for individ-

Transforming Teacher Education Through Service-Learning, pages 99–117
Copyright © 2013 by Information Age Publishing

ual interactions with ELLs. In this essay, we provide a conceptual framework for distinguishing between traditional field experiences and service-learning field experiences. Additionally, we offer guiding questions regarding the efficacy of school- and community-based service-learning experiences.

INTRODUCTION

The Education Alliance at Brown University designed Project BRITE (Brown's Response to Improving Teacher Education) to advance instruction for English language learners (ELLs). This 5-year initiative (2007–2012) focused on providing ongoing professional development for 24 faculty members from four institutions in the Northeast to strengthen their capacity to prepare future teachers to work with ELLs. In June 2012, the external evaluator, Elizabeth Brach, presented some interesting results of the work being done by project participants. As part of her analysis, Brach aggregated pre- and post-survey data ($n = 114$) BRITE participants collected from the preservice teachers with whom they worked. One statistically significant finding showed that "direct interaction with an ELL student affects the growth of the teacher candidate" (p. 31). In particular, preservice teachers who interacted directly with ELLs reported greater increases in their "knowledge of instructional practice skills" (p. 31) than did preservice teachers who only learned about ELLs through course content and assignments. This finding is important as teacher education programs work to advance instruction for ELLs, particularly given the growth in the numbers of ELLs in the United States (American Association of Colleges for Teacher Education [AACTE], 2002). It is crucial for preservice teachers to work with ELLs as part of their teacher education programs in order to become culturally and linguistically responsive teachers. It can be challenging, however, to find field placements that provide meaningful experiences because school districts in urban areas are often overwhelmed with requests for field placements from teacher education programs (Goddard, 2004). In regions with limited populations of ELLs, school districts that serve ELLs can be inundated with requests for placements.

At the University of Vermont, one ongoing BRITE-related initiative (funded by a Learn and Serve America grant) is to work collaboratively with community stakeholders to advance opportunities for teacher candidates to work with ELLs through service-learning field experiences. This ELL focus was in response to the growing number of ELLs in our state (since Vermont has a substantial Refugee Relocation Program). A community-wide dialogue found that, in addition to school support structures, a number of community centers offered assistance to ELLs. Because of this community scan, the Secondary Education Program decided to expand its placements to include community sites that offer academic support for ELLs.

To supplement the traditional field experiences currently embedded in the program, a new service-learning field experience has been added to the Reading and Writing in the Content Area course that is required for all secondary candidates. In the course, teacher candidates learn about the importance of literacy as a component of student engagement because those K–12 students who are not able to enter the academic literacy space of the classroom are left behind. Given this, the principal goal of the course is to have teacher candidates think about literacy practices to enhance engagement for all students, particularly for students marginalized in traditional classrooms. By working individually with refugee students in tutoring programs, the teacher candidates are able to gain a greater appreciation for the strengths of ELLs as they navigate the English language through the various content areas. The teacher candidates also learn to implement and practice instructional strategies that support the needs of ELLs. By incorporating this practice-based service-learning field experience into the array of field and clinical experiences completed by our candidates, the secondary program has strengthened the capacity of our teacher candidates. This conceptual essay introduces a framework for designing service-learning field experiences that supplement field-based opportunities and support the development of culturally and linguistically responsive teachers.

REVIEW OF LITERATURE

A 2010 report compiled by a Blue Ribbon Panel convened by the National Council for Accreditation of Teacher Education (NCATE) called for a redesign of teacher education with a focus on clinical practice. One reason for this was raised by Ball and Cohen (1999) in "Developing Practice, Developing Practitioners: Toward a Practice-Based Theory of Professional Education" when they discussed why knowledge is not enough. They recognized that "[t]eaching occurs in particulars—particular students interacting with particular teachers over particular ideas in particular circumstances" (p. 10). This means that for teacher candidates to become highly effective teachers who truly understand learners, they need experiences that afford them an opportunity to work with individual students while those students are engaged in learning.

For many teacher education programs, an increased focus on clinical practice requires increasing field experiences, which are "defined as a variety of early and systematic P–12 classroom-based opportunities in which teacher candidates (TCs) may observe, assist, tutor, instruct, and/or conduct research. While field experiences generally occur in schools they may also take place in other settings such as community based agencies" (Capraro, Capraro, & Helfeldt, 2010, p. 131). Though it seems to follow that increasing field experiences would lead to improved preparation for teacher candidates, a report by the Task Force on Field Experiences (1999) convened by the Association of Teacher Educators (ATE) offers an important caution: "More field experiences are not the answer. Better planned and more deliberative field experiences based on program goals are more likely to influence teacher candidates in positive ways" (p. 14). Placement opportunities should be vetted according to the opportunity to gain proficiencies, and the methods have to be valued and understood by state agencies as well as national accreditation bodies.

This call for additional, well-executed experiences is also in response to the growing population of ELLs. Because of changes in student populations and accreditation requirements, many teacher education programs have articulated program goals to support the development of competencies for working with ELLs and are using field experiences to support the development of these competencies. Various studies on the impact of incorporating field experiences with ELLs find many benefits, including better understanding of students' cultures (Clark & Medina, 2000), improved attitudes toward ELLs and other facets of diversity (Nathenson-Mejía & Escamilla, 2003), an understanding of the benefits of including diversity in the curriculum (Arias & Poyner, 2001), increased knowledge of literacy strategies for working with ELLs (Xu, 2000), and increased confidence in the ability to support ELLs (Mora & Grisham, 2001).

Though increasing clearly defined field experiences and targeting experiences with particular populations of students can lead to stronger preparation for preservice teachers, school capacity can be a significant challenge. The reality is that K–12 schools cannot always absorb additional preservice teachers into their classrooms (Goddard, 2004). So, if teacher education programs want to boost field experiences for preservice teachers, they need to look beyond the school day and outside of the school compound to do so, which means using community-based field experiences (Hollins & Guzman, 2005) and service-learning field experiences to expand sites of practice. Not surprisingly, research on adopting service-learning in teacher education has found many of the same benefits (Bell, Horn, & Roxas, 2007; Billig & Freeman, 2010) as those identified in the research on field experiences with ELLs.

The notion of using or including service-learning as a field experience is gaining acceptance with accrediting bodies. In fact, "NCATE recently identified service learning as a characteristic of programs at the highest level of proficiency in terms of the design, implementation, and evaluation of field experiences and clinical practice" (Kielsmeier, 2010, p. 12), which offers important opportunities to include service-learning field experiences. As outlined in a study conducted by Anderson and Erickson (2003), the most frequently cited reason for the use of service-learning is to expose teacher candidates to the "communities in which they would serve" (p. 114). This exposure has various benefits including allowing teacher candidates to "examine their own cultural assumptions to understand how these shape their starting points for practice" (Banks et al., 2005, p. 243). However, there are often structural constraints, as noted by Erickson and Anderson (1997), who found that one reason cited by teacher educators for why they did not include service-learning in their curriculum is that "[t]here is no room in our program for anything else. If we added service-learning, what would we take out?" (p. 5). This either/or paradigm demonstrates that some teacher educators do not understand the particular benefits of service-learning, including preparing culturally and linguistically responsive teachers.

Research on service-learning, in fact, reveals that there are many multicultural benefits for teacher candidates, including an increased understanding of multiculturalism (Boyle-Baise, 2005) and improvements in cultural competency (Miller & Gonzalez, 2010). By asking teacher candidates to examine assumptions they hold about students from diverse backgrounds (Conner, 2010), multicultural service-learning can "increase the awareness of negative stereotypes, cultural diversity, and social inequality for some preservice teachers in some contexts" (Chang, Anagnostopoulos, & Omae, 2011, p. 1088). Expanding field experience opportunities through a service-learning perspective can also offer opportunities for interactions with ELLs (Tilley-Lubbs, 2011). Hale (2008) found that a service-learning experience with Latino students challenged the stereotypes that preservice teachers held and increased confidence in their ability to work with ELLs. Bollin (2007) also found that a service-learning tutoring experience with ELLs improved preservice teachers' confidence in their ability to work with ELLs. In addition, teacher candidates gained a better understanding of issues facing students and their families, which led to greater respect.

Because of this work, the field of teacher education is moving toward the idea of conceptualizing service-learning as a field experience, though the literature on service-learning as a field experience is sparse (Boyle-Baise & Kilbane, 2000; Couse & Chorzempa, 2005; LaMaster, 2001). There has been research conducted on community-based field experiences (Hollins & Guzman, 2005) that could be described as service-learning. Naidoo (2010) described a service-learning experience where teacher candidates tutored refugee students as a "community engaged practicum" (p. 49), and Coffey (2010) described a service-learning experience where teacher candidates worked with urban youth in a summer program as a "community-based field experience" (p. 335). In support of this work, the conceptual framework introduced in the next section provides a schematic of how to categorize and think about different field opportunities. This schema will further the understanding of service-learning as an important field experience for teacher candidates as service-learning offers an opportunity to advance practice grounded in the principles of culturally responsive pedagogy.

CONCEPTUAL FRAMEWORK FOR SERVICE-LEARNING FIELD EXPERIENCES

To provide an initial foundation for the framework introduced in this section, it is important to distinguish service-learning field experiences from other types of fieldwork, particularly since research conducted by Furco and Ammon (2000) with teacher educators in California found that participants were not clear about the characteristics of service-learning. In fact, teacher educators often confused it with other field experiences. Furco (2000) points out that with community service or volunteerism, the focus is primarily on the service being provided. With an internship or other kinds of field experiences, the focus is primarily on the learning of the participant. "Service-learning programs," Furco argues, "are distinguished from other approaches to experiential education by their intention to equally benefit the provider and the recipient of the service as well as to ensure equal focus on both the service being provided and the learning that is occurring" (p. 12). This balance between service and learning provides clear distinctions between traditional field experiences in teacher education and service-learning field opportunities.

Traditional Field Experiences

Figure 5.1 provides an overview of different types of traditional field experiences, which include early field experiences, study-abroad practica, and student teaching, which may also be called an internship or clinical practice. According to the literature (LaMaster, 2001), an early field experience is any field component completed before student teaching, which typically includes observing in classrooms, assisting students, and teaching small groups or the whole class. These experiences serve many purposes, but the focus tends to be on increasing the teacher candidate's knowledge of schools, teaching, and learners. Generally these field components occur within a traditional school setting. During these field experiences, "prospective teachers typically observe the cooperating teachers and assume increasingly higher levels of responsibility, from tutoring individual pupils to teaching small groups, and then to teaching whole-class lessons" (Anderson, Barksdale, & Hite, 2005, p. 97). The clear focus and emphasis is on the learning of the teacher candidate, though learning does not always occur,

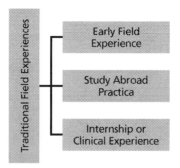

Figure 5.1 Overview of different types of traditional field experiences.

as noted by Ben-Peretz and Rumney (1991), because observational field experiences do not always help teacher candidates develop an understanding of how to teach. In fact, the mentor teacher's planning process and intentions behind instructional choices matter. If the field component does not support the teacher candidate in delving into the complexity of teaching, either through dialogue with the mentor teacher and/or dialogue with a professor and peers in a seminar, the candidate may come away from the experience with a fairly simplistic view of teaching. When writing about the practice of teacher preparation, Darling-Hammond and McLaughlin (1999) pointed out that "[n]ot only does teacher education matter, but more teacher education appears to be better than less—particularly when it includes carefully planned, extended *clinical experiences that are interwoven with course work* on learning and teaching" (p. 378, emphasis added).

Another type of field experience used in some teacher education programs are practica that are completed as part of a study abroad program. These practica can provide teacher candidates with valuable cross-cultural experiences (Clark & Flores, 1997), assist in developing a comparative education perspective (Pence & Macgillivray, 2008), and foster positive perspectives of cultural and linguistic diversity (Miller & Gonzalez, 2010). However, since the focus is again on the candidate's learning, the experience is still categorized as a traditional field experience.

The final traditional field experience is an internship or student teaching experience. Though some teacher candidates erroneously view their internship as service, the reality is that the balance between service and learning is heavily weighted toward learning. This misperception is not limited to teacher candidates as some teacher educators make a similar error. As Anderson and Erickson (2003) pointed out, some teacher educators "perceive the student teaching experience itself to be a form of service-learning" (p. 114). This points to the need for both teacher educators and teacher candidates to fully understand the distinctions between the two.

Though some teacher education programs overtly embed a service-learning component into student teaching, student teaching on its own would not typically be considered service-learning because the principal gain is to the teacher candidate.

Service-Learning Field Experiences

Figure 5.2 delineates different types of service-learning field experiences. According to Anderson (1998), service-learning experiences can be direct (providing service directly to individuals) or indirect (such as working behind the scenes to create or design something to be used by a service organization). However, for a service-learning experience to function as a field experience in a teacher education program, it must include direct service because it is through direct service that teacher candidates practice their developing skills as educators. In other words, it is through direct service that teacher candidates experience a learning environment where they work with individuals and reflect on how to mediate effective learning. This practice offers teacher candidates an opportunity to understand teaching and learning in the act of practice rather than in the contemplation of theory. It also allows for targeted experiences to enhance certain proficiencies. Not surprisingly, these learning experiences can happen in multiple settings.

School-based service-learning experiences generally happen during the school day, though they can also happen in after-school or summer

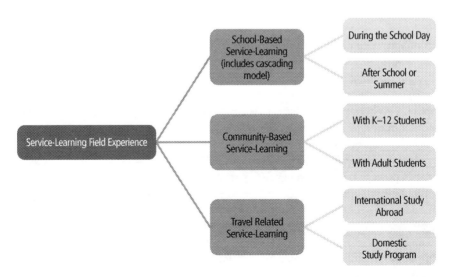

Figure 5.2 Different types of service-learning field experiences.

programs. At times they are stand-alone opportunities where teacher candidates go into schools with the expressed purpose of providing a service, such as tutoring. Sometimes teacher education programs combine a traditional field placement with a service-learning experience by having candidates complete a service activity for a portion of the time they are in the field. For example, candidates could observe in classrooms for part of the day before tutoring students one-on-one during support classes such as study halls. School-based service-learning experiences could also happen in after-school programs or summer programs; however, in order for the interaction to be considered a field experience, the service-learning requires direct service to K–12 students.

School-based service-learning experiences can also include the cascading model of service-learning. In the cascading model, teacher candidates work with K–12 teachers to design and carry out a service-learning experience with the K–12 teacher's students (Castellan, 2011), offering an opportunity for collaborative learning to happen around best practices for service-learning. In order for a cascading service-learning experience to meet the criteria for a field experience, it would require that teacher candidates work directly with K–12 students throughout the implementation of the service-learning project in order to have firsthand experience with student learning as students grapple with the service-learning process. A possible cascading service-learning project might include "doing research on a topic relevant to the elementary classroom curriculum and then involving the elementary students in preparing and implementing a lesson on that topic to a lower-level class" (Castellan, 2011, p. 4).

In addition to school-based service-learning, service-learning experiences can occur at community sites. Though teacher candidates often work with students in the age range they intend to teach, some teacher education programs include service-learning programs with adults (Anderson, 1998). Once again, the service-learning must include direct service with learners in order for the experience to be considered a field experience. In the next section of this essay, we provide a detailed description of a service-learning field experience that uses both K–12 and community-based sites.

The last category on our framework of service-learning field experiences is travel-related service-learning. In addition to international study abroad (Miller & Gonzalez, 2010), domestic study service-learning programs can happen at a location designed to provide a cross-cultural experience for teacher candidates (Stachowski & Mahan, 1998). In both cases, teacher candidates travel to new environments to grapple with cross-cultural experiences. If these cross-cultural experiences include providing direct service to learners (whether K–12 students or adults), these interactions can add to the field experience continuum in a teacher education program. Careful consideration should be given to the service side of the equation since a valid service-learning experience necessitates a careful balance of service and learning.

Conceptualizing an Array of Experiences

This conceptual framework does not argue for the exclusion of traditional field experiences and student teaching; rather, this framework seeks to expand field opportunities through service-learning to meet specific program purposes. Traditional field experiences provide learning opportunities that are integral to the development of teaching skills. This includes teaching lessons to a full class of learners and understanding how to manage the learning environment in a way that attends to the needs of all learners. Since service-learning field experiences tend to occur with individuals, it is less likely that teacher candidates will have the opportunity to manage a class through a service-learning field component. In addition, it is integral that teacher candidates understand all of the facets of a teacher's job including all the associated meetings and interactions that happen outside the classroom setting. It is only through a full-time student teaching experience that teacher candidates are fully prepared to teach.

However, service-learning provides the possibility to expand the array of field experiences to meet specific needs. One need is determining how to increase the total number of hours of field experiences without unduly burdening local schools. Though increasing clinical experiences can benefit teacher candidates (Association of Teacher Educators [ATE], 1999), schools only have limited capacity. Advancing external opportunities releases the pressure on schools while reinforcing the importance of education within the broader community. In fact, by going out into the community, teacher candidates have the potential to create and sustain change. This recognition of their ability to become change agents can be an important component to developing self-efficacy as emerging teachers (Lane, Lacefield-Parachini, & Isken, 2003). Moreover, interactions with learners offer teacher candidates an opportunity to more fully understand the individuality of learners and how to teach and reteach until a learner understands (Tinkler, hannah, & Miller, 2011).

As mentioned earlier, an additional opportunity provided by service-learning field experiences is the possibility to target experiences with particular populations of students, specifically English language learners. In many traditional field placements, teacher candidates may spend time in classrooms with a few ELLs. Though having the experience of planning a lesson for a full class while attending to the needs of ELLs can be valuable, teacher candidates must first understand the unique needs of ELLs. Though good teaching that reaches a variety of learners can support ELLs, good teaching alone is not enough (de Jong & Harper, 2005). Teacher candidates need to develop an understanding of the language acquisition process and how language acquisition can vary based on a variety of factors such as first language literacy development and exposure to English in academic and nonacademic settings. Teacher candidates need to learn the challenges specific language groups face when learning English so that they can plan ahead for these challenges. Finally, teacher candidates benefit from working one-on-one with individual ELL students. It is by way of such work that teacher candidates begin to understand how much of presumed prior knowledge is based on their own cultural background and understanding of U.S. schools.

USING SERVICE-LEARNING TO PROVIDE EXPERIENCES WITH ELLS

In the Reading and Writing in the Content Area course mentioned earlier in this chapter, teacher candidates tutor students at community sites as well as during after-school tutoring programs. In each placement, there is a concentration of ELLs seeking tutoring support, so teacher candidates have consistent opportunities to interact students at each of the four sites. In fact, the service-learning experience is structured intentionally to enhance the constancy of the interactions. One way this happens is by having teacher candidates make a weekly commitment to the site over the course of a semester (rather than an hourly commitment that allows students to bundle their hours). Because teacher candidates arrive the same time each week, community youth become familiar with the teacher candidates' schedules, offering opportunities for teacher candidates and community youth to develop relationships. Because this service-learning structure works to the benefit of community youth, it is not surprising that both the community centers and the after-school academic support programs welcome teacher candidates.

Since most of the community youth are English language learners, these service-learning experiences offer candidates the opportunity to work one-on-one with ELLs to more fully understand the strengths and challenges students face as they learn academic content while learning a new language. This is a complex process, and by working one-on-one with ELLs teacher candidates gain an appreciation of the assets community youth bring to the learning opportunity. Teacher candidates and community youth learn together the instructional strategies that work best for individual students. There is also, of course, the benefit of developing cultural and individual connections, as such connections "have often led to increased achievement" (Banks et al., 2005, p. 244). Though it should come as no surprise, it is worth noting that teacher candidates work more effectively with refugee and immigrant students once they learn more about their backgrounds (Hones, 2002). Making this intentional during the service-learning and the accompanying reflection activities is important to allow teacher candidates to reflect on the experience and the complexity of their developing pedagogical skills.

In addition to examining instructional practices, working one-on-one offers teacher candidates an opportunity to consider the importance of individual assessment practices because formative assessment is an integral piece of the process, and such assessment needs to be responsive to individual experiences and cultural knowledge (Shepard et al., 2005). This individualized assessment is at the core of developing effective literacy strategies since strategies work by augmenting and enhancing students' strengths. By placing teacher candidates at sites where they are participating in a real-world learning experience, students are able to test and reflect on the efficacy of various practices with youth. This attention to individualized formative assessment also allows teacher candidates to test their assumptions and dispositions. In other words, careful formative assessment allows teacher candidates to become more efficacious as their practice develops.

Reflection also allows individual teacher candidates to learn more about themselves, which is important because "[a]ctivities or experiences that place students face to face with their entering beliefs and assumptions both about themselves and others, and about learning, schooling, and intelligence, are essential as novice teachers prepare to teach students who are often different from themselves" (Banks et al., 2005, p. 266). Because the interactions are in a new setting (rather than during a typical school placement), the novelty provides teacher candidates an opportunity to engage in reflection that allows them to develop a strengths-based approach to developing academic literacies. There is a unique opportunity to share individual stories and life histories because the experience is one-on-one. The sharing is dialogic, offering teacher candidates a chance to share their stories as well. In other words, through dialogue (and the development of relationships), all parties enjoy an opportunity to examine assumptions and beliefs. It should be noted that in the Reading and Writing in the Content Area course, time is spent on the importance of narrative, so teacher candidates construct a literacy autobiography that affords them a chance to examine their own literacy experiences. This autobiography allows teacher candidates to recognize their literacy strengths. Since the literacy autobiography asks teacher candidates to incorporate the current semester as well, it also offers the candidates an opportunity to reflect on the literacy strengths of community youth.

This commitment to a strengths-based approach is in line with the approach advocated for by the World-Class Instructional Design and Assessment (WIDA) Consortium. Demonstrating a core commitment to a strengths-based approach (2010), WIDA has developed performance definitions that identify what English language learners are able to do by way of their CAN DO sequence: entering, beginning, developing, expanding, bridging, and reaching. For example, an ELL student who is at the developing level in reading should be able to "Differentiate between fact and opinion in text." This strengths-based sequence of standards and principles is used within each content area across the curriculum, which allows teachers to share a common understanding around literacy. This commitment to literacy across the content areas is also at the core of the Reading and Writing in the Content Area course that includes secondary students from all content areas. By recognizing that academic literacy is not confined to the language arts classroom, all teacher candidates gain an appreciation for their role in the process of developing academic literacy across all content areas. As part of the reflection process, in fact, time is spent reflecting on such cross-content learning because learning in the real world is rarely limited to one content area.

Learning is also never limited to one location. Not only do teacher candidates experience students outside the traditional classroom because there are four sites, teacher candidates can share experiences with teacher candidates at the same site and across the sites. This dialogue structure offers teacher candidates an opportunity to think about and develop an understanding of the community-wide context for enhancing the academic literacies of ELLs. To put this differently, teacher candidates begin to gain an appreciation for the community-wide systems that are (or are not) in place to support students, and they begin to recognize their responsibilities as emerging teachers. After all, it is important for the field of teacher education to "build collegiality within the profession and create a set of relations rooted in shared intentions and challenges" (Ball & Cohen, 1999, p. 13).

This community-wide approach is also useful given that learning in the 21st century is no longer limited to the traditional content-area classroom. As such, the traditional practicum placements do not offer the necessary insights into 21st century learning experiences because students in such placements only witness school supports, and in such structures, there are limited opportunities for engagement with the broader community. After-school programs can provide a sort of middle space between schools and community and there is the potential for teacher candidates to interact with parents. However, candidates who work with community organizations gain a view into learning opportunities across the community, and they develop an understanding of how schools are situated in the community. Since parents are often visible at community centers, candidates have the additional opportunity to engage with adult ELLs to develop an understanding of the sociocultural context of ELLs in the community. Teacher candidates begin to develop culturally responsive teaching practices through such experiences.

By moving through the community and identifying community-based service-learning opportunities, the service-learning practicum serves to expand social capital. This expansion comes from the forming of links that are being established between and among community youth, parents, schools, the teacher education program, and others in the community. These connections provide a real strength to the community. As such, the community's social capital is increased. This growth in capital continues even after the semester is complete because a number of teacher candidates continue their service in the community even after the semester ends. For those students who do not continue, they have entered the community-wide conversation around literacy, which means that they are positioned to advance opportunities for community youth and their families. This commitment to a collective strategy is designed "to transform those conditions in public schools which are alienating particular groups of learners, in this case, refugee learners" (Naidoo, 2010, p. 54). With this community-wide commitment to engagement, it is easier for the community to be advocates for change. For the teacher candidates, understanding the important community intersections also helps to prepare them for their work as teachers in the rapidly changing global environment of the 21st century. As mentioned earlier, NCATE recognizes this imperative, witnessed by their acknowledgment of service-learning as a valued practice. We have to move beyond the traditions of the past to realize the opportunities available to us in the present to inform our future.

QUESTIONS FOR RESEARCH

When considering a shift to service-learning field experiences, there are important questions that provide opportunities for research around service-learning as a field experience. The first question relates to developing competencies for working with ELLs. Though there is research that demonstrates that having one-on-one interactions with ELLs can improve teacher candidates' knowledge and skills (Xu, 2000), it is important to examine whether these improved skills translate into better teaching when ELLs are integrated into the regular classroom. We are exploring research to examine this transition as candidates move into student teaching.

Another important question relates to the difference between school-based and community-based service-learning experiences. Research by Bell et al. (2007) compared outcomes of students completing different types of service-learning experiences. Some teacher candidates tutored students at a school site, while some mentored youth and that mentoring happened in multiple contexts including in the community. The authors rated the students at the beginning of the semester using a framework that looks at developmental levels in relation to diversity. Both groups demonstrated similar developmental levels at the beginning of the semester. However, at the end of the semester, those who mentored showed more growth on the developmental continuum. The authors state, "we believe that the opportunities to learn in the mentoring service learning—seeing students in multiple contexts, doing activities with non-traditional power dynamics, and connecting ideas to teaching and learning—facilitated the development of more complex understandings of diversity" (p. 130). We are exploring research to determine what the differences are in learning gains between candidates placed at school sites for service-learning versus candidates placed at community sites. Understanding learning distinctions between different sites will allow us to make placement decisions based on programmatic goals.

IMPLICATIONS

A recent article by Zeichner (2010) points to the need for a closer connection between campus-based teacher education courses and field experiences. Because service-learning is based on the premise that the service experience is tied directly and intimately to course learning goals, adopting service-learning opportunities as field experiences can support this connection. In addition, using service-learning field experiences offers a release valve for school-based field placements as teacher education programs seek to expand field opportunities.

Service-learning field experiences can provide valuable cross-cultural experiences since underserved populations are often concentrated at community service sites. The advantage to these kinds of experiences is that "pre-service teachers see functioning communities and everyday cultural patterns first-hand, form relationships with people, confront stereotypes, and hear stories of lives that reflect abstractions they may have read about in textbooks" (Sleeter, 2008, p. 564). Through these experiences, teacher candidates can also begin to realize that teaching ELLs requires a specialized skill set. In particular, teachers candidates need to understand the "process of learning a second language, the role of language and culture as a medium in teaching and learning, and the need to set explicit linguistic and cultural goals" (de Jong & Harper, 2005, p. 118). When teacher candidates recognize that there is a specialized skill set, they understand that teaching strategies that are effective for other students are not necessarily effective for ELLs, and they need to modify their instruction to truly support all learners.

The importance of developing cultural competency is clear, as noted by Banks et al. (2005): "To build a culturally responsive practice, teachers need to have a broad set of teaching strategies for working with diverse children" (p. 243). Those strategies should offer opportunities to work with students on a one-on-one basis since it is by way of such individualized attention that teachers and students are able to conceptualize how to develop individualized learning plans. This opportunity is particularly important since "[i]n the real world, teachers rarely have time for one-on-one tutoring sessions or dynamic assessment that would allow them to pursue scaffolded instruction with one student" (Shepard et al., 2005, p. 279). By providing opportunities for teacher candidates to interact with students one-on-one, they may develop a more thorough understanding of the individuality of learners and their needs.

REFERENCES

American Association of Colleges for Teacher Education (AACTE), Committee on Multicultural Education. (2002). *Educators' preparation for cultural and linguistic diversity: A call to action.* Washington, DC: Author. Available at *www.aacte. org/Programs/Multicultural/culturallinguistic.pdf.*

Anderson, J. (1998). *Service-learning and teacher education.* Washington, DC: ERIC Clearinghouse on Teaching and Teacher Education. (ERIC Document No. 421481)

Anderson, J.B., & Erickson, J.A. (2003). Service-learning in preservice teacher education. *Academic Exchange Quarterly, 7*(2), 111–115.

Anderson, N.A., Barksdale, M.A., & Hite, C.E. (2005). Preservice teachers' observations of cooperating teachers and peers while participating in an early field experience. *Teacher Education Quarterly, 32*(4), 97–117.

Arias, B., & Poyner, L. (2001). A good start: A progressive, transactional approach to diversity in pre-service teacher education. *Bilingual Research Journal, 25*(4), 417–434.

Association of Teacher Educators (ATE), Task Force on Field Experience Standards. (1999). *Standards for field experiences in teacher education.* Manassas, VA: Author. Available at www.ate1.org/pubs/uploads/FieldExpStandards.pdf

Ball, D., & Cohen, D. (1999). Developing practice, developing practitioners: Toward a practice-based theory of professional education. In L. Darling-Hammond & G. Sykes (Eds.). *Teaching as the learning profession: Handbook of policy and practice.* (pp. 3–32). San Francisco: Jossey-Bass.

Banks, J., Cochran-Smith, M., Moll, L., Richert, A., Zeichner, K., LePage, P., et al. (2005). Teaching Diverse Learners. In L. Darling-Hammond & J. Bransford (Eds.). *Preparing teachers for a changing world: What teachers should learn and be able to do.* (pp. 232–274). San Francisco: Jossey-Bass.

Bell, C., Horn, B., & Roxas, K. (2007). We know it's service, but what are they learning? Preservice teachers' understandings of diversity. *Equity and Excellence in Education, 40*(2), 123–133.

Ben-Peretz, M., & Rumney, S. (1991). Professional thinking in guided practice. *Teaching and Teacher Education, 7*(5–6), 517–530.

Billig, S., & Freeman, F. (2010). *Teacher education and service-learning.* Denver: RMC Research Corporation.

Bollin, G. G. (2007). Preparing teachers for Hispanic immigrant children: A service-learning approach. *Journals of Latinos and Education, 6*(2), 177–189.

Boyle-Baise, M. (2005). Preparing community-oriented teachers: Reflections from a multicultural service learning project. *Journal of Teacher Education, 56*(5), 446–458.

Boyle-Baise, M., & Kilbane, J. (2000). What really happens? A look inside service-learning for multicultural teacher education. *Michigan Journal of Community Service Learning, 7*(1), 54–64.

Brach, E. (2012, June). *Summary project BRITE.* Presented at the final BRITE cohort meeting of the Education Alliance at Brown University.

Capraro, M. M., Capraro, R. M., & Helfeldt, J. (2010). Do differing types of field experiences make a difference in teacher candidates' perceived level of competence? *Teacher Education Quarterly, 37*(1), 131–154.

Castellan, C. M. (2011). Service-learning in teacher education: Does the model matter? *Journal of Research on Service Learning and Teacher Education, 1*(2), 1–19.

Chang, S., Anagnostopoulos, D., & Omae, H. (2011). The multidimensionality of multicultural service learning: The variable effects of social identity, context and pedagogy on pre-service teachers' learning. *Teacher and Teacher Education, 27*(7), 1078–1089.

Clark, C., & Medina, C. (2000). How reading and writing literacy narratives affect preservice teachers' understanding of literacy, pedagogy, and multiculturalism. *Journal of Teacher Education, 51*(1), 63–76.

Clark, E. R., & Flores, B. B. (1997). Instructional Snapshots (IS) in Mexico: Pre-service bilingual teachers take pictures of classroom practices. *Bilingual Research Journal, 21*(2–3), 273–282.

Coffey, H. (2010). "They taught me": The benefits of early community-based field experiences in teacher education. *Teaching and Teacher Education, 26*(2), 335–342.

Conner, J. O. (2010). Learning to unlearn: How a service-learning project can help teacher candidates to reframe urban students. *Teaching and Teacher Education, 26*(5), 1170–1177.

Couse, L.J., & Chorzempa, B. (2005). Service learning: Field experience for advanced early childhood degree candidates. *Journal of Early Childhood Teacher Education, 26*(1), 47–58.

Darling-Hammond, L. & McLaughlin, M. (1999). Investing in teaching as a learning profession: Policy, problems, and prospects. In L. Darling-Hammond & G. Sykes (Eds.), *Teaching as the learning profession: Handbook of policy and practice* (pp. 376–412). San Francisco: Jossey-Bass.

de Jong, E., & Harper, C. (2005). Preparing mainstream teachers for English language learners: Is being a good teacher good enough? *Teacher Education Quarterly, 32*(2), 101–124.

Erickson, J.A., & Anderson, J.B. (Eds.). (1997). *Learning with the community: Concepts and models for service-learning in teacher education.* Sterling, VA: American Association for Higher Education, Stylus Publishing.

Furco, A. (2000). *Service-learning: A balanced approach to experiential education.* Washington, DC: Campus Compact.

Furco, A., & Ammon, M. S. (2000). *Service-learning in California's teacher education programs: A white paper.* Berkeley: University of California, Service-Learning Research and Development Center. Available at www.servicelearning.org/library/resource/5151

Goddard, C. (2004). The field placement dilemma. *Education Week, 23,* 49–52.

Hale, A. (2008). Service learning with Latino communities: Effects on preservice teachers. *Journal of Hispanic Higher Education, 7*(1), 54–69.

Hollins, E.R., & Guzman, M.T. (2005). Research on preparing teachers for diverse populations. In M. Cochran-Smith & K.M. Zeichner (Eds.). *Studying teacher education: The report of the AERA panel on research and teacher education.* (pp. 477–548). Mahwah, NJ: Erlbaum.

Hones, D.F. (2002). *American dreams, global visions: Dialogic teacher research with refugee and immigrant families.* Mahwah, NJ: Erlbaum.

Kielsmeier, J.C. (2010). Building a bridge between service and learning. *Phi Delta Kappan, 91*(5), 8–15.

LaMaster, K. (2001). Enhancing preservice teachers' field experiences through the addition of a service-learning component. *Journal of Experiential Education, 24*(1), 27–33.

Lane, S., Lacefield-Parachini, N., & Isken, J. (2003). Developing novice teachers as change agents: Student teacher placements "against the grain." *Teacher Education Quarterly, 30*(2), 55–68.

Miller, K., & Gonzalez, A. (2010). Domestic and international service learning experiences: A comparative study of pre-service teacher outcomes. *Issues in Educational Research, 20*(1), 29–38.

Mora, J. K., & Grisham, D. L. (2001). ¡What deliches tortillas!: Preparing teachers for literacy instruction in linguistically diverse classrooms. *Teacher Education Quarterly, 28*(4), 51–70.

Naidoo, L. (2010). Engaging the refugee community of greater western Sydney. *Issues in Educational Research, 20*(1), 47–56.

Nathenson-Mejía, S., & Escamilla, K. (2003). Connecting with Latino children: Bridging cultural gaps with children's literature. *Bilingual Research Journal, 27*(1), 101–116.

National Council for Accreditation of Teacher Education (NCATE), Blue Ribbon Panel on Clinical Preparation and Partnerships for Improved Student Learning. (2010). *Transforming teacher education through clinical practice: A national strategy to prepare effective teachers.* Washington, DC: Author. Available at www.ncate.org/LinkClick.aspx?fileticket=zzeiB1OoqPk%3D&tabid=715

Pence, H. M., & Macgillivray, I. M. (2008). The impact of an international field experience on pre-service teachers. *Teaching and Teacher Education, 24*(1), 14–25.

Shepard, S., Hammerness, K., Darling-Hammond, L., Rust, F., Snowden, J.B., Gordon, E.,...Pacheco, A. (2005). Assessment. In L. Darling-Hammond & J. Bransford (Eds.). *Preparing teachers for a changing world: What teachers should learn and be able to do.* (pp. 275–326). San Francisco: Jossey-Bass.

Sleeter, C. E. (2008). Preparing White teachers for diverse students. In M. Cochran-Smith, S. Feiman-Nemser, & J. McIntyre (Eds.). *Handbook of research in teacher education: Enduring issues in changing contexts* (3rd ed., pp. 559–582). New York: Routledge.

Stachowski, L. L., & Mahan, J. M. (1998). Cross-cultural field placements: Student teachers learning from schools and communities. *Theory into Practice, 37*(2), 155–162.

Tilley-Lubbs, G.A. (2011). Preparing teachers for teaching immigrant students through service-learning in immigrant communities. *World Journal of Education, 1*(2), 104–114.

Tinkler, B., hannah, c.l, & Miller, E. (2011). *Using a social justice service-learning field experience to strengthen the argument for social foundations coursework.* Paper presented at the annual meeting of the American Educational Research Association, New Orleans, LA.

World-Class Instructional Design and Assessment (WIDA) Consortium. (2010). *The WIDA CAN DO philosophy.* Madison, WI: WIDA. Available at www.wida.us/aboutUs/AcademicLanguage/index.aspx

Xu, H. (2000). Pre-service teachers in a literacy methods course consider issues of diversity. *Journal of Literacy Research, 32*(4), 505–531.

Zeichner, K. (2010). Rethinking the connections between campus courses and field experiences in college- and university-based teacher education. *Journal of Teacher Education, 89*(1–2), 89–99.

Alan S. Tinkler is an Assistant Professor in the Department of Education at the University of Vermont. In addition to his research on service-learning, he writes fiction.

Barri Tinkler is an Assistant Professor in the Department of Education at the University of Vermont. Her research interests focus on service-learning in teacher education with an emphasis on social justice.

PART III

PRESERVICE TEACHERS LEARN THROUGH TUTORING

Joseph A. Erickson

INTRODUCTION

When integrating service-learning, teacher preparation professionals have an array of choices from which to choose. But how will I know which approach is right for my students and their unique needs? This section examines several models of service-learning that have shown promise in diverse situations across the United States.

Another major quandary for service-learning practioners is how to document and evaluate their work. Using Stufflebeam's Context, Input, Process, Product (CIPP) model (2003), the authors of Chapter 9 make a compelling case for the use of CIPP to more holistically evaluate our work.

LEARNING ABOUT SERVICE-LEARNING THROUGH TUTORING

One very popular choice for service-learning integration in the initial stages of a teacher preparation sequence is to employ service-learning as a teaching technique in our courses. The rationale has been that in order to prepare teacher candidates to teach using service-learning, they first have

Transforming Teacher Education Through Service-Learning, pages 119–122
Copyright © 2013 by Information Age Publishing
119

to experience it as *service-learners*. Many teacher preparation programs use tutoring experiences for this task. This choice is an obvious one as most teacher licensure programs feature tutoring experiences as part of their licensure sequence. The important distinction is that the standard fieldwork tutoring experience is not in and of itself service-learning but tutoring experiences have been successfully adapted so that they exhibit the principles of good practice proposed by Anderson and Hill (2001) for integrating service-learning into preservice teacher education. By intentionally specifying various aspects of their tutoring experiences, teacher candidates' tutoring experiences become much more than merely volunteering in a P–12 classroom. They can become authentic service-learning experiences.

DIVERSE MODELS TO CONSIDER

In this section of our book, we have the opportunity to review three exemplary models of service-learning integration using tutoring.

Middle school model. The first approach involves the use of service-learning in a middle-level setting. Middle schools pose unique challenges to educators in general, and teacher candidates in particular. The needs and expectations for middle schools are distinct from those for older and younger children, and yet despite the hurdles candidates face in learning how to provide exemplary middle-level learning experiences, Ruppert and colleagues lay out a model service-learning experience tailored to the unique needs of middle schoolers.

The authors find that high-quality middle-level education can be combined with rigorous service-learning, but programs attempting to do so need to be aware of unique impediments found in the middle-level setting. Those roadblocks include the difficulty in finding placements in schools that exhibit *all* of the components of a high-quality middle school. The researchers also discovered that teacher candidates found out-of-classroom activities such as advisory and after-school programming to be the most helpful and satisfying.

Models for diverse populations. American schools also face increasing diversity and a recognition that "one-size-fits-all" education does not match the needs of many children in our schools. This caveat also applies to service-learning. Our next two chapters investigate approaches to the use of service-learning with Latino/a teacher candidates (Bussert-Webb) and African American candidates (Barber et al.).

Bussert-Webb looks closely at the experiences of Latino/a teacher candidates working in a South Texas colonia, an unincorporated settlement. Even though the ethnicity of the teacher candidates apparently mirrored that of the colonia residents, the authors found that social justice perspectives were often complex and didn't easily translate from classrooms to personal consciousness.

Barber and colleagues approached service-learning with African American teacher candidates through a teacher leadership lens. Their work reveals some promising approaches that challenge more passive approaches to teacher preparation.

An evaluation model worthy of consideration. Many evaluators have struggled to capture the multifaceted and complex nature of the relation between service-learners, institution structures, community expectation, and so on. In the final chapter of this section, Zhang and colleagues demonstrate the use of Shufflebeam's (2003) CIPP approach and attempt to model this well-documented standard for exemplary evaluation as a tack well suited for service-learning practioners who seek to understand the often difficult challenge of capturing all of the complexity of service-learning.

OVERCOMING CHALLENGES TO SUCCESSFUL SERVICE-LEARNING INTEGRATION

Service-learning integration into teacher preparation continues to be difficult under the best of circumstances. With the increased pressure of high-stakes testing (both of our teacher candidates and the students with whom they will work), sometimes it appears that service-learning gets pushed even further into the margins. More than ever, we need clear models that demonstrate success for candidate preparation and P–12 student success. We hope you find these models and approaches to help with this important task.

REFERENCES

Anderson, J., & Hill, D. (2001). Principles of good practice for service-learning in preservice teacher education. In *Service-learning in teacher education: Enhancing the growth of new teachers, their students, and communities* (pp. 69–84). Washington, DC: AACTE.

Stufflebeam, D. L. (2003). The CIPP model for evaluation. In D. L. Stufflebeam & T. Kellaghan (Eds.), *The international handbook of educational evaluation.* Boston: Kluwer Academic.

CHAPTER 6

IMPACT OF SERVICE-LEARNING IN AN UNDERGRADUATE MIDDLE SCHOOL PRINCIPLES AND PRACTICES CLASS

Nancy Ruppert

ABSTRACT

In the spring of 2012, preservice teachers participated in over 50 hours of service-learning experiences in three separate schools to engage in middle school concepts. While middle schools in our area had individual expertise, there was no middle school that contained all elements of middle school curriculum. Thus, three schools were used. Each middle school had a specific expertise (advisory, after-school enrichment, and integrated teaching) that allowed candidates to work directly with middle school students in authentic settings. Throughout the experience candidates reflected on the knowledge, skills, and dispositions gained. Results suggest that using multiple sites provides candidates with insight into the different ways young adolescents respond to activities in advisory, after-school enrichment, and classroom settings, and include candidates' perceptions of what it takes to teach young adolescents and be a middle school teacher.

Transforming Teacher Education Through Service-Learning, pages 123–144
Copyright © 2013 by Information Age Publishing
All rights of reproduction in any form reserved.

PURPOSE

Research on preparing middle school teachers recommends using authentic middle school settings and using multiple avenues for teaching candidates how to work with young adolescents (AMLE, 2006). But what happens when middle schools in our local areas do not have all the components of middle school curriculum? Is it possible to use multiple service-learning experiences to address different aspects of middle school or is it too time-consuming to create such experiences? In other words what is the value of multiple service-learning experiences for candidates?

This study addresses how one university used multiple service-learning experiences to prepare middle level teacher candidates' knowledge skills and dispositions. In the district where this study took place, three different schools were used to teach middle level candidates about specific middle school curriculum. By diversifying field experiences candidates were engaged in the strengths of each school, and came away with a deeper understanding of content, advisory, and enrichment as well as what it takes to be a middle school teacher. This study includes candidates' perceptions of three service-learning experiences (after-school enrichment, advisory, and content teaching) in three different schools, identifying the impact each had on knowledge, skills, and dispositions associated with effective middle school teaching.

This study is unique in that we did not have a middle school in the area that addressed all aspects of exemplary middle schools. However, we had individual middle schools in our area that were doing a good job addressing specific aspects (instruction, advisory, and enrichment). The result was to take the best elements offered by these schools and create experiences for preservice teachers to be involved in each of them.

Using authentic middle school settings, preservice teachers in an introduction to middle schools course engaged in 50 hours of service. Within each setting, candidates recorded knowledge, skills, and dispositions observed and gained. This study provides insight into the value of choosing specific service-learning experiences based on the strengths of the schools in your area on preservice teachers. Results provide evidence that multiple placements provide candidates with more depth and breadth of middle school concepts, how to address middle school students, and what it takes to be a middle school teacher.

REVIEW OF LITERATURE

This study addresses a combination of activities and reflections associated with using multiple service-learning experiences to develop candidates' understanding of middle-level students, instruction and classroom management skills, and dispositions needed to be an effective middle school teacher. This knowledge base is supported in literature on what makes effective middle schools.

Understanding and working with young adolescents are the heart of middle level education (George, 2008). A middle school focuses specifically on the social, emotional, and intellectual needs of young adolescents (Powell, 2010). Specific experiences associated with middle school success include "advisory," "interdisciplinary units," and "exploratories" (Alexander & George, 1982). However, middle schools do not always have these elements associated with exemplary middle school curriculum and organization (George, 2008). Therefore, in an attempt to provide candidates with knowledge of three elements of middle school curriculum (advisory, after-school enrichment, and content strategies) these service-learning experiences took place in three different schools.

Knowledge refers to knowledge of young adolescents and knowledge of middle school concepts. According to the Association of Middle Level Education, an essential attribute of a middle school is to have an adult advocate for every child (NMSA, 2010). Knowledge of young adolescents begins with the notion of finding ways to build relationships (Niska, in Dore 2011). In our course we focus on young adolescents as "becoming" (Powell, 2010). To that end our goal as educators is to teach candidates how to build relationships with students. This starts with an understanding of learners and an opportunity to participate with them (Donahue, Bowyer, & Rosenberg, 2003). We address knowledge in three settings: a school that participated in an advisory program, a school that included an after-school enrichment program, and a school whose teachers worked to find ways to meet the needs of young adolescents in content-area classes.

An advisory program is a middle school program that involves teachers creating experiences for young adolescents that teach them social and emotional skills (Powell, 2010). Candidates participated in an advisory experience to observe and participate with teachers who provided insight into ways to build relationships with and among children. Research supports the use of advisory as a time in the day that is devoted for helping students develop their interpersonal skills and their self-concepts (Niska, in Dore, 2011).

A second service-learning experience took place in an after-school enrichment program designed to provide young adolescents with opportunities to develop self-concepts, goal setting, academic performance and health and wellness (Harvard Family Research Project, 2012). In this setting, candidates worked with a diverse group of students and service providers. Bell, Horn, and Roxas (2007) examined preservice teachers' responses and found that candidates developed a deeper understanding of diversity when they participate in service-learning. According to Akos (2006), students who participate in enrichment indicate a sense of belonging and are more likely to experience academic success.

A third experience involved candidates working directly with teachers in their content area of interest to explore ways to engage young adolescents in learning content. Developing authentic activities that meet the interests and needs of young adolescents is a strategy for teaching content (Powell, 2010). Mahoney and Carnes (1997) report that students who engage in activities they are interested in are less likely to get into trouble and more likely to stay in school.

In each of the settings the focus was to help young adolescents find a place to belong and experience caring adults. For each experience candidates identified specific knowledge, skills, and dispositions they developed.

Knowledge

This study focused on knowledge of young adolescents and three middle school concepts: advisory, exploratories, and instructional strategies. Clark and Clark (2007) report the importance of implementing all elements associated with the middle school concept. McKewin and Greene (2010) and George (2008) identify the current status of middle school in the United States and Florida, respectively. In describing exemplary middle schools they found that not all schools had advisory, teaming, and after-school enrichment. Knowledge of middle school concepts and exemplary practices are described by the National Forum for the Acceleration of Middle Grades Reform (2013). Schools that are designated as "exemplary" identify ways they address the following criteria: academic excellence, developmental responsiveness, social equity, and organizational structures (*SchoolsToWatch. org* [STW], 2012). While these schools provide a rich environment for preservice teachers, not all districts contain STW middle schools. Thus, providing candidates with service-learning experiences must happen in multiple settings in order for them to gain the knowledge of young adolescents and exemplary practices.

INSTRUCTIONAL SKILLS

Candidates who participate in service-learning experiences develop their skills associated with teaching and managing students (Brown & Howard, 2005; Carrington & Saggers, 2008; Chen, 2004; Lu, 2010). We know that children who participate in multiple activities after school are more successful students. Skills in this study refer to instructional tools and classroom management strategies. *This We Believe* identifies exemplary teachers in terms of their abilities to create challenging, integrated, and relevant lessons (NMSA, 2010). Stevenson (1992), Tomlinson (1999), and Marzano, Pickering, and Pollock (2001) provide middle school preservice teachers with tools and strategies that relate instructional strategies to the needs and interests of students. Tang (2004) indicates "The strength of the teaching self, the richness of the teaching repertoire and the appropriate mix of challenge and support are important variables that constitute student teachers' productive learning experiences" (p. 201). Lee, Smith, Perry, and Smylie (1999) conducted research in Chicago middle schools and found that those that focused on student needs and academic achievement had increased test scores from those that focused on one or the other. While preservice teachers participated in multiple service-learning experiences, for each they were asked to identify classroom management and instructional strategies they experienced that met the needs of their students.

Professional Dispositions

A third focus of this study was to identify the professional dispositions needed to work with young adolescents. Lounsbury (1991) shares that teaching is more than knowing our students and creating engaging lessons. He describes teaching in terms of how our attitudes toward students influence their performance. We know that service work is associated with candidates' development of purpose and insight into their own abilities (Bollin, 2007; Cone, 2009). Powell (2010) provides strategies and resources for meeting the professional standards as outlined by the Association of Middle Level Education on being a good role model, coach, and mentor. The National Council for the Accreditation of Teacher Education Middle Level Specialty Area standards describe professional dispositions as "Middle level teacher candidates understand the complexity of teaching young adolescents, and they engage in practices and behaviors that develop their competence as professionals" (2012, Standard 7).

Research supports the notion of university and school partnerships in preparing teachers. Service-learning experiences help candidates develop personal dispositions (Levesque-Bristol, Knapp, & Fisher, 2010) and a sense of civic responsibility (Miller & Gonzalez, 2009). Sandholtz and Dadlez (2000) found that candidates who work within a comprehensive experience gain more insight into the professional dispositions that were needed to work in a classroom. Sexton (2008) conducted a study on student teachers and found that their sense of identity as a teacher forms is based on the experiences they encounter. In her research she used multiple activities during student teaching to focus on candidates' development of ideas.

What the research does not share is the value of multiple experiences on candidates.

Our national standards, our current research, and our literature provide us with strategies and support for training middle school teachers. Service-learning when combined with reflections provides a place for candidates to observe and practice knowledge gained. The difficulty for some districts is that all schools may not have all the components of exemplary middle schools (McKewin & Greene, 2010). In an effort to provide candidates with a wide range of opportunities, this research examines how to use three separate service-learning experiences on candidates' knowledge, skills, and dispositions and to determine if there is a difference in what candidates' gain from each. Reflections were used during a semester to glean candidates' views of each of the experiences.

The Value of Reflection in Research

Milam (2007) describes the power and influence of reflections as they relate to cognitive development. Using research, literature, and the tool of reflection, this study provides insights into how to transform middle level candidates' knowledge, skills, and dispositions by engaging in multiple experiences associated with working with middle school students. This project seeks to look deeper at the value of three service-learning experiences on candidates using reflections and to determine the strengths of each. Several questions are being addressed in this research:

- Is it possible to create, implement, and evaluate multiple service-learning experiences for one class.
- Do the experiences impact knowledge, skills, and dispositions differently?

The Partnerships

There were three partnerships associated with this study. Students participated in an after-school enrichment program called "*In Real Life*" for 12 weeks, a charter school's advisory program for 4 weeks, and in a content-specific middle school classroom for 10 weeks. Candidates spent more than 40 hours total working alongside teachers and service providers to advocate for young adolescents.

In Real Life is an after-school enrichment program that takes place for 12 weeks during the spring semester. It is based on the Providence After School Activities (PASA) and is funded by a grant. Students sign up for activities that take place after school ranging from cooking to debate, to exercise, homework enrichment, science, and technology. The activities run Monday through Friday from 3:00 until 5:30. Candidates chose the day of the week and the activity they participated in.. They spent 2.5 hours a week in the program serving as an adult advocate, helping with management of children, and participating with the service provider to implement activities. The purpose of this project was to allow candidates to interact with students, work alongside another adult while implementing a program, and learn the behaviors of young adolescents.

A second service-learning experience involved candidates working directly with advisory teachers at a local charter school. During the month of February candidates spent 9 of the 12 class periods working in pairs with an advisory group. Advisory meets on Mondays, Wednesdays, and Fridays for 50 minutes at this charter school. In the month of February the schoolwide topic was "Hungry Bowls." In this setting, candidates were able to experience a service-learning project within an advisory setting. Preservice teachers spent three days a week with their advisory groups and participated in all the activities for a total of 12 hours.

A third field experience was included in this class as well. Candidates were placed with a classroom teacher one 90-minute class period a week for 12 weeks. Candidates were given the opportunity to teach several lessons. The purpose of this project was to help teachers help struggling learners once a week. They worked with individual students and taught mini-lessons three times during the semester.

METHODOLOGY

A case study design was used (Bogdan & Biklen, 1982). This case study analyzed student journal prompts and responses within a semester course. Candidates at a small liberal arts college participated in three specific service-learning experiences while taking an introductory middle school course. Candidates participated in an advisory program, an after-school enrichment program, and worked alongside a teacher in their content area. These three experiences, while they were intensive, provided candidates with insight into understanding and working with young adolescents, skills teachers use to manage and instruct students, and dispositions necessary for working with young adolescents.

Candidates engaged in multiple assignments related to the service-learning experiences. They were taught specific knowledge using current research and readings, lectures, and activities associated with young adolescents, advisory, and instructional strategies for working with young adolescents. They were trained by administrators from each of the service-learning settings to learn about the children involved, the strategies used, and worked specifically with an adult in each setting.

A narrative qualitative approach was used to gather students' reflections (Clandinin & Connelly, 2000). Data from 20 candidates were collected in the spring of 2012. Milam (2007) addresses the power of reflections in helping people gain knowledge and retain information. Candidates provided their views of knowledge, skills, and awareness of dispositions needed to be a middle school teacher weekly throughout the semester. In addition they engaged in monthly focus group discussions about what they were learning based on the experiences. Focus groups as a research tool is defined in Gibbs (1997).

According to Coffey (2011), candidates who participate in reflective practices and group processing of experiences gain much insight into the link between theory and practice. Studies that assess the impact of service-learning usually use surveys, journals, and questionnaires (Brown & Howard, 2005; Carrington & Saggers, 2008; Chen, 2004; Harkavy & Hartley, 2010; Kirtman, 2009; Miller & Gonzalez, 2009).

Candidates' knowledge, skills, and dispositions were analyzed to look for common themes including young adolescent development, middle level philosophy and school organization, middle level instruction, and middle level professional roles. These themes relate to what current research and literature identify as what preservice teachers need to be successful as middle school teachers (NCATE, 2012).

DATA COLLECTION

Narrative inquiry is a qualitative tool for gathering information about experiences (Clandinin & Connelly, 2000). Candidates in this setting worked in three different service-learning projects. Each week they were instructed to focus on each experience separately considering the knowledge, the skills, and the dispositions they were gaining from the experience. Throughout the semester they engaged in discussions, readings, and lectures on young adolescent development, components of exemplary middle schools, interdisciplinary instruction strategies, and working with families and community.

Knowledge was defined as what candidates observed about the characteristics of young adolescents and middle school concepts. Skills were defined as management techniques and instructional strategies candidates observed and/or experienced. Dispositions related to what candidates were learning about "what it takes to be a middle school teacher." As candidates reflected on the service-learning experiences, they were to address each of these elements and provide evidences based on observations and class experiences and readings.

At the midterm, candidates' reflections were collected and coded to look for patterns and themes in their narratives. Part of narrative inquiry involves engaging participants in the findings of the study. To that end, the results of the data were shared with the candidates allowing them to elaborate and/or dispute any of the findings that had been identified. At the end of the experience all data were separated by each service-learning experience.

A total of 205 comments were coded and provide evidence of candidates' knowledge of young adolescents, middle school concepts, classroom management, instructional tools, and dispositions associated with becoming a teacher.

Data Analysis

Candidates' reflections from each experience were examined to look for common themes. Bogdan and Biklen (2007) describe this method of looking for patterns and descriptions as a method of data analysis. The first set of coding took place at midterm.

Once responses were coded, candidates were asked to validate the findings. Comments from candidates describe findings and similarities. If a candidate's response mentioned "I was surprised at how small they were," the response was coded as "adolescent development." From the data two themes emerged relating to knowledge (adolescents and middle school concepts). Two themes emerged relating to skills (management, instruction).

After coding the responses, tally marks were set up in a table to identify the number of candidates who commented on each of the themes. Comments were separated according to knowledge, skills, and dispositions to see if there were differences among the responses to each of the projects. Finally, findings were summarized for each of the programs and at least one comment was included from the candidates to illustrate the summary.

Outcomes of the Work

Throughout the experiences candidates reflected on knowledge, skills, and dispositions gained. Knowledge refers to knowledge of young adolescents and middle school processes. Skills relate to instructional strategies and classroom management. Dispositions refer to what it takes to be a middle school teacher.

Responses were collected and coded according to common themes and patterns. Table 6.1 is a summary of the findings.

TABLE 6.1 Candidates' Knowledge, Skills, and Dispositions of Working with an Afterschool Enrichment Experience (IRL), Advisory, and Academic Content

Places and number of responses	Overall sets of data (N = 49)		IRL (N = 16)		Advisory (N = 16)		Academic content (N = 17)	
	% of total	% within	% of total	% within	% of total	% within	% of total	% within
Knowledge	40%		43%		43%		37%	
Adolescents		67%		81%		53%		58%
Content		17%		8%		7%		32%
Middle school concepts		16%		11%		40%		10%
Skills	36%		31%		31%		43%	
Management		46%		70%		36%		31%
Instructional strategies		54%		30%		64%		69%
Dispositions	23%		26%		2%		20%	
Total comments	205		86		35		84	

THEMES: KNOWLEDGE, SKILLS, AND DISPOSITIONS

Knowledge

When candidates reflected on their knowledge, three themes emerged: adolescents, content, and middle school concepts. Most often candidates were able to identify the social, emotional, intellectual, physical, and moral characteristics of young adolescents. The *In Real Life* and *Advisory* experience most often revealed candidates' observations of students' social and emotional development. The *content* experience reflections gave more information about students' intellectual development but also included social descriptions of young adolescents. The middle school concept mentioned most was knowledge about advisory. Advisory is a curriculum component of middle schools that provides students with an adult who advocates for them socially and emotionally. Candidates participated in lectures on advisory and activities that relate to middle school students' social and emotional development. Advisory is also time for team building and service. Candidates did not acknowledge other middle school organization or curricula such as exploratories, teaming, integration, or middle school philosophy even though these topics were part of the course. The following are comments related to knowledge candidates shared.

> We had an incident right at the beginning of our session. One of the girls wandered away during snack time. She seemed to have some kind of flirtation going on with two boys in another group, and followed that group to the door when they went to line up for the busses. When I got back to the cafeteria, she was there, and thought it was funny that I'd gone to look for her. I told her that next time she needed to make it clear to Melanie or me if she was going to leave the room for anything. She emphatically insisted that she had told me where she was going. After this, she was insolent and lacked interest in participation for the rest of our session. She's going to be a big challenge. I'm going to have to work really hard to avoid power struggles with her, because once you're in a power struggle, you've already lost. (IRL)

> Sixth graders are squirmy! They move around so much! This is an inclusion class, though, so they may be even squirmier than normal. In class, they are working on the differences between fact and opinion. I noticed a really interesting phenomenon with them. They can tell what a fact is, and what an opinion is. When they are asked to state their own facts, they do very well. When they are asked to state an opinion, however, they believe that any statement that starts with "I think..." counts as an opinion. I wonder how this happened? (Content)

> Today, the students were assigned a debate in which research was necessary for their topic. They will be debating on school uniforms and if, in fact, do they make a difference in behavior and academics. The students seemed ex-

cited about doing this project. We took them to a computer lab and assisted them in research. We have a group of smart kids. They could tell the difference between credible and unreliable references. I was blown away by how savvy they were with technology. It really put things into perspective for me. We are really bringing up a generation that is globally aware and ready to conquer the world. (IRL)

One of the kids in our group threw kind of a tantrum today. It started with her simply stating, "All of my teachers hate me." Ms. A asked her why. She launched into a tirade that began with her saying that she felt that she was labeled as a bad kid and that she got blamed when other students misbehaved. She said that some students even thought that they could act out and blame it on her. This progressed into her expressing her feelings that her friends had been unfairly punished for a bullying incident—at other schools, you were expected to defend yourself, and people threw footballs at her, too, and no one got punished for that. Ms. A interrupted to ask if she felt that she was being bullied. "No! They're just messing around! That's the point!" (Advisory)

Skills

A second theme relating to knowledge was specific instructional strategies related to content middle school teachers presented such as "box and whisker plots" and "students were giving reports on the Holocaust." There was only one comment about the difficulty of managing students in the advisory program. The theme of the service project in that experience was on hunger. One of the students shared knowledge from one of the presenters and the impact of guest speakers. In the *In Real Life* experience, one of the candidates shared insight into how to run debates.

Candidates' views of "skills" were coded. Two themes emerged: management and instructional strategies. In each of the settings candidates identified both themes. However, candidates observed and participated in more "management" experiences during the after-school enrichment program. The advisory focus on "Empty Bowls" as well as the fieldwork partnership allowed candidates to identify specific instructional strategies as well as management strategies. The following are comments related to skills.

Being social creatures, talking became an issue at times. Whenever the class became rowdy, she quickly brought attention back to her and she went over the assignment and the expected behaviors for the assignment. She also said whenever they became rowdy, "Eyes on me so that I know you are listening." The ones who did not look up at that moment, she gently called them out about it. Her students respected the learning environment that she had set up for them. (Content)

I feel like the behavioral skills that I developed in the first month are being implemented in the same way each time. I do believe that I have a lot to learn from Coach Williams. His discipline precedes him and has a calming effect on the students. The rest of my profession skill has been devoted to learning names faster. I feel like I've found the maximum development in this program already and this is why this has become a volunteering experience. I like to think that the kids are becoming better behaved from my interactions with them but there are so many people involved here, including five students from WWC, that I have no way of conducting valid action research. (IRL)

Today, the kids started out on the wrong foot. According to Mrs. Britt, at least. The way they entered the classroom today didn't strike me as particularly different from last week. Maybe I should take notes on how they enter each time and look for differences. Anyway, she made them all line up outside the classroom and start over. When they entered the room the second time, they were almost completely silent and very subdued. (Advisory)

Dispositions

The least responses had to do with candidates' dispositions. The majority of the comments related to the importance of showing compassion toward students and starting each day "fresh." The experience did provide candidates with either validation of their decision to be middle school teachers or gave them second thoughts on where their passions are. The following are comments related to dispositions:

I realized that I immediately made judgments against the student for bringing [it] into class, the type of judgment that might prevent him from improving academically if he was in my class. I think that I need to learn to tolerate this type of behavior for the sake of the student. I have to remember that students are capable of change for better or worse and that my actions have the potential to have a great effect or no effect at all and that there is very little I can do to change that if the student is unwilling to work toward a goal. (Content)

One thing that really became clear to me about ArtSpace was how dependent everyone is on each other. It was Ms. B's group's turn to clean up the common area after lunch this week, and if they hadn't done it, it wouldn't have been done. After delivering the food packs, we went outside for a "check-in" before tribes ended. It was interesting how much Ms. B knew about the girls, and how comfortable sharing with her they were. She knew about their boy problems, and about stuff going on at their homes. It was really cool. How does she foster that kind of relationship with the girls? I'll have to watch her closely to see what kinds of things she does. (Advisory)

I got a girl's name completely wrong for the first time today. I felt kind of silly but I apologized and she corrected me and it didn't seem to bother her. I'm glad that I get to make these small mistakes in a low-stakes environment. If I had made a few of these mistakes at once while trying to maintain a classroom and learn a new job and lifestyle in teaching it might have stressed me a bit more than it should have. I think that minimizing the stress of these small mistakes and understanding that students will forgive a large number of errors if you're honest helps a lot and might be the one of the highlights of this particular service-based learning program. (IRL)

CONCLUSIONS

Multiple studies suggest that service-learning is a very powerful tool for helping students understand the diverse needs of learners (Jenkins & Sheehey, 2009; and Novak, 2010). Brownell, Ross, Colon, and McCallum (2003) suggest that when experience such as service-learning is integrated into coursework and includes reflections, students view it as successful in identifying their own knowledge. Survey data of the impact on students learning reveal that students who participate in service-learning gain content knowledge (Kirtman, 2009; Kramarski and Michalsky, 2009). This study reveals the knowledge, skills, and dispositions candidates gained by working in specific service-learning settings.

Knowledge of Young Adolescents

In each of the settings candidates were able to identify characteristics of young adolescents. By participating in a classroom setting, an after-school enrichment setting, and an advisory setting, candidates were able to describe the different ways young adolescents interact with peers, adults, and experiences. In academic settings, candidates focused more on how young adolescents interact with intellectual challenges. "I worked with a student who was so shy and found that she was embarrassed that she did not know how to read the material" (Content).

Knowledge of Middle School Concepts

Candidates were able to identify the value of advisory and how this experience relates to students' interests in participating in service-learning experiences. They were able to articulate the value of integrating content based on the experiences in the teaching segment of the class. And they were able to articulate the importance of finding ways to allow students to participate in enrichment experiences.

Skills

Candidates realized that working with middle school students can be challenging and the best way to work with students individually. Brown and Howard (2005), Carrington and Saggers (2008), Chen (2004), and Lu (2010) studied the importance of using service-learning to enhance skills of management and instruction. Candidates in this study realize that building relationships takes time and that considering structures as well as the individual needs of students allow for teachers to build a community that is based on high expectations and student interests. This study also supports Lee et al. (1999), who discovered that when students are engaged in something they are interested in, they participate well.

Professional Dispositions

Like Sexton (2008) suggests, candidates were able to identify their own identity as teachers by using multiple settings. Candidates are aware that having content knowledge and planning lessons is important. They discovered that working with other teachers was a very valuable tool. They revealed that knowing their students and taking the time to learn about them socially, emotionally, and intellectually was important for building community and supporting the research and literature of what it means to be a middle school teacher as identified by Lounsbury (1991), Niska (in Dore, 2011), and Powell (2010). They also gained knowledge that middle school students are curious and want to play and that building time to engage in content in multiple ways (beyond lecture) will benefit their students.

DISCUSSION

Two questions were addressed in this study. First, is it possible to create, implement, and evaluate multiple service-learning experiences for one class?

Based on the findings of this study, using three service-learning experiences do indeed impact candidates' insights into middle level education. Thus, this experience suggests three things to consider. The first is the reality that not all middle schools engage in all forms of exemplary practice. The second is that using reflections as a tool for assessment can be very insightful for students. Finally, conducting service-learning experiences is time intensive and must include all partners in creation, implementation, and evaluation.

While Clark and Clark (2007) and George (2008) suggest it is important to implement all levels of middle school curriculum, not all middle schools do. By using multiple schools, these candidates were able to see the value of three middle school elements: teaming, advisory, and enrichment. McKewin and Greene (2010) also describe the most effective middle schools include multiple components of exemplary middle schools the reality is that we can provide candidates with exemplary experiences by tapping into the strengths of the middle schools in our area. Ideally we would have professional development schools that provide candidates with a comprehensive experience (Sandholtz & Dadlez, 2000). The reality for some districts is that there may be middle school that have exemplary *components* but do not house *all* the evidences of exemplary middle schools. This study suggests that when candidates can participate in exemplary programs within multiple schools they can gain insight into exemplary practices.

Because each of the activities was unique to the three schools, candidates had opportunities to experience an advisory, an after-school exploratory, and interdisciplinary instruction. Thus, as professors of education, we need to consider where the best practices are taking place in our district so that our candidates are receiving the best practices. Had candidates only participated in the after-school enrichment program they would have worked with a wonderful program for students and worked with community members; however, they would not have had the interactions they had with classroom teachers in the other two settings who worked as advocates of an advisory program and exemplary teachers. They were able to identify characteristics of young adolescents as described by Donahue, Bowyer, and Rosenberg (2003). They were able to consider the power of interdisciplinary teaching as described by Brown and Howard (2005), Carrington and Saggers (2008), and Chen (2004). In addition, they were able to articulate the dispositions needed to be a successful teacher (Powell, 2010).

Furthermore, reflections were an excellent tool. Reflection has often been a tool used in qualitative research (Bogdan & Biklen, 2010). Milam (2007) examined how media literacy tools can be enhanced and retained longer using the tool of reflection. Gibbs (2007) provided insight into the strength of focus groups. Candidates in this study used reflection and discussion as tools for thinking about knowledge, skills, and dispositions. They used reflection in group conversations and summaries of what they were gaining. In addition, they used their reflections over time to complete a case study and write letters of advice to young adolescents. Reflection provided evidence of candidates' knowledge of characteristics as described in theory and literature; they also applied their own ideas of how to serve young adolescents. What I found was giving candidates specific categories (knowledge, skills, and dispositions) provided them with tools for inquiry that gave me more insight into what they were learning. By giving them constructs for knowledge, skills, and dispositions and time to reflect in small groups about their findings, candidates were able to articulate their thoughts more clearly.

Finally, the service-learning experiences and projects are time intensive. It would have been much easier to use a professional development site to allow candidates to interact on multiple levels as described by Sandholtz and Dadlez (2000). However, what I discovered in my own district was that there were good things happening in multiple sites that would benefit our candidates. The relationships that are being built at multiple sites are allowing us to advocate for teachers and principals in multiple schools. We are in our third year of working with these different faculty/administrators. As we develop relationships we are finding new ways to work together. Thus, a recommendation is to continue to work with individual schools and community partners and continue to look for ways to engage candidates in activities that will benefit them in the classroom. Engaging our candidates in multiple ways to analyze their impact on student learning is a continuing goal of each of these projects.

The second question was, do the experiences impact knowledge, skills, and dispositions differently?

By examining the responses of candidates about what they learned, it is evident that candidates were able to reflect on young adolescent characteristics most through the IRL, after-school enrichment program, and the advisory program. They identified the most management techniques in IRL and the most instructional techniques in the advisory and content reflections. These two components reflect middle level instruction that address the needs of middle school students. Disposition reflections were most often represented in IRL responses. Each of these experiences contributed to the professional roles that are needed to work with young adolescents. By combining the learning outcomes from all three experiences, candidates were able to articulate a range of knowledge, skills, and dispositions as they related to three elements of middle school curriculum. The following are summaries of themes addressed in each element of the curriculum.

In Real Life

The most positive experiences were revealed in the after-school enrichment program. Candidates were able to identify young adolescent characteristics and commented on the social, physical, and emotional development of young adolescents. A few comments revealed deeper understanding of specific content and the middle school concept of exploratories.

In addition, the exploratory program provided candidates with practical suggestions for managing students and allowed them to identify the importance of hands-on activities and engaging students in active learning.

Advisory

The advisory experience had the least amount of comments. Candidates spent the least amount of time in this experience. They were able to identify the characteristics of young adolescents and the experience gave them insight to advisory programs and how to implement service-learning as part of an advisory program. The instructional strategies they gathered related specifically to the service-learning project "Empty Bowls." They were able to articulate the importance of allowing students to work together and how the advisory program supported the notion of building relationships as a management tool.

Content Setting

Candidates were able to identify characteristics of young adolescents within the specific academic classes. The experiences gave them insight into the intellectual disparity that exists in classrooms. Teachers in the field were able to provide candidates with instructional strategies for differentiating classrooms and several of the students were able to participate in an interdisciplinary unit the eighth-grade team was conducting on the Holocaust.

I believe that using multiple experiences and having candidates create a view of exemplary middle schools based on these experiences and the research that is available will prepare them well for working with young adolescents. I also believe that having preservice teachers in middle schools provides professional development for middle school teachers.

APPENDIX
Assignments Associated with the
Service-Learning Experiences

The following assignments are associated with this service-learning course.

1. Research the value of service-learning. Read one article, summarize the findings, share your findings with one another. Participate in a workshop on service-learning.

2. Participate in training from the leaders of IRL, ArtSpace, and R. Middle School. These trainings take place at each of the school settings. They provide an overview of their program (middle school organization), young adolescent characteristics, and expectations (professional roles). Take notes at each of these trainings. Use the insights you gain as you reflect on the experience throughout the semester.

3. Each week reflect on knowledge, skills, and dispositions gained. Separate each setting. Once a month summarize your findings and share them with others.

4. Complete a case study of one of the students you are working with using the following format.
   a) Young adolescent characteristics are described
   b) The study shows a student's development/progress/behaviors over time
   c) Strategies teachers/service providers use to interact with the student and that appear to be effective ways to communicate with the young adolescent
   d) Your views of how to engage students
   e) Three pieces of advice you would give to the students

5. Create an exploratory course that could take place in an after-school program. Consider how to use local community agencies in your after-school program. Include a description of what you could do each week for 12 weeks. Be sure and include a way to assess the impact of the course.

6. Work in a team to brainstorm an interdisciplinary unit that has as its centerpiece a service-learning experience.

7. At the end of the experience choose the three most important things you have gained from the experiences you have had. Describe them and share why they are the most important things to consider in working as a middle school teacher.

REFERENCES

Akos, P. (2006). Extracurricular participation and the transition to middle school. *Research in Middle Level Education, 29*(9).

Alexander, W., & George, P. (1982). *The exemplary middle school.* Fort Worth, TX: Holt, Rinehart and Winston, Inc.

AMLE. (2006). AMLE position statement on the professional preparation of middle level teachers. Retrieved from www.amle.org/aboutamle/position statements/professionalpreparation/tabid/287/default.aspx.

Bell, C., Horn, B. & Roxas, K. (2007). We know it's service, but what are they learning?: Preservice teachers' understandings of diversity. *Equity and Excellence in Education, 40*(2), 123–133.

Bogdan, R., & Biklen, S. (1982). *Qualitative research for education: An introduction to theory and methods.* Boston: Allyn & Bacon.

Bollin, G. (2007). Preparing teachers for Hispanic immigrant children: A service learning approach. *Journal of Latinos and Education, 6*(2), 177–189.

Brown, E., & Howard, B. (2005). Becoming culturally responsive teachers through service learning: A study of five novice teachers. *Multicultural Education, 12*(4), 2.

Brownell, M. T., Ross, D. R., Colon, E. P., & McCallum, C. L. (2003). *Critical features of special education teacher preparation: A comparison with exemplary practices in general teacher education* (COPSSE Document No. RS-4). Gainesville: University of Florida Center on Personnel Studies in Special Education.

Bruce, W. C. (1975). *Field-based teacher education: Past, present, and future.* Stanford, CA: Stanford University. (ERIC Reproduction Service No. 109070)

Carrington, S., & Saggers, B. (2008). Service-learning informing the development of an inclusive framework for beginning teachers. *Teaching and Teacher Education, 24*(3), 795–806.

Chen, D. (2004). The multiple benefits of service learning projects in pre-service teacher education. *Delta Kappa Gamma Bulletin, 70*(2), 31–36.

Clandinin, D., & Connelly, F. (2000). *Narrative inquiry: Experience and story in qualitative research.* San Francisco: Jossey-Bass.

Clark, S., & Clark, D. (2007). Using the knowledge base on middle schools and leadership to improve the quality of young adolescent learning. *Middle School Journal, 38*(2), 55–61.

Coffey, H. (2010). "'They' taught 'me'": The benefits of early community-based field experiences in teacher education. *Teaching and Teacher Education: An International Journal of Research and Studies, 26*(2), 335–342.

Cone, N. (2009). Community-based service-learning as a source of personal self-efficacy: Preparing preservice teachers to teach science for diversity. *School Science and Mathematics, 109*(1), 20–30.

Donahue, D., Bowyer, J., & Rosenberg, D. (2003). Learning with and learning from: Reciprocity in service learning in teacher education. *Equity and Excellence in Education, 36*(1), 15–28.

Dore, E. (2011). *Keeping middle schools successful.* Kennesaw, GA: NaPOMLE. Retrieved from: http://www.napomle.org/KeepingMiddleSchoolsSuccessful/index.html

George, P. (2008). *Special report: Status of programs in Florida middle schools.* Gaines-ville: University of Florida and the Florida League of Middle Schools.

Gibbs, A. (1997). Focus groups. *Social Research Update, 19.* Retrieved from http://sru.soc.surrey.ac.uk/SRU19.html.

Harkavy, I., & Hartley, M. (2010). Pursuing Franklin's dream: Philosophical and historical roots of service learning. *American Journal of Community Psychology, 46*(3/4) 428–427.

Harvard Family Research Project. (2012). Secrets of successful after school pro-grams: What research reveals. Retrieved from: www.uknow.gse.harvard.edu/learning/LD314-608.html.

Jenkins, A., & Sheehey, P. (2009). Implementing service learning in special educa-tion coursework: What we learned. *Education, 129*(4), 668–682.

Kirtman, L. (2008). Pre-service teachers and mathematics: The impact of service-learning on teacher preparation. *School Science and Mathematics, 108*(3), 94–102.

Kramarski, B., & T. Michalsky (2009). Three metacognitive approaches to train preservice teachers in different learning phases of technological pedagogical content knowledge. *Educational Research and Evaluation, 15*(5), 456–485.

Lee, V., Smith, J., Perry, T. E., & Smylie, M. A. (1999). *Social support, academic press, and student achievement: A view from the middle grades in Chicago.* Chicago: Con-sortium on Chicago School Research, University of Chicago.

Levesque-Bristol, C., Knapp, T., & Fisher, B. (2010). The effectiveness of service-learning: It's not always what you think. *Journal of Experiential Education, 33*(3) 208–224.

Lounsbury, J. (1991). *As I see it.* Westerville, OH: National Middle School Association.

Lu, Y. (2010). Beyond the undergraduate classroom: Factors influencing service learning's effectiveness at improving graduate students professional skills. *College Teaching, 58*(4), 118–126.

Mahoney, J., & R. Cairns (1997). Do extracurricular activities protect against early school dropout? *Developmental Psychology, 33,* 241–253.

Marzano, R., Pickering, D., & Pollock, J. (2001). *Classroom instruction that works.* Alex-andria, VA: Association for Supervision and Curriculum Development.

McKewin, K., & Greene, M. (2010), Results and recommendations from the 2009 national surveys of randomly selected and highly successful middle level schools, *Middle School Journal, 42*(1), 49–63.

Milam, P. (2007). The power of reflection in the research process. *School Library Media Activities Monthly, 21*(6), 26–29.

Miller, K., & Gonzalez, A. (2009). Service learning in domestic and international settings. *College Student Journal, 43*(2), 527–536.

National Forum for the Acceleration of Middle Grades Reform (2013). http://www.middlegradesforum.org/

NCATE. (2012). Specialty area standards. Available at www.ncate.org/Standards/ProgramStandardsandReportForms/tabid/676/Default.aspx.

NMSA. (2010). *This we believe: Keys to educating young adolescents.* Columbus, OH: Author.

Novak, J. (2010). Learning through service: A course designed to influence posi-tively students' disability-related attitudes. *Journal of Education for Teaching, 36*(1), 121–123.

Powell, S. (2010). *Introduction to middle school.* Upper Saddle River, NJ: Pearson.

Rock, T. C., & Levin, B. B. (2002). collaborative action research projects: Enhancing preservice teacher development in professional development schools. *Teacher Education Quarterly, 29*(1), 7–21.

Sandholtz, J., & Dadlez, S. (2000). Professional development school tradeoffs in teacher education and renewal. *Teacher Education Quarterly, 27*(1), 7–27.

SchoosToWatch.org (2012). http://www.schoolstowatch.org/

Sexton, D. (2008). Teachers negotiating identity, role, and agency. *Teacher Education Quarterly, 35*(3), 73–88.

Stevenson, C. (1992). *Teaching ten to fourteen year olds.* White Plains, NY: Longman.

Tang, S. (2004). The dynamics of school-based learning in initial teacher education. *Research Papers in Education, 19*(2), 185–204.

Tomlinson, C. (1999). *The differentiated classroom: Responding to the needs of all learners.* Alexandria, VA: Association for Supervision and Curriculum Development.

Nancy B. Ruppert is the middle grades coordinator at the University of North Carolina Asheville where she is an associate professor. She was one of the first Key Fellow Service-learning Scholars at UNC Asheville. Her work in service-learning stems from experiences she had as an undergraduate where she developed a tutoring project as part of her 100 hours of service to graduate. She taught middle school for 15 years and regularly engaged her students in service-learning. Most recently she returned to an inner-city K–8 school where she engaged students in service-learning to help them learn the value and importance of civic engagement. When she returned to the university she worked to create service-learning experiences for undergraduates who want to be teachers so they can, first, experience the power of service-learning and, second, teach them how to consider service-learning as tools for helping young adolescents become responsible citizens.

CHAPTER 7

LATINO/A PRESERVICE TEACHERS AND COMMUNITY SERVICE-LEARNING

Justice Embraced, Dodged, and Troubled

Kathleen Bussert-Webb

ABSTRACT

This chapter explores 12 Latino/a preservice teachers' divergent social justice views during a service-learning project. Some participants believed they should promote social justice, some did not discuss it, and others did not feel promotion of it was their role as teachers. This chapter prepares teacher-researchers interested in service-learning and social justice for respondents' possible disagreements and it demonstrates the power of teacher candidates' dialogue regarding their fieldwork. Also, this study shows how socioeconomic, immigration, and neighborhood factors relate to discrimination among people of the same race and ethnicity, which demonstrates the complex nature of culture. Data gathering took place in a south Texas colonia, or unincorporated settlement, with a high poverty level. Data sources for this grounded theory study were structured written reflections, daily logs, a focus group discussion, a visual metaphor activity, and participant observations.

Transforming Teacher Education Through Service-Learning, pages 145–177
Copyright © 2013 by Information Age Publishing
145

What were the social justice beliefs of 12 Latino/a preservice teachers during a service-learning project in a south Texas neighborhood? If preservice teachers gain experiences in service-learning, they are more likely to provide service opportunities and to motivate other teachers to implement service-learning (Wasserman, 2010) and are more able to realize injustices (Carrington & Selva, 2010). If they engage in dialogue at the collegiate level, they are more likely to embrace contested views in their classrooms (Edwards-Groves & Hoare, 2012). Indeed, service-learning, social justice, and dialogue relate to the 21st-century skills of critical thinking, collaboration, cross-cultural communication, flexibility, and initiative (Partnership for 21st Century Skills, 2011). Yet the studies cited were about white middle-class students. What about service-learning involving Latino/a preservice teachers? How does service-learning affect them? Are the service-learning experiences as transformative for them as they are for some white students? Do they come to the service-learning experience with social justice perspectives? Social justice, often used as a theoretical framework in service-learning (Wasserman, 2010), signifies a desire to change society's structures to make them more just (Giroux, 2004).

The preservice teachers, tutees, and the colonia residents for the present study were Latinos/as; this population is the fastest growing U.S. group (U.S. Census Bureau, 2011) and many U.S. rural areas now have Latino communities. The 2010 Census revealed that 50% of U.S.-born babies were from minority parents, 25% of whom were Latinos (Frey, 2012). Thus, this study can be applied to many geographic areas. Next, the changing face of U.S. children necessitates more ethnically diverse teachers. However, the 100% Latino/a preservice teacher population in this study are not the national norm; most U.S. teachers are white (National Center of Education Statistics, 2009). Indeed, teacher candidates of color are often excluded in the bulk of U.S. multicultural teacher education research, but this population has much to contribute to the field (Montecinos, 2004).

PERSPECTIVES

Featured in this section are the theoretical frameworks of social justice and dialogue, which were integral to this service-learning research project.

Social Justice

It is common for those interested in service-learning research to use a social justice framework because of the structural inequalities resulting in the need for service (Hart, 2006; Parker-Gwin & Mabry, 1998). Social justice includes individuals' fight against systemic inequalities and a desire to change society's structures to make them more just (Lin, 2001); also, teachers as transformative intellectuals can foster social justice (Giroux, 2004). Thus, a systems-based view of oppression takes precedence over inequalities as individual problems (Freire, 1994, 2000). Social justice also involves a critical orientation to race, ethnicity, and economic inequalities (Boyle-Baise, 1998) and should encourage service providers' self-understanding of privilege and oppression (Boyle-Baise & Langford, 2004).

Service-learning exposes preservice teachers to cultural diversity and helps them to empathize with others; however, often teacher candidates do not perceive poverty as related to structural inequalities (Boyle-Baise, 1998) and do not change their perceptions of social justice (Simons, Blank, Russell, Williams, & Willis, 2009). Boyle-Baise and Langford (2004) stated that most white college students do not understand social justice: "Activist views are rarely held by white students" (p. 56). Indeed, service-learning projects in which white middle class students work with diverse children of poverty may be from deficit models; those providing the service may perceive themselves as saving the disadvantaged (Hess, Lanig, & Vaughan, 2007; Sperling, 2007). Indeed, having white college students tutor diverse children of poverty may perpetuate racial and social class stereotypes if providers do not examine the children's cultural strengths (González, Moll, & Amanti, 2005) and question the service providers' power and privilege related to race (Cahill, 2009). Prevalent mainstream views relate to the poor's responsibility to overcome poverty, as well as perceptions of the poor's inherent deficits (Payne, 2005). However, examinations of unequal educational opportunities and power should be the norm when one enters into conversations about poverty (Gorski, 2008). Although researchers have found that cross-ethnicity pairings during service-learning experiences perpetuate class deficit myths, they continue to advocate for the same types of dyads (Sperling, 2007). After dismal social justice results, Simons et al. wrote: "Students should engage in service activities with recipients who differ from them in class and race..." (2009, p. 211).

Alternatively, some researchers have found same-ethnicity pairings to be promising for service-learning and classroom experiences (Robinson, Ward-Schofield, & Steers-Wentzell, 2005). Yet, adult–child ethnic matching is not a silver bullet for social justice. Although some Latino/a children may have teachers of the same ethnicity, it does not mean these educators perceive themselves to be change agents or that these adults have had culturally affirmative educational experiences. According to Weisman, Flores, and Valenciana (2007), "Latino teachers are often the victims of an educational system that stresses assimilation and adoption of the cultural values of the dominant group, including adherence to traditional educational practices..." (p. 192).

Indeed, sharing the same ethnicity did not mean sharing the same culture for 15 new teachers of color; conflicts between the teachers and students of the same ethnicities related to gender, social class, age, and language (Achinstein & Aguirre, 2008). Moreover, both African American students in a service-learning project sometimes expressed deficit views of families being served (Boyle Baise & Langford, 2004). Indeed, some culturally diverse people may have oppressive views toward their own ethnicity as a result of internalized racism (Valenzuela, 2008) or the dearth of strengths-based educational experiences (Weisman et al., 2007). Indeed, bilingual preservice teachers from the same geographic area as those in the present study discussed being discriminated against in K–12 settings because they spoke Spanish and looked Mexican (Sarmiento-Arribalzaga & Murillo, 2009–2010).

Thus, because participants and the children they tutored were of the same ethnicity and race, this study focuses on oppression related to immigrant status, neighborhood type, and social class to highlight the multidimensional nature of culture. For example, Mexican American females in another study stated that social class was the most difficult obstacle for other Latinas to overcome; these nine respondents either had doctoral degrees or were advanced doctoral students (Briscoe, 2009). Nieto (2008) stated that culture is a complex human creation involving "ever-changing values, traditions, social and political relationships, and worldview created, shared, and transformed by a group of people bound together by a combination of factors..." (p. 129). Because culture involves similar and dissimilar beliefs, even Mexican American preservice teachers who grew up in poverty can have divergent social justice perspectives.

Dialogue

How is it possible for teacher-researchers to have a social justice perspective and still invite dialogue? For both perspectives, Butin's (2010) notion of social justice in doubt is essential; he argued if social justice becomes our priority in service-learning classes, we may narrow discussions and alternative theoretical constructs. Butin believed we should position ourselves in uncertainty, or from epistemological doubt, the opposite of rigid thinking and defensiveness (Foucault, 1972). This open systemic model may help students to come to their own understandings so their learning is profound and sustained. Butin believed students must have service-learning experiences and class discussions that disturb their perceptions and help them to reflect at deeper levels.

Similarly, Bakhtin (1997), a literary critic and philosopher, believed a single consciousness cannot exist. According to Bakhtin, dialogue helps people to outgrow themselves: "I am conscious of myself and become myself only while revealing myself for another, through another, and with the help of another" (p. 287). Hence, dialogue is essential to de-privilege any particular culture, language, or utterance (Bakhtin, 1996). This is because knowledge is socially constructed and deconstructed from people's differing viewpoints. Because we cannot grow from consensus only, divergent perceptions are essential to understand phenomena at deeper, more critical levels (Bopry, 2002). Yet understanding is not enough; dialogue must propel us to positive action for the social good (Freire, 1994, 2000). Freire, an educator and philosopher, believed dialogue could be a tool to make society more democratic. He argued that if students were not allowed to come to their own conclusions, then the result would be a form of banking education, whereby another's thoughts were deposited into learners. Freire envisioned an alternative through respect, conversation, and informed action, or praxis. Both Freire and Bakhtin believed dialogue to be a moral imperative.

However, political and technical orientations permeate service-learning research (Butin, 2010) and appear to be the antithesis of dialogue. A few scholars have included respondents' disagreements about service-learning projects and social justice viewpoints. For example, in an alternative spring break experience as part of a diversity course, university students worked with culturally diverse children (Boyle-Baise & Langford, 2004). Rife were the college students' contested views. White middle-class students perceived talks by community informants to be enlightening, but two African Americans, the only students of color in the course, found the same talks to be degrading and racist. However, the same two suggested that people of poverty were to blame for their situations. Many of the white students made it obvious they did not want to be at the camp and most did not deeply connect the experience to their own lives: "They went into the field with limited awareness of their own privilege or oppression" (p. 64). Indeed, participants bit back (Clifford, 1986) and many did not leave the service-learning course with a social justice perspective. In conclusion, this section described the theoretical frameworks of social justice and dialogue, which were integral to the study, and which talked back to each other.

SETTING

The Research Site

The setting for this service-learning project is the focus of this section. Esperanza, a pseudonym for the Texas colonia in which the service-learning project took place, has faced discrimination by local officials, and ironically, the region has been marginalized at the state and national levels. No Veterans

Affairs hospital exists in over 250 miles, although there are over 100,000 veterans in this area, the Rio Grande Valley (Janes, 2010). Also, federal and state officials have not provided a major interstate north or west of the county to accommodate a major hurricane evacuation (Webb, 2006; Texas Department of Transportation, 2012). Next, the university in which the teacher candidates were enrolled has received no Permanent University Fund (PUF) endowment, even though many public Texas campuses receive this financial support from west Texas land profits (University of Texas Austin, 2010). Related to education, 76% of the county's population 25 years old and older has less than a high school degree and the county's poverty and unemployment rates are double the U.S. average (U.S. Census Bureau, 2010).

The region's problems may explain why city officials do not want to incorporate Esperanza, a colonia with a poverty rate of 53% and an average per capita income of less than $6,000 (U.S. Census Bureau, 2010). Officials may perceive this unincorporated settlement of 7,000 people to be a tax drain for an overburdened local budget. Although Esperanza is within city limits and has existed for over 50 years, it does not receive city services, such as police protection or electricity. A company, not the city or county authorities, covered the energy costs for 84 Esperanza street lights (Martinez, 2008). Also, less than 18% of Esperanza residents over age 25 have a high school degree or equivalent (U.S. Census Bureau, 2010). Esperanza shares many of the same socioeconomic and environmental challenges of other colonias, located along the U.S.–Mexico border (Anderson & Gerber, 2007). According to the Federal Reserve Bank of Dallas (n.d.), most colonias lack "basic water and sewage systems, paved roads, and safe and sanitary housing" (p. 1).

Despite obstacles, Esperanza exudes strengths. Home ownership in Esperanza is above the Texas average (U.S. Census Bureau, 2012). Home ownership may help neighborhood stability, which is played out in families (Migrant Health Promotion, 2012). Other Esperanza strengths include shared Latino origins (99%), Spanish language spoken at home (97%) (U.S. Census Bureau, 2010), faith (Migrant Health Promotion), and many locally owned businesses. Most Esperanza children attend nearby public school campuses, rated as recognized and exemplary by the Texas Education Agency (Long, 2010). Moreover, the after-school tutorial agency, where the study took place, has thrived for over 12 years. Because of efforts from children, their parents, and the caring tutorial director, almost all who attend the tutorial center pass to the next grade level and graduate high school.

The University, Course, and Service-Learning Project

The university, located in a border city of 180,000, is 10 miles south of Esperanza. This primarily commuter campus, which serves mostly Latinos of Mexican descent, received the 2010 Community Engagement classification. Community engagement relates to reciprocal collaboration between an institution and community (Driscoll, 2008). Mathematics, science, and English majors who wish to be certified secondary teachers must take the methods course, Teaching Reading to the English Language Learner (ELL), but others may take it as a literacy course substitution. Students can enroll on our campus during the spring or fall, or they may also take an intensive 3-week version in May in Esperanza. This upper-division class consists of English as a Second Language (ESL) and literacy theories, concepts, and methods, pair strategy presentations, role-plays, and discussions. Teacher candidates should leave the course knowing how to help emergent bilinguals (García, Kleifgen, & Falchi, 2008) to succeed academically and apply ESL and literacy methods to their disciplines, and tailor instruction to children's contexts (González et al., 2005). Assigned readings included an ESL textbook (Herrell & Jordan, 2008), a social justice article about an adolescent emergent bilingual who struggled with academic literacy (Rubenstein-Avila, 2003), an article about alternative paths to literacy (Cline & Necochea, 2003), a novel about a community garden (Fleishman, 2004), and a course packet I developed.

I started this tutoring and gardening service-learning project in May 2006 as part of this course. Local businesses and organizations have provided donations and our institution's Center for Civic Engagement has provided grants. This course and service-learning project took place for 4 days weekly for 3 weeks in 2008. Under the supervision of the tutorial director and myself, preservice teachers tutored Esperanza children on homework; they implemented lessons from 3:30 to 5:00 P.M. and then planted native plants around the tutorial center with the children and some of the children's mothers. After the families left, the preservice teachers participated in the course until 9:00 P.M. Tutoring and gardening facilitated common goals between university students and their tutees. Each preservice teacher created and executed two lessons involving the gardening project. Math majors developed lessons about volume, estimating, comparing, and solving geometric problems; science students created lessons on the water cycle, ecology, and botany; and English candidates engaged tutees in reading and writing about different facets of gardening. Last, as part of the culminating celebration, the preservice teachers and the children participated in a scavenger hunt to match native plants to the butterflies they attracted.

This section focused on the neighborhood, university, and course in which the preservice teachers were enrolled, as well as details about the service-learning project. Highlighting community strengths, as well as structural inequalities, is important from a social justice framework to avoid deficit conceptualizations (González et al., 2005; Gorski, 2008). Also, a detailed description of the context is important because the preservice teachers tutored the children, gardened with them, ate snacks with them, and participated in the methods class and service-learning project at the same site. Last, from a perspective of dialogue, context is essential to understand any phenomenon (Bakhtin, 1997).

METHODS

This section explains the qualitative data-gathering methods and data analysis used in this case study. Of 12 students enrolled in this service-learning course in May 2008, all agreed to participate: one male and 11 females. Five sought middle school certification, six high school certification, and one elementary certification. Four math majors, three science, four English, and one Special Education major participated. One, in our alternative certification program, had completed a year of teaching, but needed this class for her certificate. Others were juniors and seniors in a traditional teacher education program. All were Mexican Americans; all but two were bilingual. For dialogic collaboration, commonly referred to as peer debriefing, I also sought the viewpoints of the tutorial director and parent volunteers, as well as colleagues who have done service-learning projects and research at the same tutoring center.

Oral and written reflections were essential to demonstrate learning in this service-learning (Rowls & Swick, 2000). During our first session, respondents completed a pre-reflection. They wrote other reflections outside of class time. Essay criteria were following directions and demonstrating effort and depth. Each participant also completed learning logs; volunteers read their logs aloud daily. At the end of the course, they engaged in a tape-recorded focus group discussion; my roles were scribe, question-poser, and synthesizer. As students talked, I typed responses. When students created and presented visual metaphors in groups, I took notes and photographed the posters and group members.

Initially I thought I was using the Constant Comparative Method (Glaser, 1965) as a grounded theory approach to data analysis. However, I now believe I was looking for confirmations of technical and political viewpoints of service-learning (Butin, 2010). Initial themes were social justice, bias reduction, caring, hope, joy, collaboration, impact on teaching, and personal growth. Initially I did not notice any disagreements regarding social justice because I was focused on proving that service-learning was worthwhile. Those interested in the impact of service-learning on preservice teachers may read Bussert-Webb (2008, 2009). This technical orientation to service-learning was visible when I looked for instances of respondents' improved knowledge and skills in teaching. A political orientation was made manifest when I searched for ways in which the teacher candidates noticed structural inequalities, realized their own biases, or expressed desires to become change agents (Butin, 2010). When I reanalyzed the data by combining social justice and dialogue, I realized some disagreed with political and technical orientations to service-learning. Their disagreements were anomalies or deviations from the expected (Buchler, 1955). Although I still found a plethora of examples of participant growth in many areas, I began to recognize incongruities vis-à-vis dialogue. Because I did not feel I had anything to prove to myself or others, I moved away from trying to substantiate the merit of service-learning (Butin, 2010).

A reanalysis based on the same data consisted of marking and arranging into patterns participants' divergent perceptions of social justice: supporting it, ignoring or not mentioning it, and disagreeing with it. Sometimes their social justice views were inconsistent; thus this analysis includes participants *dialogizing* against themselves (Bakhtin, 1997). From lenses of social justice and dialogue, it was important for me to reread several times the data of participants who did not talk much during the focus group interview to make their dialogue manifest. Thus, I sought to bring to the forefront what they wrote but did not vocalize. Mazzei (2007) explicated this interplay of social justice and dialogue during data analysis: "We must always be aware of our power as researchers to construct narratives from the poetic expressions of our participants if we do not sufficiently trouble the complex and competing texts" (p. 60). Thus, in order to unpack power relationships (Clifford, 1986), especially in the interplay of race, class, and gender (Gorski, 2008), data analysis included my self-questioning about participants' silence. Furthermore, although I analyzed individuals' perceptions of social justice, I could not do so without explaining the context of their lives and this service-learning project. This is because ideology is the result of social processes (Bakhtin & Medvedev, 1978). This segment related to methods used to gather and interpret the data, and how.

DATA SOURCES

Data sources were pre-, process, and final reflections, daily learning logs, visual metaphors, participant observation, and the focus group discussion. I modified essay prompts from Rowls and Swick (2000). The pre-reflection consisted of the preservice teachers' demographics, as well as their impressions of Esperanza, the center, director, and children; perceived skills for tutoring and planting; possible commonalities and differences with tutees; anticipated learning from the tutees; and anxieties or questions about the service-learning project.

Each of the three process reflections consisted of each participant's description, reaction, and an application to course concepts. The final entry contained these questions: What have you learned about teaching and learning, service-learning, this program, the tutee, the neighborhood, social justice, structural inequalities, and yourself? What commonalities and differences did you have with your tutee(s)? What service-learning projects could you get future students involved in? The 6:00 P.M. learning log focused on the tutoring and gardening sessions and the 8:45 P.M. log was on course content. Questions were: What did you learn since the moment you arrived? What was said or done that impacted you? How do you feel about this? The metaphor activity involved pairs writing, drawing, and presenting visual and verbal metaphors, which related gardening and tutoring to teaching and learning. For the focus group discussion, respondents answered six questions, which began with the phrase, "Can you speak about...?" The topics were the gardening project, tutoring, having a university class taught outside of campus, service-learning, caring, and social justice. This segment centered on data sources.

RESULTS

The topic of social justice dominated participants' responses during the group interview and students' written reflections. Respondents revealed different approaches to social justice, which were embracing social justice, dodging it, and troubling it. Some critiqued structural inequalities, had specific service-learning plans as teachers, and saw themselves as change agents. However, others rarely mentioned social justice issues and expressed no concrete plans to continue service-learning. Others disagreed with a justice orientation; they did not see poverty as systemic and did not perceive social justice to be part of their roles as teachers. The focus group discussion is featured because it demonstrates how participants disagreed about social justice promotion; thus, this discussion caused me to think about social justice in doubt and also Bakhtin's notion of learning from contested viewpoints. Esperanza's context and the service-learning project are interwoven in the findings; in fact, this in situ service-learning course in a colonia cannot be separated from the results.

Embracing Justice

This section relates to the positive social justice stances that some participants took up during the service-learning course. Ojojona, who shared the immigrant experience with many tutees, demonstrated a passion for social justice from this service-learning project: "I learned I have the power to contribute to make a difference in our society." Also, Ojojona grew close to the children during the service-learning and was outraged her tutees' teachers had such low expectations and that they did not assign homework. She connected systemic inequities to the unincorporated status of the colonia as well:

> I learned about the structural inequality we have in [city]. I do not understand the reason this neighborhood is not included as part of the city. It is unfair for the people that live here. It is sort of discrimination. The city of [name] is neglecting this neighborhood.

Ojojona realized poverty related to structural inequalities and she saw herself as a powerful change agent.

Like Ojojona, Nina said the service-learning project empowered her to help other Latinos fight against social injustices:

> I have learned I can help someone. As a teacher, I have a voice, and I should use it for the betterment of my people. I want to make a difference. I want to set an example for my students. They do not have to just take no for an answer.

Nina was quick to act after I opened a tiny box of ragged, thin paperback books that another social services agency donated for our project; since that agency was so generous in 2007, I did not ask other entities for books in 2008. Nina may have sensed my disappointment because before the class break she asked if she and another student could bring books from her home, adjacent to the colonia. They came back with at least $800 worth of gently used hardcover novels, many of which were Newbery winners, to give to the tutees. Nina was a paraprofessional or teacher's aide in an elementary school that discarded the books; she said she was saving them for when she had her own classroom.

Nina appeared to perceive herself as a transformative intellectual (Giroux, 2004). She not only recognized systemic inequalities, but she went out of her way during the program to redress them. One inequality relates to summer reading loss, which represents the largest cumulative factor related to low-income students' achievement gap (Downey, von Hippel, & Broh, 2004). Emergent bilinguals undergo significantly more summer reading loss than English-proficient children (Kim & Gouryard, 2010), and low-income Latino children participants experience more summer reading loss than middle-class Latino children (O'Brien, 1999). In Esperanza specifically, the tutorial children reported scant summer reading and having little access to books (Díaz & Bussert-Webb, 2013).

I believe this service-learning project in Esperanza was instrumental in Nina's words and actions related to social justice; in another course she took with me on campus the previous year, she did not mention social justice, or related concepts, nor was she as engaged or participatory. Nina's book donation also represented a connection between caring and social justice, which Wink (2005) stated is a "new dynamical pedagogical whole" (p. 167). According to Lin (2001), when people care about others they tend to recognize more quickly if the cared-for are being unjustly treated and "they find ways to treat them justly, fairly, and equitably" (p. 110). Nina appeared to understand the structural inequalities of Esperanza residents, many of whom lacked legal status: "I honestly believe the reason why this neighborhood is in this condition is because nobody helps them. They do not qualify for many of the programs of assistance because of their residential status." Because many Esperanza residents do not have legal status, they cannot receive many social services and federal financial aid; also, they are less likely to report crimes against themselves and others, file complaints, fight for causes, sign petitions, or stand up to authorities for fear of deportation and separation from family.

Like Nina, Daisy could emphasize with the marginalization of Esperanza residents; she said her tutee was discriminated against because she was from Esperanza. Daisy crossed the Mexican border when she was age 6 and then lived in another economically disadvantaged neighborhood in our city. Daisy wrote about fighting for opportunities and helping her students and the world outside of her classroom; she also mentioned engaging future students in a service-learning project at a women's shelter. These instances demonstrate that Daisy saw herself as a change agent and that she perceived poverty to be a matter of structural inequalities. Weisman et al. (2007) stated that Latino preservice teachers' "familiarity with the realities that students face living in subordinated communities can give them crucial insight into many issues related to class, race, culture, and discrimination that affect these students and their communities" (p. 192).

Related to participants' critique of the city's unfair treatment of Esperanza residents were realizations of their own biases; this self-reflection about prejudice and privilege is an important aspect of social justice vis-à-vis service-learning (Boyle-Baise & Langford, 2004). Many, like Seina, said their biases about the neighborhood changed when they got to know the colonia residents on a personal level:

> I was a little wary at first when I heard we were going to be doing a project at [neighborhood]. I have heard only horrible things that happen there.... The remarkable thing is that I instantly liked my student and my surroundings. The center is really nice, clean, and organized.

I interpreted Seina's comment about the center's cleanliness to be either a personal interest or a preconception that a tutorial center in a high-poverty area would be dirty. In her pre-reflection Seina also thought her tutees would be less smart because of where they lived, but wrote she was wrong, demonstrating initial low expectations for culturally diverse children (Haycock, 2001) and a deficit perspective (Gorski, 2008).

In her final reflection Seina stated the service-learning project had a dramatic effect on her and it taught her not to stereotype children of poverty or to blame their parents:

> Before I judge a student about why he may be asleep in my class, or why his clothes are dirty and why his parents never come for meetings, I will take into account the things I saw in [Esperanza] and the struggles so many families face there.

Besides bias reduction, the service-learning experience helped Seina to realize the structural inequalities her tutees faced: "I have seen these children sometimes experience social injustice because of their race, social status, and environment." Perhaps Seina consistently embraced social justice during the service-learning experience because she appeared much older than the others and had more life experiences. However, Rosenberg, Reed, Statham, and Rosing (2012) found a statistically significant difference between older and younger college students' appreciation for the value of service-learning; older students and first-generation college students were less enthusiastic about this approach. In conclusion, this segment related to the preservice teachers' affirmations of a social justice positioning.

Dodging Justice

Not all Mexican American participants expressed a social justice stance, which is the focus of this section. Some of the preservice teachers wrote and said very little about structural inequalities, any biases others had against Esperanza, or being change agents. Most revealed that they grew up economically disadvantaged, but this did not appear to affect some in terms of social justice stances. Others came to the United States without legal documents when they were children, but this did not appear to affect their positioning about structural inequalities either.

This section is not meant as a critique of some participants. Instead, I believe they attended to other course aspects. Cana Lilly, Contenta, and Sol wrote and discussed caring, enjoying the service-learning project, and applying concepts to their teaching; Guy focused on teamwork and mentoring his tutees, two ornery preadolescent twins. These preservice teachers did not demonstrate deficit views of people of poverty. Cana Lilly wrote that service-learning helps not only those being served, but it also assists the ones providing the help, which indicates she was learning from the experience and the children. Cana Lilly's humble stance as a learner is the opposite of paternalism, which assumes moral and intellectual superiority (Gorski, 2008). Also, Contenta wanted to prove to her tutees and to their classroom teachers that the children were intelligent, "I had the opportunity to prove one more time how bright they are" and Guy referred to the twins he tutored as shining stars. Thus, the remarks these preservice teachers made toward the children, neighborhood, and people of poverty focused on strengths. This is different from the African American college students in another service-learning study (Boyle-Baise & Langford, 2004), who saw poverty as individual and who had deficit views of the families being served, for example, "Just because you are low-income does not mean you have to act low-income. Opportunities are out there. Some people don't want a job" (p. 60) and "You can't blame society for bad parents" (p. 62).

In the present study, Contenta wrote just a few words in her learning logs while others wrote at least 200 words. She moved from Mexico only a few years prior to data gathering and appeared to have difficulty writing extended reflections in English. An alternative interpretation is that she may have been reluctant to be too critical of systemic inequalities in the United States as a new member of its workforce. Also, she was teaching at a local middle school during data gathering and may have had little time to reflect on the course because of other responsibilities.

However, as I reread the data from these participants, I began to ponder some respondents' silence regarding social justice. Maybe they did not trust me. Weisman et al. (2007) stated, "To have confianza in your teachers is to trust that you will do well by them and to believe that your best interests are protected by them" (p. 199). Contenta failed another course with me the previous term because of excessive absences and missing assignments; also she did not pass my evaluation of her lesson execution when I observed her teach in her classroom the previous semester. Thus, perhaps Contenta was scared I would not evaluate her fairly if she revealed too much. Indeed, perhaps some disagreed with a social justice stance, but did not publicly do so because of respect or deference to me, fear of a lower grade, possible disapproval from peers or me, or they simply were not used to voicing disagreeing with people they deemed to be in authority; this could demonstrate power and powerlessness (Mazzei, 2008). Mazzei's (2008) conceptualization may also apply to some participants' silence in terms of the perceived difference between them and me, their privileged professor. Although my mother arrived in the United States when she was 19 and I grew up working class, I am white and am now upper middle class. Indeed, *confianza*, or trust, relates to perceived commonalities (Weisman et al., 2007).

Nonetheless, Contenta, Guy, and Cana Lilly did write about the structural inequalities of healthcare after watching a segment in *Sicko* (Moore, 2007); the segment we watched related to the lack of affordable health care for Esperanza residents. Moreover, Cana Lilly referred to colonia residents' legal statuses vis-à-vis their inabilities to obtain food stamps, Medicaid, and health and life insurance. Also, Guy mentioned the importance of voting to change governmental policies related to poverty and he commented on the lack of established police protection in Esperanza because of its unincorporated status. However, a pattern did not exist throughout their writing or class discussions signaling consistent social justice positioning, perhaps because they were taught to have an uncritical worldview. In another upper-division course several years ago at the same university, I asked preservice teachers, mostly Mexican Americans, to write complaint letters to people in authority for an authentic literacy act; one student said Mexican Americans in our geographic area were not comfortable writing to governmental officials about societal ills. I interpreted this to mean she did not perceive herself to have the social capital or authority to make suggestions for social change. According to Gorski (2008), a reluctance to suggest societal changes could relate to paternalism, even in a geographic area that is numerically Mexican American: "And this is what paternalism does by arming the privileged with the power to control social policy while rendering the oppressed, labeled incapable of advocating for themselves, silent and powerless" (p. 142).

I believe one reason some dodged social justice issues related to my failure as a professor to present enough course content on structural inequalities and, at the same time, to explicitly welcome dialogue (Butin, 2010; Freire, 1994, 2000). Based on my 2008 findings, I have since changed the direction of this methods course; I now integrate social justice into group presentation projects and have students read and respond to Gorski's (2008) critique of Ruby Payne's (2005) ubiquitous work and articles about funds of knowledge (Dworin, 2006; Rios, 2006), based on the theoretical framework of González et al. (2005). We now discuss Bakhtin in depth and the importance of disagreements as ways to outgrow ourselves and to truly value multiculturalism because culture involves shared and contested beliefs and values. Nieto (2008), like Bakhtin, believed that cultures are "dialectical, conflicted, and full of inherent tensions" (p. 139). Nowadays I constantly search for ways to help students to feel comfortable in disagreeing with each other and me. In summary, this part centered on participants' lack of consistent social justice positioning.

Troubling Justice

Highlighted in this section are some participants' disagreements with social justice promotion. Some finished the intensive service-learning course in one of America's poorest neighborhoods believing they were not change agents who would fight against structural inequalities. As the focus group discussion demonstrates, some believed poverty was an individual phenomenon, that their roles as teachers did not involve affecting social change, and that they should not discuss oppression with future students. Yet from a perspective of dialogue, the service-learning project in Esperanza and our focus group discussion began much-needed conversations about justice. In this section I show how students who appeared against a social justice orientation during the focus group took opposite viewpoints in other instances; this demonstrates the importance of dialogue for people to articulate their beliefs and to learn from others. Cana Lilly's written reflection demonstrated the contested nature of the focus group: "I've learned about social justice and structural inequalities.... Many people don't understand the importance of these. The other night we had an important discussion over this issue and I could tell from just a small number of people in the room they have different views." The following dialogue represents participants' responses to my question, "Can you speak about social justice?"

> **Mona:** I noticed prejudice between the children.
> **Belle:** They were comparing their shoes.
> **Mona:** The community doesn't help another community to prosper so they can be one bigger prosperous community. It's like Berlin not wanting to help the other side of Berlin, except we don't have a wall. The wall is poverty stricken. If we work together as a community to bring up a better community and break down that wall, we'll all be better for it.
> **LB:** We can't have everybody prosper. And I thought it was really neat that [Mona] wants to donate to United Way and [name of tutorial center] if she has the money, and if she wants to, but that this isn't what a teacher should focus on. But we can't have everybody prosper. We realize we do have poor people.

By repeating herself, LB emphasized a belief that the poor would always exist. However, those with a social justice orientation would disagree. Gans (1995) stated, "The principal subject of poverty research ... ought to be the forces, processes, agents, and institutions ... that 'decide' that a proportion of the population will end up poor" (p. 127, cited in Gorski, 2008, p. 140). Since those who have the resources can eliminate poverty, not doing so is classism (Gorski, 2008). Indeed, poverty is not a culture (Payne, 2005), and as Mona pointed out in her response to LB, teachers, authorities, and the entire community can work together to eradicate injustices:

Mona: Yeah, but it's just like segregation. This is an area segregated by another community that's segregated and it's going back to what the Civil Rights were. Are we all practicing what we preach again? If we're all going to be teachers and if we're all going to be involved in a community, we have to come together and break down those barriers.

LB: Uh huh, but that's what happens in *your* classroom. Like I understand what you're saying and that's how we can get united in our classroom, but when you say that [indistinguishable]. You're going to be nice, but how many teachers are going to practice what they preach? You might. You can probably afford it.

LB's retort implied that Mona's desire to contribute time and money to help United Way (a social service agency) and the tutorial center was Mona's choice, not something she, LB, felt compelled to do. Perhaps LB thought Mona had the economic means to donate to charities because Mona told us she collected art and she also brought a nice reproduction of Leonardo da Vinci's *Mona Lisa* to class during artifact sharing the second class night. Mona had also donated freshly sliced ham because the peanut butter sandwiches we made before did not go over well with the children. Last, Mona bought a tree for our program, which we planted. These generous gestures may have caused LB to interpret Mona as rich. LB's comment also signified that helping others as teachers involved giving them money, or quick fixes.

As the focus group continued, Seina, a nontraditional preservice teacher like Mona, appeared to take Mona's side and saw that helping the world involved using the word. As Freire (2000) stated: "But while to say the true word—which is work, which is praxis—is to transform the world" (p. 88).

Seina: Even as teachers we should get the word out, also. Help each other.

Mona: Yeah.

Belle: You can't fight for everybody, for the whole community. I mean you can, but you're like ... [indistinguishable].

Mona: I think we can bring an awareness of the segregation in this city, in this town. It's a big element because if we don't practice the awareness, that it's there.

LB: They know it already though. Really, they know that.

Seina: I think it has improved or there have been improvements. I mean, somebody's helping out, or ...

LB: I remember coming with my mom when I was little and she's a nurse and [indecipherable, but my field notes indicate she is discussing destitute conditions when visiting Esperanza homes with her mother].

Bussert-Webb: [Mona], I think I hear you saying teachers need to be more like activists, and [LB], I think you're saying it's not important in school, that basically it's in their classroom.

Mona: Of course I'm going to be active. Of course you're going to be practicing in a classroom.

LB: They shouldn't be told they're segregated until after a certain grade.

Bussert-Webb: You don't think we should tell the kids what's going on in society?

A female participant: They know.

Mona: No, they don't know.

LB: You have to start in your classroom. You shouldn't tell them they're segregated ... I don't tell them because you live in [Esperanza], that's totally different where my family lives. They already know. They will be like, "I don't need you to tell me."

[Indecipherable. Several students are talking at once.]

Bussert-Webb: Right, but I can really see that one point is the kids should understand, like Paulo Freire says, understand their oppression, so they can fight against it. That's what Paulo Freire basically says, but [LB], the point I think you're making is if the kids know, they might feel, like, depressed about it, and they might feel you think less of them. So there are two different points of view here, but I need to stop it because it's already 9:00.

I mentioned Freire because Rubenstein-Avila (2003) highlighted him in an article students read and we had discussed Freire's social justice themes. I also try to validate both viewpoints to show openness to alternative beliefs. However, I decided to end the discussion because it was already 9:00 P.M. and we were supposed to have left already. Students had not started writing their logs and they had to prepare for coursework the next day. Later, I realized that, because of time constraints, I had shut off the very dialogue I was trying to promote. I was irritated at myself for doing so and I should have asked the students if they wanted to stay to continue dialoguing. Instead, I made an autocratic decision as their instructor. However, when I read their learning logs, which they completed at the end of our discussion, I was pleased they reflected on the conversation. For example, Nina wrote: "There were a lot of things said that impacted me at [sic] the group focus. There were two students with really good points emphasizing the segregation and poverty." Although their study was about the challenges between novice teachers of color and their students, Achinstein and Aguirre's (2008) findings are still applicable in terms of intracultural dynamics because they discuss variations within an ethnicity as sources of cultural conflict (e.g., age, social class, gender, and immigration).

Belle demonstrated unclear positioning about social justice. I interpret her statement "You can't fight for everyone" to signify a lack of interest in eradicating inequalities on a macro level. Nevertheless, she demonstrated a consideration of others' viewpoints in her log that night: "I loved the discussion we had at the end of class. It was very interesting. Valid points on all sides [sic] discussed." This demonstrates dual-voicing (Bakhtin, 1981, 1996) and *inner dialogue*, or what transpires in student writing after classroom discussions. Sperling (2004) stated, "To incorporate contradiction is, in fact, to take Bakhtin quite seriously" (p. 250). In another part of the same log, Belle was appalled that many of the ELL testing laws I had mentioned that evening (Texas Education Agency, 2005), such as teachers translating for bilingual designated students during state-mandated tests, were not widely practiced in our local schools: "I think it's very important for teachers to know this and to fight for their children because I don't think parents know this information." Belle mentioned teachers fighting for their children, which I take to mean Belle's students and Belle's people, since Belle was a Latina preservice educator who wished to teach in our geographical area. Vying for one's students regarding schoolwide injustices is indeed a social justice practice. In her final reflection, Belle also wrote about how she could identify with Esperanza children, "I was poor growing up so I can relate to many children living in that area."

Perhaps Belle's experience growing up in poverty caused her to mention how the children rank-ordered their wealth by their shoes. In a reflection Belle wrote:

> Although the children in the program are Hispanic, they are still segregating each other. They talk about who has more than the other, the cars they have, how their house looks, anything that is better than the other. Sometimes they argue and start picking on each other.

Belle's observations may also demonstrate how people of the same race, ethnicity, and geographic area can discriminate against each other. Similarly, Sarmiento-Arribalzaga and Murillo (2009–2010) found preservice teachers were discriminated against in K–12 schools because they spoke Spanish and looked Mexican; these schools, approximately an hour west of Esperanza, served mostly Latino/a children. Also, according to Valenzuela (2008), "Teachers too rarely notice the wounds that students of color inflict upon one another" (p. 50). Valenzuela discussed her collusion in marginalizing another Mexican American middle school student because, in part, of the girl's cheap-looking clothes. Valenzuela attended schools that focused on cultural erasure and English-only policies that led her and her peers to create a pecking order. Belle recognized structural inequalities, the children's discrimination against each other in terms of social class, and she saw the importance of teachers fighting for marginalized youth. However, she did not appear interested in being a change agent (Giroux, 2004) outside of her classroom door (e.g., "You can't fight for . . . the whole community").

LB's social justice stance also appeared uneven. Even though she said it was not her role as a teacher to raise issues of oppression with students, she seemed greatly affected by her service-learning experiences in Esperanza. The day of the focus group discussion, we had gone on a walkabout though Esperanza's narrow, dusty streets with no sidewalks; the tutorial director pointed out the tutees' homes so participants could better understand the children's contexts. After our walk, the director presented a portion of *Sicko,* which featured an Esperanza resident's unsuccessful fight against cancer (Moore, 2007). Although the patient's wife had consistent employment, they were not able to pay for treatments and he died. LB wrote: "Everything was going OK until the caption underneath Joe's portrait read 1965–2007. Up until the end of the video, I was feeling hot, but happy and then everything went downhill [sic] I was a little suicidal."

This learning log from LB, an English major with usually impeccable grammar, demonstrated a stream of consciousness; she did not add a period before the last sentence. Her log also showed care and empathy for Esperanza residents. She also recognized discrimination or biases against its people. In one part of our focus group discussion she said I discriminated against some young men along the street during our community walkabout. LB said my moving to the other side of the street when we got close signaled to the men that I thought they were dangerous. I realized her point and agreed with her in front of the class. Additionally, LB lamented during the focus group about the injustice of immigration laws because an honor student who attended the center's tutorials could not be present for a scholastic award in another part of Texas. The honor student was undocumented and could not clear the immigration checkpoint an hour north of our city. Also, in a process reflection LB discussed the need for more people to get involved:

> The only thing that saddens me about this whole situation is there are not enough people giving back to the community (not just specifically [Esperanza]). Our community in general needs and should have more of the "Mrs. [tutorial director]" and "Dr. Webb's." My mom, since I was 13, "forced" me to start volunteering because she didn't like that in the summers I was only doing sports and so I started volunteering at a lot of different places.

However, LB did not mention *she* should volunteer. In fact, the community workers she cited, the tutorial director and myself, were at least 25 years older than her, not people her own age. Also, when she was a 13-year-old, she did not help others on her own volition or get inspired after she started. It was as though LB saw the need to make the world more just, but did not see it as her responsibility. This interpretation is supported by LB's response to Mona's activist stance. Perhaps LB's time constraints were also barriers to deep, sustained reflections about justice. She was taking another May intensive class in the morning and was also a foster parent.

As her instructor, I sensed LB's deep level of caring for her particular tutees. However, she did not want to have children recognize their oppression. I interpreted LB's remarks to mean that if we draw students' attention to how others oppress them; they will believe we think less of them, which will do more harm. Throughout her learning logs and process and final reflections, LB showed a strong bond with her tutees and often called them her children. She also went into surprising detail about them and pondered how she could help each one the best in their limited time together; indeed, she wrote more about them than any other participant, devoting over two pages to tutee interests, strengths, and needs. Was it possible LB's care for her tutees clouded her notions of justice? Wink (2005) stated that caring and justice are interrelated, but is it possible for a tutor or teacher to avoid the truth about structural inequalities to avoid hurting the children? Do caring and social justice collide in these cases, and if so, why?

LB's reluctance to discuss structural inequalities with students reminded me of when I worked with African American females whom counselors placed in the lowest track at an urban Midwestern high school. I had established a strong bond with the freshmen and felt they needed to fight to get into academically challenging classes, so I told them my perceptions of their tracking (Oakes, 2005). I wonder if I made the right decision because a counselor at the school worried that I hurt their self-esteem by telling them. Perhaps LB believed children's knowledge about their oppression would devastate them at impressionable ages. Perhaps this is what LB meant when she said, "They shouldn't be told they're segregated until after a certain grade." Do we speak with children about ways they are oppressed, and if so, who tells them and when? Vasquez (2004) explored critical issues with young children and Shor (1996) asked his working-class college students to reflect on their oppression. I attempted these discussions as well with pregnant middle school females in another study, but my attempts backfired. Black participants were angered that a privileged white woman was pointing out instances of racism, classism, and sexism (Bussert-Webb, 2001).

When answering the social justice questions in her final reflection, LB said she learned injustices were too common, but gave no further explanation. Yet she appeared to see poverty as individual versus structural because she only mentioned individual tutees: "Now I can defend my kids and tell others to get to know them before they start judging." Also, her comment that we cannot have everyone prosper might give the impression LB was an upper-middle-class student whose social positioning did not help her to see poverty as systemic. However, in her final reflection, LB discussed how she, too, grew up in poverty:

> As a child I was considered to be dirt poor. I mean living off of food stamps, in housing, Medicaid, etc. So in some way we have that in common; after my mom graduated from nursing school, she moved us out of the apartment and into a house. Now I live in a comfortable house.

Even though LB lived part of her life in dire poverty, her mom became a nurse and moved the family out of this condition. Perhaps this experience convinced LB that others could pull themselves out of poverty by individual effort and education, a bootstrap approach to overcome barriers (Gorksi, 2008). Also, LB appeared to believe in meritocracy because she thought an individual, through her own merits, could pull herself out of poverty, as her mother did (Gorski, 2008). According to Briscoe (2009): "If successful Latinas were perceived as possessing characteristics representative of their group, rather than as exceptions, then the perceiver would be forced to . . . [realize success] is not based solely upon one's merits" (p. 245). Although LB did not perceive herself to be a change agent (Giroux, 2004), she wanted to do everything to protect her own students from harm, even the harm of realizing the truth. She also saw that wealthy people could help, if they wanted to, but there was no moral obligation.

On the other hand, Mona often wrote about growing from the service-learning experience and felt morally obligated and passionate about being an activist. In her final reflection she thanked me for exposing her to structural inequalities. She also wrote: "The city does nothing to create some kind of social and economic stability in this area. Just a community being swept under the rug, so to speak, makes me mad to see this here from our own ethnic race." Mona's realization of socioeconomic factors among Latino/as was important. Cahill (2009) and Mazzei (2008) perceptively stated that those in favor of social justice need to question their own power and privilege associated with whiteness. However, power and privilege also occur within any race and ethnicity. Power and privilege may relate to immigration status, socioeconomics, educational attainment, language, literacy, skin color variations within an ethnicity (Rodriguez, 2004), or neighborhood status (Bussert-Webb, 2008, 2009). Thus, service-learning research, from justice and dialogic perspectives, should focus on opening up dialogue about oppression, whoever practices it (Sperling, 2007).

To understand Mona's perspective on social justice, it is important to mention she had been in the U.S. Navy and had traveled extensively while serving. She grew up in an economically disadvantaged section of Chicago and worked for many years in that culturally diverse city. In her first process reflection Mona wrote about her tutee, "I was once in his shoes, so what am I afraid of? I grew up poor." She decided to become a teacher a few years before data gathering. Yet, her father was from this area and her parents had returned, which gave her an insider perspective. Her unique positioning as an insider/outsider enabled her to challenge class members more than I could have as a white professor. She was much closer to their ages than me and, like most participants, she had not started teaching on a full-time basis. Also, as their peer, Mona was on the threshold of respondents' consciousness, at a place I could not enter as their professor. Mona was "on the *boundary* between one's own and someone else's consciousness, on the *threshold*" (Bakhtin, 1997, p. 287, original emphasis).

Indeed, Mona said Esperanza was the other side of Berlin because state and national leaders excluded our city, which ironically excluded the colonia. I believe Mona was alluding to an onion peel of segregation. For the layers of inequalities to be exposed, she wanted to inform people that the nation and state have excluded our city. Once people in our city realized this prejudice, Mona believed they would stop discriminating against Esperanza. Perhaps some participants did not realize the marginalization of our city in the state and country because of their young ages, their insider perspectives, and a lack of extensive U.S. travel; the latter may relate to economic difficulties. Mona's conceptualization of social justice appeared the most consistent and profound. She recognized structural inequalities and believed every teacher was obligated to help. She also wanted her future students to realize how they were oppressed so they could fight their oppression. Next, she saw the need for educators, including herself, to be activists inside and outside of the classroom. Mona, like participants in Carrington and Selva's (2010) study, was transformed by the service-learning experience, was able to critique her world, and saw herself as a change agent. However, the results indicate that the service-learning experience was not transformative for all participants. Also, Mona's peers had contested views about social justice promotion.

LIMITATIONS

Described in this part are the limitations of the study vis-à-vis credibility, confirmability, dependability, and transferability (Lincoln & Guba, 1985). In terms of credibility, or congruence between the findings and reality, I may not have captured all participants' views because parts of the focus group tape were unintelligible and I could not hear all of the speakers. Someone sat the recorder close to Mona because she was talking and this is where it stayed; this could be solved with a more sophisticated recorder. Also, I could not hear everything during the discussion because I was busy typing responses; a solution is to have students take turns typing as others talk, which would allow me to pose follow-up questions, to extend the dialogue, and to listen more carefully. Also, this could add a level of member checking because participants may be more willing to critique each other's typed notes. Another threat to credibility was that some participants may have written or said things to please me, their professor, while others may have been silent because of fear; these instances of power between students and teachers and between researchers and respondents affect the results and this cannot be overlooked in research (Mazzei, 2007). A solution is to be open about dialogue from the onset of a course. Despite these limitations, I believe the findings are credible because of the multiple data points, my several years' experience in conducting this service-learning research at the tutorial center, and the peer debriefing I performed with the tutorial director and parent volunteers, as well as colleagues who have engaged in research at the same center; these techniques make it more likely that the findings are credible (Lincoln & Guba, 1985).

In terms of confirmability, or the degree to which others can confirm the findings, I only received a few responses, albeit positive, from participants. I had emailed them the results and asked for comments and disagreements. This was disappointing from a dialogic perspective and from the standard of confirmability. A solution is to type initial results before the last class and to ask specific follow-up questions and reflections at that time. Another idea is to tell each respondent in private what her or his pseudonym is; in this way they may be interested in looking for their names in the document I send. Also, I could ask the students to respond to the themes I found of embracing, dodging, and troubling justice, for more thorough member checking. Despite the low response rate to my member-checking requests, the results do have a level of confirmability because I documented how I reread the data several times and looked for confirming and disconfirming cases. Also, others have found that even college students of color did not finish service-learning courses with social justice positioning (Boyle-Baise & Langford, 2004); even more researchers have found that some culturally diverse people may have oppressive views toward their own ethnicity as a result of internalized racism (Valenzuela, 2008) or the dearth of strengths-based educational experiences (Weisman et al., 2007). Even in the Rio Grande Valley, which is mostly Mexican American numerically, many teacher candidates have been discriminated against because they spoke Spanish and looked Mexican (Sarmiento-Arribalzaga & Murillo, 2009-2010).

Regarding dependability or reliability, the same results cannot be repeated because this study is about a particular place, time, group of people, and service-learning project. Nevertheless, I have provided much detail about data gathering and analysis so that those interested in conducting a similar study may do so. In terms of transferability, these results might not be applicable beyond a Latino/a cultural perspective. However, hopefully my detailed description of the research context and theoretical framework can help readers to transfer these results to other situations and people (Lincoln & Guba, 1985). In summary, this section focused on the study's weaknesses, as well as my attempts to overcome these limitations throughout data gathering and analysis.

IMPLICATIONS

So, what were the social justice beliefs articulated by 12 Latino/a preservice teachers during a service-learning project in a south Texas neighborhood? They embraced, dodged, and troubled social justice. Through dialogue, participants' perspectives were "shot through with shared thoughts, points of view, alien judgments and accents" (Bakhtin, 1996, p. 276). The views of the teacher candidates were what they should have been in any service-learning project in communities with high poverty levels—contested and fraught with ideological becoming (Morson, 2004).

Next, from the focus group discussion and from LB's and Belle's written reflections, I saw they took one step backward and one step forward regarding social justice promotion during the service-learning project. This indicated that learning and beliefs are not linear, but are instead constantly evolving and in a state of flux (Freedman & Ball, 2004). Some respondents' inconsistent remarks demonstrated that they grappled with what inequalities and social justice meant to them personally and professionally. The authoritatively persuasive, or official, socially privileged discourse they had heard throughout their lives was being challenged by the internally persuasive discourse of their peers and their personal experiences (Bakhtin, 1981), which demonstrates the power of group discussions about the service-learning project, as well as having students write reflections connecting the service-learning project to their lives and course content (Rowls & Swick, 2000). As Bakhtin (1997) stated: "And everything internal gravitates not toward itself, but is turned to the outside and dialogized..." (p. 287). Indeed, profound learning comes when we help students to question phenomena, versus convincing them of our views (Butin, 2010).

Boyle-Baise (1998) lamented that college students did not question the poverty witnessed during their service-learning experiences at various community centers and, like Mazzei (2007), Boyle-Baise troubled the silence: "A significant 'nonfinding' was the lack of a critical stance toward inequality" (p. 53). Similarly, I found some participants saw poverty as an individual versus structural phenomenon, and that they viewed themselves as having minimal change agent roles. However, respondents' disagreements in the present study demonstrated authentic learning, not just writing or saying things to please me. Also, the comfort of some in voicing disagreement led to new conversations and considerations of other perspectives. For example, the focus group discussion helped participants to unpack issues of social class, immigration, and neighborhood marginalization, which they learned about during the shared service-learning experience. Even the silence was enlightening because it caused me to dig deeper and to reflect on my own privilege and power in this service-learning project (Cahill, 2009).

Indeed, service-learning can help disrupt preservice teachers' notions of social justice (Carrington & Selva, 2010), especially if the instructor welcomes dialogue and brings social justice and diversity content into the course vis-à-vis readings, movies, and discussions (Simons et al., 2009; Boyle-Baise & Langford, 2004). Also, being able to disagree with class members and the professor, or to point out inconsistencies in our words and actions, may give preservice teachers confidence to follow suit in their own classrooms. For example, LB said I stereotyped men in the street by avoiding them during our community walkabout. Perhaps students' freedom and lack of fear during class discussions is why Freire (2000) believed dialogue could make the world more democratic. If preservice teachers do not experience freedom to find their voices in our classes, it will be difficult for them to encourage their students to challenge authority, to be enriched by other perspectives, and to reexamine their own points of view vis-à-vis dialogue (Morson, 2004).

Applications of 21st-century learning skills relate to collaboration, critical thinking, cross-cultural communication, and flexibility and are imperative in preservice teacher preparation. Teacher candidates must experience the type of learning environment that we expect them to bring into their own classrooms. In their study of 150 Australian preservice teachers, Edwards-Groves and Hoare (2012) found that a talking to learn project helped participants to share knowledge, build on each other's understanding, and to apply interactive practice with children. With this in mind, what would happen if we engage our students in focus group discussions in every service-learning course, not just courses set aside for our research? Edwards-Groves and Hoare stated, "Understanding the nature of classrooms as interactive spaces and the influence of talk on its participants is a core dimension of practice development which requires an overt place in teacher education courses" (p. 97). Therefore, as teacher educators, we must rethink our pedagogy to allow time during our service-learning courses for teacher candidates to unpack in class what they are learning in the field and to challenge each other and us intellectually.

This long-term service-learning project has helped me to explore and change my teaching and research methods, and even my theoretical orientation, during service-learning courses. In previous years I was set on showing how service-learning changed my students. However, my students and the service-learning project in Esperanza inspired me to invite dialogue about social justice in all of my courses. Indeed, during service-learning experiences, those served and those providing services will experience different perspectives and practices. However, by encouraging dialogue we can help service providers and recipients to change the world.

Next, even though participants were Mexican Americans, they still had a diversity of perspectives and experiences; hence, dialogue helped them to learn from each other and to enrich their viewpoints in a process of ideological becoming (Morson, 2004). The diversity of social justice beliefs within a race and ethnicity is important for white middle-class preservice teachers to realize, given the paucity of research on preservice teachers of color (Montecinos, 2004). Also, cultivating social justice orientations in Latino/a preservice teachers is essential to their empowerment and, in turn, their empowerment of students (Weisman et al., 2007; Sarmiento-Arribalzaga & Murillo, 2009-2010). For example, in a service-learning study, both Latino and Anglo preservice teachers gained a deeper level of understanding of Latinos' struggles as U.S. immigrants (Hale, 2008).

Last, I have been teaching this course for 8 years on campus and in Esperanza, but my students' learning has been so much deeper and more profound during our group service-learning project in the colonia. During the academic year, teacher candidates place themselves in schools and in community centers for service-learning requirements. However, in the May session, we are together in the same after-school tutorial center during the service-learning project and class sessions. My students' written reflections and comments during the May session experience have convinced me that they learn much more about social justice and dialogue through this group service-learning experience than through individual placements. They see the structural inequalities the children face; additionally, their shared experience in the same neighborhood provides them with common ground to unpack what they have heard, seen, and experienced. Thus, this group-based service-learning experience at one site, with the instructor present, is recommended, especially if the instructor has a long-term relationship with the agency staff and community members.

REFERENCES

Achinstein, B., & Aguirre, J. (2008). Cultural match or culturally suspect: How new teachers of color negotiate sociocultural challenges in the classroom. *Teachers College Record, 110*(8), 1505–1540.

Anderson, J., & Gerber, J. (2007). *Fifty years of change on the U.S.–Mexico border: Growth development, and quality of life.* Austin: University of Texas Press.

Bakhtin, M. M. (1981). Discourse in the novel. In M. Holquist (Ed.), *The dialogic imagination: Four essays* (M. Holquist & C. Emerson, Trans.) (pp. 259–422). Austin: University of Texas Press.

Bakhtin, M. M. (1996). *The dialogic imagination, four essays by M. M. Bakhtin* (10th ed.) (M. Holquist, Ed.; C. Emerson & M. Holquist, Trans.). Austin: University of Texas Press. (Original work published 1975)

Bakhtin, M. M. (1997). *Problems of Dostoevsky's poetics* (7th ed.) (C. Emerson, Trans. & Ed.) Minneapolis: University of Minnesota. (Original work published 1929)

Bakhtin, M. M., & Medvedev, P. N. (1978). *The formal method in literary scholarship: A critical introduction to sociological poetics* (Albert J. Wehrle, Trans.). Cambridge, MA: Harvard University Press.

Bopry, J. (2002). Semiotics, epistemology, and inquiry. *Teaching and Learning: The Journal of Natural Inquiry and Reflective Practice, 17*(1), 1–20.

Boyle-Baise, M. (1998). Community service learning for multicultural education: An exploratory study with preservice teachers. *Equity and Excellence in Education, 31*(2), 52–61.

Boyle-Baise, M. (2002). Saying more: Qualitative research issues for multicultural service learning. *Qualitative Studies in Education, 15*(3), 317–331.

Boyle-Baise, M., & Langford, J. (2004). There are children here: Service learning for social justice. *Equity & Excellence in Education, 37*(1), 55–66.

Briscoe, F. M. (2009). "They make you invisible": Negotiating power at the academic intersections of ethnicity, gender, and class. *Equity & Excellence in Education, 42*(2), 233–248.

Buchler, J. (Ed.). (1955). *Philosophical writings of Peirce* (2nd ed.). New York, NY: Dover.

Butin, D. W. (2010). *Service-learning in theory and practice: The future of community engagement in higher education.* New York, NY: Palgrave Macmillan.

Bussert-Webb, K. (2001). I won't tell you about myself, but I will draw my story. *Language Arts, 78,* 511–519.

Bussert-Webb, K. (2008, Fall). Gardening hope: How a tutoring and native garden project impacted preservice teachers. *Journal for Civic Commitment, 11.* Retrieved from www.mc.maricopa.edu/other/engagement/Journal/.

Bussert-Webb, K. (2009). Gardening, tutoring, and service by and for Latinos: La Esperanza. *Education Research and Perspectives Journal, 3*(2).

Cahill, C. (2009). Beyond "us" and "them": Community-based research as a politics of engagement. In M. L. Diener & H. Liese (Eds.), *Finding meaning in civically engaged scholarship: Personal journeys, professional experiences* (pp. 47–57). Charlotte, NC: Information Age.

Carrington, S., & Selva, G. (2010). Critical social theory and transformative learning: evidence in pre-service teachers' service-learning reflection logs. *Higher Education Research and Development, 29*(1), 45–57.

Clifford, J. (1986). *Writing culture: The poetics and politics of ethnography.* Berkeley: University of California Press.

Cline, Z., & Necochea, J. (2003). My mother never read to me. *Journal of Adult and Adolescent Literacy, 47*(2), 122–126.

Díaz, M. E., & Bussert-Webb, K. (2013). Reading and language beliefs and practices of Latino/a children in a border colonia. *Journal of Latinos and Education, 12*(1), 59–73.

Downey, D. B., von Hippel, P. T., & Broh, B. A. (2004). Are schools the great equalizer? Cognitive inequality during the summer months and the school year. *American Sociological Review, 69*(5), 613–635.

Driscoll, A.(2008, January/February). Carnegie's community-engagement classification: Intentions and insights. *Change.* Retrieved from www.carnegiefoundation .org/sites/default/files/elibrary/Driscoll.pdf.

Dworin, J.E. (2006). The family stories project: Using funds of knowledge for writing. *The Reading Teacher, 59*(6), 510–520.

Edwards-Groves, C. J., & Hoare, R. L. (2012) "Talking to learn": Focusing teacher education on dialogue as a core practice for teaching and learning. *Australian Journal of Teacher Education, 37*(8), 82–100. Retrieved from http://ro.ecu.edu .au/ajte/vol37/iss8/6.

Federal Reserve Bank of Dallas. (n.d.). *Texas colonias: A thumbnail sketch of the conditions, issues, challenges and opportunities.* Dallas, TX: Author. Retrieved from www.dallasfed.org/ca/pubs/colonias.html.

Fleishman, P. (2004). *Seedfolks.* New York, NY: HarperTrophy.

Foucault, M. (1972). *The archeology of knowledge* (A. M. Sheridan Smith, Trans.). New York, NY: Pantheon Books/Random House. (Original work published 1969)

Freedman, S. W., & Ball, A.F. (2004). Ideological becoming: Bakhtinian concepts to guide the study of language, literacy, and learning. In A. F. Ball & S. W. Freedman (Eds.), *Bakhtinian perspectives on language, literacy, and learning* (pp. 3–33). New York, NY: Cambridge University Press.

Freire, P. (1994). *Pedagogy of hope: Reliving pedagogy of the oppressed* (R. R. Barr, Trans.) New York, NY: Continuum.

Freire, P. (2000). *Pedagogy of the oppressed.* (4th ed.) (M. Bergman Ramos, Trans.). New York, NY: Continuum.

Frey, W. H. (2012). The 2010 Census: America on the cusp. *The Milken Institute Review,* pp. 47–58. Retrieved from www.milkeninstitute.org/publications/ review/2012_4/47-58MR54.pdf.

García, O., Kleifgen, J. A., & Falchi, L. (2008). From English language learners to emergent bilinguals. *Equity Matters: Research Review No. 1.* New York, NY: The Campaign for Education Equity, Teachers College, Columbia University. Retrieved from http://www.tc.columbia.edu/i/a/document/6468_Ofelia_ ELL._Final.pdf.

Giroux, H. (2004). Teachers as transformative intellectuals. In A. S. Canestrari & B. A. Marlowe. (Eds.), *Educational foundations: An anthology of critical readings* (pp. 205–212). Thousand Oaks, CA: Sage.

Glaser, B. (1965). The constant comparative method of qualitative analysis. *Social Problems, 12*(4), 436–445.

González, N., Moll, L., & Amanti, K. (2005). *Funds of knowledge: Theorizing practices in households, communities and classrooms.* Mahwah, NJ: Erlbaum.

Gorski, P. (2008). Peddling poverty for profit: Elements of oppression in Ruby Payne's framework. *Equity and Excellence in Education, 41*(1), 130–148.

Hale, A. (2008). Service learning with Latino communities: Effects on preservice teachers. *Journal of Hispanic Higher Education, 7*(1), 54–69

Hart, S. (2006). Breaking literacy boundaries through critical service-learning: Education for the silence and marginalized. *Mentoring & Tutoring, 14*(1), 17–32.

Haycock, K. (2001). Closing the achievement gap. *Educational Leadership, 58*(6), 6–12.

Herrell, A. L., & Jordan, M. (2008). *Fifty strategies for teaching English language learners* (3rd ed.). Boston: Pearson.

Hess, D. J., Lanig, H., & Vaughan, W. (2007). Educating for equity and social justice: A conceptual model for cultural engagement. *Multicultural Perspectives, 9*(1), 32–39.

Janes, J. (2010, May 16). Veterans start letter writing campaign for hospital. *The Monitor.* Retrieved from www.themonitor.com/articles/veterans-38636-hospital-south.html.

Kim, J. S., & Guryanm J. (2010). The efficacy of a voluntary summer book reading intervention for low-income Latino children from language minority families. *Journal of Educational Psychology, 102*(1), 20–31.

Lin, Q. (2001). Toward a caring-centered multicultural education within the social justice context. *Education, 122*(1), 107–114.

Lincoln, Y. S., & Guba, E. G. (1985). *Naturalistic inquiry.* Beverly Hills, CA: Sage.

Long, G. (2010, July 31). TEA: District recognized; all 52 schools recognized or exemplary. *Brownsville Herald.* Retrieved from www.brownsvilleherald.com/articles/recognized-114910-district-morning.html.

Martinez, L. B. (2008, January 31). Let there be light. *Brownsville Herald,* pp. A1, A12.

Mazzei, L. A. (2007). *Inhabited silence in qualitative research: Putting poststructural theory to work.* New York, NY: Peter Lang.

Mazzei, L. A. (2008). Silence speaks: Whiteness revealed in the absence of voice. *Teaching and Teacher Education, 24*(5), 1125–1136.

Migrant Health Promotion. (2012). *The lower Rio Grande Valley: Community strengths.* Weslaco, TX: Author. Retrieved from www.migranthealth.org/index.php?option=com_content&view=article&id=39:the-lower-rio-grande-valley&catid=8:farmworker-communities&Itemid=31.

Montecinos, C. (2004). Paradoxes in multicultural teacher education research: Students of color positioned as objects while ignored as subjects. *International Journal of Qualitative Studies in Education, 17*(2), 167–181.

Moore, M. (Director). (2007). *Sicko* [Film]. Los Angeles, CA: Weinstein Company.

Morson, G. S. (2004). The process of ideological becoming. In A. F. Ball & S. W. Freedman (Eds.), *Bakhtinian perspectives on language, literacy, and learning* (pp. 317–331). New York, NY: Cambridge University Press.

National Center of Education Statistics. (2009). *Characteristics of public, private, and bureau of Indian education elementary and secondary school teachers: Results from the 2007–2008 schools and staffing survey.* Washington, DC: U.S. Department of Education. Retrieved from http://nces.ed.gov/pubs2009/2009324.pdf.

National Education Association. (2003). *Status of the American public school teacher, 2000–2001.* Washington, DC: Author.

Nieto, S. (2008). Culture and education. In G. D. Festenmacher (Ed.), *Yearbook of the National Society for the Study of Education* (pp. 127–142). New York, NY: Wiley-Blackwell.

Oakes, J. (2005). *Keeping track: How schools structure inequality* (2nd ed.). New Haven, CT: Yale University Press.

O'Brien, D. M. (1999). *Three essays on early academic achievement of minority and disadvantaged students.* Unpublished doctoral dissertation, University of Texas at Dallas.

Parker-Gwin, R., & Mabry, J. B. (1998). Service learning as pedagogy and civic education: Comparing outcomes for three models. *Teaching Sociology, 26*(4), 276–291.

Partnership for 21st Century Skills. (2011). *Framework for 21st century learning.* Washington, DC: Author. Retrieved from www.p21.org/overview.

Payne, R. K. (2005). *A framework for understanding poverty* (4th ed.). Highlands, TX: Aha! Process.

Rios, A. (2006). *Exploring the everyday math practices in Latino families.* Tucson, AZ: Center for the Mathematics Education of Latinos/as (CEMELA). Retrieved from http://math.arizona.edu/~cemela/english/content/workingpapers/Rios_Everyday_Math-1.pdf.

Robinson, D. R., Ward-Schofield, J., & Steers-Wentzell, K. L. (2005). Peer and cross-age tutoring in math: Outcomes and their design implications. *Educational Psychology Review, 17*(4), 327–362.

Rodriguez, R. (2004). *Hunger of memory.* New York, NY: Bantam Books.

Rosenberg, H., Reed, S. C., Statham, A., & Rosing, H. (2012). Service-learning and the nontraditional student: What's age got to do with it? In J. Hatcher & R. Bringle (Eds.), *Understanding service-learning and community engagement: Crossing boundaries through research* (pp. 157–178). Charlotte, NC: Information Age.

Rowls, M., & Swick, K. J. (2000). Designing teacher education course syllabi that integrate service learning. *Journal of Instructional Psychology, 27*(3), 187–196.

Rubenstein-Avila, E. (2003). Conversing with Miguel: An adolescent English Language Learner struggling with later literacy development. *Journal of Adolescent & Adult Literacy, 47*(4), 290–301.

Sarmiento-Arribalzaga, M. A., & Murillo, L.A. (2009-2010). Pre-service bilingual teachers and their invisible scars: Implications for preparation programs. *SRATE Journal, 19*(1), 61–69.

Shor, I. (1996.). *When students have power: Negotiating authority in a critical pedagogy.* Chicago: University of Chicago Press.

Simons, L., Blank, N., Russell, B., Williams, E., & Willis, K. (2009). An exploration of the value of cultural-based service-learning for student and community partners. In B. E. Moely, S. H. Billig & B. A. Holland (Eds.), *Creating our identities in service-learning and community engagement.* (pp. 189–214). Charlotte, N.C.: Information Age.

Sperling, M. (2004). Is contradiction contrary? In A. F. Ball & S. W. Freedman (Eds.), *Bakhtinian perspectives on language, literacy, and learning* (pp. 232–251). New York, NY: Cambridge University Press.

Sperling, R. (2007). Service-learning as a method of teaching multiculturalism to white college students. *Journal of Latinos and Education, 6*(4), 309–322.

Texas Department of Transportation. (2012). *Hurricane evacuation contraflow publications: Rio Grande Valley hurricane evacuation routes.* Austin, TX: Author. Retrieved from www.txdot.gov/driver/weather/hurricane-contraflow.html.

Texas Education Agency (2005). *LPAC Decision-making process for the Texas Assessment Program (Grades 3–12).* Austin, TX: Author. Retrieved from www.tea.state.tx.us.student.assessment/resources/guides/lpac/index.html.

University of Texas Austin. (2010). *Permanent University Fund: Investing in the future of Texas.* Austin, TX: TxTell, UT Stories, University of Texas. Retrieved from http://txtell.lib.utexas.edu/stories/p0002-full.html.

U.S. Census Bureau. (2000). *American FactFinder.* Washington, DC: Author.

U.S. Census Bureau. (2011). *Hispanic heritage month 2011: Sept. 15–Oct. 15: Profile America facts for features.* Washington, DC: Author. Retrieved from www.census.gov/newsroom/releases/archives/facts_for_features_special_editions/cb11-ff18.html.

U.S. Census Bureau. (2012). *State and county quickfacts.* Washington, DC: Author. Retrieved from http://quickfacts.census.gov.

Valenzuela, A. (2008). Uncovering internalized oppression. In M. Pollock (Ed.), *Everyday antiracism: concrete strategies for successfully navigating the relevance of race in school.* (pp. 50–55). New York, NY: New Press.

Vasquez, V. (2004). *Negotiating critical literacies with young children.* Mahwah, NJ: Erlbaum.

Wasserman, K. N. (2010). Elementary teacher utilization of service learning as methodology during student teaching placements. *Issues in Educational Research, 20*(1). Retrieved from www.iier.org.au/iier20/wasserman.html.

Webb, R. B. (2006). *Category 5 hurricane evacuation analysis of the Rio Grande Valley of Texas: Maximum flow problem.* Unpublished master's thesis, University of Texas at Brownsville.

Weisman, E. M., Flores, S. Y., & Valenciana, C. (2007). Building bilingual–bicultural learning communities: Experiences of Latino teacher candidates. *Journal of Hispanic Higher Education, 6*(3), 191–208.

Wink, J. (2005). *Critical pedagogy: Notes from the real world.* Boston: Pearson Education.

Kathy Bussert-Webb, PhD, is an Associate Professor with tenure at University of Texas Brownsville, where she teaches in the Department of Language, Literacy, and Intercultural Studies and is also the Graduate Reading Program Coordinator and Coordinator/Writer for the nationally accredited English Middle School and High School Programs under NCATE. Dr. Bussert-Webb was UTB's Director of the Center for Civic Engagement and she played a key role in UTB's Community Engagement Classification, awarded by the Carnegie Foundation in 2010. She served in the U.S. Peace Corps in Honduras, and has been an educator of culturally diverse students for over 28 years.

Dr. Bussert-Webb has published numerous peer-reviewed articles on service learning and for several years she has been actively engaged with the Service Learning and Experiential Special Interest Group (SIG) of the American Educational Research Association (AERA). She has served as the SIG's co-program chair and has presented her papers for this SIG and other AERA divisions yearly since 2006. Her research interests are social justice, service learning, disciplinary literacy, and digital literacy.

CHAPTER 8

WALKING THE WALK AND SHOWING HOW

University Students Learning to Lead Through Service

**Elizabeth Barber, Tom Smith, Sharon Jacobs,
Karen Thompson, Blayre C. Penn, Bethany S. Penn,
Carl B. Redd, Destenie Nock, Brianna Cooke, Brittany McLean,
Donald R. Thompson, and Ahmod Camp**

ABSTRACT

This research traces outcomes of a service-learning experience in which student volunteers from a historic black university engage after school twice weekly, 2 hours each session, as tutors for third to fifth graders from urban impact schools in Greensboro, North Carolina. Bounded only by as many semesters as students choose to participate—and many return term after term—this supported engagement provides them with ongoing opportunities to actualize the cultural strengths and dispositions they bring with them to the university as they develop into culturally competent practitioners, members of a professional learning community, and leaders. In this project university tutors learn to teach and lead through service, and employ service-learning as a

Transforming Teacher Education Through Service-Learning, pages 179–210
Copyright © 2013 by Information Age Publishing
All rights of reproduction in any form reserved.

pedagogy of promise with children. Children have opportunities to catch up academically, and university students take up the stance of *African American teacher leader:* they embody expertise about teaching black and other global majority children (Robinson, 2011; Ball, 2009). Our chapter explores these outcomes and contributes to the ongoing dialogue on service-learning as a form of leader development.

TRACING POSSIBILITIES WITHIN A LONG-TERM LEARNING COMMUNITY

University service-learning experiences typically last a semester at most and are closed-ended—when the term is over the experience ends, and so does the opportunity to continue crafting an identity within a community of individuals working toward similar goals. Open-ended, longer-term, self-chosen service-learning experiences in which university students select their own levels of involvement provide a broader window into the meanings and uses of participation that they may construct for themselves over time. This chapter examines outcomes of long-term engagement with urban learners for tutors from a historic black university (HBCU) that include academic gains for children and the development of culturally centered identities as teachers and leaders for student participants.

In 2006 when university and public school partners planned for a service-learning tutoring program at North Carolina A&T State University, we fashioned it around themes of **S**ervice, **M**entoring, **A**chievement, **R**esponsibility and **T**eamwork. SMART PATH Tutoring and Enrichment is an afterschool program in which student volunteers engage twice weekly, 2 hours each session, with third to fifth graders from urban impact schools in East Greensboro, North Carolina. The program serves as an early course-related field experience alternative, as well as an option for fulfilling university service-learning requirements for graduation. In this chapter, written 10 semesters after SMART PATH's inception, we update an earlier examination of program outcomes (Barber & Smith, 2011) to include a focus on how SMART PATH appears to be growing its own student leadership.

SMART PATH provides opportunities for African American university students to walk the walk and show others how. At the most basic level university tutors model for children the rich array of possible identities that they, too, may take up as they craft selves as young people moving through school. Tutors share their majors with tutees, perform classical violin and talk about the physics of how you hold your finger on the strings, or sing for the children as members of the university's male chorus. Children get the chance to be tutored for several years in a row by a black female electrical engineering major, or a black male animal science major. At another level, experienced tutors show the next new group of tutors how to do these things at a virtuoso level, and student site directors guide whole tutoring sites and train new student leaders. Finally, the torch is passed to the child, who, when ready, shows other children "how to" through the program's emphasis on metacognition and voicing aloud "how you figured that out." Children get opportunities to catch up academically, and tutors embody expertise about how to teach black and other global majority children (Robinson, 2011; Ball, 2009), as well as to teach white children about living in a diverse world.

Since its first term in action in spring 2007 SMART PATH has fostered the development of cultural competence, best practice teaching, membership in a supportive learning community, and leadership skill for more than 500 university tutors. Our chapter documents how tutors learn to teach and lead through culturally resonant service that builds onto the cultural strengths and dispositions they bring to the endeavor, while employing service-learning as a pedagogy of promise with children. Our work, authored with the partners whose dedicated effort makes SMART PATH possible— university students and faculty along with public school and community agency representatives, contributes to the ongoing dialogue on service-learning as a form of teacher preparation.

SITUATING COGNITION WITHIN CONNECTED AND CONNECTING EXPERIENCES

As learners, practitioners, leaders, and scholars we ground this work within Lave and Wenger's (1991) definition of learning as an apprenticeship taking place within a specific and located community of practice (Rogoff & Lave, 2002; Brown, Collins, & Diguid, 1989), which in our case is held together by bonds of affection. Learners need opportunities to make personal connections to concepts and information, organize new knowledge to facilitate retrieval and application, metacognitively reflect upon and control their learning (Bransford, Brown, & Cocking, 2000), engage in authentic, discipline-based work, and uncover difficult aspects of a topic or concept. Within SMART PATH learners of all ages accomplish these things through engaging affectively (Wiggins & McTighe, 2005).

The affective environment is critical in anchoring development for SMART PATH tutors and student leaders. Coursework and student teaching can fail to adequately scaffold preservice teachers for working in culturally diverse contexts (Borko & Putnam, 1996). These teacher preparation experiences aim to prepare the homogenized, raceless, cultureless teacher for success with all children. While some teacher education programs adequately focus on the cultural and socioeconomic history within which schooling is located, teaching *about* the situated nature of teaching and learning can be insufficient. Novice teachers tend to place their faith in the teaching practices they experienced in school, and in those they observe in their placement classrooms, above what they are taught in university coursework (Zeichner & Hoeft, 1996). To become successful teachers for diverse learners, novices need *connected and connecting experiences* with children and their communities (Hunter-Quartz & TEP Research Group, 2003). Studies of relationships among children and teachers, the implications of these relationships for teaching and learning, and how these relationships are affected by teacher dispositions (Brown, 2002; Murrell, 2002) demonstrate the need for teachers who view urban learners as children of promise (Boykin, 2000), possess the cultural competencies needed for work in diverse classrooms (Ladson-Billings, 2001), and view themselves as efficacious.

DOCUMENTATION AND DATA SOURCES

Participatory action research (McIntyre & Lykes, 2004) and critical theory (Freire, 2004) constitute both perspective and methodology for our work. We employ case study methods (Flyvbjerg, 2011) to collect layered evidence for thick description (Geertz, 1973) of the shaping of attitudes, actions, and knowledge bases. Photo-ethnography, video-ethnography, and other ethnographic techniques including field notes (Emerson, Fretz & Shaw, 2011), pre- and post-surveys, interviews (Briggs, 1986), and power-sensitive conversations (Haraway, 1988), along with collections of program artifacts and other forms of institutional documentation (Peraklya & Ruusuvuori, 2011), provide data for multifaceted analysis (Denzin, 2011).

Populations

Urban learner participants. Participating elementary school populations are characterized as living in low-income neighborhoods, with 33% living below the poverty line and 88–90% qualifying for free lunch (http://newsroom.cigna.com/article_display.cfm?article_id=434). In 2009 their schools performed at approximately the 30th percentile on state tests, with 27% of pupils scoring on grade level (Health Resources & Services Administration, 2009). Elementary, middle, and high school students from this sector of the city who were retained in grade or dropped out totaled 1,764 in 2010 (www.co.guilford.nc.us/publichealth/divisions/wp-content/uploads/2008/12/mb_intro.pdf). At the high school into which these children's schools eventually feed, only 56% of students of color graduated in 2008, and based on new state math requirements, only 20% were projected to graduate in 4 years.

Partner school teachers send home family consent forms for the children who participate, most of whom originate from the bottom 25th percentile upon entrance to SMART PATH. We agree that no child should be removed from the program once they are successful, but continue until they move to middle school. Between 35 and 200 children participate per term, depending on need and number of university tutors available.

University tutors. New tutors are recruited each term by student leaders and experienced tutors who are invited by university faculty to speak to their classes or to student organizations on campus such as the Psychology Club or Young Men on the Move. Ideal tutor recruits are freshmen, who can serve if they wish for multiple semesters throughout their university experience. After their first experience in SMART PATH, many tutors organize their course schedules around tutoring days and times so they can stay with their tutee group for several years. Some tutor every semester from entering the university as freshmen to their student teaching term or graduation.

Like many students attending HBCUs, our university tutors identify their families as of low socioeconomic status (below $20,000 annual income). A significant number of our students self-identify as first-time college attenders. Our tutors report high levels of experience with diversity as children and in school prior to coming to the university. Almost all have worked with children as Sunday school teachers, sports or club leaders, camp counselors, and mentors or tutors before coming to college. Nearly all our tutors work in paid jobs to help finance their university educations. The ability to pay stipends to student leaders is critical in supporting them in their development as future teachers and leaders, and providing a small income to offset hours lost to other paid work.

University faculty report that students who participate in SMART PATH are *different*. Methods courses professors indicate that tutors come with an experiential knowledge base that enriches their ability to engage with course material. Administrators note maturity and deeper understanding of and commitment to teaching that appears to result in improved persistence to graduation and certification. Currently our university graduates fewer than 50% of students who major in teacher education—many do not pass PRAXIS components and/or fail to attain the grade point average to be admitted to teacher education. Commitment to children resulting in persistence to graduation forms an aspect of documentation that we need yet to pursue.

DATA COLLECTION STRATEGIES

We document program outcomes using a variety of surveys, performance-based assessments, school-based achievement data, tutor reflection, and end-of-term focus group interviews.

Performance-based assessments. Tutors employ research-based strategies for assessing and directing tutee learning (Zemelman, Daniels, & Hyde, 2005) and guide children in keeping portfolios of their work for review at the end of each term. They administer and analyze results of the *Words Their Way* Elementary Spelling Inventory (Bear, Invernizzi, Templeton, & Johnson, 2011) to provide data for targeted word study. They learn to recognize reading performance that indicates frustration or independence and administer running records (Fountas & Pinnell, 2000) to check reading levels and make needed instructional adjustments. Tutors use the Writing Developmental Continuum (Raison & Rivalland, 1994) to evaluate writing samples and select teaching objectives. "Books I've Read" lists in child portfolios document ongoing reading levels. Tutors administer and perform item analysis using sample items from the MathSlice Math Mock Test (www.mathslice.com/mathmocktest.php) for grades 3–5 as a pre- and post-assessment for targeted instruction in math.

Surveys. Tutees complete reading and writing surveys adapted from Nancie Atwell's *In the Middle* (1998) at the beginning and end of each term. Children also complete an end-of-term program evaluation survey. During some terms tutors have completed the *Multicultural Efficacy Scale* (2005), and the *Annual Survey of Teacher Novices* (Hunter-Quartz & TEP Research Group, 2003) pre- and post-assessment each semester, although these assessments fail to capture the development toward the African American form of teacher practice and leadership that we seem to be observing.

School-based data. School achievement data, including state standardized test scores and school-based benchmark scores, provide a different layer of evidence for comparison with program data.

Tutor reflection and focus group interviews. Tutors reflect in writing after every tutoring session, share evolving perspectives and expertise both formally and informally throughout the tutoring term, and participate in end-of-term focus group exit interviews to provide critical shaping feedback to each new iteration of the program.

DATA ANALYSIS AS A COLLABORATIVE PROCESS

Before each tutoring term university, school, and community agency representatives decide on evidence needed to anchor program development. That evidence is then used for reflection at multiple levels.

Child portfolios and self-assessment. With their tutors' assistance children review their own portfolios, including work samples, survey responses, and all pre- and post-assessments at the end of each term. They then set personal learning goals and make plans for achieving these goals in the next semester. Common end-of-term program outcomes for children include knowing the names of authors and titles of books that have become favorites and being able to tell about favorite pieces of writing or new kinds of writing they have engaged in. In pre-tutoring term surveys, tutees (especially those new to SMART PATH) often evidence limited experience with children's literature and with different kinds of writing or the authoring experience per se. Favorites in terms of books, authors, and their own pieces of writing show up richly in end-of-term reading and writing survey responses, self-reports that are confirmed by school media specialists, and next-term tutors who tell about children requesting certain authors/series/genres of books. Pre-post Math Mock Test item analysis similarly helps children, tutors, and program leaders document accomplishments and needs, which are further confirmed in collaboration with the inventor of the Pathematics math component, an aeronautics engineer and community volunteer who works with tutors and children every math tutoring day.

Tutoring group data review. At the end of each term tutor pairs compile a summary of assessment data for each child in their group, which they file in each child's portfolio.

Student leaders and university faculty analysis of data. Student leaders compile tutoring group summaries into a database and then meet with university faculty to analyze program data for that term. Child end-of-term program surveys indicate favorites in terms of activities in particular. Student leaders and faculty examine survey responses, focus group interviews, and information in the tutee database. Qualitative data are indexed for thematic analysis, and numerical data are examined at the program level.

Collaborative analysis with public school and community agency representatives. Finally, student leaders and university faculty share program data with school- and agency-based colleagues for further interpretation and comparison with school-based input sources. Combined analyses then determine program adjustments for the upcoming tutoring term.

S.M.A.R.T. AS A GUIDING PHILOSOPHY

The SMART PATH program emphasizes service and mentoring, understandings and life-ways deeply ingrained in African American heritage. Helping those around you and guiding those who follow are unvoiced cultural traditions. However, the ways in which HBCU students would act out these cultural expectations could not have been predicted when we began planning the program. SMART Tutoring and Enrichment began serving urban learners in spring 2007 as a Learn and Serve America grant-funded program focused on two objectives: (1) to scaffold educational equity for learners in Greensboro's urban eastern sector and (2) to prepare teachers responsive to the needs of diverse urban learners.

University and public school representatives spent Fall 2006 planning around points of agreement and mutual need. Our strongest unifying idea was and continues to be that learning takes place through active engagement with others in a context of culturally responsive mutual responsibility.

SMART PATH places two university student tutors with a group of four to six children who read on the same level. Pairing provides needed support for inexperienced tutors and splits the teaching role. Novices struggle to get through their planned lesson, let alone observe learner progress with the needed level of care. The paired model allows one tutor to teach while the other takes field notes on observations of the children in action. At the end of each 2-hour session tutors complete written reflections together and co-plan for the next session, at which they trade roles. Small groups allow for children's situated social construction of knowledge (Vygotsky, 1978; Rogoff & Lave, 2002), provide tutors with a more realistic teaching setting than one-on-one, and facilitate rapid independent takeover of skills and strategies by learners. While the program's original focus was literacy, math was added in Spring 2009 at the request of a school partner. With that change the program began attracting tutors from across the entire university campus, rather than just education majors, and the number of male tutors for the first time equaled the number of females. The SMART acronym continues to guide program practice on a daily basis.

Service

Service-learning contextualizes and gives meaning to literacy, math, and culturally relevant pedagogy as sense-making systems. Service-learning experiences foster critical literacy—the ability to read the world as well as the word (Freire, 2004)—and a sense of self-efficacy. Service-learning repositions urban children and their university tutors as experts to positively affect their continued engagement, self-confidence, and self-esteem (Duncan-Andrade & Morrell, 2008). The academic learning (Vogelgesang & Astin, 2000), mental health and well-being (Driscoll, Holland, Gelmon, & Kerrigan, 1996), and leadership development (Eyler & Giles, 1999) of children and tutors are continually reinforced through service to others.

MENTORING

Mentoring occurs across multiple levels: university and public school educators, along with education and social work experts from Black Child Development (the community agency that now administers SMART PATH), university student leaders, and more experienced tutors guide tutor novices as they collaboratively mentor groups of children assigned to them for a minimum of one semester. Children positively identify with tutors who look like them, and tutors experience for themselves the potential of urban children, and of their own efficacy in teaching them.

Achievement

Pre- and post-assessments given each tutoring term help tutors align challenges within their group's zone of proximal development (Vygotsky, 1978) to accelerate academic learning, and provide concrete evidence of each term's accomplishments. An emphasis on metacognition—"How did you figure that out?"—provides for the quick spread of constructed knowledge across children in the tutoring group. Tutors know to capture and employ child understanding the moment it surfaces, so that children mentor other children. In this context tutors come to know children who've been labeled "at risk" in very different ways.

Responsibility and Teamwork

Responsibility and teamwork anchor program development and practice. Before each tutoring term university and public school faculty, community agency representatives, and student leaders draw on data from previous terms and share insights to make ongoing program adjustments. For example, at the beginning of the Fall 2012 term, a public school teacher who serves as a faculty liaison for the program met with tutors to discuss changes in state standards assessments resulting from the new Common Core curriculum. New requirements have implications for teachers and for the tutors who support their practice. Experienced professionals engage with university tutors as colleagues in the critical endeavor of leveling the playing field for urban learners. With the guidance of university and public school faculty, community agency experts, and student leaders, tutors craft learning experiences that are educative, participatory, socially just, and caring (Oakes, Quartz, Ryan, & Lipton, 2002). Working side-by-side on common purposes, urban children, tutors, school and university staff, and community agency representatives forge empowering bonds of affection (Noddings, 1992). Over time relationships within groups and across diverse participants in the HBCU/public school/community agency nexus have evolved to provide a culture-centered safe space (Chapman, 2007) to ground identity development for university tutors and children and to foster transformative practice.

EMERGENCE OF STUDENT LEADERSHIP

Developing student leaders was not an original program goal, but as university faculty scurried to capture tutor input at the end of the first tutoring term, one student pulled a faculty member aside and said, "Why don't you let some of *us* train the next tutors? They'll listen to one of us better than a white lady like you."

About half the original field experience tutors returned as volunteers semester after semester as their schedules allowed, requesting to work with their same groups of children. As a result, tutoring groups typically have at least one tutor remain the same over their third- to fifth-grade experience in SMART PATH, ensuring the benefits of relational and instructional continuity. Whenever possible we pair new tutors with experienced ones for a layering of expertise.

Not only do tutors find reasons to stick, but the program grows its own student leaders. Over time experienced tutors emerged as program leaders who prepare, observe, and guide new tutors; keep program records; maintain materials and give input to acquisitions; oversee the collection and review of end-of-term data; plan and adapt the program and its handbook; and serve as spokespersons in public arenas. A typical student leadership team consists of three to six experienced tutors who may be paid small stipends, depending on program funding at a given time, or serve as volunteer site directors or research assistants. Working together with university/public school/community agency representatives, student leaders moved over time from reflection to analysis to transformation of the program, and then to describing and theorizing their own practice through tutoring handbook revision, conference presentation, and publication.

PROGRAM OUTCOMES FOR CHILDREN
AND SCHOOL PARTNERS

In the beginning we prayed that SMART PATH would at least do no harm to the children tutored. Over time we've learned that child participants make solid gains:

1. On average 1.5 years in reading per year in the program.
2. 1+ Word Study level per year.
3. 1 Writing Developmental Continuum level per year.

Entering and exiting math data is less developed, as we have only recently adapted an assessment tool simple enough for novice tutors to administer in a short period of time, which yields the needed item analysis as well as a grade-level equivalent.

Tutors conduct their own pre- and post-assessments for several reasons. Many practicing teachers lack knowledge of simple assessments such as the Elementary Spelling Inventory, running records, and the Writing Developmental Continuum assessment, all of which provide information on what a child knows and needs to learn next. Most important for tutor development, however, is the opportunity to find and work from children's learning strengths, interests, and needs *for yourself*. From this locating of your own tutoring group's patterns of knowing comes a bonding with each child in ownership of the quest to move their understandings to the next sensible step. From this bonding learning emerges that gets documented for continued reflection by children and their tutors. From that reflection comes a sense of self-efficacy. Despite a lack of data on math achievement to date, state standards math assessments demonstrated that with the addition of Pathematics in Spring 2009, tutee math scores rose from the 20th percentile to the 80th. End-of-term tutee surveys regularly demonstrate that Pathematics is their favorite SMART PATH activity.

All SMART PATH partner schools have achieved and maintained Annual Yearly Progress, and our longest-term partner has been recognized as the school making the most gains in the district. Our partner schools publicly recognize the program's role in their overall success. Data suggest that SMART PATH is meeting its first goal of providing greater equity of opportunity for children in East Greensboro. Children who enter the program from the bottom quartile now move into middle school reading on or above level. During the 2010–11 year, two groups of six children each read their entire fifth-grade year at a sixth-grade level.

Tutees identify with student mentors who look like them, and write about themselves graduating from the university. The children view themselves as leaders and helpers, both locally and globally. They wrote get-out-the-vote letters to familiar adults during the 2008 and 2012 election campaigns, and are pen pals with learners in Sub-Saharan Africa who are struggling to learn English to pass school exams, among many other local service projects. Children and families vote with their feet: children who participate in SMART PATH continue to choose to participate, and families with one child in the program request it for their others. Within SMART PATH tutees develop more empowering relationships with school literacy and mathematics.

Critical is the program's framing as a *tutoring and enrichment* program, rather than remediation. Children and families identify with the power of tutoring and enrichment, as well as the program's affiliation with an HBCU. At this point families indicate that they want there to be SMART-ish programming for their children into middle school.

OUTCOMES FOR UNIVERSITY STUDENTS

Service-learning experiences have the greatest impact when they extend over longer periods of time. What is it that SMART PATH tutors are learning and experiencing that motivates them to return term after term, to keep in touch during semesters when they cannot tutor, to expand their knowledge repertoires as program needs dictate, and to step up in leadership roles to ensure its continuance? In excerpts drawn from field notes, written reflections, coursework, and exiting focus group interviews, tutors share their experiences as freshmen or sophomores tutoring for the first time, then as experienced tutors and student leaders, to answer the question of why what we had envisioned as a semester-long tutoring experience calls them back term after term to engage with peers and experienced educators in a community effort to boost the learning of urban children.

For HBCU students working as tutors and leaders of a service-learning tutoring program, learning from service and learning to lead rest upon three central factors: (1) affectionate personal connection with children as well as other tutors and school/community/university leaders, (2) recognition of their own efficacy in teaching urban learners and handling the day-to-day challenges of running a program, and (3) the development of leadership skills. This outcome should not have surprised us. As African Americans, our tutors embody knowledge and dispositions crucial to serving urban learners: they recognize covert racism and stereotyping, and are able to dismantle many of these while developing their own situated understanding of urban learners.

Understanding Where Learners Come From

Novice tutors enter SMART PATH with preconceptions about urban learners, but through their experiences come to identify with and cherish the potential within their tutees. Tutors guide the children to value themselves and their accomplishments:

> I think we are here to encourage the students. I didn't have anyone there for me when I was their age, so I was just there struggling all through school. I'm surprised I even made it here. They look up to us, so we encourage them to do better.

> I know now that teaching is what you make of it. Student failure is not inevitable if you can find a way to reach out so *all* your students can reach full potential, not just the ones that get it from the way *you* got it.

Now we know that when a child complains that the work is too hard, or too easy, to have that child screened right then. Even when it looks like a behavior issue, it's best to check the curriculum level first.

SMART affected me in terms of getting serious. Once I started working with the tutees, I felt bad for them because they were hard-working children but were not succeeding in the classroom. I understand where they come from and now I believe I can help them even more when I get my degree.

Service and mentoring are hard-wired into many African American youth from an early age. They tend to *own* children of color and difference, and accept responsibility for showing them "how to be" in a racist world. They guide children in negotiating multiple cultural contexts—school forms one of these—and know which aspects of culture will be the most significant for these children's success. As mentors they know they embody inspiration for these children.

The "Magnificent Role of Inspirer"

Tutors in our HBCU setting come to us having spent significant time working with children prior to entering the university. We argue that they need opportunities to continue to build on those experiences at the same time that they attempt to adapt to university life. Putting off continued experience with children places the graduation/certification goal too far into a distant future. These students want to do meaningful work from the moment they enter the university:

I came with the intention of helping kids in any way possible. Membership in this program enables me to be a better leader and person. When teaching, I learn a lot as well. I learn about what the kids like to do and their lives in general. Many of them just want someone to listen and give them advice. When this is incorporated, I am doing exactly what I came to do, and that is to help them so that they can be all that they can be.

I've learned so much from the student staff and from my kids as well. I look forward to working with the SMART PATH program again this year. I just can't stay away from those kids. This program has given me the opportunity to grow and develop as a leader. I have been working with SMART PATH for a year now and I have found that children are honest, and many of them are not afraid to tell you if you are being boring or ineffective in your teaching style.

I've learned how influential I can be in a kid's life. There are certain teachers I remember better than others, because of the time they took to teach me. You have such an impact on someone's life. This shouldn't be taken lightly.

SMART PATH has allowed me to educate myself by educating others, and it has also developed me into an excellent leader. President Barack Obama once said, "The great teacher *inspires*." I can say that SMART PATH has given us, A&T students, opportunities to step out of our everyday role as college students and into the magnificent role of an inspirer. The kids look up to us, they have grown to love us, and we love them. Not many students or education majors can say that they've made a difference in a child's life before they've even earned their degree. With the SMART PATH program, we have done that, we've made a difference.

However, if culturally responsive service and mentoring lead to achievement for children, the shaping process for university tutor efficacy begins with taking responsibility.

Learning to Plan and Organize

Experienced tutors emphasize the importance of getting organized and writing lesson plans to anchor their practice. Many novices tell us—during their first term of tutoring—that while they might party the night before a test, they do not party the night before they tutor.

> I have learned that I have to be organized. I can't have anything in disarray or I won't understand what I am doing. . . . I have a whole different SMART notebook. I separate my SMART stuff and my other school stuff.

> I've learned how important having a lesson plan is. I thought I was going to roll up in there and they were going to get it, but they don't. So I learned I had to break it down, this is how you do this part and this is how you do that.

While it is the immediate need to plan and be prepared to face the children each day that motivates novice tutors, experienced tutors tell us that because of the SMART PATH experience, they no longer party the night before a test, either: "Nothing *is going to get between me and being able to do this work for the rest of my life.*"

Tutors learn that as important as it is to be prepared to tutor, nothing can replace the need to be flexible, adaptable, and able to accommodate tutoring to children's sociocultural and instructional needs.

"You Can't Do It One Way"

If learning to be prepared is the first big lesson for novice tutors, learning to adapt is the second. Tutors learn quickly that being organized, though essential, is not enough in and of itself; they have to be able to adapt to learner needs and respond in the moment:

> What I've learned about teaching: you can't do it one way. You have to do a variety of things, move around, be flexible, to get your students to understand, to make sure they comprehend.

> Nobody learns the same way. You're doing one thing and you have to teach it five different ways because everybody doesn't comprehend it the same way. Maybe another tutor can explain it better and they [students] are like, "Oh I can do that, it's easy I got it."

Novice tutors know that instructional content per se is not enough— great teachers know how to motivate learners. Tutors quickly recognize the potential of service-learning to place children in the expert role of helping someone else.

Understanding Service-Learning as a Pedagogy

Tutors emphasize the importance of their SMART PATH experience when they student-teach, and later accept teaching positions after graduation, regardless of the level they teach. In particular, they cite knowledge of service-learning gained:

> Content alone is not enough.... Good educators should practice things like advocacy, service-learning, student empowerment, and integrity.... Of these four, the service-learning aspect has probably been the most misunderstood. When we were in high school . . . a lot of the work we did was simply volunteer work, doing good deeds or helping out around the school. We didn't learn anything from the service that we didn't already know. The pen pal project really revolutionized our idea of service-learning because it was exactly what it was supposed to be: service-LEARNING. The students performed an act of service by writing letters to children in Africa but also learned about Africa and enhanced their writing skills in the process.

As tutors move from novice to virtuoso teaching, they also recognize the importance of the learning environment.

THE IMPORTANCE OF RELATIONSHIPS

Tutors emphasize the role of the affective environment in accelerating children's literate development. In coursework they read that caring is vital to cognition (Cardoso, 2003), that attitude is a crucial variable in reading achievement (Walberg & Tsai, 1985), and that emotional response is the reason most readers engage in reading, as well as the reason nonreaders do not (Smith, 1988). Energy, persistence, desire, determination, and will to learn are essential in cognition. SMART PATH tutors recognize the significance of the learning environment in developing these components that ground learner resilience (Gholar & Riggs, 2004) and emphasize the intrinsic motivation that is critical in developing understanding (Wang & Guthrie, 2004). They set high expectations for children's learning, and support children in achieving these goals. Getting results with children reinforces these dispositions in tutors:

> The kids are more willing to get into a lesson and learn because they can see that I'm interested. They are more willing to get engaged.

> The relationships that emerge between the student tutors and students are strong and tutees and tutors alike are often sad when students age out of the program. But as tutors and student leaders we know we have given each one of these students 100% and also have prepared them for academic success in middle school. What those students give us, though, is much greater. We get to see these students grow academically and socially. They blossom before our eyes and show us that if we work hard for them and love them, they will succeed.

> It feels good to walk into the room and see their smiling faces and see that they are ready to learn in an environment where they won't be criticized if they are not learning at the same pace of other students. It also makes us feel good to come to students that want to learn things. I will never forget one of my students saw a word in a book, and he really wanted to learn that word. It was a word that to them is a big word. The student came to SMART PATH every day spelling the word out and letting me know what it meant. I think in a classroom he may have been too embarrassed to even ask, but since the environment is a friendly, working-together environment, he asked away.

The importance of relationships and a nurturing learning environment extended into the tutor community as well. By the second year of SMART PATH we noticed that tutors, and especially student leaders, were choosing to socialize on their own with each other, going bowling together, and supporting each other when one was sick or had a crisis at home. We never expected the importance of SMART PATH in creating a space for university tutors that they saw as their own: "Here, someone knows my name and cares what happens to me."

In such a supported and culturally congruent space, tutors come to recognize their own efficacy in handling the day-to-day challenges of teaching urban learners.

Development of Self-Efficacy

Taking responsibility for the learning of a group of four to six children who need you, and knowing their teachers and families are counting on you, is a scary thing. Tutors need to quickly gain a sense of their own efficacy. Best practices don't mean much to students in a university classroom setting, but transported to the immediacy of the tutoring table, these get translated into efficacy built on moment-to-moment decision making. Reflecting in writing at the end of every tutoring session gives tutors the chance to anchor this knowledge. Talking with each other, student leaders, university and public school faculty, and community agency experts enriches reflection and builds committed university tutors into powerful preservice teachers.

> SMART PATH is better than [other kinds of] internships because there you are just observing and not getting your hands dirty. Before SMART I wasn't really sure of how to teach. I'm now more patient and have different techniques for dealing with different children.

> When you are shadowing or being an assistant to a teacher you don't get the one-on-one feeling with the children, but when you have the children all to yourself it prepares you for the future so that when you become a certified "real" teacher you will be prepared.

> As a SMART PATH tutor you need to be able to think on your feet, engage your audience, and communicate ideas effectively. All of these skills will create a positive learning experience for the students you work with. Working in SMART PATH has shown me the importance of planning ahead with lessons, and always keeping a positive attitude. As a leader you need to be able to inspire people, and every week I get to practice inspiring these children to learn. When students are at a low reading level they can easily become discouraged, but in SMART PATH we show students how much fun learning can be. Seeing the look on the students' faces after they fully understand what they are reading you can't help but want to do more and become a better leader.

University students use the SMART PATH experience to build onto the culturally situated selves they brought with them into the university, and to flourish as teacher-people. We regularly see tutors whose grades in coursework indicate that they are struggling in the role of "student" but who find themselves astonished at the skill and empowered identity they construct in their practice with children. A goal for the university is to devise ways to scaffold these university students, in particular, for success in coursework that acts as a barrier to the teaching profession.

Most of all, tutors come to recognize that the knowledge they have constructed in collaboration with others in SMART PATH will travel with them into their futures.

> The program helps us be comfortable in our teaching, and be sure. The program has made me more sure when I am explaining things to students that I have worked with in other schools. A lot of our strategies can be used in other settings, like running records, writing workshop, and our guided-reading strategies.

The Portability of Practical Learning

University students who work their way through school want more than credentials; they are dead serious about their craft and want their money's worth in practical experiences and strategies.

> Every time I learn something new in my own classes, I use the text-to-self method [comprehension strategy tutors employ] without even thinking about it. Every time the teacher uses an example about children, I have already seen or done it with children. SMART PATH gives me a head start.

> Relationships you make with the students, the making of lesson plans, and learning how to take control of a small group of students have given me by far the most helpful sense of the field of teaching that I have received since I have been here.

> I . . . needed the program at first because of a class, but throughout the semester I began to see that it helped me out a lot more than I thought it would. I am a returning tutor and I do this on a volunteer basis now. The things I learned here, I can take with me into whatever I do in education.

OUTCOMES FOR UNIVERSITY STUDENT LEADERS

For tutors, service and mentoring lead to achievement and a sense of self-efficacy. Taking responsibility for a group of children casts significant issues in education into high relief, and the learning is portable to multiple other contexts. For student leaders, service, mentoring, achievement, responsibility, and teamwork happen on a different scale. The opportunity to tutor makes it possible for university students to shift into a new ways of understanding what it means to teach and learn. SMART PATH student leaders argue that being in the position of leader similarly breeds leadership:

After I started out just being a tutor … I then became a peer mentor. I have a true gift and saw the leadership just taking over my body, which pushed me to do everything that I could to be even better. In that position, it took a lot for me to realize that people were looking up to me for information, but when I saw that I was helping out a lot of people and giving the right instructions to people, I knew that I was a strong asset to the SMART PATH family. Once I saw that people needed help I took it upon myself to take on a bigger role and help try to take the service-learning aspect of SMART PATH and make it into my own project, get different ideas on the table, so that we could grow through the community and that is when I knew my leadership would take me far in life.

I came in the room and I just felt so happy to see the tutors sitting in their groups—I made up these groups!

Working in SMART PATH gave me the environment to develop my full potential in leadership and child development skills. As an engineer by study, SMART helped in structuring my leadership ability by way of teaching me organization, commitment, simplistic material design, and great training sessions.

For tutors, teamwork operates at the level of tutoring group. For the experienced tutors who move into leadership roles, achievement, responsibility, and teamwork take on new meanings.

Learning to Lead by Watching Others

As tutors emerge into leadership roles within SMART PATH, their solidarity among themselves appears to scaffold them:

In terms of leadership, I have learned to lead by watching others. As a first-semester tutor, I took notes and tips from the veteran tutors and leadership team. They were successful and I could see that they had made a great impression on the program and the students who participated in it. SMART PATH has been a beautiful experience for me as a future teacher and leader.

. . .

[After being a tutor] my next adventure in SMART PATH led me to being a site director, a person that worked very close with Dr. Barber dealing with presenting, being a spokesperson for the program, going to conferences, speaking at large venues. My new position as site director was one that had value and honor. Being the leader, site director, and in charge of all service-learning projects just made me feel ready to take on anything that was put into my path. Leadership in this role showed me about being organized and able to take on many different tasks. I must also say having a great group of people working with me made the work fun as well and that helped, too.

Learning to Care on a Different Scale

For student leaders, the reflection that is a hallmark of quality service-learning experience happens on a difference scale. At the end of the Fall 2012 term several new student leaders reflected on how their perspectives had changed since taking on responsibility for an entire tutoring site:

> Now all the children are ours, along with all the tutors, and the program as a whole—I really feel the weight of this greater responsibility, seeing the inner workings of the program and knowing its effects on tutors and children. I feel the responsibility to carry on leading the same way, with the same level of style and skill, as [the more experienced site directors] before me.

> I have changed, mostly in how I see things. When you tutor it feels like you are doing a lot, but nothing like this. As a site director you are responsible for everything, all the behind-the-scenes getting ready, making sure everything goes OK each tutoring day, making sure the tutors have what they need. You still know all the kids and care about each one but it is very different.

> As tutors we worried about the progress of a child and our group; now we worry about the progress of tutors, groups, and the program as a whole.

At the beginning of the Fall 2012 term, when SMART PATH transitioned from a university to a public school location after a year's hiatus, one student leader commented:

> I just realized that of all the student leaders this term, I am the only one who can bring the continuity from all those good student leaders before now—Bethany, Blayre, Erica, Donald—I am going to call them up and get some advice.

By the end of that term this student leader confirmed that his most important responsibility had been to provide continuity for the program across its transition term. Three other student leaders echoed this same insight. For student leaders, teamwork and relationships operate on a different scale, but continue to be centrally important.

"I Can Show Them How"

Operating at a higher level of responsibility deepened the level of student leader reflection, and led them to want to share what they were learning with broader audiences and to talk to others who might be doing similar work. By Fall 2008 SMART PATH student leaders had given their first conference presentation, and now regularly present at local, state, regional, national, and international venues. Topics of their presentations and papers over time indicate a continuing trajectory of development in their thinking:

Fall 2008	What SMART PATH is and how it works
Spring 2009	Program outcomes for children
Fall 2009	Why university students need SMART PATH experiences with children from urban impact schools
Fall 2010	How to start a service-learning tutoring program
Spring 2011	Learning to lead through service
Fall 2011	Helping school districts and communities start their own programs
Spring 2012	Situating a program like SMART PATH within varied micropolitical contexts

In Spring 2010 the student leaders published their first paper, which focused on the affective climate for a successful tutoring program. When the grant that initially funded SMART PATH ended, student leaders engaged in grant-writing, and in Spring 2010 received grants from the National Education Association and a local community fund. In summer 2012 student leaders, several of whom are now teaching, revised the SMART PATH tutoring handbook to prepare it for publication. Student leaders continually seek grant funding and partnerships with community agencies to support the program beyond the years of their own participation. Student leaders participated in the Clinton Global Initiative University in 2010, 2011, and 2012 to learn strategies for sustaining and developing child literacy programs both locally and globally.

As these student leaders leave the university and move into their new lives as teachers, they take something that they view as special with them:

My last job with SMART PATH, working as a research assistant, was one that I will never forget because I basically was running the program with other co-workers and Dr. B., and that was the real leadership experience that I needed to send me to the level of where I can handle everything that I set my mind to. SMART PATH has given me such a boost in getting jobs and working in the corporate world that would be a challenge for most but not for me. The program helps the kids and teaches us at the same time how to lead in the world, and I am thankful for getting this opportunity to express myself and help out in every way possible.

When I was a site director and undergraduate research assistant with SMART PATH, this is where I learned to assess and analyze student data. Foundational skills such as completing running records, creating guided reading groups, and teaching high-frequency word patterns appropriate for specific grade levels are just a few of the necessary skills I gained from working with the SMART PATH Program.

Being a four-year participant with the SMART PATH Program has helped mold me into the teacher that I am. Along with my coursework content, SMART PATH gave me the field to explore my teaching techniques, and classroom management style, and gave me the comfort of knowing how to command the attention of my students.

One student leader who graduated to become a middle school math teacher called us back to ask for the newest of the tutoring handbook: "The teachers at my school do not know how to teach literacy, so I want the newest handbook so I can show them how."

In Summer 2011 two SMART PATH student leaders were among a group of nine faculty and students working in a rural school in Malawi, in Sub-Saharan Africa, to support teachers there in the country's relatively new (since 1994) universal public school initiative. A month-long course in strategies for teaching Literacy in the Mother Tongue (LMT) had been planned. However, on the first 2 days of the LMT course, the faculty member leading it was called away to the country's capital city for a meeting with the Minister of Education. The experienced SMART PATH student leaders agreed to teach in the faculty member's place. In a crowded room of 100 African teachers, the two, one who had just graduated with her B.Ed. that May, and the second to graduate the following December with a bachelor's in engineering, conducted an introduction to Word Study that the teachers lauded as one of the most important features of the month-long course. The two leaders glanced about the room, heavy with heat and the possibility of cross-cultural misunderstanding. What they saw were the satisfied, "I got it—I can do this" expressions on the faces of their Malawian teacher audience. The engineering student smiled the smile of relief all teachers know, and whispered to an American colleague present in the room, "I love teaching this stuff."

SIGNIFICANCE

Take-aways for those of us who structure service-learning programs that aim to promote the development of teachers and leaders are abundant in the reflections of SMART PATH tutors and student leaders.

Recognizing and Drawing on Cultural Strengths

We need to know our populations of university students if we are to craft service-learning programs that maximize on their cultural strengths. While the *Multicultural Efficacy Scale* was only mildly useful to us in documenting changes in our tutor population pre and post the SMART PATH experience, it allowed us to gather demographic information that provided clues about the experiences they'd had before coming to us, who they might be as people, and the strengths they might already possess that our program might build upon. Writing "Where I'm From" poems (Christensen, 2000) as self-introductions for sharing with public school and community agency partners is an activity well worth the time.

We should listen to our students. As practitioners of service-learning pedagogy we know the significance of reflection, but we may not listen as carefully as we might to what our university service-learners are saying. We need to listen to what they tell us even if it is not what we expected them to say, or what we want to hear. Listening is the ultimate sign of respect, and the beginning point of community-building.

Once we know a little about our university students we can plan service-learning experiences that are culturally congruent. Experiential learning experiences should build onto the cultural strengths and dispositions that university student brings to the endeavor. University experiences cannot create dispositions in individuals. Experiences can be designed, however, that resonate with and facilitate the ongoing development of our university students' cultural identities. Challenges are inevitable in experiential learning experiences, and service learners respond to these using their unique repertoires of cultural sense-making.

Furthermore, the conceptual framework of a service-learning program needs to fit the service-learners. We ground our work in theories that emphasize the social nature of learning. Social learning theory (Bandura, 1983) and situated cognition and communities of practice theories (Lave & Wenger, 1991) support an understanding of learning as apprenticeships taking place through engagement with others. Service-learners construct knowledge through participation. Crafting our program around service, mentoring, achievement, responsibility, and teamwork provided us with a framework resonant with aspects of cultural heritage for our students on an HBCU campus. SMART PATH provides a space for them to continue their process of self-discovery as African Americans, and to actualize that identity through service: they walk the walk, and the children they tutor see them do so, building a high-motivation feedback loop that empowers everyone concerned.

Relationships: The Ties That Bind

Service-learning experiences should provide sufficient time for the building of relationships. Relationships form the glue that holds a program together over time, which gives meaning to service and motivates continued effort. Studies of service-learning indicate that outcomes for participants are strongest when there are regular opportunities for reflection and long-term collaborative engagements in the field (Astin, Sax, & Avalos, 1999). Building on that notion, we argue that relationships ground the development that takes place within a quality service-learning experience. University students who participate in SMART PATH for one semester benefit, but those who return term after term demonstrate a trajectory of development toward further service and leadership.

Service-learning programs should value the power of collegiality and belonging as contributing members of a community of professionals. Problem solving as high-functioning members of teams of caring adults is a heady experience for university students. University tutors in SMART PATH co-plan with educators and community agency experts whose goal is to maximize learning for children in urban impact schools. It is important for university student tutors to be recognized as colleagues, to be trusted and appreciated, and to have their work and input valued. Then they know that what they are doing is real work, right now.

Efficacy: A Lynchpin of Development

Once university student tutors see for themselves that they can be effective with urban learners, all else follows. Efficacy is as powerful for university students as it is for the children they tutor. We can't make self-efficacy happen but we can set up situations in which it can emerge. We need to make sure that university students recognize how critical their contributions are. Service-learning experiences need to provide opportunities for students to find things out for themselves. Once they experience that best practices are effective, they become critical and theoretical in their thinking. But first, they need to experience practical knowledge that works, and recognize their own efficacy in employing it.

It is important to provide opportunities for service-learners to craft identities of power in teaching, even if their own grades are low. On occasion tutors come to SMART PATH and distinguish themselves among their peers, university, public school, and community partners, but make low grades in their own university coursework. They demonstrate the knowledge and dispositions they brought with them to tutoring, as well as how they continue to construct identities and practices as educators. We wrestle with the goals of teacher education: do we want teachers who conform to the good student role, or powerful practitioners? We also observe the phenomenon of tutors who actualize their purpose and develop their own intrinsic motivation to do whatever is needed to obtain certification so they can be with children for the rest of their lives.

Service learners should conduct their own pre- and postassessments. In completing these with tutees they begin the process of claiming these children as their own. Novice tutors may initially view urban learners as chunks of malfunction too inscrutable to tackle: after all, their own experienced teachers may not have had that much success teaching them. Completing pre-tutoring assessments not only teaches tutors about the simple thumbnail tools teachers can use to unpack a child's strengths, interests, and needs. It helps them discover all that the children *know* and *can do*, what they like and enjoy and perceive as their strengths, and provides specific targets for tutoring that now appear *doable*. Through the pre-tutoring term assessment process tutors "take over" much more than claim of their tutees—they find themselves talking together like teachers. Tutors need to analyze their own group's data, and student program leaders similarly need to analyze site- and program-level data.

Service-learners need to experience for themselves the urgency of lesson plans. We need to stop talking about the importance of lesson planning and let university students discover for themselves why organizing for learning is important. They also need to discover for themselves the importance of being flexible. Long-term collaborative responsibility for the learning of a small group of children teaches the lesson of beginning with the child, rather than the curriculum. Lave and Wenger (1991) distinguish between the teaching curriculum embodied in lesson plans and guides, and the learning curriculum constructed in action by living, breathing children. The best plans mean little if teachers cannot make accommodations that fit real children's strengths, interests, and needs.

University students need to discover the meaning and power of service-learning for themselves. Our university tutors read books on how to use service-learning to teach children, but they only capture the potential of service-learning as a pedagogy of hope by enacting it with children. In future research we want to document the ways in which our former SMART PATH tutors regularly employ service-learning with children in their own classrooms.

Making Space for Leadership Development

Leadership is a natural evolutionary by-product of service-learning. Service-learning programs need to provide opportunities for university students to "show how." Within SMART PATH we capture and exploit expertise the minute it surfaces. Tutors know to put the pen in the child's hand as fast as possible—children learn the most from other children. Similarly, as soon as a tutor evidences skill with a component of tutoring, he or she provides help to other tutors, rather than the university or public school faculty member or student site director. We make sure university student knowledge gets shared in ever-widening circles. Leadership is a precious commodity and should be nurtured as quickly as it appears.

To close the achievement gap for diverse learners we need teacher leaders and a citizenry of public actors committed to leading the way, asking the critical questions, and working against the grain. African American teacher leaders embody unique expertise on teaching black and other global majority learners (Ball, 2009; Foster, 1997; Gay, 2003; Irvine, 2002; Ladson-Billings, 2001). They operate from a position of advocacy, employ culture as a literacy tool, guide learners in negotiating multiple cultural contexts, fight covert racism and stereotyping of all kinds, act as a conduit of grounding values from home and community, set consistently high expectations for all learners, and support the success of all learners toward these goals (Robinson, 2011). African American teacher leaders learn to teach through "the ties that bind"—long-term caring mentoring relationships (Robinson, 2011). They "show" as a way of demonstrating leadership. They own the world's children as *their own community*. They know their own power to dismantle stereotypes and employ this power with diverse learners to show them "how to be" in the world (Robinson, 2011).

Teachers of diversity live Boykin's (2000) "triple quandary" on a daily basis. As experienced cultural navigators themselves, they know how to help children negotiate cultural difference. African American teacher leaders constitute significant hope for guiding schools and communities to level the playing field for diverse learners. However, they form an endangered species. Cuts to financial aid for cultural minority students from the Reagan era to the present, the current economic turndown that results in tuition hikes nationwide, in North Carolina the end of the Teaching Fellows program that sought out and funded talented students of color, and the gradual demise of HBCUs continue to limit opportunities for low-income students of diversity to pursue college education and teacher certification. The existing students of diversity interested in teaching need careful nurturing and opportunities to build powerful and empowering practice from the richness they bring to their university experiences. All universities that aim to develop teachers of and for diversity need to consider ways to build on the cultural strengths and dispositions that students bring with them, in order to scaffold their maximum and unique trajectories of development for service. Aiming to create the homogenized teacher may not be the best idea. For certain, our HBCU students gain immeasurably from the service-learning and experiential education opportunities in SMART PATH.

We plan to follow the careers of as many student leaders as possible, to learn more about the long-term effects of participation in SMART PATH, from its salutary impact on motivating freshmen to persist in teacher education, to its facilitation of teacher leaders who opt to teach in urban impact schools, and choose service-learning as a pedagogy in their own practice.

Research of this nature has immediate implications. Teaching needs leaders who are critical thinkers willing to challenge the status quo in order to enrich classrooms through best practice and culturally relevant teaching that includes service-learning as a pedagogy of hope. Our findings hold relevance for university faculty wishing to implement an early field experience program that forms a coherent and ongoing initiative grounded in research-based practices, and guides university students to recognize their own efficacy as preservice teacher leaders. Perhaps even more importantly, research of this nature points to service-learning experiences that hold power to accelerate the unique developmental trajectory of teacher leaders of diversity whose impact on urban schools and the learning of black and other global majority children has yet to be fully exploited.

REFERENCES

Astin, A., Sax, L., & Avalos, J. (1999). The long-term effects of volunteerism during the undergraduate years. *Review of Higher Education 21*(2), 187–202.

Atwell, N. (1998). *In the middle: New understandings about writing, reading and learning.* Portsmouth, NH: Heinemann.

Ball, A. F. (2009). Toward a theory of generative change in culturally and linguistically complex classrooms. *American Educational Research Journal, 46*(1), 45–72.

Bandura, A. (1983). *Social foundations of thought and action: A social cognitive theory.* Cambridge, MA: Pearson.

Barber, E., & Smith, T. (2011.) "These are our babies:" University student tutors, urban learners, public school and university staff crafting community through service learning. American Educational Research Association SIG. *Journal of Urban Learning, Teaching and Research, 7*, 71–83.

Bear, D., Invernizzi, M., Templeton, S. R., & Johnson, F. (2011). *Words their way: Word study for phonics, vocabulary and spelling instruction* (5th ed.). New York, NY: Prentice Hall.

Borko, H., & Putnam, R. (1996). Learning to teach. In D. Berliner & R. Calfee (Eds.), *Handbook of educational psychology* (pp. 673–708). New York, NY: Macmillan.

Boykin, W. (2000). The talent development model of schooling: Placing students at promise for academic success. *Journal of Education for Students Placed at Risk, 5*(1&2), 3–25.

Bransford, J. D., Brown, A. L., & Cocking, R. R. (Eds.). (2000). *How people learn: Mind, brain, experience, and school.* Washington, DC: National Academy Press.

Briggs, C. (1986). *Learning how to ask.* Cambridge, UK: Cambridge University Press.

Brown, D. (2002). *Becoming a successful urban teacher.* Portsmouth, NH: Heinemann.

Brown, J., Collins, A., & Diguid, P. (1989). Situated cognition and the culture of learning. *Educational Researcher 18*(1), 32–42.

Cardoso, S. (2003). *Brain and mind: Electronic magazine and neuroscience.* Retrieved from http://www.epub.org.br/cm/no5/mente/estados.i_htm

Chapman, T. K. (2007). The power of contexts: Teaching and learning in recently desegregated schools. *Anthropology & Education Quarterly, 38*(3), 297–315.

Christensen, L. (2000). *Reading, writing, rising up: Teaching about social justice and the power of the written word.* Milwaukee, WI: Rethinking Schools.

Cooter, R. B., Jr. (1994). Assessing affective and conative factors in reading. *Reading Psychology, 15*(2), 77–90.

Denzin, N. (2011). The politics of evidence. In N. Denzin & Y. Lincoln (Eds)., *Sage handbook of qualitative research* (4th ed., pp. 645–658). Los Angeles: Sage.

Driscoll, A., Holland, B., Gelmon, S., & Kerrigan, S. (2001). Assessing the effects of including service in learning. *Academic Exchange Quarterly.*

Duncan-Andrade, J. M., & Morrell, E. (2008). *The art of critical pedagogy: Possibilities for moving from theory to practice in urban schools.* New York, NY: Peter Lang.

Emerson, R., Fretz, R., & Shaw, L. (2011). *Writing ethnographic fieldnotes* (2nd ed.). Chicago: University of Chicago Press.

Eyler, J., & Giles, D. (1999). *Where's the learning in service learning?* New York, NY: Wiley.

Flyvbjerg, B. (2011). Case study. In N. Denzin & Y. Lincoln (Eds)., *Sage handbook of qualitative research* (4th ed., pp. 301–316). Los Angeles: Sage. Foster, M. (1997). *Black teachers on teaching.* New York, NY: New York Press.

Fountas, I., & Pinnell, G. (2001). *Guiding readers and writers, grades 3–6: Teaching comprehension, genre, and content literacy.* Portsmouth, NH: Heinemann.

Freire, P. (2004). *Pedagogy of hope: Reliving pedagogy of the oppressed.* New York, NY: Continuum.

Gay, G. (2003). *Becoming multicultural educators: A personal journey toward professional agency.* San Francisco: Jossey Bass.

Geertz, C. (1973). *The interpretation of cultures.* New York, NY: Basic Books.

Gholar, C. R., & Riggs, E. G. (2004). *Connecting with students' will to succeed: The power of conation.* Glenview, IL: Pearson Education.

Haraway. D. (1988). Situated knowledges: The science question in feminism and the privilege of partial perspectives. *Feminist Studies, 14*(3), 575–599.

Hunter-Quartz, K., & TEP Research Group. (2003). "Too angry to leave": Supporting new teachers' commitment to transform urban schools. *Journal of Teacher Education.*

Irvine, J. (2002). *In search of wholeness: African American teachers and their culturally specific classroom practices.* New York, NY: Palgrave/St. Martin's Press.

Ladson-Billings, G. (2001). *Crossing over to Canaan: The journey of new teachers in diverse classrooms.* San Francisco: Jossey Bass.

Lave, J., & Wenger. E. (1991). *Situated learning: Legitimate peripheral participation.* Cambridge: Cambridge University Press.

McIntyre, A., & Lykes, M. B. (2004). Weaving words and pictures in/through feminist participatory action research. In M. Brydon-Miller, P. Maguire, & A. McIntyre (Eds.), *Traveling companions: Feminism, teaching and action research.* Westport, CT: Praeger.

Multicultural Efficacy Scale. (2005). *Multicultural Perspectives 7*(4), 27–29.

Murrell, P. (2002). *African-centered pedagogy: Developing schools of achievement for African American children.* New York, NY: State University of New York Press.

Noddings, N. (1992). *The challenge to care in schools: An alternative approach to education.* New York, NY: Teachers College Press.

Oakes, J., Quartz, K. H., Ryan, S., & Lipton, M. (2002). *Becoming good American schools: The Struggle for civic virtue in education reform.* San Francisco: Jossey-Bass.

Perakyla, A., & Ruusuvuori, J. (2011). Analyzing talk and text. In N. Denzin & Y. Lincoln (Eds.), *Sage handbook of qualitative research* (4th ed., pp. 529–544). Los Angeles: Sage.

Raison, G., & Rivalland, J. (1994). *Writing developmental continuum.* Portsmouth, NH: Heinemann.

Robinson, S. T. (2011). *African American female teachers on teacher leadership.* Unpublished dissertation, North Carolina Agricultural & Technical State University, Greensboro, NC.

Rogoff, B., & Lave, J. (2002). *Everyday cognition: Its development in social context.* Bridgewater, NJ: Replica Books.

Smith, F. (1988). Understanding reading: A psycholinguistic analysis of reading and learning to read (4th ed.). Hillsdale, NJ: Erlbaum.

Vogelgesang, L., & Astin, A. (2000). Comparing the effects of community service and service-learning. *Michigan Journal of Community Service Learning,* pp. 25–34.

Vygotsky, L. (1978). *Mind in society.* Cambridge, MA: Harvard University Press.

Wang, J. H., & Guthrie, J. T. (2004). Modeling the effects of intrinsic motivation, extrinsic motivation, amount of reading, and past reading achievement on text comprehension between U.S. and Chinese students. *Reading Research Quarterly, 39*(2), 162–184.

Walberg, H. J., & Tsai, S. L. (1985). Correlates of reading achievement and attitude: a national assessment study. *Journal of Educational Research 78*(3), 159–167.

Wiggins, G., & McTighe, J. (2005). *Understanding by design* (2nd ed.). Upper Saddle River, NJ: Prentice Hall.

Zeichner, K., & Hoeft, K. (1996). Teacher socialization for cultural diversity. In J. Sikula, T. Buttery, & E. Guyton (Eds.), *Handbook of research on teacher education* (2nd ed., pp. 525–547). New York, NY: Macmillan.

Zemelman, S., Daniels, H., & Hyde, A. (2005). *Best practice: Today's standards for teaching & learning in America's schools.* Portsmouth, NH: Heinemann.

Liz Barber, PhD, is an experienced public school teacher, literacy studies professor, and ethnographic researcher. She teaches courses on global leadership and ethnographic research methods in the Leadership Studies doctoral program at North Carolina Agricultural and Technical State University in Greensboro and conducts participatory action research projects in both Greensboro and Domasi, Malawi. Her research focuses on literacy and leadership as these develop within cultures or communities of practice.

Tom Smith, PhD, teaches courses in educational foundations and service-learning in the Department of Curriculum and Instruction at North Carolina Agricultural and Technical State University. He is coauthor of a recent book on classroom dynamics and cognition, *Chaos in the Classroom,* and has an abiding interest in social justice, critical literacy, and other empowering pedagogies of hope. His research examines learning environments that foster sustainable innovation.

Sharon Jacobs is an experienced public school teacher, former assistant principal at Hairston Middle School, Nationally Board Certified Teacher–Middle Childhood Generalist, and founding principal of Washington Montessori School in Greensboro, North Carolina. Sharon received both her undergraduate and graduate degrees from North Carolina Agricultural and Technical State University. She has worked in public schools in Rockingham County and Guilford County, North Carolina, and in Bexhill-On-Sea in East Sussex, England. Sharon is passionate about the learning process and committed to service, committed to change, and committed to children.

Karen Thompson is the executive director of Black Child Development Institute of Greensboro, North Carolina, an organization that focuses on narrowing the academic achievement gap that exists for children because of their ethnicity and socioeconomic status. Karen holds a master's degree in education and human development with a concentration in school counseling from George Washington University. She has over 22 years of experience working in nonprofit environments, specifically focusing on programs that improve the lives of children in the community.

Blayre Penn is a graduate of North Carolina Agricultural and Technical State University holding a Bachelor of Science degree in elementary education. During her entire experience as an undergraduate student she served as a tutor, student site director, and research assistant with the SMART PATH Tutoring and Enrichment Program. She is currently working toward obtaining her master's degree in reading education. Blayre is a third-grade teacher within the Winston-Salem Forsyth County School System where her daily goal is to foster a mindset of excellence and self-confidence within each student she works with.

Bethany S. Penn currently teaches second graders within the Guilford County School System. She obtained her BS degree in elementary education from North Carolina Agricultural and Technical State University. Bethany's passion for education and children was heightened while working with the SMART PATH Tutoring and Enrichment program. She gained experience and knowledge through 4 years in the program, first as a tutor, next as a student site director, and finally as a research assistant studying program outcomes. She is now pursuing a master's degree in reading education, because she knows that reading gives students endless possibilities.

Donald Thompson II s a graduate of North Carolina Agricultural and Technical State University holding a BS degree in mathematics with a concentration in secondary education. At North Carolina A&T Donald served as one of the first site directors for the SMART PATH Tutoring and Enrichment program. He is a secondary mathematics educator within the Durham Public School System where through project learning he develops his students into critical thinkers. He also serves as the assistant track coach for his high school and is currently working to expand SMART PATH from Greensboro to Durham and eventually across North Carolina.

Ahmod Camp is an alumnus of North Carolina Agricultural and Technical State University where he majored in music education and speech communications. He has worked with the SMART PATH Tutoring and Enrichment program for 9 years as a first-generation tutor, then site director, and eventually as a graduate research assistant. During these years Ahmod developed expertise in teaching literacy and math through using service-learning as a pedagogy. He continues as an emeritus consultant for the program. Ahmod is currently employed as After-School Group Leader for Chapel Hill–Carrboro City Schools in North Carolina. He seeks opportunities to enhance children's afterschool and daycare experiences by implementing methods that he perfected while working with SMART PATH. Ahmod is passionate about advancing and enriching the teaching styles that make learning intellectually and emotionally engaging for children.

Carl Redd II is a senior secondary math education major at North Carolina Agricultural and Technical University. His first role in the SMART PATH Tutoring and Enrichment program was as a tutor completing a field experience. He never imagined becoming a SMART PATH site director, or presenting at prestigious conferences such as the Lilly South and the North Carolina Association of Colleges and Teacher Educators. Carl learned about key aspects of teaching, including lesson planning and classroom management, plus gained experience in using service-learning as a pedagogy—all of which are vital in becoming an educator—through his participation in SMART PATH.

Jordan Toler is a senior liberal studies major with a concentration in Race, Class, and Culture at North Carolina Agricultural and Technical State University. She is currently serving as an AmeriCorps team member on the 2012–2013 Spirit of Excellence for Black Child Development Institute of Greensboro. She tutors children in literacy and mathematics in the Guilford County School System. She also serves as the 2013 lead site director for the SMART PATH Tutoring and Enrichment program. Jordan started in SMART PATH to fulfill a course-based field experience. She fell in love with the program and took on a role as a site director, where she developed leadership skills she will use in her career.

Brittany S. McLean is a senior child development, early education, and family studies (birth-kindergarten licensure) major at North Carolina and Technical State University. She is from Rocky Mount, a rural area in eastern North Carolina where educational resources are sparse. Participating in a program such as SMART PATH Tutoring and Enrichment only seemed right for her. She began her affiliation with SMART PATH as a field experience requirement for a class, not expecting to spend the next three semesters of her college career deeply invested in the program. SMART PATH gave her vital experience and training as a future educator and in lesson planning, various assessments, and how to relate to and connect with children of diverse backgrounds and cultures. Brittany is a member of the Student North Carolina Association of Educators and the North Carolina A&T State University Chapter of National Association for the Advancement of Colored People. Upon graduation in December 2013, she will pursue a master's degree in special education at the University of North Carolina–Charlotte, and embark upon a teaching career in a low-performing, urban school with the Charlotte Mecklenburg County School System.

CHAPTER 9

TOWARD A BETTER UNDERSTANDING

A 360-Degree Assessment of a Service-Learning Program in Teacher Education Using Stufflebeam's CIPP Model

Guilli Zhang, Christine Shea, Nancy Zeller,
Robin Griffith, Debbie Metcalf, Jennifer Williams,
and Katherine Misulis

ABSTRACT

How do we adequately capture and evaluate service-learning programs given their complexity and multifaceted outcomes? Service-learning programs often involve multiple stakeholders and generate intended main effects as well as unanticipated spillover impacts. While assessments aiming at a single aspect of impact and focusing on a single stage of a service-learning program can be informative and valuable in answering isolated questions, they often fail to provide a complete picture to fully capture the multifaceted effects that a service-learning program can generate in the process and at the end. This

Transforming Teacher Education Through Service-Learning, pages 211–232
Copyright © 2013 by Information Age Publishing
211

chapter describes an effective 360-degree assessment of a service-learning tutoring program in teacher education at a research university by following Stufflebeam's Context, Input, Process, and Product (CIPP) Evaluation Model. The process and advantages of the 360-degree assessment is described and discussed. The 360-degree assessment framework using the CIPP Evaluation Model is systematic and can help researchers to strive toward a more holistic appraisal of a service-learning program.

When evaluating service-learning programs, it's important to take into consideration their complexity and multifaceted outcomes. Learning through service is a distinctive characteristic and merit of service-learning. An effective service-learning program should demonstrate two sets of desirable outcomes: the learning gains of service providers and the positive impacts on service recipients. These outcomes tend to be both cognitive and affective and multifaceted. Additionally, service-learning programs often involve multiple stakeholders and generate intended main effects as well as non-intended spillover effects. While assessments aiming at a single aspect of service-learning impact and focusing on a single stage of a service-learning program based on either the qualitative or quantitative research method can be informative and valuable in answering isolated questions on the value of service-learning, they often fail to provide a holistic picture to truly and fully capture the multifaceted impacts that a service-learning program can generate both in the program's intermediate stages and produce at the end. This chapter describes an effective 360-degree assessment of a service-learning tutoring program in teacher education at a research university in the southeast United States by following Stufflebeam's Context, Input, Process, Product (CIPP) Evaluation Model (2003). The assessment was conducted by using the qualitative and quantitative mixed-methods approach. The need for and the process and advantages of conducting the 360-degree assessment during the four-stage CIPP Evaluation is described and discussed. The 360-degree assessment using the CIPP Evaluation Model is systematic and has the potential to serve as an ideal framework for researchers to employ in order to achieve more holistic and accurate appraisals of the outcomes and influences brought about by a service-learning program. These appraisals will afford them the information needed to make more comprehensive and better-informed judgment of a service-learning program's merit and worth, as well as the possibility to be able to compare the strengths and weaknesses of different service-learning programs.

THEORETICAL FRAMEWORK

Service-learning programs' impacts are typically multidimensional. Service-learning involves the integration of community service into the academic curriculum (Koliba, Campbell, & Shapiro, 2006). Not only does the service-learning project meet the needs of a community, but it also demonstrates the value of active community involvement and promotes the notion of caring for others (Koliba et al., 2006). In teacher education programs, pre-service teachers who participated in service-learning projects have gained confidence as professionals and engaged in leadership roles following their participation in the project (Bullard & Maloney, 1997). Preservice teachers who participated in service-learning activities have also reported increased self-awareness regarding their upcoming role as a professional teacher and feelings of empowerment and accomplishment (Chen, 2004). Further-more, preprofessionals in professional preparation programs have cited service-learning opportunities as a powerful tool to increase multicultural awareness and a sense of social justice, allowing them better able to work with students and families from diverse backgrounds (McHatton, Thomas, & Lehman, 2006).

Providing a unique learning opportunity for service-learning providers is but one aspect of a service-learning project's benefits. Participating in a service-learning project can be an important opportunity for children who are the recipients of service-learning (Scott, 2006). The service-learning experience can reinforce and strengthen children's academic skills while at the same time enhance their self-esteem and independence.

The outcomes of a service-learning program can be cognitive or affective (Eyler & Giles, 1999). Some of these outcomes are better assessed by utilizing quantitative research methods and readily available research scales; others are not so straightforward, and require the kind of inquiry that is afforded by qualitative research methods. Some of these outcomes are observable directly from the work of the service-learning participants; however, many of the impacts are not so apparent and need to be uncovered indirectly from people who work closely with the service-learning participants, including the university faculty advisors, cooperating teachers, school principals, peers, and even parents.

Effective program evaluation requires all major aspects of a program at any stage of the program be evaluated to provide a full assessment of its effectiveness (Stufflebeam, 2003). Attempting to evaluate a program from one single aspect at a single time point often can be no more effective than the blind person trying to describe an elephant after only touching one part of its body. Stufflebeam's CIPP Model encompasses four evaluation components (Context, Input, Process, and Product) and can guide the evaluation of the entire process of programs, including program planning, implementation, and conclusion.

According to Stufflebeam (2003), the Context Evaluation component assesses the need for an intervention, the overall environmental readiness for the intervention program, whether existing goals and priorities are attuned to needs, and whether proposed objectives are sufficiently responsive to assessed needs. During Input Evaluation, the experts and stakeholders provide input that allows an assessment of the environmental barriers, constraints, and resources relevant to the implementation of the program. Process Evaluation affords opportunities to assess periodically the extent to which the program is being carried out appropriately and effectively. Product Evaluation focuses on the outcome of the program, both intended and unintended outcomes. An oversimplified summary is that:

- Context evaluation identifies needs and sets goals
- Input Evaluation develops and refines project plans
- Process Evaluation monitors project implementation
- Product Evaluation assesses project outcomes

Figure 9.1 depicts the CIPP Model's key components and their associated relationships with programs (Stufflebeam & Shinkfield, 2007). As depicted in Figure 9.1, all four components of the CIPP Model play important and necessary roles in the assessment of a program.

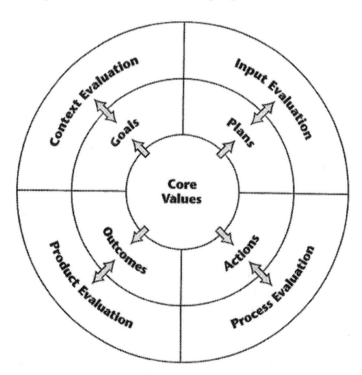

Figure 9.1   Key components of the CIPP Evaluation Model and associated relationships with programs (Stufflebeam & Shinkfield, 200, p. 333).

The CIPP Model can encompass assessments of any coordinated set of activities directed at achieving goals. The process can be repeated such that it forms a cycle that allows continued program improvement through evaluation. Figure 9.2 illustrates the CIPP model's application process and cycle.

Program evaluation needs to be executed by research methods, which are generally categorized into quantitative research methods and qualitative research methods. Quantitative research and qualitative research methods differ in many ways, and each is best suited for different types of research questions (Fraenkel & Wallen, 2008). The most noteworthy difference lies in that quantitative research is best at answering questions regarding *if a difference or relationship exists* and the qualitative research's strength lies in its ability to tackle questions regarding *why and/or how a difference or relationship exists*. In this study, the research question, "Is the motivation score of the service-learning group higher than that of the non-service-learning group?" could be best answered by quantitative research. In contrast, the question "Why did the service-learning group have higher (or lower) motivation than the non-service-learning group?" could be better explored by using qualitative inquiries.

Within the two research methods categories, specific research techniques also differ in many ways and each can offer unique advantages. For example, within the qualitative research methods category, Thomas, Mac-Millan, McColl, Hale, and Bond (2005) have noted marked differences between the focus group interview and the individual interview methodology. Focus group interviewing is ideally suited for exploring the complexity surrounding social behaviors within the context of lived experience, and in ways that encourage the participants to engage positively with the research process (Rabiee, 2004). One of the distinct features of focus group interviewing is the group dynamics; hence the type and range of data generated through the social interaction of the group are often deeper and richer than those obtained from one-on-one interviews (Thomas et al., 1995). Focus groups could provide information about a range of ideas and feelings that individuals have about certain issues, as well as illuminating the differences in perspective between groups of individuals. The uniqueness of focus group interviewing is the ability to generate data based on the synergy of the group interaction (Green, Draper, & Dowler, 2003).

Assessing the multifaceted impacts of service-learning programs often requires the researchers to investigate a service-learning program from more than one angle, use more than one research approach, and adopt more than one research method. The use of multiple assessment approaches and methods will allow researchers to "pool" the strength that each method has to offer. The 360-degree assessment is essential in capturing both service-learning's intended main impacts and other spillover effects. Additionally,

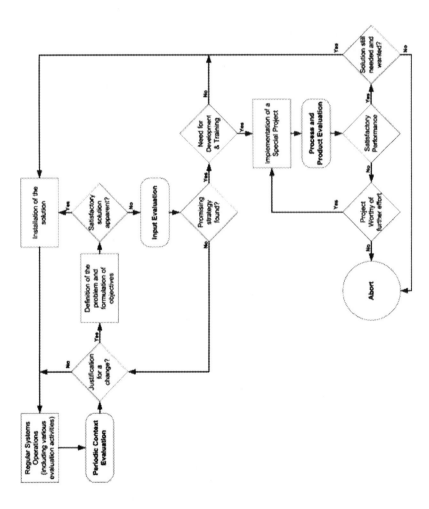

Figure 9.2   The flow of a CIPP evaluation in fostering and assessing system improvement (Stufflebeam & Shinkfield, 2007, p. 348).

the CIPP Model (Stufflebeam, 2003) is essential in guiding systematic assessments at all major stages of the service-learning programs.

METHODOLOGY AND RESULTS

During the spring semester of 2008, a service-learning tutoring program was implemented at a research university in the southeast United States. A total of 59 preservice teachers taking a course in Diagnostic/Prescriptive Teaching of Reading participated in the study. Thirty-seven preservice teachers were in the two sections of the course that were randomly selected to serve as the experimental group, while the other 22 were in the two sections that served as the control group. Two faculty advisors collaboratively provided supervision and instruction to these preservice teachers. The sections were taught by following the same course outline except the service-learning component. While the preservice teachers in the control group completed the traditional field experience, those in the experimental group completed a service-learning component by tutoring a total of 60 response-to-intervention students in kindergarten, first, and second grades at a local elementary school. The response-to-intervention students were selected because they were not receiving special education services but were working below grade level in reading and writing, therefore they can also be thought of as at-risk readers and writers. (In this chapter, the terms "students," "at-risk learners," or "readers" are used interchangeably to refer to these response-to-intervention students.) The control group implemented the course requirements in a traditional field placement setting working with students recommended by the classroom teacher. To protect participants' rights, all names used in this study are pseudonyms.

Working with the elementary school students on a weekly basis for 8 weeks, the preservice teachers in the experimental group administered literacy assessments including running records (Clay, 1993), the Qualitative Reading Inventory–4 (Leslie & Caldwell, 2006), the Elementary Reading Attitude Survey (McKenna & Kear, 1990), and the Burke Reading Interview (Burke, 1980). Based on these assessments, the preservice teachers designed and taught lessons that targeted the students' needs while building upon their strengths. They also shadowed the at-risk learners during reading and writing instruction. During the rest of the 15-week semester, the preservice teachers spent 3 hours and 30 minutes on preparation of tutoring and 1 hour and 30 minutes providing tutoring service to the at-risk learners each week.

In addition to working with the at-risk learners on a weekly basis, the preservice teachers also worked closely with cooperating teachers in the elementary school, exchanging information, providing updates, and asking for advice. Moreover, the two university faculty advisors also kept in close contact with the school principal, who took an active part in the program by overseeing the process and holding frequent conversations with the pre-service teachers and the cooperating teachers.

A 360-DEGREE ASSESSMENT OF THE SERVICE-LEARNING PROGRAM USING THE CIPP MODEL

Taking advantage of the different functions of the CIPP Model's four components, we conducted a full 360-degree assessment of the service-learning program. Specifically, we utilized the context evaluation component of the CIPP Model to help identify service providers' learning needs and the community's needs. Then, the input evaluation component helped to prescribe a responsive tutoring project that could best address the identified needs. Next, the process evaluation component monitored the project process, identified potential procedural barriers and needs for project adjustments, and prompted needed adjustments. Finally, the product evaluation component helped to measure, interpret, and judge project outcomes and interpret their merit, worth, significance, and probity.

Specifically, in order to systematically gain a full understanding of the many aspects of the impacts of the service-learning tutoring program, following the CIPP Model, the assessments were methodically conducted from multiple angles at different stages of the program using multiple assessment techniques (see Table 9.1).

Context Evaluation

We first conducted context evaluation to assess the needs for the service-learning project, and the contextual readiness for the project. The University, a research university in the southeastern United States where the preservice teachers were attending graduate school, was assessed as of its appropriateness and capability of carrying out the service-learning program. The University's College of Education offers both undergraduate and graduate programs of study in teacher preparation. All of their programs incorporated internship opportunities or capstone projects in collaboration with top-notch K–12 school professionals and community partners in state-of-the art facilities. The College continues to lead the state in the production of new education professionals. Based on data from 2006–2007, the College is proud of the fact that its teacher education graduates have the highest employment rate in the state.

TABLE 9.1   A 360-Degree Assessment of Service-Learning Program Using the CIPP Model

CIPP Evaluation Model Components	360-Degree Assessments
Context Evaluation Identifies Needs and Sets Goals	• university contextual readiness • elementary school contextual readiness • preservice teacher focus group interviews • initial quantitative assessments of preservice teachers • initial quantitative assessment of elementary students
Input Evaluation Develops and Refines Project Plans	• Serve and Learn America • national experts • university vice chancellor for service-learning • department chairperson • university faculty task force members • preservice teacher focus group interviews • elementary school stakeholders
Process Evaluation Monitors Project Implementation	• biweekly meetings of university faculty task force members • observations of program implementation • interviews • reflections • student samples
Product Evaluation Assesses Project Outcomes	• post-program quantitative assessments of preservice teachers • post-program quantitative assessment of elementary students • assessment of all other stakeholders through a variety of research approaches

Service-learning has become part of the culture at the university. The creation of a new position, the Vice Chancellor for Service-learning, has created a surge of interest in service-learning programs and service-learning opportunities on and off campus. The university has a well-established infrastructure for service-learning research activities. There are well-integrated programs within the university where students spend a semester or more in a connected series of courses linked to service-learning projects in the community.

The service-learning faculty task force consisted of one university administrator, five expert content-area faculty members, and two faculty members in research and evaluation methodology. Initial assessments of preservice teachers reveal that they were equipped with the knowledge and skills needed to provide the service. More importantly, they expressed strong curiosity and desire to participate in this program.

The service site was an elementary school that was very representative of a typical elementary school in the county. Racial and socioeconomic balance was achieved by the requirement of a policy of the county. The principal was very open to the service-learning program and embraced it immediately. The elementary teachers involved were very excited about the program and were happy to work with the preservice teachers and the university faculty.

Preservice teachers were evaluated as part of the context evaluation. Multisession focus group interviews were conducted with both the control groups and experimental groups before the service-learning intervention to explore their initial attitudes and dispositions about working with students who came from diverse backgrounds. The focus group interview guides contained six questions. The sources for these questions were three instruments cited in Bringle, Phillips, and Hudson (2004): the Community Service Self-efficacy Scale, the Volunteers Function Inventory, and the Personal Social Values Scale. The initial Interviews were scheduled in January (before the intervention). The focus groups average seven to eight participants. Two moderators conducted the focus group interviews. The assistant moderator kept notes and summarized at the end of the interviews.

In addition to qualitative assessments, quantitative instruments were used prior to the program implementation to assess the initial status of preservice teachers regarding the following constructs: community service self-efficacy, motivations regarding volunteer activity, self-esteem, and confidence in making a clinically significant contribution to the community through service. The following research instruments were used: the Self-esteem Scale (Rosenberg, 1965), the Community Service Self-efficacy Scale (Reeb, Katsuyama, Sammon, & Yoder, 1998), the Volunteer Functions Inventory (Clary et al., 1998), and the Personal Social Values Scale (Mabry, 1998). Similarly, assessments were conducted on the initial status of elementary school students' self-esteem, steps toward independence and academic achievement in reading, and oral and written language skills. Elementary students' perceptions of themselves as readers, oral communicators, and writers were assessed by student interest inventories and the Elementary Reading Attitude Scale (McKenna & Kear, 1990) administered by the tutors.

Input Evaluation

Expert input was sought to judge the feasibility of the service-learning tutoring program before its implementation and adjustments were made to improve the program. The program plan and research evaluation plan were written in great detail and were submitted to Serve and Learn America, the funding agency of the program, to evaluate their potential merit and feasibility. In addition, an email was sent to several nationally recognized experts in the area of service-learning asking for opinions and suggestions. University administrators including the Vice Chancellor for Service-learning and the department chairperson further judged the plans. Based on the input received, the service-learning faculty task force held face-to-face discussions as well as Delphi studies to refine both plans. The improved plans were also shared with the elementary school principal and cooperation teachers for their input. Furthermore, the focus group interview data mentioned earlier not only serve as part of the context evaluation, but also as input evaluation of the preservice teachers.

Process Evaluation

We closely monitored the project's implementation process with ongoing process evaluation effort. The service-learning task force members held biweekly meetings to give updates on the program implementation. They also shared positive stories as well as discussed any potential problems that needed to be addressed.

Preservice teachers' self-reflection served as a window to look into the process of the program. Reflection is recognized to be an essential link between community experience and academic learning (Felten, Gilchrist, & Darby, 2006). Reflection can also serve as a mirror reflecting the inner changes in the service providers and make these changes visible. Following each of the tutoring sessions, the preservice teachers spent 15–20 minutes to reflect on what they gained from the interactions with and what they contributed to the students and the cooperating teacher. This served as an informal form of ongoing self-evaluation. Moreover, these reflective journal entries were collected and entered into NVivo 8, and analyzed independently by two experienced researchers.

A list of questions was provided to guide the preservice teachers' reflections (see Table 9.2). These questions were designed to promote reflective

---

TABLE 9.2   Reflection Questions for Service-Learning Logs

Reflection #1	What happened? Did anything take you by surprise? What are you contributing? What are you receiving?
Reflection #2	What did you contribute to the students and teachers at Western Elementary this week? What did you gain as a result of your work at Western Elementary this week?
Reflection #3	How has your work with your case study student changed since the first week?
Reflection #4	In your service-learning experience, you may be working with individuals who are culturally different from you. Identify ways that you are similar to and ways that you differ from your case study student. How do these cultural differences impact the work you do with the student?
Reflection #5	Describe at least two ways you have helped your case study student. Describe at least one thing you have learned from your case study student. How will this knowledge help you in the future?
Reflection #6	What will you take away from this service-learning experience? What do you hope your case study student will take away from this service-learning experience?

thinking about what the preservice teachers were learning and what they were contributing to the students in the public school setting.

To ensure the trustworthiness of the findings from the qualitative analysis of the reflection logs, the codes and findings from the two independent researchers were analyzed for percentage agreement and evidenced a high reliability. Among several other themes that emerged from the reflections were the preservice teachers' continually intensified passion toward their students and their heightened sense of responsibility. The analysis also indicated that preservice teachers involved in service-learning projects were able to learn course content better while engaging in activities that met the needs of the community, in this case at-risk readers and writers.

To monitor impacts on the elementary students, formal academic assessment, as well as informal academic assessment (e.g., content analysis of samples of student work), structured observations, curriculum-based measures, and students' reflective journals were employed during the project. Observations were conducted by faculty advisors and cooperating teachers regularly.

Product Evaluation

The Product Evaluation was centered on two overarching questions: (1) Did the service-learning experience make any difference on preservice teacher's learning? (2) What impacts did the service-learning program have on others, especially the at-risk learners? To better organize the Product Evaluation, the project's impacts on the preservice teachers' learning were examined separately from its other impacts. This was done because learning outcomes are typically the main intended outcome of service-learning programs. Because service-learning providers' learning is at the center of service-learning programs, it deserves a full 360-degree assessment of itself. The assessment of preservice teachers' learning was centered around the preservice teachers and conducted from the following angles: preservice teachers' own reflections, direct quantitative assessments using survey research scales, focus group interviewing of preservice teachers, sample course work, course performance, faculty observation of tutoring sessions, input from university faculty advisors, elementary school principal, cooperating teachers, Reading Recovery teachers, and the elementary at-risk learners. The assessment of other impacts of the service provided in the service-learning program attempts to uncover all noteworthy impacts on involved community partners, with an emphasis on the at-risk readers being tutored. Figure 9.3 depicts the elements of the 360-degree assessment we conducted during the Product Evaluation.

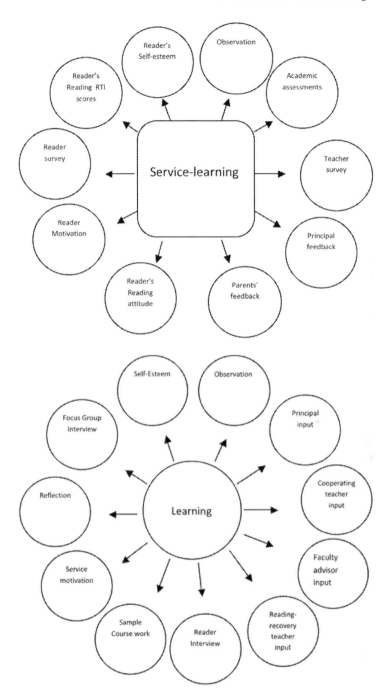

Figure 9.3   A 360-degree assessment of learning outcomes and other service impacts.

A 360-Degree Assessment of Preservice Teachers' Learning

Reflection. Findings from analysis of preservice teachers' reflections revealed that preservice teachers' language changed over time as a result of engaging in service-learning, particularly the words the preservice teachers chose to describe their case study students. At the beginning of the service-learning experience, the preservice teachers used words like *sweet, polite, talkative, enthusiastic,* and other general terms to describe the elementary school students. After four weeks of working with these students in one-on-one tutoring sessions, the preservice teachers were better able to articulate their case study students' strengths and needs and were able to describe techniques they used to address those needs. For example, preservice teacher Trisha described her work with 6-year-old ELL student Manuel in this way:

> In the first 2 weeks, Manuel and I were just going through the motions it seems. I didn't know what to do with him and he couldn't tell me. Now, though, I think he is comfortable with me and I can see him improving. Last week, he only knew two letters in his name and this week he knows all but two. We are working on an English/Spanish alphabet book and I think that really helps him.

In addition, the preservice teachers made frequent comments and inquires about the most effective approaches for addressing the case study of students' individual needs. Ishawna stated, "I want Josh to go beyond his current reading level, so I'm constantly looking for other ways to help him. I take what we learn in class and try to figure out what is appropriate for him." When unsure about the best way to reach a student, the preservice teachers often initiate consultations with the classroom teachers, Reading Recovery teachers, and course faculty advisor. The preservice teachers were so invested in their students' success that a number of them chose to continue tutoring after the semester ended.

By the fifth week of the service-learning project, the researchers noted a marked change in the confidence level of the preservice teachers. Instead of comments like "I don't think I really contributed much, except in keeping some of the students focused," preservice teachers began to write the following comments in their reflection logs:

> One way that I have helped Zanijah [case study student] is by helping her comprehend the text. I have done this by asking her questions while we are reading and preparing her for ways she can do this when reading on her own.

> I have helped Robert [case study student] by giving him strategies to solve unknown words. I taught him to check the picture, repeat the sentence, and start sounding out the word before he asks for help.

The reflections indicate an increasing level of sophistication in the preservice teachers' understanding of the reading process but also an increased awareness of their roles in supporting the development of effective reading processes in elementary school students.

Focus group interview. Focus-group interviews, as a means of qualitative data collection, are becoming increasingly popular among professionals in research for exploring what individuals believe or feel as well as why they behave the way they do. The main aim of this qualitative research method is to understand, and then explain, the meanings, beliefs, and cultures that influence the feelings, attitudes, and behaviors of individuals.

Multisession focus group interviews were conducted with both the control groups and experimental groups before and after the service-learning intervention to explore whether service-learning had made a difference in students' level of confidence in making a difference and/or personal social values related to community service, and whether there was a change in their attitudes and dispositions about working with students who come from diverse backgrounds.

The focus group interview guides contained six questions. The sources for these questions were three instruments cited in Bringle et al. (2004): the Community Service Self-efficacy Scale, the Volunteers Function Inventory, and the Personal Social Values Scale. Interviews were scheduled in January (before the intervention) and April (after the intervention); the interview guides for January and April were very similar, with only minor modifications relating to the fact that participants had in April experienced and implemented in their tutoring the service-learning training. Questions in the April interview guides prompted participants more than in January to tell stories or anecdotes about their experiences. In both times there were two moderators. In January the assistant moderator kept notes and summarized at the end of the interviews; in April, the second moderator played a more active role with follow-up questions. She also kept notes, but summarized at the end of each question rather than at the end of the interviews. The focus groups averaged seven to eight participants in both January and April.

Following are the questions from the focus group interview guide(s). The material in parentheses illustrates how questions were modified in April versus how they were phrased in January:

What are your memories from childhood regarding volunteering?
   (Tell a story about a time when you volunteered.)
Why do you think people volunteer? (Focus on one person you know
   who has volunteered: why do you think she or he does it?)
What are your expectations about working one-on-one with children?
   (How were your expectations met? What went right? Wrong?)

React to this statement: "People who receive social services have only themselves to blame!" (Describe an anecdote or story about working with a child or children from a different background than your own.)

Why do you think kids drop out of high school? (Think of the child/children you worked with—is he or she a potential dropout?)

If you are in a leadership role in school, how would you deal with the dropout problem? What strategies would you use for your school? Your classroom?

These interviews were video-recorded directly to DVD and transcribed and analyzed using NVivo 8. The initial, tentative findings indicate that service-learning preservice teachers care more than the control group preservice teachers about acquiring the knowledge and skills in the preservice classes involved in the study because they realize that the materials are not just the kinds of things that they might take a test on, but would actually apply to real people: they discovered that they could make a real difference. They felt more confident and that their work was more appreciated.

The following are quotes from some of the service-learning participants in the focus group interviews:

> At first, my students did not get along. By me taking the time to talk with them and be sure to never show favoritism, I was able to get them to work together. That made me feel really good.

> Taking the time to show each student that you care and having a reward system worked for me . . . had I not had this experience, I may not have thought to do this in my own classroom. I have learned that I can manage a group of students and still have them like and respect me.

The preservice teachers initiated, discussed, and made many comments about the value of the service-learning experience. Alyson stated that as a result of the service-learning experience, she realized that she could actually make a difference in the life of a student. Katherine noted that she was no longer scared to work with struggling readers because she now had some proven techniques she could use. Finally, the preservice teachers noted that the service-learning experience made the course content "real." Shakira wrote, "Learning about teaching reading [from a textbook] is completely different than reading with an actual student." For the preservice teachers in this study, the service-learning experience afforded them the opportunity to apply course content in authentic learning environments while the elementary school students benefited from the extra one-on-one time.

Quantitative assessments of affective learning. In addition to the informal qualitative self-assessments, quantitative instruments were used in a pre-test/post-test control group design to assess changes in preservice teachers regarding the following constructs: community service self-efficacy, motivations regarding volunteer activity, self-esteem, and confidence in making a clinically significant contribution to the community through service. The following research instruments were used: the Self-esteem Scale (Rosenberg, 1965), the Community Service Self-efficacy Scale (Reeb et al., 1998), the Volunteer Functions Inventory (Clary et al., 1998), and the Personal Social Values Scale (Mabry, 1998). For each of the constructs, a gain score was calculated for preservice teachers by subtracting their pre-test score from their post-test score. An independent samples t-test was used to conduct a gain score analysis (also known as change-score analysis) to investigate whether there was a difference between the amount of changes in service-learning group and the control group in each of these constructs. A t-test on gain score analysis is one of the effective ways to take into consideration the potential preexisting differences between the two comparison groups, and improve the validity of the findings (Maris, 1998). These direct quantitative investigations revealed higher growth in service-learning participating preservice teachers' confidence in making a clinically significant contribution to the community through service ($p < .05$) and motivations regarding volunteer activity ($p < .05$).

Other assessments of preservice teachers' learning. While participating in service-learning, preservice teachers' course-related academic performance should not be compromised by the service-learning component. Rather, their academic performance should be enhanced. Preservice teachers' academic performance was monitored throughout the process. University faculty advisors regularly conducted nonparticipatory observations of the tutoring sessions. Samples of preservice teachers' coursework, faculty observation field notes, curriculum-based measures, and reflective journals were collected and assessed by the university faculty advisors to explore the preservice teachers' understandings and mastery of the reading process and reading instruction. Both advisors reported more refined coursework, seemingly higher dedication to the course, superior level of mastery of the reading instruction skills, and deeper understanding of the course content.

Input from community partners. Community partners working closely with preservice teachers were interviewed regarding their feelings about the participating service-learning preservice teachers. These include university faculty advisors, the elementary school principal, the cooperating teachers, and the elementary students. From these sources, researchers gained firsthand information that was not available through other means of assessment. The cooperating teachers reported initial resistance to these service-learning preservice teachers. They said that they thought these service-learning preservice teachers may require more attention and more time on their part, and later discovered that that was not the case, and were surprised that it was actually quite the opposite. The reading-recovery teachers, in particular, commented on the apparent higher level of interest in the subject matter and skills and greater eagerness to learn demonstrated by preservice teachers in the service-learning group compared with those in the control group. Researchers were informed of the preservice teachers' sense of pride and devotion, which translated into increased diligence and greater awareness of responsibility. They were "easier to work with, more willing to work, and more determined to make a difference in the (elementary) students."

A 360-Degree Assessment of Service Impact on Elementary Students and Other Community Partners

Using similar approach and mixed methods, the program's impacts on elementary students were also continuously assessed formally and informally. To assess the effect of the service-learning project on the elementary school students' self-esteem, steps toward independence and to document students' growth and academic achievement in reading and oral and written language skills, formal academic assessment, informal academic assessment (e.g., content analysis of samples of student work), structured observations, curriculum-based measures, and students' reflective journals were employed both during the project and at the end. Elementary students' perceptions of themselves as readers, oral communicators, and writers were pre- and post-assessed by student interest inventories and the Elementary Reading Attitude Scale (McKenna & Kear, 1990) administered by the tutors.

Improved attitude toward reading and significant increase in students' perceptions of themselves as readers were evidenced in the results of t-tests on the pre- and post-assessment scores. Students' scores on the RTI tests demonstrated a consistently increasing trend. The t-test on students' self-esteem using the Self-esteem Scale (Rosenberg, 1965) did not show a statistically significant difference between pre- and post-test ($t = .128$, $p = .899$).

A survey of elementary school teachers was conducted to measure their beliefs about the impact of the program regarding each individual elementary student who was the recipient of the service-learning tutoring program. The results indicate that the majority of the students demonstrated improvement in reading, writing, spelling, problem solving, motivation, confidence, and attendance. However, roughly only 50% of the students showed increased self-esteem and critical thinking skills.

A random sample of parents was also interviewed regarding whether any changes in their children were observed. The teachers and most parents noted observed positive changes in the students related to reading and writing.

Feedback from community partners was obtained to discover any impact the service-learning program had on them. These partners include cooperating teachers, reading-recovery teachers, and the school principal.

CONCLUSION AND DISCUSSION

This chapter demonstrates the importance of performing a 360-degree comprehensive assessment of service-learning programs in order to fully evaluate and understand their impacts. It illustrates the value of following a systematic evaluation model and using multiple research methods. In the reported service-learning project, direct quantitative investigations revealed several important changes in preservice teachers' cognitive learning and in their affective growth. The differences on many other factors did not reach statistical significance, possibly partially due to the small sample size (Zhang & Algina, 2008, 2011) and the insensitivity of the research instruments. However, the qualitative data collected through preservice teacher self-reflection, cooperating teacher and faculty advisor's observation of the preservice teachers, focus group interviews of the preservice teachers, and interviews of the elementary students, the cooperating teachers, the reading-recovery teachers, and the principal served very well as informative supplementary evidence providing rich, more in-depth information that was not available through the quantitative inquiries. These qualitative data afforded researchers the eyes and ears to truly see and hear about the positive impacts this program had made on its participants. It was evident that certain changes sometimes do not easily translate into statistically significant numbers. The assessments of the impacts on elementary students worked in a similar way.

Orchestrating the 360-degree assessment throughout the service-learning program is not an easy task but a worthwhile and necessary one. It is very hard to image one could fully appreciate the impacts that the service-learning program have on both the service-learning providers (the preservice teachers) and the service recipients (the elementary students) without looking at the program from multiple angles.

From passionately embracing service-learning to seriously adopting a service-learning program as a routine practice in education requires evidence of merits gathered from careful, objective, and effective assessment of all its major aspects. The assessment of service-learning programs is not a simple task. The snapshot type of assessment from a single angle using a mono-method is unlikely to provide a complete picture of the many facets of service-learning's effects. The 360-degree assessment following Stufflebeam's CIPP Model described in this research provides researchers and practitioners an example of how a service-learning program can be systematically assessed more fully, deeply, and effectively.

REFERENCES

Bringle, R. G., Phillips, M. A., & Hudson, M. (2004). *The measure of service learning.* Washington, DC: American Psychological Association.

Bullard, J., & Maloney, J. (1997). Curious Minds after-school program: A creative solution to a community need. *Michigan Journal of Community Service Learning, 4,* 116–121.

Burke, C. (1980). The reading interview. In B. P. Farr & D. J. Strickler (Eds.), *Reading comprehension: Resource guide.* Bloomington: School of Education, Indiana University.

Chen, D. W. (2004). The multiple benefits of service learning projects in pre-service teacher education. *Delta Kappa Gamma Bulletin, 70*(2), 31–36.

Clary, E. G., Snyder, M., Ridge, R. D., Copeland, J., Stukas, A. A., Haugen, J., et al. (1998). Understanding and assessing the motivation of volunteers: A functional approach. *Journal of Personality and Social Psychology, 74,* 1516–1530.

Clay, M. M. (1993). *An observation survey of early literacy achievement.* Portsmouth, NH: Heinemann.

Eyler, J., & Giles, D. E. (1999). *Where's the learning in service-learning?* San Francisco: Jossey-Bass.

Felten, P., Gilchrist, L. Z., & Darby, A. (2006). Emotion and learning: Feeling our way toward a new theory of reflection in service-learning. *Michigan Journal of Community Service Learning, 12*(2), 38–46.

Fraenkel, J. R., & Wallen, N. E. (2008). How to design and evaluate research in education. New York, NY: McGraw-Hill.

Gelmon, S. B. (2000). Challenges in assessing service-learning. *Michigan Journal of Community Service Learning, Special Issue,* pp. 84–90.

Green, J. M., Draper, A. K., & Dowler, E. A. (2003). Short cuts to safety: Risk and "rules of thumb" in accounts of food choice. *Health, Risk and Society, 5,* 33–52.

Koliba, C. J., Campbell, E. K., & Shapiro, C. (2006). The practice of service learning in local school-community contexts. *Educational Policy, 20*(5), 683–717.

Leslie, L., & Caldwell, J. (2006). *Qualitative reading inventory – 4.* Boston, MA: Pearson.

Mabry, J. B. (1998). Pedagogical variations in service-learning and student outcomes: How time, contact, and refection matter. *Michigan Journal of Community Service Learning, 5,* 32–47.

Maris, E. (1998). Covariance adjustment versus gain scores—revisited. *Psychological Methods, 3,* 309–327.

McHatton, P. A., Thomas, D., & Lehman, K. (2006). Lessons learning in service learning: Personnel preparation though community action. *Mentoring and Tutoring: Partnership in Learning, 14*(1), 67–79.

McKenna, M. C., & Kear, D. J. (1990, May). Measuring attitude toward reading: A new tool for teachers. *The Reading Teacher, 43*(8), 626–639.

Rabiee, F. (2004). Focus-group interview and data analysis. *Proceedings of the Nutrition Society, 63*, 655–660.

Reeb, R. N., Katsuyama, R. M., Sammon, J. A., & Yoder, D. S. (1998). The Community Service Self-Efficacy Scale: Evidence of reliability construct validity, and pragmatic utility. *Michigan Journal of Community Service Learning, 5*, 48–57.

Rosenberg, M. (1965). *Society and the adolescent self-image.* Princeton, NJ: Princeton University Press.

Scott, V. G. (2006). Incorporating service learning into your special education classroom. *Intervention in School & Clinic, 42*(1), 25–29.

Stufflebeam, D. L. (2003). The CIPP model for evaluation. In D. L. Stufflebeam & T. Kellaghan, (Eds.), *The international handbook of educational evaluation.* Boston: Kluwer Academic.

Stufflebeam, D. L., & Shinkfield, A. J. (2007). *Evaluation theory, models, and applications.* San Francisco, CA: Jossey-Bass.

Thomas, L., MacMillan, J., McColl, E., Hale, C., & Bond, S. (1995) Comparison of focus group and individual interview methodology in examining patient satisfaction with nursing care. *Social Sciences in Health, 1*, 206–219.

Zhang, G., & Algina, J. (2008). Coverage performance of the non-central F-based and percentile bootstrap confidence intervals for Root Mean Square Standardized Effect Size in one-way fixed-effects ANOVA. *Journal of Modern Applied Statistical Methods, 7*(1), 56–76.

Zhang, G., & Algina, J. (2011). A robust root mean square standardized effect size and its confidence intervals in one-way fixed-effects ANOVA. *Journal of Modern Applied Statistical Methods, 10*(1), 77–96.

Guili Zhang, PhD, is an Associate Professor in Research and Evaluation Methods in the Department of Special Education, Foundations, and Research at East Carolina University. She is a recipient of the Frontiers in Education Benjamin J. Dasher Best Paper Award, the American Society for Engineering Education Best Paper Award, and the Edward C. Pomeroy Award for Outstanding Contributions to Teacher Education from the American Association of Colleges for Teacher Education.

Nancy Zeller, PhD, is a Professor in the Department of Special Education, Foundations, and Research at East Carolina University. She is also Research Area Program Coordinator in the department.

Christine Shea, PhD, is a Professor in the Foundation of Education in the Department of Special Education, Foundations, and Research at East Carolina University.

Robin Griffith, PhD, is an Assistant Professor in the College of Education at Texas Christian University.

Katherine Misulis, PhD, is an Associate Professor and Interim Chairperson in the Department of Literacy Studies, English Education, and History Education at East Carolina University.

Debbie Metcalf, MAEd, is a National Board Certified teacher and Teacher-in-Residence in the Department of Special Education, Foundations, and Research at East Carolina University.

Jennifer Williams, PhD, is an Associate Professor in Special Education in the Department of Special Education, Foundations, and Research at East Carolina University.

PART IV

THE PEDAGOGY OF SERVICE-LEARNING FOR IMPLEMENTATION IN P–12 CLASSROOMS

Virginia M. Jagla

INTRODUCTION

Besides experiencing service-learning as direct service endeavors, teacher candidates should be taught to use the pedagogy with their P–12 students. We feel this is a major aspect of transforming teacher education. Service-learning offers a unique opportunity for students to get involved with their communities in a tangible way by integrating service projects with classroom learning. Service-learning engages students in the educational process, using what they learn in the classroom to solve real-life problems. Students not only learn about democracy and citizenship, they become actively contributing citizens and community members through the service they perform.

At National Louis University we involve many of our teacher candidates in residencies or year-long internships in schools, where they are expected to plan and implement service-learning pedagogy. Several of these programs place candidates in urban schools. The intention of service-learning is to experience democracy in action. Students learn through the experiences themselves as well as reflection on the process. The powerful pedagogy of service-learning empowers those who participate. Some think of inner-city youths as the recipients of service. Students in any neighborhood

Transforming Teacher Education Through Service-Learning, pages 233–236
Copyright © 2013 by Information Age Publishing

strengthen their sense of altruism and self-esteem through helping others. Teacher candidates need to learn more about this powerful pedagogy to assist in teaching students in similar situations. By providing teacher candidates with service-learning experiences in a school setting to design and implement service-learning projects with their students, we impart the knowledge, skills, and dispositions to empower these candidates to be able to continue to develop such projects in their future schools in other blighted urban neighborhoods for years to come.

Our teacher candidates coach and work alongside their students within community organizations to truly reconceptualize the notion of learning in these urban areas. The urban education candidates acquire a wealth of experience and have a good conception of what these types of projects entail. They experience firsthand the integrative properties of the pedagogy of service-learning and are ready to fine-tune such ideas in future classrooms. As one of our candidates put it, "I have decided to make service-learning a staple in my future curricula and will be an advocate for the acceptance and growth of the service-learning movement ... an educator is responsible for one thing: finding the most relevant, efficient and meaningful ways to teach children, to enlighten young people, and to inspire our future leaders."

To strengthen the understanding of service-learning pedagogy for our teacher candidates, it is important for us to cultivate partnering schools where the candidates can put this theory into practice. While we are doing that with individual schools, our partnership with Chicago Public Schools (CPS) (housing over 600 public schools) deepens continually, with regard to service-learning pedagogy. Members of our faculty meet regularly with CPS personnel along with faculty members from other Chicago colleges and universities. Together, this consortium has helped develop sustainable projects within CPS throughout Chicago. Collectively, we are strengthening the teacher education programs in many colleges of education through this partnership.

CPS now requires that all students complete at least three service-learning projects that are embedded in classroom instruction before they graduate from high school. CPS defines service-learning as a *teaching strategy that links classroom curriculum to projects that service the community. Students build academic, civic, and social-emotional skills as they serve their community.*

While the graduation requirement is directed toward students, it expects schools and teachers to offer multiple opportunities for students to participate in service-learning projects. An Environmental Science teacher might link instruction in principles of biodiversity and ecologies with a stewardship project at a local wetland area. A Social Science teacher might link a study of the progressive era with a service project for senior citizens at a historic settlement house. We believe that classroom learning is extended and enhanced through a meaningful service project and that the service project is enriched through rigorous academic preparation and reflection.

Chicago Public Schools is now contemplating asking its university partners to provide a foundation in service-learning pedagogy and practices for their teacher candidates. There is a proposal that would expect that all universities seeking to send student teachers to CPS classrooms would ensure that their teacher candidates have appropriate preparation, including participation in service-learning experience at the university level; instruction in the pedagogy and principles of service-learning in a university class; exposure to the core requirements of service-learning for CPS students; opportunity to develop a unit, lesson, or project that incorporates service-learning pedagogy; and completion of a community asset mapping/knowledge assignment.

Completing each of these steps would ensure that student teachers would arrive at CPS prepared to facilitate or co-facilitate a service-learning project with the students. While in the student teaching assignments, Chicago Public Schools might expect all student teachers complete a community asset mapping/knowledge experience, facilitate or co-facilitate a service-learning project, and complete a service-learning project design for review based on content area/coursework.

As Chicago Public Schools has made an important shift from community service to service-learning, it has made a significant investment in preparing teachers to initiate curriculum-based projects with their students. The possibility for teacher candidates to come to CPS prepared to implement service-learning projects represents an extraordinary opportunity both for CPS and for our college of education. Now more than ever, CPS needs its newest teachers to begin their careers in the classroom cognizant of the history and issues of the school's community and skilled in increasing academic and social-emotional learning through pedagogical practices such as service-learning, which bridge the divide between school and community.

Some of the previous chapters in this book allude to the use of service-learning pedagogy with P–12 students. If we are to truly transform teacher education, it is extremely important to teach the pedagogy of service-learning to our teacher candidates to use with their future students. In the chapter, "TeacherCorps: Transforming Teacher Education through Social Justice, Service-Learning, and Community Partnerships," we learn about a program that prepares teacher candidates to provide community-based service-learning experiences for K–12 students. Learning the skills to teach for social justice, including the implementation of course based service-learning, is clearly delineated throughout this final chapter of the book. Social justice is a major aspect of the chapter (Agarwal, Epstein, Oppenheim, Oyler, & Sonu, 2010; Borrero, 2009; Brooks & Thompson, 2005; Cochran-Smith, 2004, 2010; Cochran-Smith et al., 2009; Enterline, Cochran-Smith,

Ludlow, & Mitescu, 2008; Puig & Recchia, 2012). Deeper understanding of social justice perspectives is one of many insights gained through service-learning. This powerful pedagogy has impressive and effective impact on students of all grade/age levels from preschool through graduate school. Colleges of education owe it to their teacher candidates both to provide service-learning experiences for them and to teach candidates how to embed the pedagogy into their future classrooms.

REFERENCES

Agarwal, R., Epstein, S., Oppenheim, R., Oyler, C., & Sonu, D. (2010). From ideal practice and back again: Beginning teachers teaching for social justice. *Journal of Teacher Education, 61*(3), 237–247.

Borrero, N. (2009). Preparing new teachers for urban teaching: Creating a community dedicated to social justice. *Multicultural Perspectives, 11*(4), 221–226.

Brooks, J., & Thompson, E. G. (2005). Social justice in the classroom. *Educational Leadership, 63*(1), 48–52.

Cochran-Smith, M. (2004). Defining the outcomes of teacher education: What's social justice to do with it? *Asia-Pacific Journal of Teacher Education, 32*(3), 193–212.

Cochran-Smith, M. (2010). Toward a theory of teacher education for social justice. In M. Fullen, A. Hargreaves, D. Hopkins, and A. Lieberman (Eds.), *The international handbook of educational change* (2nd ed., pp. 445–467). New York: Springer.

Cochran-Smith, M., Shakeman, K., Jong, C., Terrell, D. G., Barnatt, J., McQuillan, P. (2009). Good and just teaching: The case for social justice in teacher education. *American Journal of Education, 115*(3), 347–377.

Enterline, S., Cochran-Smith, M., Ludlow, L. H., & Mitescu, E. (2008). Learning to teach for social justice: Measuring change in the beliefs of teacher candidates. *The New Educator, 4*(4), 267–290.

Puig, V. I., & Recchia, S. L. (2012). Urban advocates for young children with special needs: First-year early childhood teachers enacting social justice. *The New Educator, 8*(3), 258–277.

CHAPTER 10

TEACHERCORPS

Transforming Teacher Education Through Social Justice, Service-Learning, and Community Partnerships

**Marjori Krebs, Kiran Katira, Swechha Singh,
and Neil Rigsbee**

ABSTRACT

TeacherCorps is a partnership program at the University of New Mexico (UNM) among the Department of Teacher Education faculty, the Community Engagement Center staff, and several elementary and secondary schools located in federally designated "pockets of poverty." We work with these teacher candidates as TeacherCorps members as they complete their teacher preparation coursework, field experience, and serve as members of AmeriCorps. The goal of TeacherCorps is to provide a transformative learning experience for Teacher Education candidates. The program prepares these future teachers to provide community-based service-learning experiences for K–12 students who utilize both university and community assets to address critical community-identified needs. Each candidate also earns work-study dollars and volunteer hours toward an AmeriCorps Education Award. The guiding principles of the TeacherCorps experience include a three-pronged approach of

Transforming Teacher Education Through Service-Learning, pages 237–261
Copyright © 2013 by Information Age Publishing
237

Academics, Community Engagement, and Leadership Development. Several key themes guide the TeacherCorps program and are interwoven throughout the teacher candidates' field experiences, reflection sessions, and professional development workshops. These themes include community-based service-learning and civic engagement; antiracism and social justice; partnerships with families, community leaders, and community-based organizations; and interdisciplinary teaching methods. This chapter provides the theoretical underpinnings of the program juxtaposed with qualitative research that evaluates the TeacherCorps members' preparation conducted through this approach. We, as researchers, found that as a result of their service in TeacherCorps, the participants developed their understanding of how to implement community-based service-learning in their classrooms, teach through the lens of social justice, focus on the assets of a community, and engage parents and community members in student learning.

Ms. Altus begins her day in the school cafeteria at the tribal community school, supervising students eating breakfast. Before heading to her first period math class, she meets with a group of students to listen to their ideas on feeding homeless people in the park across the street with vegetables from the school's community garden.

Mr. Devan begins his Spanish class by asking students to submit their family recipes that they translated into Spanish for their class Family Cookbook, and then students meet in small groups to share the lessons learned about their own family histories by listening to family conversations around these recipes.

Ms. Albertson returns her kindergarten students back into the classroom from the school community garden. They have just picked their first green chilies from the seeds they planted earlier in the school year. As part of their science unit on the five senses, the students discussed when they will roast the chilies and invite family and community members for a community harvest celebration.

These teacher candidates are members of TeacherCorps, a teacher preparation program where teacher candidates, who are also AmeriCorps members, implement community-based service-learning into their field experience classrooms. With the theme of social justice front and center in this teacher preparation program, these teacher candidates face complex decisions and situations from moment to moment during the school day, and with guidance and reflection opportunities, they begin to understand the social justice issues behind these decisions and situations (Cochran-Smith, 2004). TeacherCorps members are integrating social justice in their classrooms and school communities every day. The most important goal in teaching for social justice is to promote student achievement and enhance their opportunities and changes in the world (Cochran-Smith, 2010). Cochran-Smith and colleagues state, "Teaching for social justice is not an option, but a crucial and fundamental part of just and good teaching" (2009, p. 375).

This chapter presents a unique combination of social justice education infused into teacher education with service-learning as a tool of civic engagement. In addition, this chapter incorporates TeacherCorps members' feedback on their experiences.

HISTORY OF TEACHERCORPS AND AMERICORPS CONNECTION

TeacherCorps was originally established through the Higher Education Act of 1965 to improve teaching in predominantly low-income neighborhoods. Following *Brown vs. Board of Education*, schools were more integrated and teachers were looking for ways to teach multiracial classes. Through this original model, interns, under the supervision of master teachers, attended workshops led by local colleges, public schools, and community organizations, which gave the interns a more clear understanding and context of low socioeconomic communities of color, thus enabling them to be more effective teachers in inner-city elementary schools. The interns and their team leaders then participated in and developed community engagement and service-learning activities in these neighborhoods (Eckert, 2011). The University of New Mexico's Department of Teacher Education, partnering with the University's Community Engagement Center, has revitalized this TeacherCorps idea in conjunction with AmeriCorps. This current TeacherCorps initiative emphasizes social justice, critical pedagogy, and community-based service-learning as its core themes. There are other programs that connect teaching and AmeriCorps, namely the TEAMS Project in San Francisco, California (Borrero, 2009), and Growing Together in Columbus, Ohio (Partnerships Make a Difference, 2012), but the teacher candidate and classroom teacher populations and program configurations differ greatly.

The TeacherCorps–AmeriCorps connection is important because the program allows for teacher candidates to serve in the neighborhoods where they teach, giving them the opportunity to earn an hourly wage through federal work-study funds. All these additional hours beyond their required field experience hours allow the teacher candidates the opportunity to earn as they go through school, but in a way that enhances their future careers. Upon completion of their terms of service, they are eligible for an Education Award of up to $2,700 for their 900 hours of service. This Education Award is to be used to pay for college, graduate school, or pay back student loans (Corporation for National Service, 2012a). AmeriCorps is a national program of the Corporation for National and Community

Service (CNCS), an independent federal agency. The mission of the CNCS is to "improve lives, strengthen communities, and foster civic engagement through service and volunteerism" (Corporation for National and Community Service, 2012b, para. 1). TeacherCorps members carry out this mission every day in the before- and after-school time in their urban elementary and secondary schools.

Faculty members in the University of New Mexico Department of Teacher Education and staff members at the University's Community Engagement Center (CED) created TeacherCorps as an extension of the UNM Service Corps program. The intent of TeacherCorps is to focus on service-learning in the area of education and teacher preparation in lower socio-economic neighborhoods. Teacher candidates are recruited from these or similar neighborhoods in which they serve. They complete their field experience requirements and implement community-based service-learning activities as part of their teacher licensure programs. Additionally they serve as role models for younger members of their communities, demonstrating the importance of attaining a college education.

Preparing teacher candidates for careers in teaching children in urban areas is a concern around the country. According to Smith and Smith (2009),

> Better preparation of teachers for urban districts could lower teacher turnover rates...good teacher preparation for urban districts could be one missing link to generate school reform through stabilizing the teacher workforce and creating greater continuing and a greater sense of community within the schools. (p. 336)

Helping future teachers understand social justice issues is critical, and "occurs all too rarely, and is especially uncommon in urban and other schools with large numbers of students who are poor, minority, immigrant, or have special learning needs" (Cochran-Smith et al., 2009, p. 374).

Teachers in urban school districts find their jobs rewarding because they are experiencing the enjoyment of diversity, making a positive difference, and having a sense of accomplishment (Smith & Smith, 2009). Teacher preparation programs must embrace their role in preparing teachers to focus on enabling students of color to live out the theme of social justice by accessing the educational opportunities they deserve. This focus must begin early in teachers' careers (Borrero, 2009) and must include "advocating for students, their parents, communities, and others involved in larger social advocacy movements" (Cochran-Smith, 2010). TeacherCorps strives to bring these major constructs together by preparing our teachers to fully understand the context of their student's lives and the potential for transformation through civic engagement.

NEEDS ADDRESSED BY THE COMMUNITY-BASED
SOCIAL JUSTICE TEACHERCORPS PROGRAM

Teacher candidates in TeacherCorps complete their field experience requirements in urban schools in Albuquerque, New Mexico. They work in schools located in federally defined "pockets of poverty." Poverty affects almost one-third of children in New Mexico; 30% of children under the age of 18 are living in poverty (New Mexico Voices for Children, 2011). Most of the schools served by TeacherCorps are designated as Title I Schools by the U.S. Department of Education, where 40% or more students come from families that are designated as low-income families. In addition, most of the participating TeacherCorps schools did not meet annual yearly progress (AYP) as defined in the federal No Child Left Behind legislation. Statewide, as of 2012, New Mexico ranked 49th in the nation in overall child well-being, with the following sub-category rankings: 49th in health, 49th in education, 49th in family and community, and 48th in economy (Annie E. Casey Foundation, 2012). In addition, New Mexico ranks 47th in the national high school dropout rankings, with 34% of New Mexico high school students failing to graduate. Dropout rates vary according to race and ethnicity: white students (25%), Hispanic (37%), African American (39%), and Native American (42%). In addition, 80% of fourth graders are rated as "below proficient" in reading (New Mexico Voices for Children, 2010).

There are great needs in New Mexico, and our teachers are actively engaged in addressing these disparities. Teacher candidates must be trained to work with children in these high-need areas in order to be prepared to teach in New Mexico schools. New teachers can expect to struggle with issues of social justice as they begin their careers (Agarwl, Epstein, Oppenheim, Oyler, & Sonu, 2010); however, most teacher candidates and new teachers know little about teaching with culture and community in mind, and understand even less about how their responses can be degrading and oftentimes offensive to students. These attitudes can result from teacher education programs short-changing important topics such as community, culture, and social contexts in their preservice teacher instruction (Smith & Smith, 2009).

THE TEACHERCORPS PROGRAM

The Goal of TeacherCorps

We created TeacherCorps at the University of New Mexico based on a need to prepare teachers who have a greater understanding of the root causes of the achievement gap and the social determinants of equity. Teacher Education faculty and Community Engagement Center staff believe this knowledge, informed by direct experience in urban communities of color and coupled with critical reflection, will equip the teacher candidates to better serve these students. The goals of TeacherCorps are to transform the teacher candidates' preparation experience by utilizing community knowledge and leadership; providing coursework and professional development experiences through an antiracism, social justice lens; and training teacher candidates to implement community-based service-learning projects with K–12 students to address community-identified needs.

Teaching is a social and cultural practice, and we expect teacher candidates to interact with the cultures of the schools in various and complex ways. Teachers must also know and understand the communities in which they teach (Cochran-Smith, 2012; Puig & Recchia, 2012). Similarly, teachers must purposefully involve families in their children's education, creating a sense of family empowerment through partnering with the classroom teacher and the school (Bailey, 2001; Puig, 2011). Introducing the topics of the importance of families in teacher candidate training creates a firm foundation for these future teachers to act on these practices and beliefs when they have their own classrooms (Puig, 2011).

Philosophical Beliefs: Social Justice, Service-Learning, and Authentic Community Engagement

Those of us who have worked together to create TeacherCorps believe that classroom teachers who understand and incorporate into their teaching the lives and community contexts of the children they teach will have greater success in engaging and motivating children in their own education. We also believe that teachers need to themselves understand and help children understand the foundational root causes of social inequities, and to create service-learning and civic engagement opportunities to address community-identified needs.

The program provides training in service-learning strategies for both TeacherCorps members and their cooperating teachers. In connecting the academic content, the Common Core State Standards, and community needs, we are helping to create cultures in schools where partnerships with community members and organizations are valued and these partnerships are incorporated throughout the service-learning process. We are also building meaningful bridges to connect communities, families, and schools in local problem solving and service-learning.

It is important to provide opportunities for teacher candidates to expand their perceptions of teachers' roles not only as leaders of specific classrooms, but also as collaborators with other teachers to raise concerns about the system's reinforcement of "privilege and disadvantage based on race, culture, language, background, and gender" (Cochran-Smith, 2004, p. 207). Teacher education curricula should combine effective classroom practice with a focus on equity and participation by community members. This combination is essential for teachers dedicated to social justice (Borrero, 2012). According to Puig and Recchia (2012),

> Ensuring that all children's needs are met in an appropriate learning environment is a social justice issue for young children, ensuring that all teachers are prepared to enter these environments ready to identify and address their students' educational needs may also be considered a social justice issue for preservice teachers. (p. 275)

Teacher preparation programs should work with intentionality to provide the social, intellectual, and organizational contexts through teaching curriculum processes, field experience placements, and specifically designed student-initiated community involvement to prepare their teacher candidates to teach for social justice, and then commit to supporting them as they try to deliver on this commitment during their beginning classroom experiences (Borrero, 2009; Cochran-Smith et al., 2009).

Key Themes and Guiding Principles

TeacherCorps provides field experiences, reflection sessions, and professional development workshops to incorporate the following themes not only for their TeacherCorps members who are teacher candidates, but also for their cooperating teachers:

- Innovative Teacher Preparation with a Focus on Community-Based Service-Learning and Civic Engagement;
- Viewing of Community Issues through an Assets-Based, Antiracism, Social Justice Lens;
- Partnerships with Families, Community Leaders, and Community-Based Organizations; and
- Creation of Classroom Communities of Caring Learners and Thinkers through Interdisciplinary Teaching Methods

The guiding philosophy of the program utilizes the Praxis approach where Knowledge, Action, and Reflection are practiced in a cyclical process (Friere, 1974) through the following key program components: Academics (teaching licensure requirements and before- and after-school tutoring/family engagement program support), Community Engagement (federal and state work-study funding opportunities and AmeriCorps Education Award scholarship opportunities), and Leadership Development (service-learning professional development workshops, creation of cultures of service-learning in schools, and social justice through reflection sessions). A description of each of these program components is provided below.

Academic Experiences. *Teaching licensure requirements.* TeacherCorps prepares teacher candidates to complete their State of New Mexico elementary (K–8) or secondary (7–12) teacher licensure requirements through coursework and field experiences. Our goal is to prepare teacher candidates who teach through a social justice lens, so we agree with Brooks and Thompson (2005) that purposeful connections between their classroom experiences and methods coursework and the curriculum must be clearly addressed.

Before- and after-school tutoring/family engagement program support. These same TeacherCorps members serve as tutors in before- and after-school programs or support the family engagement programs at the community-based learning centers connected to the schools in which they student-teach. In research conducted by Smith and Smith (2009), urban teachers expressed a common thread regarding connecting with students in urban schools: "their neighborhoods, their families, their culture" (p. 347). TeacherCorps members working in before- and after-school community settings are directly connected with these elements. TeacherCorps members implement service-learning as a pedagogy and also study the principles of quality service-learning in their reflection sessions and methods courses (Anderson, 2001).

Community Engagement. *Federal and state work-study funding opportunities.* TeacherCorps members are also eligible to earn federal and state work-study dollars for their extra time outside of their required field experience hours in their placement classrooms and in before- and after-school community settings, providing the teacher candidates with various experiences in diverse settings (Anderson, 2001). This income allows TeacherCorps members to focus on their teacher preparation and not work in minimum-wage jobs that do not further their career goals.

AmeriCorps Education Award scholarship opportunities. Each TeacherCorps member may earn an AmeriCorps Education Award of approximately $2,700 for 900 extra hours of service in their schools and before- and after-school programs.

Leadership Development. *Service-learning professional development workshops.* TeacherCorps faculty and staff, who are former classroom teachers, lead three day-long professional development workshops for TeacherCorps members and their field experience cooperating teachers. Not all cooperating teachers attend because participation on their parts is voluntary. Once we attain more funding, we plan to provide stipends to increase cooperating teacher attendance at these workshops. The participants learn about implementing community-based service-learning projects with their students, in partnership with community members and organizations. Program coordinators of TeacherCorps work to provide grant funds to pay for substitute teachers so cooperating teachers can attend with no cost to their school. Participating in professional development and having substitutes paid for by outside entities are motivators for teachers to participate in such workshops (Krebs, 2012).

In order for teachers to teach with passion and dedication, they need to be able to participate in professional development sessions that are meaningful, meet their direct needs, and provide opportunities for collaboration with other teachers (Anderson, 2001; Cochran-Smith, 2010; Smith & Smith, 2009). Collaborations such as these between teachers in schools, teacher candidates, community leaders, and university representatives with a focus on the teacher candidates' field experiences can support strong, meaningful, seamless connections between teacher education and professional development, thus allowing an authentic space for theory and practice to inform each other (Puig, 2011). In addition, when teachers implement service-learning they find they are able to foster deep and meaningful connections with numerous constituencies, such as among themselves and other people with whom they work, themselves and their students, themselves and other teachers, the different areas of the curriculum, and themselves and members of the community-at-large (Krebs, 2012).

Creation of cultures of service-learning in schools. TeacherCorps members and their cooperating teachers work together to provide training and assistance for other teachers in their schools to implement service-learning. TeacherCorps members participate in year-round, regularly scheduled day-long professional development opportunities along with their cooperating teachers on the topic of implementing service-learning in their field experience classrooms.

These workshops are designed around the themes of Partnerships Make a Difference (2012) of "creating a legacy, identifying and demonstrating gifts, fascinations, and positive character traits, understanding and becoming part of a community, taking action that matters, engaging in reflection, and envisioning the future" (para. 2). In addition, teacher candidates and their cooperating teachers gain experience in creating service-learning projects that follow the Elements of High Quality Service Learning (National Youth Leadership Council, 2008), which include "meaningful service, link to curriculum, reflection, diversity, youth voice, and partnerships" (para. 1–6).

Billig (2002) captures the essence of the professional development provided to TeacherCorps members when she highlights the importance of academic connections, partnerships, and reflection:

> Students who engage in high quality service-learning activities typically have some choice in the service they provide, work cooperatively with each other and with members of the community, receive at least some cognitive guidance from adults and/or peers as they reflect on and make sense of their experiences, and acquire a new knowledge or skills that recognizably link to academic content areas. (p. 246)

Researchers report that students derive personal, interpersonal, social, and academic benefits from participation in service-learning (Aquila & Dodd, 2003; Eyler & Giles, 2002; Melchior & Bailis, 2002; Scales, Blyth, Berkas, & Kielsmeier, 2000; Scales & Roehlkepartain, 2004; Search Institute, 2000). In the area of personal development, students self-report increases in self-confidence, self-esteem, leadership skills, personal decision-making skills (Aquila & Dodd, 2003), career benefits, and spiritual growth (Eyler & Giles, 1999). Socially, students who participate in service-learning report a positive impact on their own social responsibility (Scales, et al., 2000), civic attitudes, and volunteerism (Brandeis University, 1999). Students see themselves as valuable resources for their organizations and their communities (Eyler & Giles, 1999; Search Institute, 2000). Students express that taking care of others who experience difficulties is truly everyone's responsibility (Melchior & Bailis, 2002).

A well-designed service-learning program can contribute to students' attainment of important values, knowledge, skills, and commitment necessary for good citizenship (Eyler & Giles, 1999; Melchior & Bailis, 2002). When participating in service-learning, students are given opportunities to practice and nurture social skills by interacting with different types of people (Search Institute, 2000). Interpersonally, teachers and administrators note an improvement in students' abilities to work with others. The students themselves report that it was rewarding to help others (Eyler & Giles, 1999). Students showed support and concern for the well-being of others (Search Institute, 2000) and tended to maintain that concern over time more than students who did not participate in service-learning (Scales et al., 2000). Students also tended to develop a greater tolerance and appreciation for other cultures (Eyler & Giles, 1999) and those students who participated in service also reported talking more often with their parents about school than students who did not participate (Scales et al., 2000).

When teachers in K–12 classrooms and faculty in higher education settings incorporate service-learning into their coursework, they tended to fulfill both personal and professional needs (Ammon, 2002; Palmer, 2004). Teachers found service-learning to be personally rewarding because they could relate the curriculum and service to their own interests and experiences.

Service-learning also met faculty needs for their belief in promoting civic engagement in their classes (Palmer, 2004). Professionally, teachers could relate service-learning to their educational philosophies and to their teaching goals (Ammon, 2002) as well as to solve pedagogical problems such as the need to connect content to current worldly events (Palmer, 2004).

Social justice context through reflection sessions. Program coordinators of TeacherCorps facilitate the TeacherCorps Reflection Seminar course (EDUC 493) to provide space for conversation and context of their school and community experiences through a social justice lens. "A commitment to social justice teacher education must be partnered with a commitment to self-study and self-reflection" (Agarwl et al., 2010, p. 237). According to Cochran-Smith, teachers should teach based on a deep political consciousness, purposefully garnering the role of "advocate and activist... [with a] deep respect for differences, and commitments to diminishing the inequities of American schooling and society" (2010, p. 457).

The TeacherCorps Reflection Seminar creates a unique opportunity outside of the school, outside of the methods classroom, and outside of the typical teacher preparation classroom management seminar to address important topics such as race and oppression. When focusing on social justice in teacher education, programs must be prepared to deal with tensions that arise from diversity issues of teachers, and to also focus on perspectives of those who have been oppressed or marginalized in society (Cochran-Smith, 2010).

Through these seminars, TeacherCorps members are able to focus on these structural inequalities by reading articles, learning from guest speakers, and participating in discussions. Guest speakers include interdisciplinary faculty, community leaders, teachers, principals, and other school leaders. Advocacy for social justice is a developing process—one that relies on experiences and reflection to put social justice attitudes into practice (Puig & Recchia, 2012). Teachers should see teaching for social justice as a process, not an attained skill. The Reflection Seminar provides a strategic opportunity for TeacherCorps members to reflect on their experiences and to see their thinking processes. This type of social reconstructionist thinking and reflection is imperative in order to effectively educate teachers to be social justice practitioners (Agarwl et al., 2010).

Teacher candidates are not typically prepared to be activists; however, they are capable of engaging in preparation programs with social justice agendas wherein they are expected to make decisions in their classrooms that reflect a larger educational system that structures inequalities (Cochran-Smith et al., 2009). In the TeacherCorps Reflection Seminars, teacher candidates engage with faculty experts across campus in conversations ranging from community schools, achievement gap disparities, community gardens, bilingual education, Native American education, African American education, restorative justice, funds of knowledge, and numerous other topics.

METHODOLOGY

Participants and Data Collection

TeacherCorps members at UNM are students accepted into the Teacher Education program, who have applied to become a part of a special

TeacherCorps cohort. Twelve TeacherCorps members responded to the initial written online survey (see Appendix) at the beginning of the program, and six responded at the end of the program regarding its impact and effectiveness. The participants represented teacher candidates in grades K–12, with almost half the participants completing their field experiences in grades K–5. Both graduate and undergraduate students participated in the study. The self-identified racial makeup of the participants of Caucasian, Hispanic, white-Hispanic, Native American-Hispanic, and Asian-Filipino closely resembled the diversity of the teacher candidates overall.

Surveys were administered prior to the beginning of the program and nearing completion of the program. Participants responded to both quantitative and qualitative survey questions in the pre- and post-surveys. Survey questions were identical to understand changes in knowledge and experiences as a result of their participation in TeacherCorps over their 18-month experience. Survey questions ascertained candidates' understanding of social justice, service-learning, the achievement gap, and working with parents and other community members. The researchers for this study are current Teacher Education faculty, Community Engagement Center staff members, and graduate students.

Strategies for Analyzing Data

As a descriptive study, a combination of analysis methods were employed (Creswell, 1998). The methods used involved inductively developing codes, categories, and themes (Strauss & Corbin, 1998), including the horizontalization process of qualitative analysis. In analyzing the data and coding for significant themes, researchers implemented Moustakas's (1994) modifications of the Stevick-Colaizzi-Keen Method of Analysis of Data. Researchers considered each statement with respect to significance for description of the experience, then listed each nonrepetitive, nonoverlapping statement as a means of horizontalization, or invariant horizons of the meaning units of the experience of the data. Researchers then related and clustered the invariant meaning units into themes, including verbatim examples to give depth to the thematic coding process and descriptions (Moustakas, 1994). To increase the depth of the data, researchers met in small groups to conduct initial analysis and determine findings for each of the key questions asked on the surveys. One researcher then reconciled the groups' analyses and formulated the results found below.

FINDINGS: WHAT DID TEACHERCORPS MEMBERS SAY ABOUT THEIR EXPERIENCES?

Initial survey responses were brief and displayed limited knowledge of community-based service-learning, the achievement gap, and engaging parents and the community in the education process.

TeacherCorps members responded as they neared the end of their experience that they had grown in many areas that are typical of the growth of teacher candidates during their field experiences, including appreciation of the support they received, and that the faculty listened to them and gave them constructive feedback on their teaching. The members felt that faculty addressed the concerns they had in their classrooms and that the assistance with classroom management was valuable. However, because of the TeacherCorps Reflection sessions they attended, they gained valuable information about a variety of topics, including service-learning, hunger, and community assets. Students commented that "TeacherCorps allows us to take what we've learned and take it to another level" and "the extra advice and guidance has been wonderful."

TeacherCorps members also voiced an appreciation and recognition of the financial support they received in comments such as, "TeacherCorps cooperates well with teacher education in order to ensure a valuable experience for the student teachers that builds off of the university curriculum and student teachers are compensated through work study and their ServiceCorps stipend."

Understanding Community-Based Service-Learning

At the beginning of the TeacherCorps program in August, teacher candidates had limited understanding of *community-based service-learning* and surface-level understanding of the reasons behind the achievement gap. Early definitions of community-based service-learning weighed on the side of the TeacherCorps members "helping" those in the community with their problems, and seeing themselves as the ones doing the work in these communities for the benefit of those who live there. Other themes identified in their definitions of community-based service-learning included solving community problems, involvement in the community, making learning meaningful, increasing self-efficacy, and thinking critically. Noticeable attitudes were emerging regarding the importance of recognizing community assets through statements such as, "Working with the assets of a community to improve the lives of those living within the community," thus creating, identifying, and acknowledging the assets and personal connections with the community. A nod toward working with families also emerged in this quote from a participation: "Working with and for the community along with the students and families improves all aspects of the community."

Nearing completion of the program, their views of community-based service-learning advanced to include ideas such as the importance of "using community assets where I teach" and "connecting to the community where I teach." They had taken note of local museums and parks they could use when identifying community-based service-learning projects. A TeacherCorps member summed it up this way:

> I love the idea of community learning. When students are learning something that is relevant to them, they are more than likely to understand. When they create the relationship of what is being taught, they are totally into learning without realizing that they are learning!

TeacherCorps members also observed that people wanted to help and support their communities, and they recognized local programs, agencies, and assets were available to help solve community-based needs. "People want to make changes for the better." In addition, teacher candidates observed that residents had a sense of pride in their communities and they felt welcomed into these communities. One TeacherCorps member comment summarized the strong curricular connections students made during the project:

Our project [focuses] on food and nutrition and allows the students to have a say after researching what goes into the breakfasts and lunches they are served on campus. Through this project we will have students that can make educated decisions about what goes into their bodies and how it will affect their energy, their overall heath.

The Achievement Gap

Likewise, students had brief responses when asked about their thoughts on why there was an achievement gap between different racial and ethnic groups. The themes that emerged here included lack of relevant curriculum, parents not valuing education, low socioeconomic status of students, racial and ethnic differences, and lack of community and school resources. Responses included "perception," "less money for materials," "the academics may not relate to their lives," and the misconception that different racial and ethnic groups do not value education.

TeacherCorps members nearing the end of their program are beginning to voice concerns that the *achievement gap* is really an *opportunity gap* and have observed their students facing numerous challenges outside the classroom, but see their skills increasing to approach such challenges alongside their students, by being "better able to manipulate my teaching several different ways for each one of my students to learn." They are beginning to recognize that parents actually *do* want their "kids to succeed" and they "support a quality education."

One teacher candidate responded thoughtfully about the lack of opportunity for students:

> I believe there is an achievement gap for a couple reasons. I know there are times that students have a language barrier and are unable to be successful in an English-only setting. Some students may not have all the educational resources available to them, which creates achievement gaps. Teachers need to advocate for their students so they can be successful.

Teacher candidates valued the additional information they had learned during the reflection sessions, specifically the information about poverty and diversity. As one teacher candidate commented, "I know how to really look at socioeconomic status and the needs of an area." The infusion of service-learning into their field experience was valuable also, "I now know how to teach through service." They also appreciated the "inspiration" they gained from the presenters at the reflection sessions.

TeacherCorps members were also positive about learning in a cohort community with other students who care about each other and share similar values about the community. One student also commented on how the compensation through work study and AmeriCorps was an asset to her as she had to work to get through school.

Challenges in Working with Parents and Community

Initially in survey responses TeacherCorps members predicted challenges such as parents' unwillingness to participate, challenges with "time" and "commitment" for parent availability to attend meetings and be directly involved in the classroom: "The parents are too busy to be involved." They also predicted language barriers that may exist, and they feared being blamed for their students' lack of performance. Several identified their lack of skills in "convincing and encouraging" parents to participate, intimating that there is an inherent unwillingness by parents to participate and it is the TeacherCorps member's job to persuade parents to take an active role in their children's education. Several also indicated that their previous methods courses had not prepared them to connect with parents and they lacked the skills to do so. In their final evaluation, all participants responded that they benefitted from their participation in TeacherCorps. They believe they have not only improved their teaching through their participation, but also have better skills to handle social issues that arise in the classroom. They know and understand the diversity of their school communities, are aware of the assets of those communities, and have made significant connections with parents and other family members. One member stated:

> In the community at my school the assets are abundant. We have a variety of teachers and a freedom to discuss difference and how they work in our favor. We have different community groups that work with our school and have formed many partnerships that are outside of the basic things you would expect to have at a school.

Regarding connections with the community, the TeacherCorps members' overall evaluative comments expressed their enthusiasm around the relations they had established with the school staff and community members. They now know the community and value their community. They expressed observing the power of people working together and believe they are "better equipped to handle social issues." Comments such as "learning what is important to the community and working together is amazing" expressed their comfort levels with community engagement and their newfound motivation to do such work. They also observed greater skills in teaching culturally diverse students, including English language learners. "I am excited to get to know the people, places, traditions, and needs of the students and communities I am surrounded by." Another member summarized:

> I am nothing but grateful to this program for showing me that there is more than one way to become a better teacher. You can study all you want, but until you open up and learn who you are teaching, you cannot grow enough to be your best.

Challenges and Suggestions

In the follow-up survey, TeacherCorps members identified the challenges they encountered during their TeacherCorps experience, including the extra time required of them in the schools and reflection sessions, and a perceived lack of organization of the reflection sessions. Because some reflection sessions were held in community settings, travel time and transportation proved challenging to some. Interestingly, none of their challenges related to their school setting or experience, but to logistics of the university requirements. The third challenge expressed was the lack of involvement of the cooperating teachers, who had not committed to TeacherCorps, but just to having a student teacher. One participant commented, "It was tricky trying to convey everything [i.e., community-based service-learning] to someone who had none of the same experiences."

Their suggestions for improvement centered on working more closely with their cooperating teachers and logistics of the program. One student commented, "I think they [the cooperating teachers] would love the speakers and topics [at the reflection sessions] and will be more apt to participate in the final [service-learning] project if they have a broader understanding of what the program is really about." None of their challenges or suggestions focused on their previously identified fears of working with parents and the community, or on the lack of parental support or involvement. Those relationships seemed to be vibrant.

LESSONS LEARNED AND RECOMMENDATIONS

Learning the skills to teach for social justice can be "constructed as a legitimate outcome of teacher education and thus expand the larger agenda to make teacher education accountable for the quality of teachers it prepares" (Enterline, Cochran-Smith, Ludlow, & Mitescu, 2008, p. 267). TeacherCorps is working to do just this. For Teacher Education programs considering a deep and thoughtful focus on social justice, spaces must be created in the Teacher Education program for this type of specialized knowledge attainment and deep reflection. Simply alluding to social justice in teaching methods courses and then expecting students to be able to implement such a philosophy is short-sighted and ineffective. There are some instructors of methods courses who whole-heartedly incorporate a social justice focus into their teaching methods instruction, which does enhance the work of TeacherCorps; however, this is not uniform across the program. Teacher candidates need time to share and reflect on their specific classroom experiences, and receive feedback from mentors who are sensitive to the social justice issues at play in those scenarios. The use of service-learning as a tool to implement the lessons learned is invaluable, as it provides the engaged pedagogy needed to truly motivate the teachers and students alike. The need for knowledge about social inequities, the true opportunity deficits that can result in the achievement gap, and the importance of leadership necessary to truly teach for social justice are areas in which we are just beginning to understand from our TeacherCorps members' viewpoints. Continued research is necessary to understand the teacher candidate experience in teaching for social justice.

We are certainly in the infancy stages of purposefully working with our TeacherCorps members to teach for social justice; we are all still learning the meaningful, emotional, stressful intricacies of this work. Argawl et al. (2010) established a set of criteria for those of us who are brave enough to take on this task:

Educators who teach for social justice a) enact curricula that integrate multiple perspectives, question dominant Western narratives, and are inclusive of racial, ethnic, and linguistic diversity in North America; b) support students to develop a critical consciousness of the injustices that characterize our society; and c) scaffold opportunities for students to be active participants in a democracy, skilled in forms of civic engagement and deliberative discussion. (p. 238)

If teachers actually reach this level of teaching for social justice it is usually not until they enter a master's-level program. Our children, especially those in diverse, high-poverty areas, cannot wait this long. These students need teachers who are prepared to teach them now—who have a keen understanding of not only the knowledge of social justice, but also the skills to enact social justice in the classroom. We are working to accomplish this by preparing our teacher candidates to implement community-based service-learning and other strategies that mainstream prepared teacher candidates do not typically have. TeacherCorps is working to prepare new teachers for these roles, but much is yet to be learned about this process and we are anxious to continue to work at the task. The assumption is that non-TeacherCorps programs are NOT working to prepare initial certification teachers for this work.

A central challenge [to teacher education] is how to prepare teacher candidates who can demonstrate what some consider "best" instructional practices, but also know how to challenge those practices when they exclude certain children or fail to serve particular groups of students. (Cochran-Smith, 2004, p. 205)

As researchers and as teacher educators, we strongly recommend other teacher education programs to face social justice issues head on and implement programs that purposefully prepare teachers for working in challenging neighborhoods.

Key Recommendations

Internally within the university, we recommend that coordinators set clear goals for content and experiences: (1) determine what teacher candidates need to understand about social justice, and what they need to know to enact it in the classroom; (2) engage experts across campus who can deepen teacher candidates' knowledge of important topics for teaching with a social justice lens; (3) create a course to teach this content and to formalize the processes and the expectations of the students; (4) within that course, model strategies for engaging parents and other community members to make positive gains in their local neighborhoods; (5) solicit support from community engagement and partnership organizations on campus to assist with establishing service-learning relationships in the community; and (6) establish some way to fund teacher candidates for the extra time they spend in their community settings so they do not have to leave their schools for a part-time job, but rather are receiving funds from work-study and/or AmeriCorps to continue their preparation.

Externally, we recommend that coordinators establish relationships and follow through on commitments with community organizations and schools: (1) locate principals and schools who have community-based service as a part of their culture; (2) strategically place teacher candidates in these settings; (3) obtain funds to provide meaningful stipends for cooperating teachers above what they already receive for being cooperating teachers so they are required to attend professional development sessions with their teacher candidates, and (4) obtain funds to pay for substitutes so the time cooperating teachers spend outside the school day is kept to a minimum.

We have far to go in our journey of perfecting this approach to transforming teacher preparation, but we are continuing to make improvements to move forward. For the upcoming cohort, we are hoping to make the following specific changes based on lessons learned: (1) holding regular meetings with cooperating mentor teachers at the school, (2) holding regular meetings with school principals, (3) building a reflection session curriculum that builds on the professional development skills, and (4) giving leadership roles to members in their second year of the program. It seems that these are the findings and recommendations here—make more of them, including ways to illustrate each idea.

One student's summary comment gives insight into the power of TeacherCorps:

> Even though it's demanding with time and patience, I wouldn't change my experience for the world. . . . I always tell my mom . . . I was supposed to graduate two years ago. If that would have happened, I obviously wouldn't have experienced TeacherCorps since it wasn't around. The experience I have had is unbelievable. I leave [school] every day knowing that I'm making a positive impact on those children's lives—and that's what makes me smile.

APPENDIX
TeacherCorp Pre- and Post-Survey

Thank you for taking the time to complete this questionnaire. By answering the following questions you are indicating that you are voluntarily agreeing to participate in this study and that you understand that (1) your answers will be kept confidential and anonymous, (2) your responses will be analyzed, and (3) your responses may be included in further program evaluation and documentation.

1. Please indicate your primary role in TeacherCorps:
    a) Elementary Education Preservice Teacher
    b) Secondary Education Preservice Teacher
    c) Elementary Education Cooperating Teacher
    d) Secondary Education Cooperating Teacher
    e) School Principal
    f) Parent of a child in a classroom with a TeacherCorps Member
    g) Community Member in a school with a TeacherCorps Member
    h) Other (please specify)

2. Please indicate your age range:
    a) 18–22
    b) 23–30
    c) 31–40
    d) 41–50
    e) 51–60
    f) 61–70
    g) 71 or over

3. *For teacher candidates and cooperating teachers only:*

    Please indicate the grade range for which you are primarily responsible:

    Kindergarten–3rd grade
    4th–5th grade
    6th–8th grade
    9th–10th grade
    11th–12th grade
    Other (please specify)

4. Please identify yourself with regard to race and ethnicity:

5. Please explain your role in working with TeacherCorps:

6. Please indicate your perceived level of involvement with Teacher-Corps in any capacity:
    a) Low
    b) 1
    c) 2
    d) 3 Medium
    e) 4
    f) 5
    g) 6 High
  Please comment:

7. What is your current confidence level in working with children? ("Working with" includes developing projects, facilitating, teaching, etc.)
    a) Low
    b) 1
    c) 2
    d) 3 Medium
    e) 4
    f) 5
    g) 6 High
  Please comment:

8. What is your current confidence level in working with parents?
    a) Low
    b) 1
    c) 2
    d) 3 Medium
    e) 4
    f) 5
    g) 6 High
  Please comment:

9. What is your current confidence level in working with community members?
    a) Low
    b) 1
    c) 2
    d) 3 Medium
    e) 4
    f) 5
    g) 6 High
  Please comment:

10. What do you believe is the purpose of education?

11. What is your personal definition of "community-based service-learning"?

12. Why do you think there is an achievement gap between the academic achievement of children of different racial and ethnic groups?

13. What challenges do you notice in working to connect children's learning in classrooms to parents?

14. What challenges do you notice in working to connect children's learning in classrooms to parents?

15. What do you believe gets students excited about learning?

16. What assets do you see in your community?

17. How do you believe teachers and schools could help children know and understand these assets?

18. What issues do you see in your community in which school-age children could be involved in working toward a solution?

19. How would you explain TeacherCorps to someone not familiar with the program?

20. What are your observations regarding TeacherCorps at this time?

21. What other comments or feedback do you have for TeacherCorps?

Thank you for taking the time to complete this survey. We so appreciate your feedback!

REFERENCES

Agarwal, R., Epstein, S., Oppenheim, R., Oyler, C., & Sonu, D. (2010). From ideal practice and back again: Beginning teachers teaching for social justice. *Journal of Teacher Education, 61*(3), 237–247.

Ammon, M. S. (2002). Probing and promoting teachers' thinking about service-learning: Toward a theory of teacher development. In S. H. Billig & A. Furco (Eds.), *Service-learning through a multidisciplinary lens* (pp. 33–53). Greenwich, DT: Information Age.

Anderson, J. (2001). *Service-learning in teacher education: Enhancing the growth of new teachers.* New York, NY: AACTE.

Annie E. Casey Foundation. (2012). *Kids Count data book: State trends in child well-being.* Retrieved from www.aecf.org.

Aquila, F. D., & Dodd, J. M. (2003). *Learn and serve Ohio: Annual evaluation report.* Cleveland, OH: Cleveland State University.

Bailey, D. B. (2001). Evaluating parent involvement and family support in early intervention and preschool programs. *Journal of Early Intervention, 24*(1), 1–14.

Billig, S. H. (2002). Adoption, implementation, and sustainability of K–12 service-learning. In A. Furco & S. H. Billig (Eds.), *Service-learning: The essence of pedagogy.* Greenwich, CT: Information Age.

Borrero, N. (2009). Preparing new teachers for urban teaching: Creating a community dedicated to social justice. *Multicultural Perspectives, 11*(4), 221–226.

Brandeis University. Center for Human Resources. (1999). *Summary report: National evaluation of learn and serve America.* Waltham, MA: Author.

Brooks, J., & Thompson, E. G. (2005). Social justice in the classroom. *Educational Leadership, 63*(1), 48–52.

Brown, K. M., Benkovitz, J., Muttillo, A. J., & Urbvan, T. (2011). Leading schools of excellence in closing achievement gaps. *Teachers College Record, 113*(1), 57–96.

Cochran-Smith, M. (2004). Defining the outcomes of teacher education: What's social justice to do with it? *Asia-Pacific Journal of Teacher Education, 32*(3), 193–212.

Cochran-Smith, M. (2010). Toward a theory of teacher education for social justice. In M. Fullen, A. Hargreaves, D. Hopkins, & A. Lieberman (Eds.), *The international handbook of educational change* (2nd ed., pp. 445–467). New York, NY: Springer.

Cochran-Smith, M., McQuillan, P., Mitchell, K., Gahlsdorf Terrell, D., Barnatt, J., D'Souza, L., et al. (2010). A longitudinal study of teaching practice and early career decisions: A cautionary tale. *American Educational Research Journal, 49*(5), 844–880.

Cochran-Smith, Shakeman, K., Jong, C., Terrell, D. G., Barnatt, J., & McQuillan, P. (2009). Good and just teaching: The case for social justice in teacher education. *American Journal of Education, 115*(3), 347–377.

Corporation for National and Community Service. (2012a). AmeriCorpsVISTA. Retrieved from www.americorps.gov/for_organizations/apply/vista.asp.

Corporation for National and Community Service. (2012b). Our mission and guiding principles. Retrieved from http://www.nationalservice.gov/about/role_impact/mission.asp.

Creswell, J. W. (1998). *Qualitative inquiry and research design: Choosing among five traditions.* Thousand Oaks, CA: Sage.

Eckert, S. A. (2011). The national teacher corps: A study of shifting goals and changing assumptions. *Urban Education, 46*(5), 932–952.

Enterline, S., Cochran-Smith, M., Ludlow, L. H., & Mitescu, E. (2008). Learning to teach for social justice: Measuring change in the beliefs of teacher candidates. *The New Educator, 4*(4), 267–290.

Eyler, J., & Giles, D. E. (1999). *Where's the learning in service-learning?* San Francisco, CA: Jossey-Bass.

Eyler, J., & Giles, D. E. (2002). Beyond surveys: Using the problem solving interview to assess the impact of service-learning on understanding and critical thinking. In A. Furco & S. H. Billig (Eds.) *Service-learning: The essence of pedagogy* (pp. 147–159). Greenwich, CT: Information Age.

Friere, P. (1974). *Education for critical consciousness.* New York, NY: Sheed & Ward.

Krebs, M. M. (2012). Crossing boundaries in service-learning professional development: Preservice and inservice teachers learning together. In J. A. Hatcher & R. G. Bringle (Eds.), *Understanding service-learning and community engagement: Crossing boundaries through research* (pp. 129–156). Charlotte, NC: Information Age.

Melchior, A., & Bailis, L. N. (2002). Impact of service-learning on civic attitudes and behaviors of middle school and high school youth: Findings from three national evaluations. In A. Furco & S. H. Billig (Eds.), *Service-learning: The essence of pedagogy* (pp. 201–222). Greenwich, CT: Information Age.

Moustakas, C. (1994). *Phenomenological research methods.* Thousand Oaks, CA: Sage.

National Youth Leadership Council. (2008). *K–12 service-learning standards for quality practice.* Retrieved from http://www.nylc.org.

New Mexico Voices for Children (2011). *2011 Kids Count in New Mexico.* Retrieved from 222.nmvoices.org

Palmer, B. (2004, November). *Promoting innovative teaching: Faculty motivations for pursuing a service-learning teaching fellowship.* Paper presented at the annual meeting of the Association for the Study of Higher Education, Portland, OR.

Partnerships Make a Difference. (2012). "Growing together" service learning network. Retrieved from http://www.partnershipsmakeadifference.org.

Puig, V. I. (2011). Cultural and linguistic alchemy: Mining the resources of Spanish-speaking children and families receiving early intervention services. *Journal of Research in Childhood Education, 26*(2), 325–345.

Puig, V. I., & Recchia, S. L. (2012). Urban advocates for young children with special needs: First-year early childhood teachers enacting social justice. *The New Educator, 8*(3), 258–277.

Scales, P. C., Bluth, D. A., Berkas, T. H., & Kielsmeier, J. C. (2000). The efforts of service-learning on middle school students' social responsibility and academic success. *Journal of Early Adolescence, 20*(3), 332–359.

Scales, P. C., & Roehlkepartain, E. C. (2004). *Community service and service-learning in U.S. public schools, 2004: Findings from a national survey.* Minneapolis, MN: National Youth Leadership Council.

Search Institute. (2000). *An asset builder's guide to service-learning.* Minneapolis, MN: Author.

Smith, D. L., & Smith, B. J. (2009). Urban educators' voices: Understanding culture in the classroom. *Urban Review, 41*(4), 334–351.

Strauss, A. L., & Corbin, J. (1998). *Basics of qualitative research.* Thousand Oaks, CA: Sage Publications.

Marjori M. Krebs is a teacher educator at the University of New Mexico. Marjori works with preservice and inservice teachers, with her passion in the area of service-learning professional development.

Kiran Katira is an East-African, Asian-Indian woman, born in Kenya and raised in England. For the past 15 years she has worked to utilize university and community assets to meet community-identified needs in inner-city Albuquerque. As director of University of New Mexico's Community Engagement Center, she facilitates the growth and development of university students serving in community-initiated projects. The students apprentice with strong leaders who have a holistic approach to the health and well-being of the children, youth, families, and community. Kiran has also taught courses to graduate and undergraduate students at the University of New Mexico, with a focus on race relations and education, community-based initiatives, and critical multicultural education.

Swechha Singh is currently pursuing a PhD in Language, Literacy, and Sociocultural Studies at the University of New Mexico. Swechha has been actively involved in community-based work for nearly 10 years. As an assistant director of UNM's Community Engagement Center, she designs and implements community-based programs in collaboration with faculty and community partners. She provides professional development to university students serving in community-based projects through courses, workshops, and other educational opportunities with a focus on critical pedagogy.

Neil P. Rigsbee is a doctoral student in the Counselor Education Program at the University of New Mexico. His minor emphasis is in educational psychology. His research interests include suicide assessment training in counselor education, assessment, intervention, and prevention of suicide among elementary-age children, humanistic-counseling effectiveness, and quantitative and qualitative research design and data analysis in counseling and education. Neil is a licensed clinical mental health counselor who works at a community mental health clinic in downtown Albuquerque where he provides counseling services to primarily low-SES, psychiatric outpatient, and court-referred clients. He is also a clinical supervisor for counseling interns at this agency and at the University of New Mexico's LGBTQ Resource Center.

FINAL REFLECTION

THE VISION WE HOLD

The introduction to this volume on transforming teacher education asks the question, *Why service-learning now?*

This question is elegant because it is both simple and complex, as it allows us an opportunity to examine service-learning as a pedagogy to advance the transformation of teacher education while engaging in the philosophical inquiry about the purpose of education. Its beauty also stems from the implied urgency because the question could quite easily be read as an imperative. As a philosophical inquiry, the question could be rewritten: Why education now? The answer to this question is crucial as society tackles the incredible challenges of the current global ecology. As Dewey stated in *Democracy and Education,* education offers "individuals a personal interest in social relationships" (p. 56). This utterance, while accurate, seems strangely distant.

To examine the broader mission of schools in a more personal way makes sense. "Education enables our children to do more than make a living; it enables them to *make a life*" (Erickson, 2011). To make a life is a complex journey, and service-learning—a multifaceted pedagogy that allows students a chance to work within complex and dynamic communities—offers a way to transform teacher education with an eye toward this broader purpose of education at a time when there is astonishing inequity.

Because the vision we hold becomes the reality we experience, it is imperative to consider the question—*Why service-learning now?*—as we adjust

Transforming Teacher Education Through Service-Learning, pages 263–264
Copyright © 2013 by Information Age Publishing

teacher preparation programs to promote engaging opportunities for today's youth.

REFERENCES

Dewey, J. (2011). *Democracy and education.* New York: Simon and Brown. (Original work published 1916)

Erickson, J. (2011). *When reforming teacher preparation, don't forget service-learning.* Retrieved from http://www.ecs.org/clearinghouse/91/31/9131.pdf.

ABOUT THE EDITORS

Virginia M. Jagla is Associate Professor of Education at National Louis University in the Chicago area. She has been a teacher and administrator in urban schools, museums, and arts organizations. She has taught for various colleges and universities. Currently Dr. Jagla leads the NLU Civic Engagement Team. She is an editor of the online journal *i.e.: inquiry in education.* She is the chair of the Middle Level Educators SIG of the Association of Teacher Educators and the chair of the Service-Learning and Experiential Education SIG of the American Educational Research Association. Dr. Jagla is the series editor for *Advances in Service-Learning Research* (Information Age Publishing). She also wrote a book, *Teachers' Everyday Use of Imagination and Intuition: In Pursuit of the Elusive Image* (SUNY Press). Dr. Jagla has numerous published chapters and articles in various juried journals. She is a frequent presenter at local, national, and international conferences and symposia. Her research interests include imagination and intuition in education, the use of the visual and creative arts in education, urban education, and service-learning, particularly as it applies to middle-level education.

Joseph A. Erickson is Professor of Education at Augsburg College in Minneapolis, Minnesota. He is also a licensed psychologist in private practice. He earned his doctorate in educational psychology at the University of Minnesota. In 2006, Erickson was honored as one of the "District Leaders for Citizenship and Service-Learning" by the Education Commission of the States' National Center for Learning and Citizenship for his leadership in civic education and commitment to community service-learning. He was a member and former chair of the Minneapolis School Board. He currently

Transforming Teacher Education Through Service-Learning, pages 265–266
Copyright © 2013 by Information Age Publishing

teaches, provides psychotherapy and conducts research primarily in effective teaching strategies, attitude change, and the use of technology for enhancing learning.

Alan S. Tinkler is Assistant Professor in the Department of Education at the University of Vermont in Burlington. He is also co-coordinator of the Partnership for Change, a school remodeling effort funded by the Nellie Mae Foundation. When not engaged in research and teaching, he writes fiction. His doctoral dissertation, "Malaria Journal," is a novel loosely based on his experiences in Papua New Guinea where he lived for 2 years as a Peace Corps volunteer.